Positive and Constructive Contributions for Sustainable Development Goals

Cristina Raluca Gh. Popescu
University of Bucharest, Romania & The Bucharest University of Economic Studies, Romania

A volume in the Practice, Progress, and Proficiency in Sustainability (PPPS) Book Series

IGI Global
PUBLISHER of TIMELY KNOWLEDGE

Published in the United States of America by
IGI Global
Engineering Science Reference (an imprint of IGI Global)
701 E. Chocolate Avenue
Hershey PA, USA 17033
Tel: 717-533-8845
Fax: 717-533-8661
E-mail: cust@igi-global.com
Web site: http://www.igi-global.com

Library of Congress Cataloging-in-Publication Data

Names: Popescu, Cristina Raluca Gh., 1983- editor.
Title: Positive and constructive contributions for sustainable development goals / Cristina Raluca Gh. Popescu, editor.
Description: Hershey, PA : Engineering Science Reference, [2023] | Includes bibliographical references and index. | Summary: "This book aims at providing an updated view of the newest trends, novel practices and latest tendencies concerning the benefits, advantages, opportunities, and challenges that building an international successful process of making positive and constructive contributions for Sustainable Development Goals (SDGs) in terms of: (a) finding robust, sustainable, and inclusive development solutions capable to foster individuals' human rights, and generally make sure that no one is left behind in the Post-COVID-19 Era; (b) ensuring healthy lives and promoting well-being globally, for all at all ages, no matter the individuals' level of income, age, race, or gender; (c) promoting sustained, inclusive and sustainable economic growth in the Post-COVID-19 Era, based on equitable quality education for all people, thus promoting lifelong-learning opportunities capable to help individuals develop new skills, become more independent, and offer the opportunity to develop and to progress"-- Provided by publisher.
Identifiers: LCCN 2022040884 (print) | LCCN 2022040885 (ebook) | ISBN 9781668474990 (hardcover) | ISBN 9781668475003 (paperback) | ISBN 9781668475010 (ebook)
Subjects: LCSH: Sustainable development. | Social responsibility of business.
Classification: LCC IIC79.E5 P669255 2023 (print) | LCC HC79.E5 (ebook) | DDC 338.9/27--dc23/eng/20220913
LC record available at https://lccn.loc.gov/2022040884
LC ebook record available at https://lccn.loc.gov/2022040885

British Cataloguing in Publication Data
A Cataloguing in Publication record for this book is available from the British Library.

All work contributed to this book is new, previously-unpublished material. The views expressed in this book are those of the authors, but not necessarily of the publisher.

For electronic access to this publication, please contact: eresources@igi-global.com.

Practice, Progress, and Proficiency in Sustainability (PPPS) Book Series

Ayman Batisha
International Sustainability Institute, Egypt

ISSN:2330-3271
EISSN:2330-328X

Mission

In a world where traditional business practices are reconsidered and economic activity is performed in a global context, new areas of economic developments are recognized as the key enablers of wealth and income production. This knowledge of information technologies provides infrastructures, systems, and services towards sustainable development.

The **Practices, Progress, and Proficiency in Sustainability (PPPS) Book Series** focuses on the local and global challenges, business opportunities, and societal needs surrounding international collaboration and sustainable development of technology. This series brings together academics, researchers, entrepreneurs, policy makers and government officers aiming to contribute to the progress and proficiency in sustainability.

Coverage

- E-Development
- Knowledge clusters
- Technological learning
- Sustainable Development
- Outsourcing
- Environmental informatics
- Innovation Networks
- Intellectual Capital
- Green Technology
- ICT and knowledge for development

IGI Global is currently accepting manuscripts for publication within this series. To submit a proposal for a volume in this series, please contact our Acquisition Editors at Acquisitions@igi-global.com or visit: http://www.igi-global.com/publish/.

The Practice, Progress, and Proficiency in Sustainability (PPPS) Book Series (ISSN 2330-3271) is published by IGI Global, 701 E. Chocolate Avenue, Hershey, PA 17033-1240, USA, www.igi-global.com. This series is composed of titles available for purchase individually; each title is edited to be contextually exclusive from any other title within the series. For pricing and ordering information please visit http://www.igi-global.com/book-series/practice-progress-proficiency-sustainability/73810. Postmaster: Send all address changes to above address.

Titles in this Series

For a list of additional titles in this series, please visit: www.igi-global.com/book-series/practice-progress-proficiency-sustainability/7381

Leadership Approaches to the Science of Water and Sustainability
Kristin Joyce Tardif (University of Arkansas, Fort Smith, USA)
Engineering Science Reference • © 2022 • 219pp • H/C (ISBN: 9781799896913) • US $215.00

Eco-Friendly and Agile Energy Strategies and Policy Development
Mir Sayed Shah Danish (University of the Ryukyus, Japan) and Tomonobu Senjyu (University of the Ryukyus, Japan)
Engineering Science Reference • © 2022 • 272pp • H/C (ISBN: 9781799895022) • US $240.00

Handbook of Research on Global Institutional Roles for Inclusive Development
Neeta Baporikar (Namibia University of Science and Technology, Namibia & University of Pune, India)
Information Science Reference • © 2022 • 398pp • H/C (ISBN: 9781668424483) • US $270.00

Analyzing Sustainability in Peripheral, Ultra-Peripheral, and Low-Density Regions
Rui Alexandre Castanho (WSB University, Poland)
Engineering Science Reference • © 2022 • 334pp • H/C (ISBN: 9781668445488) • US $240.00

Frameworks for Sustainable Development Goals to Manage Economic, Social, and Environmental Shocks and Disasters
Cristina Raluca Gh. Popescu (University of Bucharest, Romania & The Bucharest University of Economic Studies, Romania)
Engineering Science Reference • © 2022 • 296pp • H/C (ISBN: 9781668467503) • US $240.00

Handbook of Research on Building Inclusive Global Knowledge Societies for Sustainable Development
Cristina Raluca Gh. Popescu (University of Bucharest, Romania & The Bucharest University of Economic Studies, Romania)
Information Science Reference • © 2022 • 405pp • H/C (ISBN: 9781668451090) • US $295.00

Handbook of Research on Principles and Practices for Orchards Management
Waleed Fouad Abobatta (Horticulture Research Institute, Agriculture Research Center, Egypt) Ahmed Farag (Central Laboratory for Agricultural Climate, Agriculture Research Center, Egypt) and Mohamed Abdel-Raheem (National Research Center, Egypt)
Engineering Science Reference • © 2022 • 382pp • H/C (ISBN: 9781668424230) • US $295.00

IGI Global
PUBLISHER of TIMELY KNOWLEDGE

701 East Chocolate Avenue, Hershey, PA 17033, USA
Tel: 717-533-8845 x100 • Fax: 717-533-8661
E-Mail: cust@igi-global.com • www.igi-global.com

The editor would like to joyfully and to warmly dedicate this book entitled *Positive and Constructive Contributions for Sustainable Development Goals* to the ones that will choose to read this valuable work, namely to the academics, scientists, researchers, students, PhD scholars, Post - doctoral students, managers, and leaders. In this matter, the editor is full of gratitude to those who will dedicate their time and their energy in analysing the aspects and the case studies comprised in the book chapters of this research project, since they are the ones who will make possible the continuous promotion of the values comprised in the Global Goals (GG) and will contribute to our existence in a responsible and in a sustainable manner.

Also, the editor would like to heartily and to kindly dedicate this book entitled *Positive and Constructive Contributions for Sustainable Development Goals* to all the IGI Global Team Members as a sign of great respect for the great effort put every single time in creating wonderful scientific projects capable to help individuals and communities appreciate life, happiness and health at their true value. Besides all these, the editor strongly believes that the IGI Global Team Members are valuable promoters of the Corporate Social Responsibility (CSR), Corporate Governance (CG), and Sustainable Development Goals (SDGs) in the knowledge society and in the Digital Era, providing valuable insights on what business performance (BP) ought to look like when relying on the power of intangible assets (IA) – such as, for instance, on human resources (HR) and intellectual capital (IC).

Let us hope that the IGI Global book on *Positive and Constructive Contributions for Sustainable Development Goals* will bring balance in your lives and will make you aware of the vital importance played by nature in our daily activities! Also, let us hope that this pivotal scientific work will determine you to act more responsibly and more sustainably, since happiness, health, and well-being are easy to target and hard to gain in the challenging and changing times we live in now!

Table of Contents

Detailed Table of Contents

achievement is evident, due to the fact that it is closely related to food, food waste, and healthy diets. Taking this into account, the objective of this research is to find out how Spanish supermarket chains are communicating their CSR strategies based on SDG 12 through their social networks. A survey of 300 people has been carried out to understand the level of importance that the Spanish population gives to supermarkets complying with and communicating their commitment to SDG 12. Thanks to the results of this research, companies will be able to carry out specific communication and social marketing strategies through social networks with which they will enhance their brand image and reputation.

The current chapter focuses on the scope of employee happiness and resilience which will be examined in detail, and the importance of happiness and resilience for organizational sustainability in the post-COVID-19 pandemic period are discussed through research and reports. Then recommendations are provided based on the results of scientific studies to protect and increase employee happiness and resilience. This chapter aims at revealing the importance of wellbeing and resilience in the workplace highlighting the aftereffects of COVID-19 in the organizational ecosystem.

All prominent leaders, managers, researchers, and specialists worldwide position the positive and constructive contributions for Sustainable Development Goals (SDGs) in the centre of their activities and interests due to the power that the international community holds in reaching all SDG targets and achieving a global partnership for sustainable development (SD). The focal point of this study is represented by individuals' self-belief to fight against climate change and utilizes valuable data from the European Social Survey (ESS) Wave 10 in 2020 on two main areas: the impact that large numbers of people limiting their energy use might have on climate change and the causes of climate change which could be represented by natural processes, human activity, or both. The findings show that more than half of those individuals in the sample are taking bold and transformative steps towards a better future for all choosing sustainability, being more likely to have positive attitudes about individual efforts to control climate change, centering on reducing their energy consumption.

In the digital age, the COVID-19 pandemic and the COVID-19 crisis uncovered entities' pressing top-priority to reimagine and to reinvent themselves, thus embracing the unrivalled benefits and the unmatched opportunities offered by digital transformation. Hence, the advantages revealed by digital transformation helped shape the "new normal" and addressed the Sustainable Development Goals (SDGs) beyond compare, bringing inimitable changes and challenges to organizational culture and employee motivation. On the one hand, the aim of this novel and original study is to highlight the importance of digital transformation for all, now and for the future generations, thus ensuring better and more complex ways to communicate and to connect. On the other hand, the objective of this up-to-date and eye-opening chapter is to display the trends that come to fuel digital transformation in order to create new business processes and develop new cultural paths, thus accentuating customers' experiences, diversifying market requirements, and intensifying the need for better organizational security.

Corporate social responsibility (CSR) refers to a business approach that takes into account economic, environmental, and social issues in a balanced, holistic, and long-term manner for the benefit of current and future stakeholders. However, when did the term emerge? How has it evolved since its inception? Under what theoretical perspectives has it been approached? Through a narrative review of the literature, the research addresses these research questions to bring clarity to the field of study. The results of the research show that the term emerged in the 1950s, having evolved to include the economic, social, and environmental dimensions and that there are five motivations that drive its implementation: (1) alignment of interests between agents and principal, (2) satisfaction of stakeholder demands, (3) compliance with the institutional context, (4) obtaining a competitive advantage, and (5) maintaining congruence between the objectives of society and the objectives of the organization.

This chapter addresses the following questions: What are the organizational gaps in achieving the SDGs indicators in the hilly ethnic groups, and how are they looking forward to sustainable development? This chapter also shows the organizational structure and its challenges concerning coping with SDGs and unfolding the links within ministries in Bangladesh. The Sustainable Development Goals are a burning issue worldwide, and they have significant consequences on economic growth as well as on public administration, either sound or immoral management. The Ministry of Chittagong Hill Tracts Affairs (MoCHTA) is mandated to ameliorate and ensure social safety and security in the life settings of the different ethnic people in the Chittagong Hill Tracts (CHT) area after signing an accord on 2nd December 1997. Methodologically, it is a neoliberalism study, and the authors conducted this chapter based on secondary data analyzed and reviewed, such as Ministry's APA, Citizen Charter, project or development activities, reports, and interviews with senior bureaucrats and ethnic leaders.

Social aspects, management, and development are important in all the industries including the pharmaceutical industries. Sustainability management is necessary to be followed even in pharmaceutical industries, and there are many measures or pharmaceutical management practices that will help to achieve social management of pharma products. The chapter will cover the effective pharma products management through proper disposal of medicines and their use by sustainable approach.

No creed has called for education for peace. Instead of revealing the world of injustices, such an assertion emerged since the 1970s by Paulo Freire, Frantz Fanon from French, Syed Hussein Alatas from Malaysia, Vine Deloria from the American Indians. Later, Gayatri Spivak, Walter Mignolo, Eve Tuck, and Yung have pointed out the system's problem. This chapter demonstrates an unorthodox, non-linear discussion with UNESCO's (in effect, the SDG 4) educational program references. The inspiration came from different masterpieces—Spivak's Righting Wrong, Vine Deloria's Indigenous Metaphysics, Frantz Fanon's Black Skin White Mask, Darryl Macer's Bioethics for Love. In terms of gnoseology, the authors followed Sadia Gaon's phrase—a polymath said in 872 AD: 'observe the unobserved' in the new normalcy—a part of practical philosophy—and the analytical or conceptual domain. This chapter contains three parts: first the motivation, then the analytical framework, and finally, established argument. The authors conclude that the education system shapes mental faults that shape our activation.

Acid violence is not only a violation of human rights, women's rights, and humanity, but also a terrible crime regardless of location. The chapter seeks to concentrate the overall picture with a historical description of acid crime across the world with a succinct and critical review of acid violence from an activist's perspective, including its background history, contributing factors, consequences on victims' lives, and national and international perspectives on acid burn rehabilitation and treatment from Bangladesh context. A proposal is given for future study, which, understandably, will be under the SDGs regime and local legal provision in achieve social justice and human rights.

Foreword

These days specialists chose to point out that the importance and the role of the 17 Sustainable Development Goals (SDGs) is growing at a rapid pace and it is vitally linked to the way in which the achievement of these goals is done in order to better adjust to the intended purposes stated by the countries and the United Nations (UN) – in particular, the UN Department of Economic and Social Affairs.

In the same vein, it ought to be mentioned that the Global Goals (GG) empower individuals to reflect more on their actions towards the environment while considering not only themselves and the close family members but, also, the people around them and the future generations and their capacity to enjoy the benefits and the advantages of life on Earth at its greatest meaning and potential (United Nations Development Programme (UNDP), 2022).

Hence, the targeted outcomes implicated by the 17 Sustainable Development Goals (SDGs) should embody all the characteristics specific to the sustainable development (SD) of our nations, with long run implications in terms of creating a more balanced economy and society, built on responsible environmental actions, and promoted with the aid of creativity, education, innovation, knowledge, knowhow, research, technology, and financial resources (United Nations Development Programme (UNDP), 2022).

In this matter, António Guterres – Secretary-General of the United Nations (UN) brought to the attention of the leaders and governments worldwide in the latest Report on the evolution of the Sustainable Development Goals (SDGs), that the aims intended by the 2030 Agenda for Sustainable Development were subjected lately to constant and serious threats due to numerous crisis and conflicts (United Nations (UN), 2022, p.2). In the same Report, it was pointed out that, due to the fragile nature of the socioeconomic and political environment, humankind finds itself at a crossroad which implicates the fact that the national and international commitments assumed by all United Nations Member States in 2015 may not find an immediate equivalent among the anticipated future accomplishments of the regions and of the countries worldwide (United Nations (UN), 2022, p.2).

Nevertheless, Scott Vaughan – CEO and President of the International Institute for Sustainable Development (IISD) highlighted in 2016 the fact that, over the years, the 17 Sustainable Development Goals (SDGs) have managed to gather numerous critics, displaying specialists' worry that the aims proposed will not be accomplished in the intended timeframe and with maximum efficiency (International Institute for Sustainable Development (IISD), 2016, p.3).

The IGI Global book entitled *Positive and Constructive Contributions for Sustainable Development Goals* provides a fresh and pivotal perspective on the current status of the Global Goals (GG), offering a challenging and an interesting perspective coming from specialists worldwide, which intends to capture best the leaders, researchers and practitioners recommendations and solutions in terms of bringing to life the intended international aims.

What is more, the IGI Global book entitled *Positive and Constructive Contributions for Sustainable Development Goals* shows the engaging role of the Global Goals (GG) for the individuals' well-being as well as for the Planet's health.

Furthermore, the IGI Global book entitled *Positive and Constructive Contributions for Sustainable Development Goals* tackles in a unique and in a robust manner both the benefits and the challenges of the Global Goals (GG), since the authors of the book chapters have chosen very interesting topics of analysis and very engaging case studies that come to support the themes of debate.

Under these circumstances, the IGI Global book entitled *Positive and Constructive Contributions for Sustainable Development Goals* has the intention of finding answers to key questions, such as the following ones (but not only limited to the ones below):

- Which are the 17 Sustainable Development Goals (SDGs) and how are all these aims defined?
- What does sustainable development (SD) implicate and what examples of good international practices could be offered in this matter?
- Which are the advantages of the 17 Sustainable Development Goals (SDGs) for the developed countries while compared to the ones belonging to the developing countries?
- What make these intended targets special for individuals' lives and for the Earth's future development and existence?
- Which are the steps that businesses worldwide should consider in order to become a great support in terms of the achievement of the 17 Sustainable Development Goals (SDGs)?
- Which are the advantages and the disadvantages of the 17 Sustainable Development Goals (SDGs)?
- In what way will humankind benefit from the 17 Sustainable Development Goals (SDGs)?
- How the future of people and of the Planet does look like through the eyes of the present generations and which are the responsibilities that individuals hold in order to ensure the resources preservation and life on Earth?

This is a great moment for all of us, since this current scientific project supports development, innovation, intellectual capital (IC), intellectual property (IP), education, knowledge, knowhow, novelty, and research, being done with great effort from the authors of the book chapters, the Review Board Members (RBM), the Editorial Advisory Board Members (EABM), the editor, and the publisher.

That is the reason why I would like to take this opportunity to congratulate the authors of the book chapters, the Review Board Members (RBM), the Editorial Advisory Board Members (EABM), the editor, and the publisher for a job well-done and for a successful scientific project that is intended to make all of us more aware of both the opportunities as well as the changes that the Global Goals (GG) managed to bring so far and will continue to bring in our daily activities.

Besides the aforementioned aspects, the target audience of the IGI Global book entitled *Positive and Constructive Contributions for Sustainable Development Goals* is represented mainly by the following categories: academics, scientists, researchers, students, PhD scholars, Post-doctoral students, managers, and leaders.

In particular, I would like to emphasize the extensive and the tremendous contribution of the editor, namely of Professor Dr. Cristina Raluca Gh. Popescu, from the University of Bucharest, Bucharest, Romania and The Bucharest University of Economic Studies, Bucharest, Romania, to the success of the IGI Global book *Positive and Constructive Contributions for Sustainable Development Goals*. Also, I would like to mention that the editor has shown through the scientific research done over the years, a spectacular dedication and an extraordinary attachment towards the 17 Sustainable Development Goals (SDGs), in general, and to the sustainable development (SD) principals, in particular.

In continuation, it should be taken into consideration the fact that Professor Dr. Cristina Raluca Gh. Popescu effectively and proficiently edited until now numerous books with IGI Global that fall under the following classifications: Business and Management; Computer Science and Information Technology; Education; Environmental, Agricultural, and Physical Sciences; Library and Information Science; Medical, Healthcare, and Life Sciences; Media and Communications; Security and Forensics; Government and Law; Social Sciences and Humanities; Science and Engineering. Also, it ought to be pointed out that Professor Dr. Cristina Raluca Gh. Popescu dedicated, over the years, significant time and effort in writing several book chapters that were published as single author or co-author with IGI Global.

All in all, the United Nations Global Compact (UNGC) stressed in 2022 the importance of doing business responsibly and sustainably, while centring on the ways in which the Global Goals (GG) could be successfully achieved by the year 2030 with a clear focus mainly on: "gender equality", "disarmament", "sustainability", "accessibility", and "civil society" (United Nations Global Compact (UNGC), 2022; United Nations Geneva (UNG), 2022). These have the tendency to make all of us both aware and responsible not only for ourselves and the close ones, but also for the people that will soon continue our mission on this Planet.

I wish you all a pleasant reading! In addition, I hope that the IGI Global book *Positive and Constructive Contributions for Sustainable Development Goals* will help (re)discover the wonderful possibilities that we all have to make a notable contribution to leaving in a responsible and in a sustainable manner with care to all people and with concern to the environment.

Jarmila Duháček Šebestová
Department of Business Economics and Management, Silesian University in Opava, Czech Republic & Moravian Business College Olomouc, Czech Republic

Jarmila Duháček Šebestová, *Associate Professor, is an experienced researcher focusing on Small Businesses. She has participated in a number of international projects, including IPREG (Innovative Policy Research for Economic Growth) and the E-WORLD project (International Entrepreneurs Network). She is Vice President of the European Council of Small Businesses for the Czech Republic. Research interests: small business performance, small business dynamics, social and sustainable entrepreneurship.*

REFERENCES

International Institute for Sustainable Development (IISD). (2016). *Sustainable Development Goals. IISD Perspectives on the 2030 Agenda for Sustainable Development*. Retrieved September 26, 2022, from https://www.iisd.org/system/files/publications/sustainable-development-goals-iisd-prespectives.pdf

United Nations (UN). (2022). *The Sustainable Development Goals Report 2022*. The Department of Economic and Social Affairs (DESA). United Nations Publications. Retrieved September 26, 2022, from https://unstats.un.org/sdgs/report/2022/The-Sustainable-Development-Goals-Report-2022.pdf

United Nations Geneva (UNG). (2022). *Sustainable Development Goals*. Retrieved September 26, 2022, from https://www.ungeneva.org/en/topics/sustainable-development-goals

United Nations Global Compact (UNGC). (2022). *Making Global Goals Local Business*. Retrieved September 26, 2022, from https://www.unglobalcompact.org/sdgs

United Nations Development Programme (UNDP). (2022). *What are the Sustainable Development Goals?* Retrieved September 26, 2022, from https://www.undp.org/sustainable-development-goals

Foreword

The International Institute for Sustainable Development (IISD), "an award-winning independent think-tank," focused on the individuals' needs and the Planet's preservation, stated in the most recent reports published in September 2022 the fact that moving beyond the Gross Domestic Product (GDP) ought to represent a key priority for all countries worldwide (International Institute for Sustainable Development (IISD), 2022a).

What is more, building an inclusive future for all should become an important aim due to be targeted by all nations at a global level, implicating combined tremendous and urgent policy efforts from governments officials (International Institute for Sustainable Development (IISD), 2022b).

Furthermore, specialists believe that, in particular, international businesses might have the power to become the very drivers for sustainability under the circumstances in which "integrated actions" would be taken in terms of reducing inequalities, taking care of nature, and focusing on people's health, happiness, and well-being (World Business Council for Sustainable Development (WBCSD), 2022).

Nevertheless, there are several doubts that some international specialists and some reputed entities expressed while referring to the real benefits and opportunities that the Sustainable Development Goals (SDGs) should reflect now and for the future. In this matter, for instance, among the critique brought to the Sustainable Development Goals (SDGs) we can find the following ones: first of all, the Sustainable Development Goals (SDGs) are considered limited in terms of the current international situation and the indicated deadline for their achievement represented by the year 2030 is much too far in time (Future Learn, 2022); second of all, even though the Sustainable Development Goals (SDGs) point out to the inequalities between individuals in terms of the access to different resources or facilities, they should also consider the inequalities that can be found in the international system, based on the argument that by trying to ensure sustainability in one region another region might suffer and might end up by being ignored in the process (Future Learn, 2022); third of all, the Sustainable Development Goals (SDGs) might be considered by some as being bureaucratic and seem to address the global picture and not the real local problems with which nations have been confronting themselves, in some cases, for years and, in other situations, even for decades (Future Learn, 2022); fourth of all, the Sustainable Development Goals (SDGs) are seen by some individuals and organizations more like "wishes" rather than specific targets, probably because of their uncertain, global nature and the fact that they offer enough room for interpretation in terms of the instruments and methods due to be used for their achievement and success (Future Learn, 2022); fifth of all, the lack of data in terms of the results regions and countries are obtaining while focusing on the Sustainable Development Goals (SDGs) represents a real problem for specialists, thus showing there are no concrete ways of knowing the true benefits of the Sustainable Development Goals (SDGs) at a small case – at a local, national level (Future Learn, 2022); sixth of all, the World Bank's international poverty line (IPL) of $1.90 a day is seen by numerous economists and financial advisors as being far too low, since choosing such levels will not be able to support the end of poverty or of hunger in the affected regions and nations, and the population of those areas will not be able to live with dignity, protected, and safe (British Educational Research Association (BERA), 2021); and seventh of all, some of the declared Global Goals (GG) are contradictory – namely, putting an accent on "sustain economic growth" is, in fact, in contradiction with other Sustainable Development Goals (SDGs), such as, for example, combatting climate change (Alston, 2020; British Educational Research Association (BERA), 2021).

The IGI Global book entitled *Positive and Constructive Contributions for Sustainable Development Goals* published by IGI Global comes with a fresh approach of the Global Goals (GG), bringing to life leaders, researchers, and specialists perspective on the benefits offered to our Planet by accelerating progress with the aid of the instruments and the frameworks based mainly on Sustainable Development (SD).

In my opinion, the dedication and the effort of the authors of the book chapters, the Review Board Members (RBM), the Editorial Advisory Board Members (EABM), the editor, and the publisher in order to create such a visionary and wonderful scientific project on *Positive and Constructive Contributions for Sustainable Development Goals* should be noted.

Also, it ought to be prompted that this scientific project includes not only the theoretical background that should usually address the advantages and the benefits of Sustainable Development (SD) and Sustainable Development Goals (SDGs), but also the disadvantages and threats that reside in focusing on the aim specific to the Sustainable Development Goals (SDGs) as well as the most relevant examples and case studies that provide vital information on the best practices due to be followed in terms of the achievement of the Sustainable Development Goals (SDGs).

In particular, I would like to underline the vital and valuable contribution of the editor, namely of Professor Dr. Cristina Raluca Gh. Popescu, from the University of Bucharest, Bucharest, Romania and The Bucharest University of Economic Studies, Bucharest, Romania, to the success of the IGI Global book project *Positive and Constructive Contributions for Sustainable Development Goals.*

In the same line with the aforementioned aspects, I would like to stress that the editor has shown through the scientific research performed over the years (making reference to the books edited and published, as well as to the book chapters, articles and conference papers authored) a great dedication in analyzing the 17 Sustainable Development Goals (SDGs) and to the sustainable development (SD) principals.

In continuation, I would like to congratulate the publisher, IGI Global, for the book *Positive and Constructive Contributions for Sustainable Development Goals* and to wish the publisher great accomplishments and tremendous success in promoting this powerful project at an international level.

I wish you all to enjoy reading the book chapters part of the book project *Positive and Constructive Contributions for Sustainable Development Goals* and, as a result, to act more responsible in your actions and activities! Sustainability should become part of our nature as individuals and a way of living for all of us!

Amr Radwan
Universidad Estatal de Milagro (UNEMI), Ecuador

Amr Radwan *is an enthusiastic young African economist with more than 20 years of experience in the field of applied economics in general with a broad research interest focusing on Bio Trade, Water Economics, Agricultural Economics, Food Economics, Agro-Food Marketing, Sustainable Tourism, Obesity and Health Economics. Also, with a broad geographical coverage in African countries such as Egypt, European ones such as Spain and American ones such as Ecuador and the United States of America combining teaching, academic as well as professional experience. Dr. Radwan obtained his B. Sc. with a specialization in agricultural economics from Cairo University in June of 2002 ranking first with a grade of excellent with honor. Accordingly, he was appointed as an assistant lecturer at the department of agricultural economics by March of 2003. As a demonstrator, he has been involved in the applied section of several courses including principles of agricultural marketing, principles of microeconomics, and farm management. When he got an opportunity to continue his postgraduate studies in Spain, he did not hesitate in doing so with the aim of helping his continent with new experience and skills in his field. He finished his master thesis on food safety issues which have been chosen as the best master thesis presented at IAMZ during 2009, also, he obtained another Master of Science in Economics from Barcelona University in 2010. On September 2014 he obtained his Ph.D. at Barcelona University which concentrates on the role of Economic factors on Obesity prevalence and diet quality in Spain. Since 2005 Dr. Radwan is working in a multidisciplinary and multicultural environment and has participated in many competitive projects, three of them were collaboration projects conducted in Egypt and Financed by the Spanish agency for international cooperation and development (AECID). Also, he published some articles in peer reviewed international journals and presented his research results in many international conferences. Dr. Radwan is publishing in three languages: English, Spanish and Arabic. Moreover, he got a scholarship as a visiting researcher at the Economic Research Services of the US Department of Agriculture (ERS-USDA) from April until September of 2011. Since 2015, Dr. Radwan has been working in Ecuador where he has collaborated as professor and researcher with several Ecuadorian universities and research centers. During these years he teaches several courses, at undergraduate as well as postgraduate levels, including Microeconomics, Macroeconomics, Agricultural Economics, Agro-Food Marketing, Research Methods and Social and Environmental Management. He worked as head of the social environmental area, Director of the Bio-trade B.Sc. program, member of the Agro ecology B.Sc. program management committee and the postgraduate committee at Universidad Regional Amazónica (Ikiam) in Tena (Ecuador). Dr. Radwan was the creator and first director of the Bio-trade B.Sc. program which is innovative and unique Bio-trade B.Sc. program in Latin America. Also he headed the actualization and creation of strategic lines of the integral development plan for Ecuadorian Amazon.*

REFERENCES

Alston, P. (2020). *The parlous state of poverty eradication: Report of the Special Rapporteur on Extreme Poverty and Human Rights.* Human Rights Council. https://chrgj.org/wp-content/uploads/2020/07/Alston-Poverty-Report-FINAL.pdf

British Educational Research Association (BERA). (2021). *Embedding sustainability education in practice. Are the Sustainable Development Goals sustainable?* Retrieved September 26, 2022, from https://www.bera.ac.uk/blog/are-the-sustainable-development-goals-sustainable

Future Learn. (2022). *Are the Sustainable Development Goals the Best Approach to Sustainability?* From the online course: "Achieving Sustainable Development" created by Trinity College, The University of Dublin. Retrieved September 26, 2022, from https://www.futurelearn.com/info/courses/achieving-sustainable-development/0/steps/35496

International Institute for Sustainable Development (IISD). (2022a). *Moving Beyond GDP to Achieve the SDGs.* Retrieved September 26, 2022, from https://www.iisd.org/

International Institute for Sustainable Development (IISD). (2022b). *Moving Beyond GDP: A Stock-Flow Approach To Measuring Wellbeing For The G20.* Retrieved September 26, 2022, from https://www.iisd.org/publications/report/moving-beyond-gdp-stock-flow-approach-g20

World Business Council for Sustainable Development (WBCSD). (2022). *How we drive sustainable development*. Retrieved September 26, 2022, from https://www.wbcsd.org/

Preface

Specialists these days position a particular emphasis on the meaning, on the importance and the role of the Sustainable Development Goals (SDGs), especially in the case in which there exist certain expectations towards their achievement, so that regions and countries worldwide could learn to become more orientated towards the good of individuals and the Planet, rather than centred on increasing the Gross Domestic Product (GDP) at any price (SDG Progress Report, 2022). Moreover, it is believed that the Sustainable Development Goals (SDGs) are extremely broad and bold aims, which have the purpose, on the one hand, to become more dedicated to ensuring their own well-being as well as others state of comfort, and which target, on the other hand, to show a sustainable path to emerging and developing countries towards acting more responsibly (United Nations (UN), 2022). Furthermore, these Global Goals (GG) provide valuable insights on the manner in which the individuals and the society could be of help and could take real action in order to become more sustainable at an international level, displaying care towards everything surrounding us (The Global Goals, 2022).

The World Health Organization (WHO) pointed out that inequalities represent one of the most dangerous threats in the society we live in, since it leaves some categories of individuals behind which my lead to serious damage for all involved parties and not only for the people that live in poverty, unable to enjoy health, a good justice system, and protect themselves and all the dear ones (World Health Organization (WHO), 2022). Also, although the Global Goals (GG) are general and address all individuals, all countries, and all regions at an international level, there are certain concerns when it comes to taking targeted action in order to ensure putting in practice these aims, since (World Health Organization (WHO), 2022): (a) the countries have certain particularities and certain priorities, thus the Millennium Development Goals (MDGs) should take into consideration the rhythm of development of each region and country (World Health Organization (WHO), 2022); (b) the people have different needs and different ways of expressing their desires, which should be reflected in the way in which they address the Millennium Development Goals (MDGs) as long as they focus on sustainability, sustainable development (SD), prosperity for the present as well as the future generations (World Health Organization (WHO), 2022).

Nevertheless, the Human Resources (HR) represent the most vital Intangible Asset (IA) that entities possess and specialists believe that these resources should benefit from a particular attention when it comes to address the Sustainable Development Goals (SDGs), based on the following key arguments (Karapınar Kocağ et al., 2022; Šebestová & Popescu, 2022): (a) first of all, life on Earth depends on individuals state of health, well-being, and level of happiness, the general satisfaction of individuals' requiring correlation with the level of health of the ecosystems (Karapınar Kocağ et al., 2022; Šebestová & Popescu, 2022); (b) second of all, nature influences people and has the capacity to make them more connected to the Planet's needs especially in the context in which people get their vitality and their strength from the environment in which they live in (Popescu, 2020); (c) third of all, the Intellectual Capital (IC) has the force to drive organizations and businesses at the highest levels of profitability and prosperity possible, since it targets efficiency as well as increased levels of development and innovation on medium and long term (Popescu & Popescu, 2019); and (d) fourth of all, Corporate Social Responsibility (CSR) and Corporate Governance (CG) that act in accordance with the Sustainable Development Goals (SDGs) have the capacity to increase business performance (BP) at levels, especially in the case in which the intangible asset (IA) are the ones that provided the necessary edge capable to lead to prosperity and growth (Popescu, 2019).

Besides all the aforementioned issues, there are numerous questions due to be considered when it comes to the Sustainable Development Goals (SDGs) achievement and the book on "*Positive and Constructive Contributions for Sustainable Development Goals*" tries to offer an answer in the best and comprehensive way possible to them:

- What are the Millennium Development Goals (MDGs) and in what manner do they contribute to our lives and our aims?
- Should the Global Goals (GG) be analysed and considered different from one region to another and from one country to another, depending on their possibilities to develop and to cope with change?
- What makes the Sustainable Development Goals (SDGs) unique and how will they be able to address international crisis, conflicts and problems?
- What is the importance of coping with inequalities and which role play in this matter equity and the respect for human rights?
- Is the Universal Health Coverage (UHC) a real desiderate for the future in terms of ensuring powerful and reliable health systems now and for the years to come?
- What is the place of sustainable financing when it comes to addressing scientific research and innovation focused on accomplishing the Sustainable Development Goals (SDGs)?

The main objective of this reference book on *Positive and Constructive Contributions for Sustainable Development Goals* is to provide valuable insight of today's context concerning the process of making positive and constructive contributions for Sustainable Development Goals (SDGs). This valuable book tackles today's progress in terms of achieving the Sustainable Development Goals (SDGs) that were set in 2015 by the international community as part of the UN 2030 Agenda for Sustainable Development. In this matter, the focus of this novel book is to present possible solutions capable to address the latest economic, social, political and demographical global challenges by tackling all the dimensions of Sustainable Development, in a balanced and integrated manner.

This book aims at providing an updated view of the newest trends, novel practices and latest tendencies concerning the benefits, advantages, opportunities, and challenges that building an international successful process of making positive and constructive contributions for Sustainable Development Goals (SDGs) in terms of: (a) finding robust, sustainable, and inclusive development solutions capable to foster individuals' human rights, and generally make sure that no one is left behind in the Post-COVID-19 Era; (b) ensuring healthy lives and promoting well-being globally, for all at all ages, no matter the individuals' level of income, age, race, or gender; and (c) promoting sustained, inclusive and sustainable economic growth in the Post-COVID-19 Era, based on equitable quality education for all people, thus promoting lifelong-learning opportunities capable to help individuals develop new skills, become more independent, and offer the opportunity to develop and to progress.

The target audience is represented by the following key categories, as follows: academics, scientists, researchers, students, PhD scholars, Post - doctoral students, managers, and leaders.

The main objective of this reference book is to provide a platform for sharing researchers' and professionals' most recent ideas, findings and works concerning the process of finding solutions to make positive and constructive contributions for Sustainable Development Goals (SDGs), while addressing global challenges and tackling all dimensions of sustainable development, in a balanced and integrated manner. In this context, researchers and professionals are kindly invited to submit their contributions in form of original research papers, case studies or essays, in particular on the following topics (but not limited to the following topics) highlighted below. It should also be stated that interdisciplinary and cross section contributions are welcomed as long as they fall in the area specific to the theme of this current book. Some of the reference topics are stated below, but the themes could be broader than the ones mentioned:

- Competency-Based Education
- Constructing Modern Knowledge
- COVID-19 Domains
- Entrepreneurship and Greening Economy
- Entrepreneurship Measuring Indicators
- Entrepreneurial Finance
- Environmental sustainability and justice
- Financial security and safety
- Food security
- Future Energy Scenarios, with Focus on Smart Energy Markets
- Health Education and Awareness
- Intellectual Capital, Sustainability and Resilience
- International Entrepreneurship
- Intelligence
- New and Sustainable Agribusiness Management Models
- Pandemic-Related Domains
- Resiliency
- Risk Assessments for Coronavirus Threats
- Smart Cities
- Stability
- Sustainable Conservation Management
- Sustainable Development in Business Reporting
- Sustainable Entrepreneurship
- Sustainable Entrepreneurship Skills and Competences
- Sustainable Human Resource Development
- Sustainable Rural Community Development
- Global Entrepreneurship
- Social Entrepreneurship
- Corporate Social Responsibility
- Creativity

- Creating an Inclusive And Competitive Entrepreneurship
- Information Technology
- Innovation
- Innovative Business Models
- Intellectual Capital
- Leadership
- Knowledge Management
- Organizational Performance
- Responsible Innovation, Performance and Excellence for a Sustainable Future
- Responsible Consumption and Production
- Social Responsibility
- Sustainable Entrepreneurial Ecosystems
- Sustainable Energy, with Responsible Consumption and Production
- Sustainability Practices
- Sustainable Society, with Responsible Consumption and Production
- Technologies and Policies for a Sustainable Society
- Technological and Social Innovation for Sustainable Business
- Innovative Applications of Artificial Intelligence in Business and Management
- Artificial Intelligence for Business and Management in the Big Data Era
- Artificial Intelligence in Value Creation for Business and Management
- Artificial Intelligence in Business and Management: A Modern Approach
- Artificial Intelligence in Business and Management: A New Synthesis
- Applications of Artificial Intelligence in Business and Management
- Artificial Intelligence Techniques in Business and Management
- Foundations of Artificial Intelligence in Business and Management
- Artificial Intelligence in Business and Management: An Exploration
- The Impact of Artificial Intelligence on Business and Management
- Understanding Artificial Intelligence in Business and Management
- The Use of Artificial Intelligence in Business and Management
- Artificial Intelligence and the power to influence the future
- Business Excellence and Innovation
- Circular Economies
- Cybernetics

The keywords that are specific to this book entitled *Positive and Constructive Contributions for Sustainable Development Goals*, published by IGI Global – International Academic Publisher – are the following ones:

- Sustainable Development Goals (SDGs)
- United Nations (UN) 2030 Agenda for Sustainable Development
- Development of the 2030 Agenda
- International Community
- Sustainable and Inclusive Development Solutions
- Global Challenges

- All dimensions of Sustainable Development
- Balanced and Integrated Manner for Achieving Sustainable Development
- The Post-COVID-19 Era
- Traditional Knowledge
- International Cooperation
- Sustained, Inclusive and Sustainable Economic Growth
- Development-Oriented Policies
- Productive Activities
- Decent Job Creation
- Entrepreneurship
- Creativity and Innovation
- Growth of Micro-, Small- And Medium-Sized Enterprises
- Financial Services
- Sustainable Consumption and Production
- Healthy Lives
- Well-Being for All at All Ages
- Social Protection Systems
- Policies Capable to Encourage EU Countries
- International Poverty
- Mobilization of Resources
- Mental Health
- Gender Equality
- Human Rights
- Enhanced Development Cooperation
- Climate-Related Extreme Events
- Sustainable Management of Water
- Wastewater Treatment, Recycling and Reuse Technologies

ORGANIZATION OF THE BOOK

The book is organized into 13 chapters. A brief description of each of the chapters may be found below, as it results based on the authors' own statements:

Chapter 1 focuses on the benefits of Artificial Intelligence (AI) and the power of sustainability in a game-changing Post-COVID-19 Era, addressing the key drivers for economic development, social development, and environmental protection. The keywords in this matter are the following ones: Business, Knowledge, Human Resources, Innovation, Intangible Assets, Intellectual Capital, Sustainable Development Goals, Digitalization, Global Economic Environment, Restart the Economy, and COVID-19.

Chapter 2 targets the ways to Communicate SDG 12 in Social Media, catering on the case of Distribution Channels. The keywords in this matter are the following ones: Sustainable Development Goals (SDG's), Supermarkets, Hypermarkets, Consumer, Instagram, Social Media, Sustainability, and Corporate Social Responsibility (CSR).

Chapter 3 centres on answering to an intriguing question, namely: "Can employee wellbeing and resilience contribute to organizational sustainability after Covid-19?" The keywords in this matter are the following ones: Employee Wellbeing, Happiness, Resilience, Organizational Sustainability, Workplace Happiness, COVID-19, and Post Pandemic.

Chapter 4 tackles the dynamics of self-belief to fight against Climate Change (CC), providing valuable evidence from the European Social Survey (ESS). The keywords in this matter are the following ones: Climate Change, Energy, Human Activity, Knowledge, Education, Health, Well-Being, European Social Survey, Sustainable Development Goals (SDGs), Global Economic Environment, Statistics, and Sustainability.

Chapter 5 brings to the attention Corporate Social Responsibility versus Corporate Sustainability, mention that these are different concepts for a common goal. The keywords in this matter are the following ones: Corporate Social Responsibility; Corporate Sustainability; Narrative Review; Similarities; and Differences.

Chapter 6 brings to light the aspects surrounding the data driven behaviour finance for mutual fund investment decision making. The keywords in this matter are the following ones: Investor Biases, Behaviour Finance, Rational Decision Making, and Crisis.

Chapter 7 aims to present the theoretical perspectives on Corporate Social Responsibility, under the form of a narrative review. The keywords in this matter are the following ones: Corporate Social Responsibility; Narrative Review; Agency Theory; Stakeholder Theory; Institutional Theory; Resource and Capabilities Theory; and Legitimacy Theory.

Chapter 8 highlights the Digital Transformation (DT) impact on organizations' culture and employees' motivation, while centring on shaping the "New Normal" and addressing Sustainable Development Goals (SDGs). The keywords in this matter are the following ones: Business, Knowledge, Human Resources, Innovation, Intangible Assets, Intellectual Capital, Sustainable Development Goals, Digitalization, Global Economic Environment, Organizational Culture, and COVID-19.

Chapter 9 addresses the topic of Corporate Social Responsibility, while providing a comprehensive analysis of the concept. The keywords in this matter are the following ones: Corporate Social Responsibility; Historical Evolution; Narrative Review; Agency Theory; Stakeholder Theory; Institutional Theory; Resource and Capabilities Theory; Legitimacy and Theory.

Chapter 10 takes into consideration the particularities of achieving Sustainable Development Goals, centring on a case study of Ministry of Chittagong Hill Tracts Affairs, Bangladesh. The keywords in this matter are the following ones: Sustainable Development Goals, Ethnic, Organizational Gap, Policy, and Bangladesh.

Chapter 11 addresses the importance of the social management of Pharma Products for Sustainable Development (SD). The keywords in this matter are the following ones: Carbon footprint, Disposal, Eco-friendly, Economical, Incineration, Needles, Syringes, and Wastes.

Chapter 12 brings to light a philosophical reflection of SDGs-4 and the education policy, centring on the case of justified self-interest versus common interest. The keywords in this matter are the following ones: Education, Utilitarian Philosophy, Neoliberal, Colonialism, Social Justice, Critical Paradigm, and Justified Self-Interest.

Chapter 13 highlights the case of the community based rehabilitation programs for acid victims' community in Bangladesh, offering a conceptual analysis aiming to including the excluded into SDGs Regime. The keywords in this matter are the following ones: Acid violence, Human Rights, Women's Rights, and Bangladesh.

Cristina Raluca Gh. Popescu

University of Bucharest, Romania & The Bucharest University of Economic Studies, Romania

REFERENCES

Karapınar Kocağ, E., Li, Y., & Popescu, C. R. G. (2022). The Determinants of Immigrants' Skill Composition. *Journal of Risk and Financial Management, 15*(9), 391. doi:10.3390/jrfm15090391

Popescu, C. R. G. (2019). Corporate Social Responsibility, Corporate Governance and Business Performance: Limits and Challenges Imposed by the Implementation of Directive 2013/34/EU in Romania. *Sustainability, 11*(19), 5146.

Popescu, C. R. G., & Popescu, G. N. (2019). An Exploratory Study Based on a Questionnaire Concerning Green and Sustainable Finance, Corporate Social Responsibility, and Performance: Evidence from the Romanian Business Environment. *Journal of Risk and Financial Management, 12*(4), 162. doi:10.3390/jrfm12040162

Popescu, C. R. G. (2020). Sustainability Assessment: Does the OECD/G20 Inclusive Framework for BEPS (Base Erosion and Profit Shifting Project) Put an End to Disputes Over The Recognition and Measurement of Intellectual Capital? *Sustainability, 12*(23), 10004.

Šebestová, J. D., & Popescu, C. R. G. (2022). Factors Influencing Investments into Human Resources to Support Company Performance. *Journal of Risk and Financial Management, 15*(1), 19. doi:10.3390/jrfm15010019

The Global Goals. (2022). *Explore Voices for Change – A Global Goals World.* https://voicesforchange.world/

SDG Progress Report. (2022). *Advanced Unedited Version. Progress towards the Sustainable Development Goal: Report of the Secretary-General.* https://digitallibrary.un.org/record/1627573. https://digitallibrary.un.org/record/3930067

United Nations (UN). (2022). *Department of Economic and Social Affairs. Sustainable Development. The 2030 Agenda for Sustainable Development. Transforming our world: the 2030 Agenda for Sustainable Development.* https://sdgs.un.org/2030agenda

World Health Organization (WHO). (2022). *Sustainable Development Goals.* https://www.who.int/europe/about-us/our-work/sustainable-development-goals

Acknowledgment

The World Health Organization (WHO) pointed out that there is stringent need for Universal Health Coverage (UHC), mentioning that social policy has become lately vital to the world we live in, which means that health financing started to occupy a key position on the agenda of leaders and specialists all around the Globe. In this matter, the COVID-19 crisis and the COVID-19 played crucial roles, displaying the problems that exist in all health system, no matter how developed the countries and regions are.

In addition, according to the World Health Organization (WHO) dedicated specialists, these are times of "extreme tension" which seem to disturb the usual rhythm in terms of the accomplishment of the Sustainable Development Goals (SDGs), leading to less solidarity among individuals and diminished concern towards the global climate emergency.

Nevertheless, the Sustainable Development Goals (SDGs) should remain a major priority to all the people and to all the countries at a global level, especially in the context in which the "New Normal" will implicate adding new challenges besides the already existing ones. For instance, in this regard, international organizations have managed to point out the vital role played in our society by Digital Transformations (DT), highlighting the implications of "the digital health plan" intended to shed a new light on how to foster Universal Health Coverage.

All in all, both individuals and entities worldwide place a tremendous value on promoting health and well-being, seeking (a) both local and international support for communities, (b) better and safer lives for the present and the future generations, (c) balance in terms of limited resources and unlimited desires belonging to individuals and businesses, and (d) better access to digitalization and technology in order to ensure more complex and more reliable levels of organization.

The editor would like to express a tremendous gratitude to the two valuable international specialists who were responsible with preparing the "Foreword" section of the book on the *Positive and Constructive Contributions for Sustainable Development Goals*, namely Associate Professor Dr. Jarmila Duháček Šebestová (from the Department of Business Economics and Management, Silesian University in Opava, SBA in Karviná & Moravian Business College Olomouc, the Czech Republic) and Dr. Amr Radwan Ahmed Radwan (Invited Researcher, Universidad Estatal de Milagro (UNEMI), Milagro, Guayas, Ecuador).

At this point, the editor would like to show the deepest appreciation to all the IGI Global Team Members for the constant support received during the publication process of the book entitled *Positive and Constructive Contributions for Sustainable Development Goals*. At all times, the IGI Global Team Members showed a tremendous dedication in bringing to life this scientific project and in creating a wonderful experience for all the parties involved in the process.

Acknowledgment

Chapter 1
Artificial Intelligence and Sustainability in a Game-Changing Post-COVID-19 Era:
Key Drivers for Economic Development, Social Development, and Environmental Protection

Cristina Raluca Gh. Popescu
https://orcid.org/0000-0002-5876-0550
University of Bucharest, Romania & The Bucharest University of Economic Studies, Romania

ABSTRACT

In this day and age, artificial intelligence (AI) places itself among the awe-inspiring forces capable to accelerate the global efforts to support economic and social development and environmental protection. Moreover, sustainability positions itself among the memorable desiderates promoted by the United Nations (UN) 17 Sustainable Development Goals (SDGs) due to the undeniable necessity to protect the environment and to conserve the planet's limited resources. Furthermore, the COVID-19 pandemic and the COVID-19 crisis severely and irreversibly altered the balance intended to be created and to be maintained with the aid of the global goals. Hence, the post-COVID-19 era has to discover answers to dazzling questions, such as: "Is artificial intelligence a tool for sustainability or is sustainability the omnipresent driver of change for digitalization?" "Does the future of inclusive and robust sustainable development (SD) rely on the artificial intelligence technologies?" and "Is humanity ready for those business practices models based on artificial intelligence for sustainability?"

INTRODUCTION

These days, Artificial Intelligence (AI) and Sustainability represent key forces in a game-changing post-COVID-19 Era and are believed to become key drivers for Economic Development (ED), Social

DOI: 10.4018/978-1-6684-7499-0.ch001

Development (SD), and Environmental Protection (EP) in turbulent times, such as the ones that humanity currently faces. It is the authors' opinion that in this day and age, Artificial Intelligence (AI) places itself among the awe-inspiring forces capable to accelerate the global efforts to support economic and social development, and environmental protection. Moreover, in times in which health, safety, and security have come to be the promoters of well-being, Sustainability positions itself among the memorable desiderates promoted by the United Nations (UN) 17 Sustainable Development Goals (SDGs), due to the undeniable necessity to protect the environment and to conserve the limited Planet's resources. Furthermore, it ought to be emphasized that the COVID-19 pandemic and the COVID-19 crisis severely and irreversibly altered the balance intended to be created and to be maintained with the aid of the Global Goals. Hence, according to the authors of the book chapter on "Artificial Intelligence and sustainability in a game-changing Post-COVID-19 Era: Key drivers for Economic Development, Social Development, and Environmental Protection", the Post-COVID-19 Era has to discover answers to dazzling questions (research questions – RQ), such as: (RQ1) "Is Artificial Intelligence a tool for Sustainability or is Sustainability the omnipresent driver of change for digitalization?"; (RQ2) "Does the future of inclusive and robust Sustainable Development (SD) rely on the Artificial Intelligence technologies?"; and (RQ3) "Is humanity ready for those Business Practices Models based on Artificial Intelligence for Sustainability?" In addition, there several keywords that the book chapter on "Artificial Intelligence and sustainability in a game-changing post-COVID-19 Era: Key drivers for Economic Development, Social Development, and Environmental Protection" revolves around, namely: business, knowledge, human resources (HR), innovation, intangible assets (IA), intellectual capital (IC), Sustainable Development Goals (SDGs), digitalization, global economic environment, restart the economy, and COVID-19.

Based on the ideas aforementioned, there are four steps that ought to accompany this current analysis and this current research, namely:

Step 1: In order to find an answer to the first key question (RQ1) – namely, to "Is Artificial Intelligence a tool for Sustainability or is Sustainability the omnipresent driver of change for digitalization?" the authors of this book chapter have mentioned the most important and the most relevant details specific to the concepts of Artificial Intelligence and Sustainability, such as: definitions, characteristics, functions, and examples.

Step 2: In order to find an answer to the second key question (RQ2) – namely, to "Does the future of inclusive and robust Sustainable Development (SD) rely on the Artificial Intelligence technologies?" the authors of this book chapter have presented the importance of the Artificial Intelligence technologies in the complex process of creating inclusive and robust Sustainable Development (SD) for all, now and in the future.

Step 3: In order to find an answer to the second key question (RQ3) – namely, to "Is humanity ready for those Business Practices Models based on Artificial Intelligence for Sustainability?" the authors of this book chapter have highlighted the importance of creating and supporting long term Business Practices Models based on Artificial Intelligence for Sustainability for all, now and in the future.

Step 4: The fourth step that characterizes this current analysis is represented by integrating several key concepts – such as, for instance, business, knowledge, human resources (HR), innovation, intangible assets (IA), intellectual capital (IC), Sustainable Development Goals (SDGs), digitalization, global economic environment, restart the economy, and COVID-19 – into the current research, in order to create the general background of this scientific work and make valuable connections with different fields of interest, such as business administration, economics, management, accounting, audit, and other interdisciplinary areas.

The European Parliament (EP) Special Committee on Artificial Intelligence in a Digital Age (AIDA) Rapporteur, Axel Voss highlighted in the "Activity Report following AIDA Mandate 2020-2022. September 2020 – March 2022", published in March 2022, the following aspects: "Artificial Intelligence is the key technology of the future. AI will determine how we work, how we move, how we do business sustainably. AI is changing our administration, our healthcare system, our defense. Every area of our lives will be affected by technological change. The consequences for our competitiveness, our prosperity and our security should not be underestimated. But this should not scare us - rather, it should encourage us, because this change can bring huge opportunities for the benefit of society as a whole" (European Parliament (EP), 2022c, p.5). Based on the aspects mentioned in the lines above, it ought to be pointed out that reputed specialists have prompted the general attention on Artificial Intelligence (AI) and the power that it currently holds to create a better future for all, since it is believed to represent a vital form of technology for these days as well as for the future. Also, digitalization has become a pivotal component in people's lives, aspect that was remarked with priority during the first months and the first years (2020, 2021, 2022) of the COVID-19 pandemic and the COVID-19 crisis. Hence, digitalization has promoted Artificial Intelligence (AI) at new levels, since Artificial Intelligence (AI) can nowadays influence at in an extensive manner: (a) the way individuals perform their daily tasks and their daily routine in their private time as well as in their work activities; (b) the way in which people decide to continue their education and their training – since education and training programs these days rely on extensive digital solutions, complex learning programs and processes; (c) the way people travel from one place to another – since going from one place to another and being flexible in this area has become highly important; (d) and the way business activities, business processes and procedures, and business management is done – since doing business has changed over the last years and decades, digitalization and sustainability becoming important and noteworthy factors in ensuring and promoting healthy and sustainable business environments for all, on the long run. In other words, Artificial Intelligence (AI) has become a powerful driver for ensuring sustainability and for promoting Sustainable Development (SD), thus having the capacity to support the achievement of all the Sustainable Development Goals (SDGs) as long as Artificial Intelligence (AI) is used with the purpose of making the right choices, the ones meant to support life, health, mental health, well-being, peace, prosperity, and an equilibrium between individuals' needs and expectations and the needs of the environment – with an accent on supporting life on Planet Earth, biodiversity, healthy ecosystems, and a bright and sustainable future for all (see, in this matter, Figure 1. Artificial Intelligence (AI) and Sustainability – General Frameworks and Objectives that Come to Support Performance and Excellence in the Post-COVID-19 Era).

In the European Parliament (EP) study on the "EU health data center and a common data strategy for public health", prepared by the Panel for the Future of Science and Technology, and published by the European Parliamentary Research Service, the Scientific Foresight Unit (STOA), in September 2021, it has been mentioned that, according to specialists: "The COVID-19 pandemic bought about such significant societal impacts in the European Union (EU) and beyond that only time and distance" might have the capacity to show the real extent of the situation both on individuals' lives and on the Planet's ability to regenerate, since the general situation generated by the COVID-19 pandemic has impacted "(…) each and every one of its millions of inhabitants in unique, unforeseen, radical and life changing (for some, unfortunately, life-taking) ways" (European Parliament (EP), 2021, p.1). Also, the European Parliament (EP) study on the "EU health data center and a common data strategy for public health" tackles the impact of the COVID-19 pandemic on the public health system – which was severely destabilized and which confronted itself with an unprecedented crisis – stating the following key aspects that require im-

Figure 1. Artificial Intelligence (AI) and Sustainability – General Frameworks and Objectives that Come to Support Performance and Excellence in the Post-COVID-19 Era. Source: the authors, based on the sources highlighted in the references section of this book chapter

mediate attention and undeniable action from the world's leaders and the individuals that possess power of decision at the highest level possible, namely: "Regarding data, its availability and comparability, the COVID-19 pandemic revealed that the EU has no clear health data architecture, and that even simple statistics on elements like intensive care beds, number of active cases under surveillance or availability of professionals, were limited by national and even regional idiosyncratic differing interpretations" (European Parliament (EP), 2021, p.1). Hence, it is believed that Artificial Intelligence (AI) has the power to change the public health system and offer better solutions in order to support sustainability and Sustainable Development (SD), in order to accomplish the aim of fostering better lives, healthier environments, happiness, and well-being for all individuals, at all ages, these days and in the future (see, in this matter, Figure 2. Artificial Intelligence (AI) in the Post-COVID-19 Era – Ways of Supporting Better Life-Styles, Healthier Environments, Happiness, and Well-Being for All Individuals, at All Ages).

In continuation to the aspects mentioned above, the European Commission (EC) highlighted in May 2022 in the "Proposal for a Regulation of the European Parliament and of the Council on the European Health Data Space" the following important ideas, namely: "The European Health Data Space (EHDS) is the first proposal of such domain-specific common European data spaces. It will address health-specific challenges to electronic health data access and sharing, is one of the priorities of the European Commission in the area of health and will be an integral part of building a European Health Union. EHDS will create a common space where natural persons can easily control their electronic health data. It will also make it possible for researchers, innovators and policy makers to use this electronic health data in a trusted and secure way that preserves privacy" (European Commission (EC), 2022, p.1). In this context, the digitalization process is highly important and the activities that are related to this process might be successfully performed with the aid of Artificial Intelligence (AI) technologies. The European Commission (EC) document entitled "Proposal for a Regulation of the European Parliament and of the Council on the European Health Data Space" pointed out other crucial elements, such as: (a) "(…) natural persons have difficulties in exercising their rights over their electronic health data, including accessing and transmitting their electronic health data nationally and cross-borders"; (b) "(…) the uneven implementation and interpretation of the GDPR by Member States creates considerable legal uncertainties, resulting in barriers to secondary use of electronic health data (…)", more specifically "(…) it creates certain situations where natural persons cannot benefit from innovative treatments and policy-makers cannot react effectively to a health crisis, due to barriers impeding access for researchers, innovators, regulators and policy makers to necessary electronic health data (…)"; and (c) "(…)

Figure 2. Artificial Intelligence (AI) in the Post-COVID-19 Era – Ways of Supporting Better Life-Styles, Healthier Environments, Happiness, and Well-Being for All Individuals, at All Ages. Source: the authors, based on the sources highlighted in the references section of this book chapter

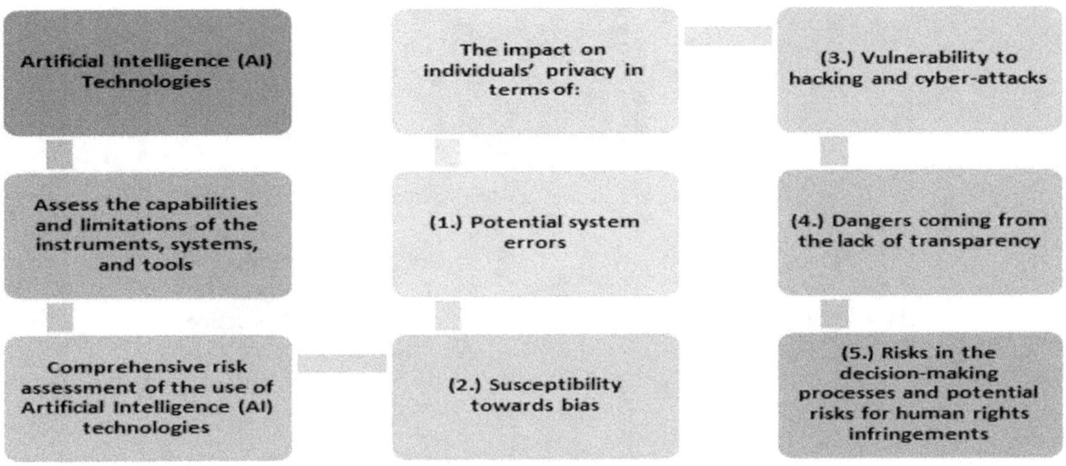

due to different standards and limited interoperability, manufacturers of digital health products and providers of digital health services operating in one Member State face barriers and additional costs when entering another one" (European Commission (EC), 2022, p.1). Based on the aspects presented in the lines above, the specialists that were responsible with preparing the European Commission (EC) "Proposal for a Regulation of the European Parliament and of the Council on the European Health Data Space" emphasized the following decisive objectives: (a) the first objective "the COVID-19 pandemic has shown" is represented by "the importance of electronic health data for the development of policy in response to health emergencies"; (b) the second objective is represented by "the imperative of ensuring timely access to personal electronic health data for health threats preparedness and response, as well as for treatment, but also for research, innovation, patient safety, regulatory purposes, policy-making, statistical purposes or personalized medicine"; (c) the third objective is "to ensure that natural persons in the EU have increased control in practice over their electronic health data"; (d) the fourth objective is "to ensure a legal framework consisting of trusted EU and Member State governance mechanisms and a secure processing environment", which is believed to "allow researchers, innovators, policymakers and regulators at EU and Member State level to access relevant electronic health data to promote better diagnosis, treatment and well-being of natural persons, and lead to better and well-informed policies", thus showing the desire as well as the necessity "to contribute to a genuine single market for digital health products and services, by harmonizing rules, and so boost healthcare system efficiencies" (European Commission (EC), 2022, pp.1-2) (see, in this matter, Figure 3. Artificial Intelligence (AI) in the Post-COVID-19 Era – Ways of Supporting Ethical Behavior and Ethical Practices in Order to Support Sustainability and Boost Performance, Productivity, and Growth).

According to the United Nations (UN) Sustainable Development Goals (SDGs) the third aim promoted is represented by the desiderate to "Ensure healthy lives and promote well-being for all at all ages", which implicates mobilizing all the resources towards "ensuring healthy lives and promoting well-being at all ages" as an essential process for fostering sustainable development, which the authors of this book

Figure 3. Artificial Intelligence (AI) in the Post-COVID-19 Era – Ways of Supporting Ethical Behavior and Ethical Practices in Order to Support Sustainability and Boost Performance, Productivity, and Growth. Source: the authors, based on the sources highlighted in the references section of this book chapter

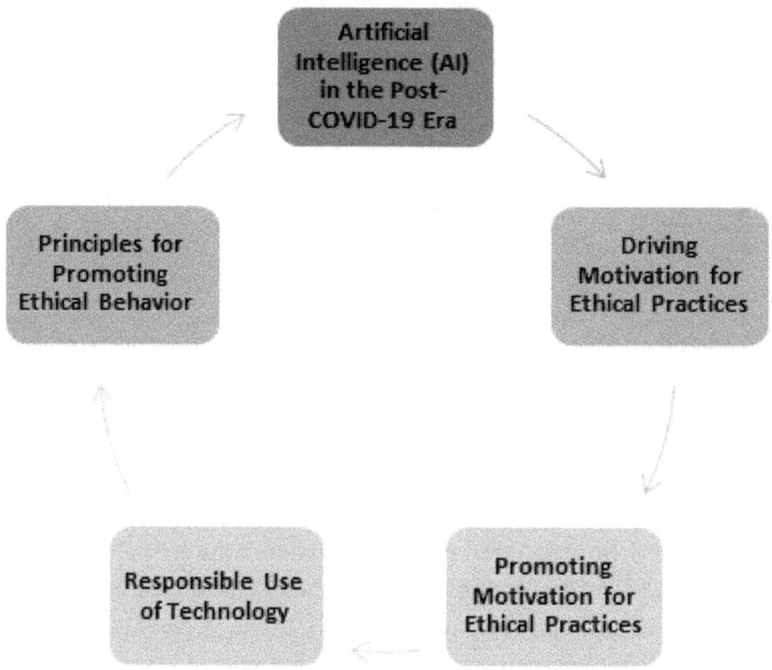

chapter believe could be facilitated with the help from Artificial Intelligence (AI) technologies (United Nations (UN), 2022).

This introductory section is followed by several other sections that come to support the importance of the theme chosen for analysis, namely: the background section of this book chapter centers on the role and on the importance of artificial intelligence and of sustainability in a game-changing Post-COVID-19 Era, since the authors believe that these two elements are key drivers for economic development, social development, and environmental protection; the main focus section of this book chapter displays the definitions and the characteristics attributed to artificial intelligence and of sustainability in a game-changing Post-COVID-19 Era, in order to demonstrate the authors' belief that these two elements are key drivers for economic development, social development, and environmental protection; the discussion and synthesis of results section of this book chapter presents the most important findings that the authors believe should be emphasized in order to show the importance of the theme chosen; the solutions and recommendations section and the future research directions section of this book chapter sheds a new light on the manner in which the authors intend to continue their analysis and their research, thus accentuating the importance of the theme chosen; and the conclusion section of this book chapter presents the most relevant aspects that ought to be considered for further research.

BACKGROUND

The background section of this book chapter focuses on the role and on the importance of artificial intelligence and of sustainability in a game-changing post-COVID-19 Era, since the authors believe that these two elements are key drivers for economic development, social development, and environmental protection. This current section focuses on the following main aspects, namely:

Step 1: This section presents the role and the importance that are believed to be specific to the concepts of Artificial Intelligence (AI) and sustainability.

Step 2: This section makes vital connections between the concepts of Artificial Intelligence (AI) and sustainability and other areas and domains, such as, for instance: (a) the health system at the European Union's (EU) level and at the international level; and (b) the information and technology systems the European Union's (EU) level and at the international level.

The authors are focused in the lines below on finding an answer to the following questions: "What is Artificial Intelligence (AI)?"; "What are the role and the importance of Artificial Intelligence (AI) these days?" and "Which are the most important domains that stand to benefit from the use of Artificial Intelligence (AI)?"

According to the European Commission (EC) document entitled "White Paper on Artificial Intelligence – A European approach to excellence and trust", published in February 2020, specialists remarked the fact that "digital technology becomes an ever more central part of every aspect of people's lives", mentioning the fact that "people should be able to trust it. Trustworthiness is also a prerequisite for its uptake. This is a chance for Europe, given its strong attachment to values and the rule of law as well as its proven capacity to build safe, reliable and sophisticated products and services from aeronautics to energy, automotive and medical equipment" (European Commission (EC), 2020, p.1). In this document the specialists defined Artificial Intelligence (AI) as follows: "AI is a collection of technologies that combine data, algorithms and computing power. Advances in computing and the increasing availability of data are therefore key drivers of the current upsurge of AI" (European Commission (EC), 2020, p.2). In the same aforementioned document, it is highlighted that "Europe's current and future sustainable economic growth and societal wellbeing increasingly draws on value created by data", which leads to the specialists' belief that "AI is one of the most important applications of the data economy", since: "Today most data are related to consumers and are stored and processed on central cloud-based infrastructure. By contrast a large share of tomorrow's far more abundant data will come from industry, business and the public sector, and will be stored on a variety of systems, notably on computing devices working at the edge of the network. This opens up new opportunities for Europe, which has a strong position in digitized industry and business-to-business applications, but a relatively weak position in consumer platforms" (European Commission (EC), 2020, pp.1-2).

In the table below, the authors have presented the most relevant ideas that can be linked with Artificial Intelligence (AI) and the benefits that can be brought to the society, with the deep emphasis on the importance of building trust in the society, based on the fact that "it is vital that European AI is grounded in our values and fundamental rights such as human dignity and privacy protection" (see, in this matter, Table 1. Artificial Intelligence (AI) and the Benefits that Can be Brought to the Society) (European Commission (EC), 2020, p.2).

It is the strong opinion of the authors that Artificial Intelligence (AI) and sustainability have both the power to enable the process of digitalization in the health system at the European Union's (EU) level as well as at a larger scale – namely, at an international level, in the interest of facilitating individuals'

Table 1. Artificial Intelligence (AI) and the Benefits that Can be Brought to the Society. Source: the authors, based on the European Commission (EC) document entitled "White Paper on Artificial Intelligence – A European approach to excellence and trust", published in February 2020 (European Commission (EC), 2020, p.2)

	Artificial Intelligence (AI)
Benefits brought in the post-COVID-19 Era	• According to specialists, Europe has today the potential to "combine its technological and industrial strengths with a high-quality digital infrastructure and a regulatory framework based on its fundamental values", targeting "to become a global leader in innovation in the data economy and its applications as set out in the European data strategy" (European Commission (EC), 2020, p.2). In this matter, the European Union (EU) needs valuable specialists trained in the field of Artificial Intelligence (AI), which will be able to make this desiderate a reality. In the same line with the aspects mentioned in the lines above, it ought to be stressed that Human Resources (HR) represent a pivotal factor in the implementation of Artificial Intelligence (AI) in the most vital domains of the society, since this type of technology is based on creativity, innovation, initiative, and desire to progress in a healthy manner, and with great respect and concern towards nature and its needs.
	• At the European level, specialists mentioned that an AI ecosystem could be developed in order to bring "the benefits of the technology to the whole of European society and economy", having in mind three areas of action, namely: (a) "for citizens to reap new benefits for example improved health care, fewer breakdowns of household machinery, safer and cleaner transport systems, better public services"; (b) "for business development, for example a new generation of products and services in areas where Europe is particularly strong (machinery, transport, cyber-security, farming, the green and circular economy, healthcare and high-value added sectors like fashion and tourism)"; and (c) "for services of public interest, for example by reducing the costs of providing services (transport, education, energy and waste management), by improving the sustainability of products and by equipping law enforcement authorities with appropriate tools to ensure the security of citizens, with proper safeguards to respect their rights and freedoms" (European Commission (EC), 2020, p.2). First of all, the authors believe that the development of technology can bring numerous advantages and important benefits to the society in which people live in these days. However, there is the paramount matter of trust in terms of using the advanced forms of technology in all domains, since Artificial Intelligence (AI) could be used not only in the benefit of individuals, thus showing how important the cyber-security is in the society that individuals live in these days. Second of all, the authors believe that sustainability relies on the development of Artificial Intelligence (AI), based on the belief that Artificial Intelligence (AI) ecosystems that are created could work in the spirit of preserving life, biodiversity, and the natural ecosystems. Third of all, Artificial Intelligence (AI) could help individuals to have access to education and training, to benefit from better health systems, to be part of smart cities and smart societies, leading prosperous lives.

access to electronic health data in order to promote healthier lives, dedicated and "well-informed policies", expected to create a health system capable to respond in a prompt and secure manner to people's needs and to strengthen a better future for all in the spirit of supporting healthy minds, healthy bodies, mental health, happiness, and well-being (European Commission (EC), 2022, pp.1-2).

In the table displayed below the authors have shown the importance of both Artificial Intelligence (AI) and Sustainability, as key forces in a game-changing Post-COVID-19 Era as well as key drivers for Economic Development (ED), Social Development (SD), and Environmental Protection (EP) in turbulent times (see, in this matter, Table 2. Artificial Intelligence (AI) and Sustainability – Key Forces in a Game-Changing Post-COVID-19 Era and Key Drivers for Economic Development (ED), Social Development (SD), and Environmental Protection (EP) in Turbulent Times).

In the same line, the European Parliament (EP) Special Committee on Artificial Intelligence in a Digital Age (AIDA) Rapporteur, Axel Voss argued the following key ideas: "After careful consideration of the benefits that AI can bring to areas of health care or our fight against climate change, we present a clear AI Roadmap on how the EU can harvest these benefits and can become a global leader in AI and overcome the barriers of legal uncertainty and an insufficient digital infrastructure. Firstly, we need a clear and future proof legislative framework that avoids regulatory burden and instead gives space for

Table 2. Artificial Intelligence (AI) and Sustainability – Key Forces in a Game-Changing Post-COVID-19 Era and Key Drivers for Economic Development (ED), Social Development (SD), and Environmental Protection (EP) in Turbulent Times. Source: the authors, based on the sources highlighted in the references section of this book chapter

	Artificial Intelligence (AI)	Sustainability
Key Forces in a Game-Changing Post-COVID-19 Era	• Represents both the present and the future of the society in which people live in these days, having the power to support the digitalization process which is highly expected and which is very important in all areas.	• Is the essence of a healthy and robust society, in which individuals show deep concern towards the quality of their lives, their mental and body health, their happiness, and the preservation and the development of the ecosystems, while taking care of the Planet in terms of ensuring biodiversity, balance, and inclusiveness in all domains.
Key Drivers for Economic Development (ED), Social Development (SD), and Environmental Protection (EP) in Turbulent Times	• Has the power to facilitate unlimited access to information and to knowledge, which is an aspect that can be valued accordingly in order to support life and to foster Economic Development (ED), Social Development (SD), and Environmental Protection (EP) now and in the future.	• Economic Development (ED) is usually analyzed together with several key economic indications, such as, for instance the Gross Domestic Product (GDP). • It ought to be considered that the Gross Domestic Product (GDP) does not always reflect in an accurate manner the Economic Development (ED) processes in a society, since this concept should be analyzed and understood through the perspective of individuals and the Planet, and not by accentuating the importance of prices, profits, and performance. • Hence, Economic Development (ED) should focus less on the ways to maximize the profits, and more on the ways to ensure the well-being of individuals and the preservation of ecosystems.
	• Has the capacity to support human beings activities, by leaving the repetitive tasks of individuals to robots, thus offering more time to people to focus on other aspects that surround their personal and their professional lives.	• Social Development (SD) makes reference to several key aspects of the daily lives and the daily activities of individuals, which means that people should keep a continuous interest throughout their lives to learn, and to get educated, since life-long training and life-long learning programs facilitate access to information and to knowledge. • In addition, Social Development (SD) implicates building respect feelings towards nature and acting in the spirit of helping the natural habitats develop and ecosystems maintained.
	• Can be regarded as a positive aspect in those situations in which it acts in the benefit of the society and of individuals, but it can, also, be seen as a negative or, at least, a questionable part of the society in which people live in these days, due to the threats that might bring in several fields: (a) it could threaten individuals jobs, leading to increased rates of unemployment, in those cases in which machines and robots are able to better perform the tasks given, by comparison to the way in which individuals might handle the same given tasks; (b) it could put in danger the security of the society, in those cases in which the security systems could be access by dangerous individuals and/or organizations seeking to act in their own benefit; (c) it could put in danger individuals lives in those cases in which machines and robots and different forms of advanced information technologies (IT) are used for combat purposes (during wars, as weapons used by armies).	• Environmental Protection (EP) is a key part of sustainability, since taking care of nature is of essence in order to support high standards of life and to foster creativity, innovation, initiative, health, happiness, and well-being.
Solutions and Examples:	• Artificial Intelligence (AI) has become more and more an integrating part of individuals' lives, bringing to the attention numerous benefits as well as disadvantages; the key to making the best of the potential advantages that these new and modern technologies have to offer in our society is to enable them to act in the benefit in individuals and nature.	• The authors strongly believe that achieving excellence in this day and age is related to the manner in which humanity will come to work together with nature, rather than find solutions and ways to "conquer" the natural forces and change the natural course of living on this Planet.
	• Artificial Intelligence (AI) and excellence go hand in hand in a society that craves for finding solutions to value better the time and/or to give a better and a more sophisticated meaning to time itself – since time is believed to be one of the most precious resources that people have, due to the fact that it is limited and it does not possess the power to regenerate.	• In like manner, the authors believe that supporting individuals' lives is highly connected with the future of this Planet, its ecosystems and its biodiversity, since people are part of the natural habitat and depend on the heath of the environment and the preservation of the environment.
	• Artificial Intelligence (AI) is expected to support those actions that are beneficial for our society and for individuals, acting as a pivotal factor for Economic Development (ED), Social Development (SD), and Environmental Protection (EP) in turbulent times.	• These days, it has become more and more pressing to position happiness, health, and well-being as top priorities for people and for organizations, since being in harmony with yourself, with your body, and with nature are believed to be of essence in order to be able to cope with the stress and with the tasks that overwhelm individuals on a constant basis.

innovation. This also includes rethinking our governance approaches and legislative processes, thus reducing the number of overlapping legislation and focusing instead on clear implementation and harmonization. Secondly, we need access to data and a competitive digital green infrastructure, requiring maximum investment in connectivity and making sure that technologies such as AI do not contribute to environmental risks but rather mitigate them. Thirdly, we need to envision an ecosystem of excellence for AI and digital skills, accessible for every citizen at all stages of life while supporting AI talent and the prevention of brain drain. Fourth, there is a clear need for an ecosystem of trust, that ensures clear ethical standards based on fundamental rights while promoting the trustworthy use of AI in governance, healthcare, security and industry" (European Parliament (EP), 2022c, p.5).

By analyzing the ideas that can be drawn from the European Parliament (EP) Special Committee on Artificial Intelligence in a Digital Age (AIDA) Rapporteur, Axel Voss, there are several connections that ought to be made, as follows:

Step 1: Based on the specialists' opinion, Artificial Intelligence (AI) is strongly connected with all the areas of individuals day to day lives and is expected to offer solutions to people's problems in all domains. In this matter, a good example is represented by the connections that can be made between Artificial Intelligence (AI) and sustainability, since with the aid of Artificial Intelligence (AI) organizations can find important solutions to cope with climate change. In continuation, another vital example is held by the connections that can be made between Artificial Intelligence (AI) and sustainability in terms of creating smart cities and in creating green economies for all.

Step 2: Also, Artificial Intelligence (AI) represents a powerful tool these days when it comes to referring to the legal systems, since it can be used in governance, where it can ensure ways to foster good governance and good leadership practices for all. Moreover, the idea of creating a New Leadership for a New Era will have a very powerful impact on the society, since it will enable entities to act in the spirit of individuals' health and nature's preservation, focusing on ensuring robust Economic Development (ED), inclusive Social Development (SD), and vital Environmental Protection (EP) in turbulent times.

In the next section represented by the main focus of the current book chapter, there are several concepts that are closely analyzed and carefully exemplified, namely: Artificial Intelligence (AI) in a game-changing Post-COVID-19 Era; Artificial Intelligence (AI) and Machine Learning (ML) on the way of transforming various industries; benefits and risks of Artificial Intelligence (AI); Sustainability in a game-changing Post-COVID-19 Era; Economic Development (ED); Social Development (SD); and Environmental Protection (EP).

MAIN FOCUS OF THE CHAPTER

This section represented by the main focus of the current book chapter on "Artificial Intelligence and sustainability in a game-changing Post-COVID-19 Era: Key drivers for Economic Development, Social Development, and Environmental Protection", addresses the case of several concepts that are closely analyzed and carefully exemplified by the authors, namely: Artificial Intelligence (AI) in a game-changing Post-COVID-19 Era; Artificial Intelligence (AI) and Machine Learning (ML) on the way of transforming various industries; benefits and risks of Artificial Intelligence (AI); Sustainability in a game-changing Post-COVID-19 Era; Economic Development (ED); Social Development (SD); and Environmental Protection (EP).

Artificial Intelligence (AI) is vital for the development of the society in which people live these days, bringing numerous advantages and creating several opportunities capable to improve life and to support Economic Development (ED), Social Development (SD), and Environmental Protection (EP) at all levels. The World Economic Forum (WEC) published in January 2018 an objective report on "Harnessing Artificial Intelligence for the Earth", as part of the "Fourth Industrial Revolution for the Earth Series", in which specialists noted that the Planets environmental problems represent the result of industrialization, mentioning the alarming levels of waste in nature as well as the dangers that can arise from climate change, high levels of air, rivers, oceans, and soils pollution, deforestation, and "loss of biodiversity" (World Economic Forum (WEC), 2018, p.3). What is more, the Fourth Industrial Revolution accentuates the vital role of innovations in a society that has come to rely more and more on technology and on individuals' desire and need to be more connected, move at a faster pace than ever before, do everything more effectively, and expect to have everything widely available any time, any place (World Economic Forum (WEC), 2018, p.3). Furthermore, the next steps due to be taken at this stage are the ones that will embody the merger between "digital, physical and biological realms", with an amazing effect on the evolution of humanity, the development of new technologies, and the transformation of all domains – with a particular emphasis on the demographical, social, economic, financial, and political ones (World Economic Forum (WEC), 2018, p.3). Hence, the effects of Artificial Intelligence (AI) in all the domains will change the values and the identities of people and will position on a different scale the opportunities that the future generations will have while compared to the past and the present ones (World Economic Forum (WEC), 2018, p.3).

The World Economic Forum (WEC) brought to light in June 2022 the "White Paper" entitled "A Blueprint for Equity and Inclusion in Artificial Intelligence" in which specialists acknowledged the importance of having a "holistic approach" when it comes to addressing the international matters surrounding the advantages and the opportunities brought by Artificial Intelligence (AI) in people's working and personal environment, mentioning that "improvements in equity and inclusion across" all Artificial Intelligence (AI) "life cycle and governance ecosystem" are expected in order to support the development of Artificial Intelligence (AI) and create vital benefits for all individuals, at all levels (World Economic Forum (WEC), 2022a, p.3).

Also, the World Economic Forum (WEC) highlighted in May 2022 in the "White Paper" on "Unpacking AI Procurement in a Box: Insights from Implementation" the fact that it is paramount for entities to find the wright sources in procuring "safe and ethical artificial intelligence and machine learning (AI/ML) tools", offering the example of several unique AI Procurement pilots, namely with the Metrô de São Paulo and the other with the Hospital das Clínicas of the University of São Paulo (World Economic Forum (WEC), 2022b, p.4). According to this report, specialists successfully demonstrated the importance of Artificial Intelligence (AI) implementation in the public sector and the governments' pivotal involvement in making the right choices in acquiring "artificial intelligence and machine learning (AI/ML) tools" capable to foster better equipped healthcare systems, expected to serve better people's needs, thus supporting lives and individuals' levels of well-being (World Economic Forum (WEC), 2022b, p.4).

In continuation, the "White Paper" on the "Responsible Use of Technology: The IBM Case Study" that was published in September 2021 by the World Economic Forum (WEC) centered the attention on the changes and the challenges that the COVID-19 pandemic brought all around the globe, mentioning that "at the heart of the Fourth Industrial Revolution" may be encountered valuable results of research and invocation programs and projects which permitted the advancement of technologies in terms of "artificial intelligence (AI), distributed ledger and cloud computing" (World Economic Forum (WEC), 2021a, p.3). Even though all the novel technologies have managed to bring a tremendous value in our society, the World Economic Forum (WEC) bring to light potential dangers and disadvantages resulted from the improper and unethical use of technologies, such as, for instance: (a) the dangers that Artificial Intelligence (AI) might bring in the business environment, in the relationship between the organizations and their customers and clients, in those situations in which the moral values of individuals could be harmed, thus affecting the potential benefits that might arise from introducing Artificial Intelligence

(AI) tools in the business world; and (b) the irresponsible use of Artificial Intelligence (AI) mechanisms and tools in the government services and in the education and the healthcare system, which could dramatically and maybe irreversibly erode people's trust in new and advanced forms of technology, which might lead to harming the individuals and the environment, and which could lead to creating inequities among individuals (World Economic Forum (WEC), 2021a, p.3).

As seen lately, the problems that can be encountered these days in the energy sector all around the globe have worrying effects upon all specialists. In this matter, the World Economic Forum (WEC) highlighted in the "White Paper" on "Harnessing Artificial Intelligence to Accelerate the Energy Transition" published in September 2021 the following key aspects: (a) the general tendency capable to define best nowadays changes in the energy sector is reflected by the nations' "transition to a low-carbon economy", which has become lately a vital and an urgent step for ensuring sustainability in a game-changing Post-COVID-19 Era, thus being able to support in a better manner Economic Development (ED), Social Development (SD), and Environmental Protection (EP); and (b) the general tendency of corporation worldwide is the one to set "carbon-negative targets", which might be possible to obtain with the aid of Artificial Intelligence (AI), thus becoming closer to facilitating the energy transition at a faster pace (World Economic Forum (WEC), 2021b, p.3).

There are several aspects to consider in this regard:

Step 1: Artificial Intelligence (AI) and the emerging technologies specific to Artificial Intelligence (AI) should be used by individuals and by entities in a responsible manner, based on coherent and robust policies and governance frameworks (World Economic Forum (WEC), 2021c, p.3). Moreover, Artificial Intelligence (AI) and the emerging technologies specific to Artificial Intelligence (AI) ought to be characterized by: positive actions and activities, transparent decisions and use, and solutions capable to support the ethics principles and global public good (World Economic Forum (WEC), 2021c, p.3).

Step 2: These days, the specialists promoting the use of "Artificial Intelligence (AI) the internet of things (IoT) and augmented reality" point out to the immeasurable benefits of these new forms of technology, stressing the fact that these novel technologies are expected to generate long-lasting benefits for the members of the society (World Economic Forum (WEC), 2021b, p.4). Nevertheless, today specialists display a great concern towards the harm that these new forms of technology might cause in those cases in which the principles of ethics are not applied accordingly and the use of "Artificial Intelligence (AI) the internet of things (IoT) and augmented reality" is not done in a responsible, inclusive, robust, and resilient manner (World Economic Forum (WEC), 2021b, p.4).

Step 3: Based on the two steps presented in the lines above, the specialists worldwide are constantly encouraging the world's leaders and the governments of all countries to work on creating and on publishing "ethical technology principles", especially for these new forms of technologies, such as the ones represented by Artificial Intelligence (AI) (World Economic Forum (WEC), 2021b, p.4). In this way, the use of these innovative and powerful forms of technology will be done with care, caution, ethics, and responsibility (World Economic Forum (WEC), 2021b, p.4) (see, in this matter, Figure 4. Artificial Intelligence (AI) and Sustainability – Ways of successfully promoting the Responsible, Ethical, and Robust Use of Technology in Turbulent Times).

In December 2020, the specialists from the World Economic Forum (WEC) published the "White Paper" entitled "Responsible Limits on Facial Recognition. Use Case: Flow Management. Part II Pilot phase: Self-assessment, the audit management system and certification" in which they stressed the importance of bringing technology to the highest levels possible in order to have access to accurate results when it comes to correctly identifying the employers, employees, customers, clients, and sellers (World

Figure 4. Artificial Intelligence (AI) and Sustainability – Ways of successfully promoting the Responsible, Ethical, and Robust Use of Technology in Turbulent Times. Source: the authors, based on the sources highlighted in the references section of this book chapter

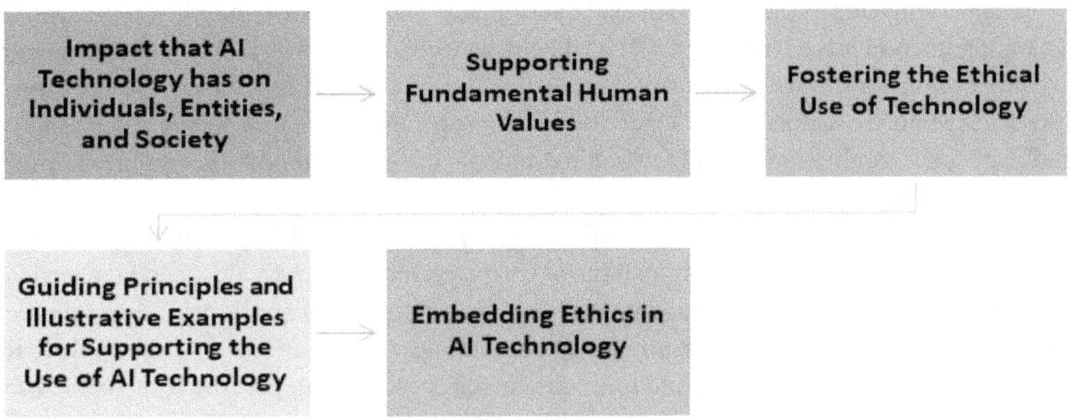

Economic Forum (WEC), 2020a, p.3). An interesting point was brought to the attention by the World Economic Forum (WEC), as a result of the COVID-19 pandemic, in terms of offering responsible access to "seamless and contactless technology" as well as of facilitating the responsible use of those frameworks capable to support "facial recognition technology and remote biometrics" in the airport industry (World Economic Forum (WEC), 2020a, p.3). It ought to be considered that Artificial Intelligence (AI) and sustainability play a crucial role in the responsible use of facial recognition technologies, since there are numerous risks and trade-offs associated with the implementation of the governance frameworks and the performance management systems specific to the facial recognition technologies in different domains, such as, for instance, in the aforementioned airport industry (World Economic Forum (WEC), 2020a, p.3).

In continuation to the aforementioned ideas, the "White Paper" published in December 2020 on "Ethics by Design: An organizational approach to responsible use of technology" mentions the importance of improving individuals' lives with the aid of technology while centering on fostering ethical and moral benefits for all individuals and for the society (World Economic Forum (WEC), 2020b, p.4). Hence, technological innovation needs to be constantly supported by up-to-date strong legal systems and transparent regulatory systems (World Economic Forum (WEC), 2020b, p.5).

Even though the times are rapidly changing and the situations encountered these days are highly challenging, specialists believe that there will always be solutions capable to support health, well-being, and sustainability in our society (Popescu, 2018; Popescu, 2019a, 2019b, 2019c, 2019d). Moreover, the Post-COVID-19 Era seeks to accentuate the necessity of finding and maintaining equilibrium between all these rapid changes and unprecedented challenges, by fostering ethical methods, good practices, good governance, corporate social responsibility, and social responsibility with the aid of new technologies – such as the ones represented by Artificial Intelligence (AI) (Popescu, V. A. et al., 2014; Popescu, V. A. et al., 2015a, 2015b, 2015c).

DISCUSSION AND SYNTHESIS OF RESULTS

The discussion and synthesis of results section of this book chapter examines the most important findings that characterize the subject under analysis.

First of all, the results show that Artificial Intelligence (AI) and sustainability represent the two game-changing instruments of the Post-COVID-19 Era as well as the key drivers for economic development, social development, and environmental protection, based on the fact that by combining the ethical principles and the policy and the governance frameworks specific to the new forms of technology with the benefits of sustainability the world in which individuals live in might have the opportunity to evolve in a safe and inclusive manner.

Second of all, taken together Artificial Intelligence (AI) and sustainability could work in the benefit of people and of the society, thus avoiding all those situations in which individuals and the environment might be harmed in any way. In this matter, leaders, governments and specialists' worldwide call for responsible innovation and research practices, ethical principles capable to successfully apply to the new forms of technology, and new methods and novel processes capable to support the responsible use of the instruments, tools and technologies associated with Artificial Intelligence (AI).

SOLUTIONS AND RECOMMENDATIONS

The solutions and recommendations section of this book chapter take into consideration the benefits supported by the Sustainable Development Goals (SDGs) at a global level.

In this matter, the first solution and recommendation brought to the attention by the authors is to foster responsible innovation capable to respond in a timely manner to the requirements imposed by the United Nations Sustainable Development Goals (SDGs), taking into consideration the following key aspects: (a) Artificial Intelligence (AI) can change the future of the society in which individuals live in by its use in responsible technology product development, in this way offering a better experience to the clients and customers, and facilitating access to improved and higher benefits for the entities; (b) Artificial Intelligence (AI) can facilitate responsible economic growth in our society as well as sustainable development, by promoting those technologies that support happiness, life, prosperity, and well-being; and (c) Artificial Intelligence (AI) can be used responsible every step of the way, its power offering the opportunity to create good in the society and help entities to develop, innovate, and achieve more goals than ever before in the history of mankind.

FUTURE RESEARCH DIRECTIONS

In this case, the future research directions might tackle the following targets: first of all, one possible research direction could be represented by presenting the correlation between the Artificial Intelligence (AI) and the Sustainable Development Goals (SDGs), with a particular emphasis on the benefits of using the new technologies in an ethical and in a responsible manner in our society, driven by entities commitment to respond to the customers' needs in an optimum manner, capable to build trust and to raise awareness in supporting happiness, life, prosperity, and well-being for all individuals worldwide; second of all, another possible research direction could be represented by the benefits of using Artificial

Intelligence (AI) in key domains in the benefit of humankind and the planet, such as, for instance: in the energy sector, the medicine field, and so on.

CONCLUSION

In conclusion, these days Artificial Intelligence (AI) represents one of the most inspiring forces capable to accelerate the global efforts to support, on the one hand, economic and social development and to ensure, on the other hand, environmental protection. In continuation, sustainability – in the form acknowledged by the United Nations (UN) 17 Sustainable Development Goals (SDGs), offers both people and entities the tremendous opportunity to protect the environment and to conserve the limited Planet's resources, by making use in an ethical and in a responsible manner of the benefits brought by new and innovative instruments, tools, and technologies embodies by Artificial Intelligence (AI). Given these unprecedented circumstances, the COVID-19 pandemic and the COVID-19 crisis severely and irreversibly disturbed the balance initially expected to have been brought by the achievement of the Global Goals. Nevertheless, these new and unprecedented changes and challenges have the power to make individuals stronger and more united in their desire to accomplish the United Nations (UN) 17 Sustainable Development Goals (SDGs) in the Post-COVID-19 Era. Hence, this book chapter encourages specialists, leaders, and governments worldwide to profoundly reflect on the following key questions and to discover answers to these important questions, such as: (a) "Is Artificial Intelligence a tool for Sustainability or is Sustainability the omnipresent driver of change for digitalization?"; (b) "Does the future of inclusive and robust Sustainable Development (SD) rely on the Artificial Intelligence technologies?"; and (c) "Is humanity ready for those Business Practices Models based on Artificial Intelligence for Sustainability?" In this way, the authors believe, that individuals will have all the necessary arguments to become more responsible in their actions and in their activities, becoming aware of the fact that, through their decisions, they may either work towards accomplishing the United Nations (UN) 17 Sustainable Development Goals (SDGs), or against the achievement of the Global Goals.

ACKNOWLEDGMENT

This research received no specific grant from any funding agency in the public, commercial, or not-for-profit sectors.

REFERENCES

European Commission (EC). (2022). *Proposal for a Regulation of the European Parliament and of the Council on the European Health Data Space (Text with EEA relevance)* {SEC(2022) 196 final} - {SWD(2022) 130 final} - {SWD(2022) 131 final} - {SWD(2022) 132 final}. COM(2022). 197 final 2022/0140 (COD). https://health.ec.europa.eu/system/files/2022-05/com_2022-197_en.pdf

European Commission (EC). (2020). *White Paper On Artificial Intelligence - A European approach to excellence and trust.* COM(2020) 65 final. https://ec.europa.eu/info/sites/default/files/commission-white-paper-artificial-intelligence-feb2020_en.pdf

European Parliament (EP). (2021). *EU health data center and a common data strategy for public health. Study Panel for the Future of Science and Technology EPRS.* European Parliamentary Research Service. Scientific Foresight Unit (STOA). PE 690.009 – September 2021. https://www.europarl.europa.eu/RegData/etudes/STUD/2021/690009/EPRS_STU(2021)690009_EN.pdf

European Parliament (EP). (2022a). *Artificial intelligence: MEPs want the EU to be a global standard-setter.* https://www.europarl.europa.eu/news/en/press-room/20220429IPR28228/artificial-intelligence-meps-want-the-eu-to-be-a-global-standard-setter

European Parliament (EP). (2022b). *Special Committee on Artificial Intelligence in a Digital Age.* https://www.europarl.europa.eu/committees/en/aida/home/highlights

European Parliament (EP). (2022c). *Special Committee on Artificial Intelligence in a Digital Age.* Committees. Activity Report. following AIDA Mandate 2020-2022. September 2020 - March 2022. European Union (EU). https://www.europarl.europa.eu/committees/en/aida/home/highlights. https://www.europarl.europa.eu/cmsdata/248838/AIDA_Committee_Activity_Report.pdf

Popescu, C. R. G. (2018). "Intellectual Capital" - Role, Importance, Components and Influences on the Performance of Organizations - A Theoretical Approach. *32nd Conference of the International-Business-Information-Management-Association (IBIMA). Vision 2020: Sustainable Economic Development And Application Of Innovation Management.*

Popescu, C. R. G. (2019a). Business Development Opportunities: Demonstrating Present And Future Performance, Auditing Intellectual Capital: A Case Study On Romanian Organizations. *33rd International-Business-Information-Management-Association (IBIMA) Conference. Vision 2025: Education Excellence and Management of Innovations through Sustainable Economic Competitive Advantage.*

Popescu, C. R. G. (2019b). Intellectual Capital, Integrated Strategy and Performance: Focusing on Companies' Unique Value Creation Mechanism and Promoting Better Organizational Reporting In Romania: A Framework Dominated By the Impact of Green Marketing and Green Marketing Strategies. *33rd International-Business-Information-Management-Association (IBIMA) Conference. Vision 2025: Education Excellence and Management of Innovations through Sustainable Economic Competitive Advantage.*

Popescu, C. R. G. (2019c). Demonstrating How Universities Extend Value Creation And Performance: Convergence Between Intellectual Capital Contributions And Research Quality - A Romanian Collective Intelligence Framework. *11th International Conference on Education and New Learning Technologies (EDULEARN). EDULEARN19: 11th International Conference On Education And New Learning Technologies.*

Popescu, C. R. G. (2019d). Using Intellectual Capital Measurements In Universities To Assess Performance - Evidence From The Romanian Education System. *11th International Conference on Education and New Learning Technologies (EDULEARN). EDULEARN19: 11th International Conference On Education And New Learning Technologies.*

Popescu, V. A., Popescu, G. N., & Popescu, C. R. G. (2014). The Economic And Social Dimensions Of Romania's Metallurgical Industry. *Metalurgija. Croatian Metallurgical Socberislaviceva, 53*(1), 113-115.

Popescu, V. A., Popescu, G. N., & Popescu, C. R. G. (2015a). The Relation Productivity - Environment In The Context Of Sustainable Development - Case Study On The Romanian Industry. *Metalurgija. Croatian Metallurgical Socberislaviceva, 54*(1), 286-288.

Popescu, V. A., Popescu, G. N., & Popescu, C. R. G. (2015b). Competitiveness And Sustainability - A Modern Economic Approach To The Industrial Policy. *Metalurgija. Croatian Metallurgical Socberislaviceva, 54*(2), 426-428.

Popescu, V. A., Popescu, G. N., & Popescu, C. R. G. (2015c). The Impact Of Global Crisis On The Dominant Sectors Of The Economy At The Romanian Industry. *Metalurgija. Croatian Metallurgical Socberislaviceva, 54*(2), 289-291.

United Nations (UN). (2022). *Sustainable Development Goals (SDGs). Goal 3: Ensure healthy lives and promote well-being for all at all ages.* https://www.un.org/sustainabledevelopment/health/

World Economic Forum (WEC). (2018). *Fourth Industrial Revolution for the Earth Series. Harnessing Artificial Intelligence for the Earth.* PwC and Stanford Woods Institute for the Environment. https://www3.weforum.org/docs/Harnessing_Artificial_Intelligence_for_the_Earth_report_2018.pdf

World Economic Forum (WEC). (2020a). *Responsible Limits on Facial Recognition. Use Case: Flow Management. Part II Pilot phase: Self-assessment, the audit management system and certification.* White Paper. https://www.weforum.org/whitepapers?platform=shaping-the-future-of-technology-governance-artificial-intelligence-and-machine-learning. https://www3.weforum.org/docs/WEF_Responsible_Limits_on_Facial_Recognition_2020.pdf

World Economic Forum (WEC). (2020b). *Ethics by Design: An organizational approach to responsible use of technology.* White Paper. https://www.weforum.org/whitepapers?platform=shaping-the-future-of-technology-governance-artificial-intelligence-and-machine-learning. https://www3.weforum.org/docs/WEF_Responsible_Limits_on_Facial_Recognition_2020.pdf

World Economic Forum (WEC). (2021a). *Responsible Use of Technology: The IBM Case Study.* White Paper. https://www.weforum.org/whitepapers?platform=shaping-the-future-of-technology-governance-artificial-intelligence-and-machine-learning. https://www3.weforum.org/docs/WEF_Responsible_Use_of_Technology_The_IBM_Case_Study_2021.pdf

World Economic Forum (WEC). (2021b). *Harnessing Artificial Intelligence to Accelerate the Energy Transition.* White Paper. https://www.weforum.org/whitepapers?platform=shaping-the-future-of-technology-governance-artificial-intelligence-and-machine-learning. https://www3.weforum.org/docs/WEF_Harnessing_AI_to_accelerate_the_Energy_Transition_2021.pdf

World Economic Forum (WEC). (2021c). *Responsible Use of Technology: The Microsoft Case Study.* White Paper. https://www.weforum.org/whitepapers?platform=shaping-the-future-of-technology-governance-artificial-intelligence-and-machine-learning. https://www3.weforum.org/docs/WEF_Responsible_Use_of_Technology_2021.pdf

World Economic Forum (WEC). (2022a). *A Blueprint for Equity and Inclusion in Artificial Intelligence.* White Paper. https://www.weforum.org/whitepapers?platform=shaping-the-future-of-technology-governance-artificial-intelligence-and-machine-learning. https://www3.weforum.org/docs/WEF_A_Blueprint_for_Equity_and_Inclusion_in_Artificial_Intelligence_2022.pdf

World Economic Forum (WEC). (2022b). *Unpacking AI Procurement in a Box: Insights from Implementation.* White Paper. https://www.weforum.org/whitepapers?platform=shaping-the-future-of-technology-governance-artificial-intelligence-and-machine-learning. https://www3.weforum.org/docs/WEF_Unpacking_AI_Procurement_in_a_Box_2022.pdf

KEY TERMS AND DEFINITIONS

Artificial Intelligence and Machine Learning on the Way of Transforming Various Industries: Artificial Intelligence (AI) represents the intelligence that the machines are demonstrating and is opposed to the Natural Intelligence (NI) which is displayed by human beings and by animals; in addition, Artificial Intelligence (AI) and Machine Learning (ML) have the great power to transform various domains and industries these days, such as, for example, business, education, law, information technology (IT), marketing, medical, technology industry (TI), manufacturing, and so on; thus, in order to support a better future for all and be part of a game-changing Post-COVID-19 Era, Artificial Intelligence (AI) should be friendly, should enable smart machines to be capable of performing tasks that are repetitive for humans, thus offering people the opportunity to center on grater and on more complex task and to be able to develop themselves and their creativity (European Parliament (EP), 2022b).

Artificial Intelligence in a Game-Changing Post-COVID-19 Era: Artificial Intelligence (AI) occupies a top position these days and is considered a hot subject due to its popularity among the representatives of the business circles and the technology circles; although many specialists argue that Artificial Intelligence (AI) represents the future of our society, it can be noted that it is, in fact, an integrating component of the present days; moreover, it represents the branch of Computer Sciences (CS) that possesses a game-changing power in the Post-COVID-19 Era and which represents the key to a better future for all, in the context in which it values the remarkable advantages and the magnificent benefits comprised by the simulation of Human Intelligence Processes (HIP) by different types of machines – with a particular accent put on the simulation of Human Intelligence Processes (HIP) by different types of computer systems and which put an accent on the development of Intelligence Machines (IM); furthermore, there are numerous applications that enable Intelligence Machines (IM) to operate, think, and work like human beings, and which are based on Artificial Intelligence (AI), which are based on Expert Systems (ES), Natural Language Processing (NLP), Machine Vision (MV), Problem-Solving (PS), Learning and Planning (LP), and/or Speech Recognition (SR); hence, Artificial Intelligence (AI) in a game-changing Post-COVID-19 Era points out the necessity of helping human beings to adapt to the digitalization processes at a quicker pace, in order to obtain major benefits into day to day lives, while finding solutions to improve, govern, and develop the application of Artificial Intelligence (AI) in the future yet to come (European Parliament (EP), 2022c).

Benefits and Risks of Artificial Intelligence: These days, Artificial Intelligence (AI) is progressing rapidly, and it brings both benefits and risks to our society; specialists believe that the impact of Artificial Intelligence (AI) on our society should be in the benefit of the society and our Planet Earth, by aligning the Artificial Intelligence (AI) goals with the Sustainable Development Goals (SDGs), thus creating a New Economic Model capable to support life, well-being, health, happiness, peace, security, and a bright future for all; nevertheless, specialists believe that the impact of Artificial Intelligence (AI) on our society could be devastating in those cases in which it will lead to threats to the safety of the communities, by making use of "lethal autonomous weapons systems" – namely, "slaughter-bots", "killer robots" (European Parliament (EP), 2022a).

Economic Development (ED): The COVID-19 pandemic and the COVID-19 crisis have made human beings more aware of the fragile nature of life and have shown that any minor inadvertence that might occur in the habitat that individuals live in could lead to immediate disasters, having irreversible consequences on our lives; Economic Development (ED) should be understood these days in a different manner that it was perceived in the past decades, since development itself should be associated with good lives, high standards of living, happiness, prosperity, security, healthier lives, and a bright future for all; Economic Development (ED) should be based on harmony with the natural ecosystems and should be understood as a way of making people's lives better without harming the environment and without affecting the Planet's resources.

Environmental Protection (EP): These days, the New Economy has proven that knowledge represents the most important asset that the society has access to and has shown that life is the most valuable good that individuals have; in the spirit of acting responsibility, Environmental Protection (EP) has become an integrating part of the New Economy, showing that the future of humanity and of Planet Earth are interrelated, and one without the other is not possible; Environmental Protection (EP) depends on Social Responsibility (SR) and on Corporate Social Responsibility (CSR) actions and initiatives, that embrace healthier lifestyles, deep concern towards nature's preservation, keeping the natural habitats safe, ensuring biodiversity, and fostering well-balanced ecosystems.

Social Development (SD): In the Post-COVID-19 Era, Social Development (SD) has become essential for the prosperity and the future of humanity; the COVID-19 pandemic and the COVID-19 crisis have shown the fragility of life itself and the importance of living in harmony with the plants, the animals, and the environment, at a general level; besides that, it is the authors opinion that Social Development (SD) relies on access to education programs and life-long training sessions, since constantly expending knowledge and having access to information provide better solutions for healthier lifestyles; in continuation, having access to education represents a tremendous asset when it comes to making the right choices and taking the right decisions in life, based on the fact that the access to information makes individuals more powerful and more capable to choose between right and wrong; these days, Social Development (SD) should reflect the level of harmony that should be encountered between the society and nature, since sustainability should accompany all the actions made by people and all the decisions that are taken.

Sustainability in a Game-Changing Post-COVID-19 Era: These days, taking care of the natural habitats and ensuring biodiversity have come major concerns for specialists; sustainability represents a must in the society in which people live in these days, since it has the power to support life and to ensure healthier ways of living; the society in which people live in today has been severely and, in some cases, even irreversibly affected by pollution, deforestation, and waste, which has led to the need to become more responsible in the actions and in the activities that take places in all areas; the future of the society is represented by green economics, with an accent on healthier habits and healthier frameworks and models in which to develop and to prosper; the old economic models based on increased prices, maximization of profit, and high benefits without showing concern towards nature and individuals, have led the society to severe crises, which means that specialists have looked for new economic models which are built on better principles than the ones before, centering on trust, respect towards life, nature, and the prosperity of the future generations due to come.

Chapter 2
How to Communicate SDG 12 in Social Media:
The Case of Distribution Channels

Pedro Cuesta-Valiño
https://orcid.org/0000-0001-9521-333X
Universidad de Alcalá, Spain

Azucena Penelas-Leguía
Universidad de Alcalá, Spain

Patricia Durán-Álamo
Universidad de Alcalá, Spain

ABSTRACT

Over recent years, companies have developed multiple corporate social responsibility (CSR) actions with the aim of being more economically, socially, and environmentally responsible with their surroundings. In this context, many of these strategies are linked to the Sustainable Development Goals (SDG) set out in the framework of Agenda 2030. As far as SDG 12 is concerned, the role of supermarkets in its achievement is evident, due to the fact that it is closely related to food, food waste, and healthy diets. Taking this into account, the objective of this research is to find out how Spanish supermarket chains are communicating their CSR strategies based on SDG 12 through their social networks. A survey of 300 people has been carried out to understand the level of importance that the Spanish population gives to supermarkets complying with and communicating their commitment to SDG 12. Thanks to the results of this research, companies will be able to carry out specific communication and social marketing strategies through social networks with which they will enhance their brand image and reputation.

DOI: 10.4018/978-1-6684-7499-0.ch002

INTRODUCTION

The social, environmental, and economic challenges facing global society have made it increasingly crucial for the companies that make up the global, national and local business fabric to commit themselves to improve the conditions of the market in which they operate, seeking to give back to society part of the benefit they derive from it. Some of the fields in which CSR actions are focused are related to climate change or with ensuring access to essential resources such as education or food.

In this context of business commitment to society, in 2015, all United Nations (UN) and the Member States adopted 17 Sustainable Development Goals (SDGs) as part of the 2030 Agenda for Sustainable Development.

The emergence of the SDGs has triggered companies worldwide to frame their CSR actions and have a common goal, directly linking their projects to achieving one goal or another. Given that companies are part of society, they must also have the ethics to contribute to achieving these goals (IESE, 2017). For example, when it comes to the commercial distribution sector, SDG 12 has become the protagonist. Concepts such as food waste or responsible, healthy and sustainable consumption enter the scene and become the protagonists of the actions carried out by commercial distribution companies such as supermarkets and hypermarkets.

However, for a company's CSR strategies to be truly understood by its audiences, they must be communicated appropriately (Illia et al., 2010). Researchers such as Pagani (2012) go so far as to question whether a company can be socially responsible without communicating. Furthermore, others such as Orjuela (2011) assert that communication determines the success or failure of a company's CSR management.

Consequently, now that CSR actions are directly linked and related to the SDGs, it is still necessary for companies to communicate them. Through such communication, companies not only demonstrate their commitment to society but also to the achievement of the SDGs set out and defined by the UN in the 2030 Agenda.

Considering the importance of communication for the consolidation and impact of CSR strategies and, consequently, of the SDGs, this research aims to analyse what CSR strategies linked to SDG 12 carry out by the leading retail companies in Spain, how they communicate these actions through social media, specifically on Instagram, and whether society is interested in the commitment of retail chains.

BACKGROUND

Corporate Social Responsibility (CSR) has been defined by many experts from the academic and business world over the last few years. Taking as a reference the definition provided by the ISO 26000 standard, CSR is the responsibility of an organisation for the impacts of its decisions and activities on society and the environment through ethical and transparent behaviour that contributes to sustainable development, including the health and well-being of society. Furthermore, it must consider stakeholder expectations and current law, be consistent with international standards of behaviour and be integrated within the company and embodied in its relationships (ISO 26000, 2010).

Therefore, CSR is considered an asset that must be managed correctly, as it directly impacts the reputation of organisations (Estanyol, 2020). Therefore, correct management, implementation and communication of CSR can generate positive changes in the company (Pabón et al., 2013) and its reputation.

Table 1. Sustainable Development Goals. Source: UN (https://www.un.org/es/sustainable-development-goals)

GOAL 1: No Poverty	GOAL 7: Affordable and Clean Energy	GOAL 13: Climate Action
GOAL 2: Zero Hunger	GOAL 8: Decent Work and Economic Growth	GOAL 14: Life Below Water
GOAL 3: Good Health and Well-being	GOAL 9: Industry, Innovation and Infrastructure	GOAL 15: Life on Land
GOAL 4: Quality Education	GOAL 10: Reduced Inequality	GOAL 16: Peace and Justice Strong Institutions
GOAL 5: Gender Equality	GOAL 11: Sustainable Cities and Communities	GOAL 17: Partnerships to achieve the Goal
GOAL 6: Clean Water and Sanitation	GOAL 12: Responsible Consumption and Production	

Furthermore, other academic research has also demonstrated the positive impact of CSR strategies on the economic growth of companies and countries (Navarro & González, 2006; Skare & Golja, 2014).

Considering its positive impact, the weight of CSR actions has increased within organisations over the last few years. Business reports such as the one launched by SERES-Deloitte in 2022 show that Spanish companies invested 4% more in CSR in 2020, reaching 1,486 million.

In addition to this context, in which the importance of CSR is growing, in 2015, all Member States of the United Nations (UN) approved the 17 Sustainable Development Goals (SDGs) as part of the 2030 Agenda for Sustainable Development (Table 1). As set out by the UN, the SDGs aim to become the roadmap that society must follow to achieve a sustainable future. It is why the UN itself highlights the importance of the involvement of the private sector and the companies that make it up.

Each of the SDGs de encompasses a series of actions and activities that, in turn, become small sub-goals with which society can identify more closely, thus facilitating their implementation (Khan, A et al., 2021). For example, SDG 12 promotes healthier and more sustainable food, eradicating food waste or more sustainable and environmentally friendly food production.

With the emergence of the SDGs and the UN's call to the private sector, more and more companies are framing their CSR actions around the SDGs. So much so that even studies and reports, such as the SERES-Deloitte 2022 report, highlight the SDGs' impact on companies' CSR strategies. As far as Spain is concerned, and according to the data in the report above, 90% of the companies participating in the study include the Sustainable Development Goals in their CSR strategy.

In the distribution and food sector, the commitment to the SDGs and CSR at the level of ecology and sustainability must be even more significant since, as different studies have shown, the food industry is one of the most polluting industries (Willett et al., 2019) along with the fashion and energy industries. In fact, according to experts such as Hartman (2011) and Genier et al. (2009), the food sector faces challenges that are closely related to natural, human and physical resources. A reality which must be the role they play in one of the population's most basic needs: their food and the care of what is consumed.

It is why supermarket and hypermarket chains should have a conscious and genuine commitment to SDG 12, carrying out specific actions to minimise the environmental impact of their activity to make it more sustainable (Schmitt et al., 2017). In addition, and following the UN guidelines for the fulfilment of SDG 12, they must also promote healthier, more sustainable and responsible consumption among their customers. Thanks to this type of consumption, they will generate a lower environmental impact (Torstensson et al., 2021), without forgetting that companies have the power to influence and boost demand for certain products (Dawson, J., 2013). Companies linked to the distribution and production sector can organise themselves to reduce food waste, thus minimising its negative impact on the environment (Bonomi and Ricciardi, 2017; Moggi et al., 2018).

Based on this reality, in Spain, the National Association of Large Retailers (ANGEM), which includes some of the most important companies in the Spanish retail sector, such as Carrefour, El Corte Inglés, Eroski and the Alcampo Group, displays on its website information related to compliance and commitment to the SDGs. In this website, they show the sector's clear commitment to CSR linked to the SDGs.

Social media as a corporate communication channel over the last few years, its importance has been increasing, leading companies to use it to develop and give more visibility to their marketing and communication actions. Experts such as Jami & Lotfiyan (2020) have highlighted that they are an indispensable advertising channel. In this new context, these platforms are postulated as a new resource to develop social marketing actions in which the commitment to the SDGs is made known. In addition to this reality, users are not only using social media as an entertainment channel, they are also using them to transmit knowledge and as an "*Internet of value*" (Porcelli, 2020). It is why companies can also share helpful content related to the SDGs (ElAlfy et al., 2020), offering their audiences information that allows them to learn about these goals that seek to build and consolidate a more sustainable society. In fact, regarding companies' use of social media to communicate CSR, research has shown that its use improves the effectiveness of CSR strategies (Wang & Huang, 2018).

In the case of retail companies and their commitment to the SDGs, social media is an exciting environment to transmit values and behaviours that encourage compliance with the SDGs among their audiences, i.e., consumers and society. It should not be forgotten that communicating internally and externally what has been done in terms of CSR and SDGs through social media feeds back into the system and creates a network for communicating sustainability in a transparent, truthful and effective manner (Cuaderno de Comercio y Sostenibilidad, 2020).

In any case, in terms of communication of concepts associated with SDG 12 through social media, authors such as Samoggia et al. (2019) have analysed the communication in social media that *retailers* make about *healthy food* or the importance of communicating consumption and local products (Kumar et al., 2021). Continuing with the communication of SDG 12 on social media, the research carried out by Pilar et al. (2021) on the presence and relationship of the term *healthy food* with other concepts on Twitter and Instagram stands out. As they indicate, "Given that young people change their behaviour about people's behaviour on social networks, it is possible to use this data to predict their future association with healthy food characteristics" (Pilar et al., 2021).

Given that CSR strategies are increasingly focused on the SDGs and that companies must communicate these CSR actions for them to be genuinely consolidated, this research shows how Mercadona, Carrefour, Lidl and Grupo Día publicise CSR actions that focus on SDG 12 through social media, specifically through Instagram. The choice of these four companies linked to the commercial distribution sector in Spain is because four accounts for almost 50% of the sector's market share (Table 2). Furthermore, the choice of Instagram is because it is the favourite social media platform in Spain (We Are Social, 2022). Besides, a survey carries out to find out to what extent the Spanish population demands a conscious and tangible commitment from these companies to CSR strategies based on SDG 12.

With the analysis of all this information, the following research questions are posed:

Table 2. Market share according to Kantar Wordpanel 2021. Source: Own elaboration

Company	Market share (%)
Mercadona	25.1
Carrefour	9.4
Lidl	5.4
Grupo Día	4.5

- Research Question 1 (RQ1): *Do the leading distribution companies operating in Spain carry out CSR actions linked to SDG 12?*
- Research Question 2 (RQ2): *Do retail companies communicate on Instagram about CSR actions linked to SDG 12?*
- Research Question 3 (RQ3): *Do women value CSR actions linked to SDG 12 more than men?*
- Research Question 4 (RQ3): *Is age a variable influencing the perception of CSR actions linked to SDG 12?*

METHODOLOGY

The methodological approach of this research is based on a dual study in which primary and secondary data sources have been used. With this combination, it hopes to obtain the necessary information to analyse the level of implementation of CSR strategies linked to SDG 12 in the leading Spanish distribution companies, as well as whether these companies communicate the actions linked to SDG 12 through social media.

In the first phase of the research, an exploratory descriptive study was carried out in which secondary data was collected on the social media activity of the four leading companies linked to the retail distribution sector in Spain. Specifically, it has been analysed how these companies have communicated CSR actions based on SDG 12 through Instagram during January, February, and March 2022. Consequently, with the qualitative information collected, it is possible to extract an overview of the level of communications that these companies make on social media about actions related to SDG 12.

In the second phase of the research, a descriptive cross-sectional study based on a survey was carried out. The survey was carried out between March and May 2022 with 300 valid questionnaires. For the validation of the questions (items) that make up the questionnaire, a focus group was carried out with the participation of a total of four consumers who regularly shop (two men and two women between 16 and 65 years old), two company executives who are linked to CSR strategies and two university professors who teach management in social media and who have also researched topics related to the SDGs and social media.

The questionnaire is composed of three blocks of questions. The first group aims to find out the respondents' current purchasing preferences. Then, different questions are posed to analyse the respondents' perception of the level of importance they attach to the commitment of retail companies to respect the environment and the achievement of SDG 12. A 5-point Likert-type scale is used for these questions, where 1 is complete disagreement and 5 is complete agreement. These questions are drawn from research conducted by Chu et al. (2020 and 2019) to analyse how CSR actions influence consumer sentiment towards a brand and Mandaric et al. (2021) on these parameters applied to the fashion industry. Based on this research, the respective adaptations have been made to retail distribution and SDG 12. The data collected in the survey were analysed with the DYANE 4 software.

MAIN FOCUS OF THE CHAPTER

Results of Secondary Data Analysis

As explained above, during the first phase of the research, an exploratory, descriptive study was carried out to analyse the activity of Mercadona, Carrefour, Lidl and Día España on Instagram. This monitoring aims to analyse the weight of the publications related to the actions. To do this, firstly it is necessary explain each of these companies' actions about SDG 12.

Mercadona. It is positioned as the leading retail distribution company in Spain. The company currently has 1,632 shops throughout Spain and 29 in Portugal, with a workforce of over 95,000 employees in both countries (Mercadona, 2022). Throughout its website, Mercadona states its commitment to fulfilling the SDGs. About SDG 12, information can find related to specific actions to ensure animal welfare, others to responsibly manage waste or commit to avoiding food waste. Despite these proposals, they lack a specific corporate framework. They do not have a unique name to unify all these actions. They are actions that they, as a company, commit to doing, but there is no involvement process for their consumers. They talk about what they do as a company but not how to translate this into everyday life in households.

Carrefour. Carrefour is a French-based company whose central sector is retail distribution. It is currently the second largest retailer in Spain, with 205 Carrefour hypermarkets, 159 Carrefour Market supermarkets, 1067 Carrefour Express supermarkets, 146 service stations and 426 travel agencies. Carrefour demonstrates its commitment to SDG 12 with the inclusion on the shelves of its various brands such as *ECO-Planet, Carrefour Veggie, Nuestra Tierra* and *Carrefour BIO*. They all reveal the company's commitment to promoting a healthier and more sustainable eating style. In addition, it has activated specific strategies such as "*Act For Good*", "*Zero Waste*", or "*Acciones para comer mejor*" (Actions to eat better), which not only serve as a platform to give visibility to the brands themselves but also promote recycling, the reuse of food packaging, as well as the end of food waste among its audiences (Carrefour, 2022).

Lild. Of German origin, Lidl has been operating in Spain since 1994 and has become the third largest retail chain. Spain has 630 shops, 11 logistics platforms and a workforce of more than 17,000 employees (Lild, 2022). Its website (Lidl, 2022) is where CSR actions and their direct link to the SDGs are visible. In the case of SDG 12, and like the previous companies analysed, they show a clear "responsible purchasing policy" with which they ensure animal welfare, the production of raw materials ecologically and sustainably, as well as the consolidation of ecological and healthy brands such as "*BIO*" or "*Vemondo*". In addition, it promotes healthy eating with its initiatives such as "*FrutiTour*" or "*Fórmula Desayuno" (Breakfast Formula),* which encourages the consumption of fruit in the family.

Dia España. The Día supermarket chain was founded in Madrid in 1979. Currently, the corporation belongs to the industrial group LetterOne, which in 2019 became the main shareholder. According to data provided by the company, DIA has 3,918 shops (2021 figure) in Spain, of which 2,851 are DIA shops and 1,067 are Clarel shops, making it the fourth largest commercial distribution group in Spain. In terms of sustainability, the company's 2021 Sustainability Plan, which has the 17 SDGs as its guid-

Table 3. Results of the analysis of the companies' information on Instagram. Source: Own elaboration based on Instagram profiles of each of the companies

Company	Nº Followers	Featured Stories	January Publicactions	February Publications	March Publications
Mercadona	586 thousand	No	1	1	0
Carrefour	809 thousand	Yes	9	13	11
Lidl	1,4 million	No	13	11	0
Día España	286 thousand	No	2	2	2

ing thread, is noteworthy. About SDG 12, initiatives related to food waste, food safety, improving the nutritional profile of own-brand products and the sustainability of raw materials stand out. In its new line of communication and *rebranding*, Día España has opted for the slogan "Nueva Calidad Día" (New Día Quality), which also gives visibility to these direct commitments to SDG 12. As has been highlighted, all the information previously analysed is accessible through the website of each of the corporations. This reality shows that all four use this digital environment to communicate their commitment to SDG 12.

Table 3 shows the number of followers each company has, whether they have featured *stories* to give visibility to the actions related to SDG 12 mentioned above, as well as the number of publications they made regarding SDG 12 during January, February and March 2022.

As can be seen, Carrefour is the company that communicates its commitment to SDG12 the most, followed by Lidl. It should be noted that while in the case of Carrefour, the link with the actions carried out about SDG12 is reflected using *hashtags* and logos created for each of the brands and initiatives, this is not the case for Mercadona and Grupo Día. In the case of Lidl, it maintains very active communication with veganism and, consequently, the consumption of vegan products of the Vemondo brand during January, as they promote the challenge they have called "Veganuary" (vega+january), which has its hashtag (#veganuary). Continuing with Lidl, February gives excellent visibility to its "BIO" products, with images where the brand logo is visible. However, it lacks its hashtag or one related to SDG 12. This commitment declines during March when no publication gives direct visibility to its CSR actions linked to SDG 12.

Mercadona and Grupo Día make publications without a marked and defined line of communication, following a more sporadic and not very specific scheme, makings it difficult for followers to relate the publication to a positive impact, for example, on the environment, food, or local development. In this case, it is only Día España which, in a bid to reinforce its new line of communication (New Quality Day), shows in some of its publications the text "New Quality Day" in the image, referring to the national origin in the written text of the publications.

Finally, in the case of using featured *stories*, once again, it is only Carrefour that uses this resource to give visibility and importance to the initiatives that they carry out about SDG 12.

These results show how the four companies carry out very similar actions in SDG 12 compliance. However, not all of them have an initiative with their name to frame them and give them visibility. However, while the website becomes, in all four cases, a resource from which information on these strategies related to SDG 12 can be obtained, the social network Instagram is only used consistently and visibly in two cases. These results show that, except in the case of Carrefour and Lidl, there is still a long way to go in using social media as a communication channel for CSR actions linked to SDG 12. Given that the

Table 4. Representativeness of the sample based on age. Source: Own elaboration based on INE data and the sample

Sample characteristics by age group	Sample		Spanish population between 16 and 65 years old	
Between 16 and 25 years old	51	17%	4.800.366	15%
Between 26 and 40 years old	138	46%	8.585.588	27%
Between 41 and 55 years old	60	20%	11.568.827	37%
Between 56 and 65 years old	51	17%	6.429.891	20%
Total	300	100%	31.384.672	100%

two companies (Mercadona and Día España) share content about their products and recipes, they could clearly and visibly highlight to their followers the part directly related to their commitment to SDG 12.

Based on the analysis, it can indicate that research questions RQ1 and RQ2 were answered in such a way that the leading supermarket and hypermarket chains in Spain are not only carrying out CSR actions linked to SDG 12 but are also taking advantage of Instagram to publicise them. The level of use among each of the companies is indeed different, with Carrefour and Lidl reporting the highest levels of use.

Results of Primary Data Analysis

As previously highlighted, alongside the exploratory, descriptive analysis, cross-sectional descriptive research was carried out based on a survey, from which a total of 300 valid questionnaires were collected. The survey aimed to determine how essential distribution companies, specifically supermarkets and hypermarkets, are to carry out and communicate actions linked to SDG 12. The data obtained were analysed using the DYANE 4 software (Santesmases, 2012)

Firstly, it should be noted that the sample can consider representative of the Spanish population between 16 and 65 years of age. The distribution is 58% women and 42% men, and with distribution by age group as shown in Table 4:

The arithmetic means of the sample based on gender reveals that both men and women respond very positively to the CSR actions linked to SDG 12. As can be seen in Table 5, the mean of the responses is always above "4.2", which shows that they are in "moderate agreement" to "complete agreement" with the items raised.

However, the cross-tabulation of mean values based on gender also reveals specific differences between the responses of men and women. Taking Snedecor's F as a reference, eight of the fifteen items analysed show statistically significant differences between men's and women's perceptions. In this sense, women are closer to "complete agreement" with the questions "use and/or produce organic products", "contribute to sustainability", "have a sustainable product line under its brand name", "have sustainable products section", "promote healthy eating habits", "promote action to minimise food waste" and "share tips on environmental care".

Based on the data obtained, it can affirm that gender directly influences the positive response to CSR actions linked to SDG 12, with women expressing a greater appreciation for this type of content and actions.

Concerning the cross-tabulation of mean values according to age, age is not a variable that influences the response. Only for the question " share tips on environmental care " is the Snedecor's F less than

Table 5. Cross tabulation of arithmetic average values concerning gender. Source: Own elaboration

Designation	Total sample	Gender		Snedecor's F
		Female	Male	
Reduce its C02 emissions in its activities	4.4600	4.5115	4.3889	F(1.298) = 1.2242 p = 0.2694
Use and/or produce organic products	4.2633	4.3736	4.1111	F(1.298) = 5.6572 p = 0.0180
Use and/or produce recycled materials	4.5700	4.6494	4.4603	F(1.298) = 3.2327 p = 0.0732
Use and/or produce biodegradable materials	4.5433	4.6149	4.4444	F(1.298) = 2.6790 p = 0.1027
Reduce the use of packaging and containers	4.5300	4.6207	4.4048	F(1.298) = 3.7984 p = 0.0522
Contribute to sustainability (e.g., by shopping local)	4.4800	4.5805	4.3413	F(1.298) = 4.8537 p = 0.0284
Have a sustainable product line under its brand name	4.3067	4.4425	4.1190	F(1.298) = 7.8005 p = 0.0056
Have sustainable products section	4.3767	4.4885	4.2222	F(1.298) = 5.6928 p = 0.0177
Promote action to minimise food waste	4.6067	4.6839	4.5000	F(1.298) = 2.7994 p = 0.0953
Promote actions to minimise waste (e.e packagings, bags, etc.)	4.6400	4.7011	4.5556	F(1.298) = 1.9269 p = 0.1661
Promote sustainable consumption habits in general	4.4800	4.5690	4.3571	F(1.298) = 3.5977 p = 0.0588
Promote healthy eating habits	4.4000	4.5690	4.1667	F(1.298) = 11.3634 p = 0.0008
Share tips on environmental care	4.2300	4.3908	4.0079	F(1.298) = 9.9014 p = 0.0018
Promote packaging recycling (e.g., how and where to recycle)	4.4800	4.5632	4.3651	F(1.298) = 3.0534 p = 0.0816
Promote responsible consumption	4.5233	4.5977	4.4206	F(1.298) = 2.5052 p = 0.1145

0.05 and therefore a significant statistical difference. In this case, the age groups "between 16 and 25" and "between 26 and 40" show a response below the sample average.

The cross-tabulation of mean values based on age reveals no significant differences between respondents' perceptions by age group, except for the case "share tips on environmental care", where it can see that the older the respondent, the more favourable the opinion of the respondents.

According to what has been analysed, in response to RQ4, it can be indicated that age is not a variable that has a determining influence on the population's response. Only in one of the items analysed can it be said that the younger population between 16 and 40 years of age, i.e., the centennials and millennials, respond less favourably to CSR actions linked to SDG 12.

Table 6. Cross tabulation of arithmetic average values concerning age. Source: Own elaboration

Designation	Total sample	age				Snedecor's F
		From 16 to 25	From 26 to 40	From 41 to 55	From 56 to 65	
Reduce its C02 emissions in its activities	4.4600	4.4118	4.3986	4.5000	4.6275	F(3.296) = 0.8023 p = 0.4934
Use and/or produce organic products	4.2633	4.0784	4.2464	4.3333	4.4118	F(3.296) = 1.1829 p = 0.3164
Use an/or produce recycled materials	4.5700	4.4314	4.5000	4.7000	4.7451	F(3.296) = 1.7457 p = 0.1577
Use and produce biodegradable materials	4.5433	4.4118	4.4783	4.7000	4.6667	F(3.296) = 1.5619 p = 0.1987
Reduce the use of packaging and containers	4.5300	4.5686	4.4420	4.5833	4.6667	F(3.296) = 0.8333 p = 0.4765
Contribute to sustainability (e.g., by shopping local)	4.4800	4.3725	4.4130	4.6000	4.6275	F(3.296) = 1.2177 p = 0.3035
Have a sustainable product line under your brand name	4.3067	4.1569	4.2029	4.4667	4.5490	F(3.296) = 2.4149 p = 0.0667
Have a sustainable product section	4.3767	4.2941	4.2899	4.5167	4.5294	F(3.296) = 1.3581 p = 0.2558
Promote action to minimise food waste	4.6067	4.6078	4.5580	4.6833	4.6471	F(3.296) = 0.2843 p = 0.8367
Promote actions to minimise waste (e.g., packaging, bags, etc.)	4.6400	4.6863	4.5362	4.7500	4.7451	F(3.296) = 1.1946 p = 0.3120
Promote sustainable consumption habits in general	4.4800	4.4118	4.3841	4.6000	4.6667	F(3.296) = 1.5120 p = 0.2115
Promote healthy eating habits	4.4000	4.2157	4.3116	4.5667	4.6275	F(3.296) = 2.2298 p = 0.0848
Share tips on environmental care	4.2300	4.1176	4.0580	4.4167	4.5882	F(3.296) = 4.1234 p = 0.0069
Promote packaging recycling (e.g., how and where to recycle)	4.4800	4.4118	4.3551	4.6333	4.7059	F(3.296) = 2.2854 p = 0.0789
Promote responsible consumption	4.5233	4.4314	4.4203	4.6333	4.7647	F(3.296) = 2.0499 p = 0.1070

SOLUTIONS AND RECOMMENDATIONS

Mercadona, Carrefour, Lidl and Día España show their commitment to the environment and society through their websites, especially about SDG 12.

According to the results obtained in this research and the literature review carried out, academic discussions have shown how many companies are directly linking their CSR strategies to the fulfilment of the SDGs. In the case of retail chains, specifically supermarkets and hypermarkets, the direct commitment should be to SDG 12, and this is what the companies analysed have shown. However, it should not be forgotten that in this commitment to SDG 12 and CSR, communication is vital. Therefore, RQ1 is confirmed, demonstrating that companies are still committed to specific communication strategies to publicise their CSR actions.

Continuing with the academic discussions, in this context, the companies analysed make use of digital environments such as the website to communicate CSR actions related to SDG12; however, in terms of social media, specifically Instagram, there is still a long way to go. Therefore, although it has been shown that social media can be a good channel for communicating retail companies' CSR commitment and SDG12 compliance (Kumar et al., 2015; Samoggia et al., 2019; Porcelli, 2020), retail companies can still make more use of its potential. Therefore, RQ2 is answered in the affirmative, although not all companies make the same use of social media.

As far as management discussions are concerned, it is confirmed that the companies analysed use Instagram to communicate with their audiences and that a large part of the content shown is linked to SDG 12 and other SDGs. Taking this into account, while Carrefour and Lidl are more committed to reflecting their SDG 12 actions on their profiles, Mercadona and Día España follow a more direct line. But, knowing that Mercadona and Día España are sharing a large amount of content related to recipes and products with some of the qualities linked to SDG 12, they could be highlighted and given greater visibility with their hashtags and designs. Both companies could use more specific content for giving more visibility to their SDFG 12 actions.

In addition, retailers are encouraged to create CSR actions linked to SDG 12 with their names, designs and hashtags (as in the case of Carrefour). This way, a common thread is created at the communication level, allowing audiences to identify each action implemented clearly. Once this exercise has been carried out, their dissemination in social media is framed and directly linked to the brand and the SDGs themselves, helping to improve and boost their dissemination.

Continuing with the management discussions, the results show that gender is a variable that influences the response to this type of action (RQ3). At the same time, age is not a relevant variable (RQ4). Therefore, when structuring their commercial promotion actions, these companies should consider that female audiences value CSR actions linked to SDG 12 more positively than male audiences. Therefore, it may be a variable when developing their marketing campaigns on social media or in other online or offline environments. However, as far as age is concerned, the research results reveal that it is not a variable that significantly influences the response. So, as a consequence, it should not necessarily influence the segmentation criteria of the campaigns.

On a social level, the interest that corporations and society have in achieving SDG 12 is genuine. It is demonstrated that the corporations analysed carry out specific actions related to reducing food waste, healthy eating and the consumption of local products. At the same time, the survey results show that Spanish society also attaches importance to supermarkets and hypermarkets carrying out actions related to SDG 12.

FUTURE RESEARCH DIRECTIONS

The main limitation of this research lies in the fact that it has only been analysed how the four leading distribution companies in Spain (Mercadona, Carrefour, Lidl and Grupo Día) communicate their CSR actions linked to SDG 12 through the social network Instagram. Future research could study how these entities use other platforms as LinkedIn, TikTok, Twitter or Facebook for communicating the CSR actions. As a result of this future research and analysis, the results obtained can compare, and new conclusions can draw.

Furthermore, a deeper content social media analysis could be done. Useful results could be appeared after analysing and comparing the copies and the information (hashtags, specific words, images, etc) that the companies use in platforms like Instagram. Knowing the content and the consumer react to this type of information (like, comments, shares, etc), other companies and sector could use the best practices. It should also be noted that this research has focused only on SDG 12. However, as previously demonstrated, the 2030 Agenda includes 17 SDGs that affect different areas of all companies that make up the global business fabric. Future lines of research could analyse how distribution companies are committed to fulfilling other SDGs and whether they communicate about these actions.

Finally, future studies could focus on analysing different sectors whose environmental, social, and economic impact is also essential, such as the energy or textile sectors. With this latter approach, comparisons between different sectors can be made. At this sense, it would be possible to study whether one sector stands out from another in terms of communicating the SDGs through specific social and social media.

CONCLUSION

The arrival of the SDGs has led many companies to link their CSR actions to achieving these goals. In this context and given the environmental and social impact that distribution chains have, it is necessary for them not only to develop CSR actions related to SDG 12 (among others) but also to give them visibility and communicate these commitments effectively. Among the tools companies can use to give visibility to their strategies and actions, social media have been demonstrating for years their potential to lead changes and become a vehicle for knowledge and training. It is why distribution companies should rely on tools such as Instagram to show their audiences the CSR actions based on SDG 12 that they are carrying out. With these communications, they will be raising awareness among the population that another type of consumption and more sustainable and ecological food is possible. Furthermore, they are contributing their bit towards the fulfilment of SDG 12. And it is that companies do not forget that the population that, as has been demonstrated during this paper, is also increasingly committed to caring for and respecting the environment.

REFERENCES

ANGEM. (2019). *Informe de Sostenibilidad* [Sustainability Report]. https://www.anged.es/wp-content/uploads/2021/01/Informe-sostenibilidad-anged-web.pdfv

Bonomi, S., & Ricciardi, F. (2017). Trasformare lo spreco alimentare in risorsa sociale: Una soluzione organizzativa [Transforming food waste in a social resource.An organizational solution]. *Impresa Progetto*, *2*, 1–20.

Cámara de Valencia. (2020). *Cuaderno de Comercio y Sostenibilidad: Comercio y la RSE* [Trade and Sustainability Notebook: Tafe and CSR]. https://www.camaravalencia.com/es-ES/informacion/publicaciones-de-interes/publicaciones-y-documentos/comercio-distribucion/Documents/CUADERNOS%20COMERCIO%202011/cuaderno_Comercio_y_Sostenibilidad.pdf

Carrefour. (2022). *Página web oficial sobre Responsabilidad Social Corporativa para Biodiversidad* [Officla Website on Corporate Social Responsibility for Biodiversity]. https://www.carrefour.es/responsabilidad-social-corporativa

Carrefour [@Carrefoures]. (2022). *Publicaciones* [Perfil en Instagram]. Recuperado el 15 de marzo de 2022, de https://www.instagram.com/carrefoures/

Dawson, J. (2013). Retailer activity in shaping food choice. *Food Quality and Preference*, *28*(1), 339–347. doi:10.1016/j.foodqual.2012.09.012

ElAlfy, A., Darwish, K. M., & Weber, O. (2020). Corporations and sustainable development goals communication on social media: Corporate social responsibility or just another buzzword? *Sustainable Development*, *28*(5), 1418–1430. doi:10.1002d.2095

España, D. [@día_esp]. (2022). *Publicaciones* [Perfil en Instagram]. Recuperado el 25 de marzo de 2022, de https://www.instagram.com/dia_esp

Estanyol, E. (2020). Comunicación de la responsabilidad social corporativa (RSC): Análisis de las campañas más premiadas en 2018 [Communication of Corporate Social Responsibility (CSR): Analysis of the most Awarded Campaigns in 2018]. *El Profesional de la Información*, *29*(3), e290334. Advance online publication. doi:10.3145/epi.2020.may.34

Grupo Día. (2022). *Página web oficial sobre Sostenibilidad*. https://diacorporate.com/vision-sostenible/

IESE. (2017). *Empresa y objetivos de desarrollo sostenible* [Company and Sustainable Development Goals]. Cuadernos de la Cátedra "la Caixa" de Responsabilidad Social de la Empresa. Nº34. https://media.iese.edu/upload/ST0438.pdf

Illia, L., Rodríguez, B., González, A., & Romenti, S. (2010). La comunicación de la RSC entre las 250 principales empresas europeas [The CSR Communication Between the Top 250 Euopean Companies]. *Cuadernos de Información*, *27*(27), 85–96. doi:10.7764/cdi.27.25

Instituto Nacional de Estadística (INE). (n.d.). https://www.ine.es/

ISO 26000. (2010). *Guidance on social responsibility. Committee Draft ISO/CD26000*. International Standards Organization. https://iso26000.info/wp-content/uploads/2017/06/ISO-26000_2010_E_OBP-pages.pdf

Jami Pour, M., & Lotfiyan, Z. (2020). A new framework of electronic word-of-mouth in social networking sites: The system-based approach. *International Journal of Internet Marketing and Advertising*, *14*(1), 48–70. doi:10.1504/IJIMA.2020.106044

Khan, A., Chen, C. C., Suanpong, K., Ruangkanjanases, A., Kittikowit, S., & Chen, S. C. (2021). The Impact of CSR on Sustainable Innovation Ambidexterity: The Mediating Role of Sustainable Supply Chain Management and Second-Order Social Capital. *Sustainability*, *13*(21), 12160. doi:10.3390u132112160

Kumar, S., Murphy, M., Talwar, S., Kaur, P., & Dhir, A. (2021). What drives brand love and purchase intentions toward the local food distribution system? A study of social media-based REKO (fair consumption) groups. *Journal of Retailing and Consumer Services*, *60*, 102444. doi:10.1016/j.jretconser.2021.102444

Lidl. (2022). *Página web oficial sobre Sostenibilidad* [Offical Website on Sustainability]. https://empresa.lidl.es/sostenibilidad

Lidl [@lidlespana]. (2022). *Publicaciones* [Perfil en Instagram]. Recuperado el 25 de marzo de 2022, de https://www.instagram.com/lidlespana/

Mandaric, D., Anica, H., & Goran, K. (2021). Perception of Consumers' Awareness about Sustainability of Fashion Brands. *Journal of Risk and Financial Management, 14*(12), 594. doi:10.3390/jrfm14120594

Mercadona. (2022b). *Página web oficial sobre Responsabilidad Social Corporativa* [Offical Website on Corporate Social Responsibility]. https://info.mercadona.es/es/cuidemos-el-planeta

Mercadona [@mercadona]. (2022). *Publicaciones* [Perfil en Instagram]. Recuperado el 25 de marzo de 2022, de https://www.instagram.com/mercadona/

Moggi, S., Bonomi, S., & Ricciardi, F. (2018). Against Food Waste: CSR for the Social and Environmental Impact through a Network-Based Organizational Model. *Sustainability, 10*(10), 3515. doi:10.3390u10103515

Navarro-Espigares, J. L., & González-López, J. M. (2006). Corporate social responsibility and economic growth. *Estudios de Economía Aplicada, 24*, 637–665.

Orjuela, S. (2011). La Comunicación en la gestión de la Responsabilidad Social Empresarial [Communication in the Managment of Corporate Societal Responsibility]. *Correspondencias & Análisis, 1.*

Pabón, M. V., Jiménez, V., & Sierra, A. (2013). Relación entre la responsabilidad social y la publicidad social en las organizaciones. *Revista Comunicación, 30*, 67–76.

Pagani, G. (2012). ¿Se puede ser una empresa socialmente responsable sin comunicar? In M. Cuervo (Ed.), *Relaciones Públicas al sur de Latinoamérica II. Una mirada regional de los nuevos escenarios y desafíos de la comunicación* (pp. 117-125). Cuaderno 40: Facultad de Diseño y Comunicación. Centro de Estudios en Diseño y Comunicación Univ. de Palermo. http://www.scielo.org.ar/pdf/ccedce/n40/n40a11.pdf

Pilar, L., Kvasnicková Stanislavská, L., & Kvasnicka, R. (2021). Healthy Food on the Twitter Social Network: Vegan, Homemade, and Organic Food. *International Journal of Environmental Research and Public Health, 18*(7), 3815. doi:10.3390/ijerph18073815 PMID:33917406

Pilar, L., Stanislavská, L. K., Kvasnicka, R., Hartman, R., & Tichá, I. (2021). Healthy Food on Instagram Social Network: Vegan, Homemade and Clean Eating. *Nutrients, 13*(6), 1991. doi:10.3390/nu13061991 PMID:34207910

Porcelli, A. (2020). El valor de las redes sociales en el progreso de los objetivos de desarrollo sostenible [The Value of Social Media in Advancing the Sustainable Development Goals]. *Lex Social, 10*(2), 2. doi:10.46661/lexsocial.5078

Samoggia, A., Bertazzoli, A., & Ruggeri, A. (2019). Food retailing marketing management: Social media communication for healthy food. *International Journal of Retail & Distribution Management, 47*(9), 928–956. doi:10.1108/IJRDM-08-2018-0178

Santesmases, M. (2012). *DYANE. Versión 4*. Editorial Pirámide.

Schmitt, E., Galli, F., Menozzi, D., Maye, D., Touzard, J. M., Marescotti, A., Six, J., & Brunori, G. (2017). Comparing the sustainability of local and global food products in Europe. *Journal of Cleaner Production, 165*, 346–359. doi:10.1016/j.jclepro.2017.07.039

Seres-Deloitte. (2022). *VIII Informe del impacto social de las empresas* [VIII Report on the Social Impact of Companies]. https://www2.deloitte.com/es/es/pages/about-deloitte/articles/informe-impacto-social-empresas.html

Shu-Chuan, C., & Hsuan-Ting, C. (2019). Impact of consumers' corporate social responsibility-related activities in social media on brand attitude, electronic word-of-mouth intention, and purchase intention: A study of Chinese consumer behavior. *Journal of Consumer Behaviour, 18*(6), 453–462. doi:10.1002/cb.1784

Shu-Chuan, C., Hsuan-Ting, C., & Gan, C. (2020). Consumers' engagement with corporate social responsibility (CSR) communication in social media: Evidence from China and the United States. *Journal of Business Research, 110*, 260–271. doi:10.1016/j.jbusres.2020.01.036

Skare, M., & Golja, T. (2014). The impact of government CSR supporting policies on economic growth. *Journal of Policy Modeling, 36*(3), 562–577. doi:10.1016/j.jpolmod.2014.01.008

Torstensson, L., Johansson, R., & Mark-Herbert, C. (2021). Food Dishes for Sustainable Development: A Swedish Food Retail Perspective. *Foods, 10*(5), 932. doi:10.3390/foods10050932 PMID:33922742

Wang, R., & Huang, Y. (2018). Communicating corporate social responsibility (CSR) on social media: How do message source and types of CSR messages influence stakeholders' perceptions? *Corporate Communications, 23*(3), 326–341. doi:10.1108/CCIJ-07-2017-0067

We Are Social. (2022). *Digital Spain 2022*. https://wearesocial.com/es/blog/2022/01/digital-2022/

Willett, W., Rockström, J., Loken, B., Springmann, M., Lang, T., Vermeulen, S., Garnett, T., Tilman, D., DeClerck, F., Wood, A., Jonell, M., Clark, M., Gordon, L. J., Fanzo, J., Hawkes, C., Zurayk, R., Rivera, J. A., De Vries, W., Majele Sibanda, L., ... Murray, C. J. L. (2019). Food in the Anthropocene: The EAT–Lancet Commission on healthy diets from sustainable food systems. *Lancet, 393*(10170), 447–492. doi:10.1016/S0140-6736(18)31788-4 PMID:30660336

KEY TERMS AND DEFINITIONS

Agenda 2030: Agreement drawn up by the United Nations for the sustainable development of the planet. It includes a total of 17 Sustainable Development Goals focused on achieving a fairer and less impoverished society.

Corporate Social Responsibility: A way of managing companies whose aim is to have a positive impact on the environment in which they operate at an economic, environmental, and social level.

Instagram: Social network with 2,000 million users who share content in image, text or video format. The main valuable point of Instagram is picture content and during the last years it has grown a lot. In

Spain, it is the most important social media platform, after WhatsApp, the messaging app. It belongs to the technology conglomerate known as Meta.

SDG 12: Sustainable Development Goal defined by the 2030 Agenda that aims to ensure responsible production and consumption of existing food resources in order to safeguard food supplies for future generations.

Social Networks: Structures formed on the Internet in which groups of people with similar interests share content, experiences, and opinions.

Sustainability: Development that can meet the needs of the present without compromising the needs of the future. To this end, it ensures a real balance between economic growth, social well-being, and care for the environment.

Sustainable Development Goals: A universal call to action to ensure the sustainability of the planet, eradicate poverty and achieve a better quality of life for people everywhere.

Chapter 3
Can Employee Wellbeing and Resilience Contribute to Organizational Sustainability After COVID-19?

Seher Yastıoğlu
Burdur Mehmet Akif Ersoy University, Turkey

Tugba Erhan
https://orcid.org/0000-0002-5697-490X
Süleyman Demirel University, Turkey

Hasan Hüseyin Uzunbacak
https://orcid.org/0000-0002-3297-1659
Süleyman Demirel University, Turkey

ABSTRACT

The current chapter focuses on the scope of employee happiness and resilience which will be examined in detail, and the importance of happiness and resilience for organizational sustainability in the post-COVID-19 pandemic period are discussed through research and reports. Then recommendations are provided based on the results of scientific studies to protect and increase employee happiness and resilience. This chapter aims at revealing the importance of wellbeing and resilience in the workplace highlighting the aftereffects of COVID-19 in the organizational ecosystem.

DOI: 10.4018/978-1-6684-7499-0.ch003

What doesn't kill you, makes you stronger.

Friedrich Nietzsche

Happiness is the meaning and the purpose of life, the whole aim and end of human existence.

Aristotle

INTRODUCTION

Unexpected events have become an inevitable part of the today's world of daily and business lives. The ability to maintain the lives and obtain sustainability have been more challenging. This is the era where most definitions have been evolving or most needs have been replacing with the ones which have not been cared much before. Managerial skills are required to include to have emotional intelligence for both managers and employees in order to show empathy and understand others better. In other words, the psychological needs of the individuals are needed to be prioritized within this rapidly changing era of pre and post pandemic period.

Individuals and organizations may share a common goal. Both of them expect to improve their welfare. The welfare of the organizations helps provide sustainability also supports the welfare of the community. However, the expectations of employees and the organizations have been increasing day by day in order to meet and satisfy the individual and organizational needs.

This chapter aims at highlighting the importance of wellbeing and resilience of the employees for sustainability considering the effects of the pandemic on employees and organizations. Also, the authors provide a critical overview of the importance of wellbeing and resilience which may be neglected in some of the today's organizational structure.

BACKGROUND

The Evolution of Wellbeing in the Workplace

It is known that individuals spend most of their productive and long periods at work, and time spent at work covers more than one-third of life apart from sleep and private life. As such, the definition and perception of work have been changed, it is not just a means of making money, but work has become the life itself. Therefore, regarding the fact that a person is in search of happiness in life, today's employees have started to look for workplaces where they will feel happy. Happiness has become as important in our work life as it is in our subjective lives.

Happiness, which is also called well-being in different studies, is a concept that is often used to express the state of psychological satisfaction or joy. Besides, instead of the concept of employee happiness or happiness at work, it is seen that there are studies that use the concepts of positive work attitudes such as general well-being, life satisfaction, positive affect, job satisfaction, job engagement or affective commitment, and even happiness is stated interchangeably with these concepts. However, happiness has its own structure. Although it is one of the most desired emotions by the employees, it is quite difficult to define a single definition and determine its structure for a subjective experience such as happiness, but it is seen that there are different perspectives in the literature.

Happiness at work has been defined as a state of pleasure and positive emotions, which enable employees to reach their potential and maximize their performance using resources at an optimum level, overcoming difficulties, finding meaning and satisfaction (Pryce-Jones, 2010; Edmunds & Pryce-Jones, 2008; Lama & Cutler, 2008). Happiness in work life is characterized by being firmly attached to a meaningful goal, looking to the future with hope, and joining daily activities supported by relationships with real friends. Employees are filled with an inner energy and add meaning to their own lives when they are engaged with the work that is compatible with their values, a work that contributes to others and serves for a higher purpose beyond payments offering them opportunities of freedom and advancement (Mckee, 2017). These positive feelings, freedom and space for advancement enable employees to perform their work happily. Fisher (2010), on the other hand, expresses happiness in the workplace as positive feelings towards the job itself, the characteristics of the job, and the organization as a whole.

Based on Fisher's conceptualization, Salas-Vallina et al. (2017) identified happiness at work considering work engagement as an umbrella concept that includes job satisfaction and organizational affective commitment. In other words, the energy and motivation of the employee combined with passion and enthusiasm for the job, satisfaction with working conditions, sense of belonging and love towards job have been considered as the determinants of happiness at work (Salas-Vallina & Alegre, 2021). Although there are high correlations between happiness and other positive work attitudes, the presence of positive work attitudes is not enough to conclude that employees are in a state of complete mental and emotional well-being (Thompson & Bruk-Lee, 2021). For example, a person may feel unhappy even if he or she loves his or her job or if there are organizational resources such as adequate wages, career opportunities that enable the employee to be satisfied with the job. Therefore, the well-being (happiness) of employees should be evaluated in a broader context. From this point of view, Warr (2013) states that organizational happiness studies mostly focus on "environmental features", namely jobs and organizations, whereas little attention is paid to people's experiences, thoughts, and personal characteristics. In order to truly understand happiness at work, it is recommended to consider both personal characteristics and organizational dimensions together.

In addition to the distinction between personal and organizational sources of happiness, the distinction between subjective well-being and psychological well-being is also used while conceptualizing workplace happiness. Subjective well-being refers to the experiences of pleasure and happiness from life, positive emotions such as joy, excitement, hope, confidence, satisfaction, pride often and negative emotions such as sadness, anger, stress, guilt less (Diener et al., 1991). If a person has supportive social relationships and work experiences at work, opportunity to engage in social interaction all day long adding value to work, feeling satisfied, performing the work with enthusiasm, feeling committed can experience high levels of subjective well-being (Kahneman & Krueger, 2006; Monnot& Beehr, 2014; Singh & Aggarwal, 2018). Psychological well-being, which is called real happiness, refers to leading a virtuous life with common sense and discipline, dominating the environment, accepting oneself in all aspects, finding meaning, serving for a higher purpose, devoting all one's potential to development, experiencing a sense of authority and autonomy, and developing positive relationships with others (Ryff & Keyes, 1995; Ryff & Singer, 2006). It is the psychological well-being of employees which provides long-term and permanent contributions to development. It would be wrong to say which well-being is more advantageous for workplace happiness. Subjective well-being and psychological well-being are concepts that have different elements but are interrelated to each other to form the basis of happiness at work.

It can be seen that there are different approaches to the elements/resources that form the structure of workplace happiness, as well as the different opinions on what workplace happiness means. Based on their extensive research, Myerson and Tind (2017) revealed that workplace happiness depends on an attentive communication style, positive work environment, supportive organizational culture, flexible workplaces, mental and emotional involvement in work/decision processes. According to another study, there are four main determinants of happiness in the workplace: work repulsive feelings, flow and intrinsic motivation, supportive organizational experiences, and unsupportive organizational experiences. Accordingly, positive organizational experiences such as support from colleagues and the organization, positive work experiences with managers, and internally satisfying experiences such as a sense of belonging to a community, personal achievements, self-improvement with new knowledge, and being useful to others through skillful work contribute to the happiness of employees. On the other hand, negative organizational experiences such as excessive workload, job insecurity, ambiguity of job description, unnecessary job changes and unfair treatment make employees unhappy (Singh & Aggarwal, 2018). Also, it is assumed that employees who are devoted to their work, emotionally attached to the organization and experience job satisfaction will also achieve happiness in their jobs (Salas-Vallina & Alegre, 2021).

Employee happiness affects the organizational context as well as the social context. In other words, employee happiness is not just related to work life. To support this view, Khatri and Gupta (2019) determined the four factors that are the source of employee happiness as work-life balance, job wellness, life purpose and physiological health. In addition to the elements that enable individuals to be satisfied with their work, such as working conditions, challenging tasks, enjoyment of work, and opportunities for development, finding a meaning in life and working for a purpose, doing work in harmony with individual values, living a social life and physical health also contribute to employee happiness which are also highlighted as important determinants.

As a result, it can be said that, in order to achieve happiness, employees should be given jobs that are compatible with them, or jobs which enable them to achieve their goals successfully, give them autonomy and responsibility by developing new business models that support them to be committed to find a meaning in their work. On the other hand, an employee needs to feel satisfied from the work itself, connect the work with a meaning and purpose, benefit others with the work, and discover resources that will increase the inner motivation.

Employee Wellbeing After Covid 19 for Organizational Sustainability

The COVID-19 pandemic, which emerged suddenly and unexpectedly in 2020, has caused numerous challenges in both business and private life. Not only the Covid-19 pandemic, but the following global and economic crises have been causing unprecedented times to overcome for both companies and employees by accelerating the inevitable changes. Changes and innovations require leaving the old routine approaches to a much more competitive and creative organizational ecosystem. It is not only business processes and the understanding of competition that have changed. The perspectives of the employees towards the organizations and the organizations towards the employees have changed. While organizations have been trying to adopt and maintain a remote and flexible working culture, they have also been protecting the motivation, well-being, personal and social rights of their employees in order to keep the qualified personnel within the organization. By doing so, organizations contemplate new working models in order to increase productivity and performance while making changes in the priorities of human resources policies.

Organizations have been attempting to create new ways to lead, work, learn and communicate. In these unexpected and dramatic circumstances, Future Workplace's HR 2021 Sentiment Survey provides evidence for the changing priorities for companies with hybrid working models. According to the report, while the most important priority of human resources managers in 2020 was the employee experience, in 2021 the most important priority of 68% of HR managers is to protect and maintain employee well-being & mental health (Future Workplace, 2021). This indicates that the organizations have shifted their focus from corporate priorities to human needs and that their way of working should be human oriented.

It's not surprising that the mental health and well-being of employees has become a top priority. The pandemic has dragged the lifestyle of the employees out of the ordinary and caused increased stress and anxiety in the employees. In addition to stress and anxiety, more than 50% of information workers dealing with computer-based office work have switched to remote work during the pandemic (Lund et al., 2021). During this transition, employees began to leave their businesses in waves. In the United States, 4.53 million employees left their jobs in November 2021, and it was a record (Cook, 2021).

An increasing sense of loneliness and social isolation from remote work has unintentionally damaged employee well-being (PWC, 2022). Some reasons for the resignations were burnout, a lack of a meaningful sense of work, toxic work cultures, and a desire for greater autonomy and flexibility in work arrangements (De Smet, et al., 2021; Henry, 2021). This new world of work appears to be causing people to question the meaning of what they do and make their well-being a priority. Therefore, there is a transformation from employees who think that material gains are goals that need to be achieved and that happiness will only come out when the goals are reached one by one, and people who say that it is enough if I make good money have turned to employees who put their happiness beyond financial gains and prioritize it.

Although the 'happy employee is a productive employee' perspective[1] is not new, it has been understood once again that in today's uncertain and competitive business environment, positive attitudes of employees have become a fundamental source of competitive advantage and success (Guest, 2017). It has become vital for the organizations to put employee well-being at the center of their strategies and adopt a more human-centered culture. As such, investing in employee happiness for organizations has become obligatory, not a necessity. Particularly, studies in the field of positive psychology suggest that happiness should come before even the success of the employee highlighting that happiness is not just a result of success but a prerequisite. Therefore, it is useful to remind organizations that: 'If you sacrifice happiness, you sacrifice success!' (McKee, 2017).

So why is the happiness of employees so important for the success and efficiency of the organizations? Scientific research and reports of the organizations have given the answer to this question. Thousands of scientific studies and studies on Fortune 500 companies have discovered that happy and positive thinking brains are more motivated, creative, resilient, and productive in their work, and thus perform higher (Achor, 2010). Employee happiness was found to be one of the ways that potentially leads to higher employee retention with higher performance.

The truth that happiness is not a luxury but a necessity for economies and companies has not been mentioned for the first time. According to a report published by the United Nations in 2012, it was declared that the unsustainable production and consumption patterns hinder sustainable development, focusing only on GDP is insufficient; also, it was discussed that a more inclusive, equitable and balanced approach is needed to promote sustainability, eradicate poverty and increase welfare. From this point of view, it was accepted that there was a need for a 'new economic paradigm based on happiness and well-being' (Royal Government of Bhutan, 2012).

Recent reports also support this. For example, according to Gallup's State of the Global Workplace report published in 2022, a lack of engagement in the workplace has a direct impact on economies worldwide. Decline in productivity and profitability, and increased turnover costs the world economy $7.8 trillion, and this accounts for 11% of global GDP approximately. Again, in the same report, only 21% of those who participated in the study reported that they were engaged, while only 1 in 3 said that they had an overall well-being. However, 63.3% of the organizations underline that retaining employee is more difficult than hiring them. This situation has been creating higher costs for the organizations. US employers spend $2.9 million a day to replace layoffs which makes $1.1 billion a year.

One of the major reasons for leaving the jobs is that the employees are not happy with their jobs, and they cannot be fully committed to their jobs in order to cope with stressful situations that they are exposed to, thus the employees cannot see the value they expect from their organizations, and this causes a conflict between employee and the organizations' expectations. In other words, this situation may result in higher undesired consequences for the organizations that do not create a supportive work environment which is compatible with the values of their employees. The work environment ensures the employee socialization, in addition employees care about equality and protection of their rights as these all will enable them to love their jobs and increase their well-being and engagement.

By looking at the increase in the number of investments for employee wellbeing it can be said that fortunately, organizations have been realizing the importance of employee welfare and creating a human-oriented work environment for productivity and sustainable performance. In 2020, the number of organizations that implemented practices that contribute to the well-being of employees doubled compared to 2019 (REBA, 2020). This investment in welfare returns the organizations as a lot of profit. For example, every £1 invested in employee welfare returns as £5 in return on investment (Deloitte, 2020). Besides, happy employees are 13% more productive in the same work time than the dissatisfied employees (Bellet, De Neve, & Ward, 2022), which leads to better performance and turns into a profit for organizations.

Organizations that aim to add value sustainability need to invest in the happiness of their employees in order to have high productivity, engagement, and loyal employees. Increasing employee happiness contributes to the sustainability of the workforce (Atan, et al., 2021). Employee happiness, which is an important determinant of employee performance, acts as a catalyst for organizational prosperity and greatly contributes to the long-term sustainability of an organization (Nassir, 2017).

EMPLOYEE RESILIENCE IN ORGANIZATIONS

Survival and sustainability are the key goals of the organizations. These goals can be achieved not only by the organizational ability but also with the endurance of the employees who may not have the same ability to cope with the challenges and adapt the changes. New era of pandemic has been highlighting the fact of the occurrence of expectancies which is inevitable and hardly avoidable. Although, the development of technology and rapid adaptation into individuals' lives may provide huge benefits, the disadvantages are required to be considered.

The criteria for organizational sustainability include employee support in addition to many tangible assets. Along with the presence of visible competitive superiorities, organizations in twenty-first century need to consider the psychological requirements of the employees as well as their sociological reflections. Also, studies indicate that resilience is essential for individuals to handle and recover from the unexpected crisis like Covid-19 (Ojo et.al., 2021). Long lasting effects of the pandemic will take time to explore, researchers of disciplines such as psychology, sociology, and organizational behavior have been focusing on the effects, however, little research is yet known on the sustainability of the organizations or the role of resilience on maintaining sustainability.

Increasing workforce need reveals different types of employee approach. In other words, employee and organization connections are required on the specific conditions in order to maintain the sustainability reciprocally. Kuntz et al. (2016) emphasizes a different perspective on resilience focusing on the resilience in stable situation (business- as-usual) contexts and adverse situations. Covid-19 pandemic can be considered as a good example of the adverse situations. The pandemic also has created an obligatory movement and changes in employees' social and work lives.

As being familiar with the resilience literature framework, it can be pointed out that some individuals are good at coping with adverse situations by showing positive approach and assessing the situation wisely, while others even cannot bear the daily adverse routines including commuting to work, establishing relationship, or communicating with other for daily needs. Regarding the daily or life's unexpected crisis or challenges, resilience is defined as a positive adaptation, or to have the ability to carry on against all the adverse or undesired situations (Wald, et al., 2006).

Resiliency after Covid-19 for Organizational Sustainability

Experiences can help individuals learn lessons from the unexpected events. The current pandemic period has created a complex uncertain life and work environment. In some cultures, and sociocultural contexts, being resilient has been perceived differently. This kind of differentiation has also created a challenge to reach a consensus on the definitions. As most studies indicate that some jobs have had the highest risk of the pandemic and located in the core. Healthcare employees has been one of these jobs included higher risks of getting infected and worried about the pandemic (Chua et al., 2004).

Individuals may experience physical, mental, and psychological effects of crisis such as pandemic or disasters when they are not ready to take an action and survive in uncertainty (Duncan, 2020). In this context psychologically resilient people have been considered that they wear a shield to be protected from the worsening effects of the traumatic periods such as pandemic. Studies provide evidence that especially healthcare employees who are more resilient than the others have coped with the burden of the pandemic more effectively and recover faster (Foster et al., 2020).

This part of the chapter attempts to reveal the importance of resilience for organizational sustainability. There are many factors that facilitate and support the sustainability of an organization. The psychology of sustainability framework highlights enhancing and providing resilient workplaces is beneficial for sustainable work settings (Sommovigo et al., 2019).

Sustainability is one of the common words used in the world of business. Covid-19 pandemic has caused several protective changes in the organizations in order to balance employment and sustainability. Managing stress and coping with the challenges of daily and work life have already been a problematic even before the pandemic period.

Individuals can experience different psychological moods or disorders. These potential personal differences may end in different reactions to different situations. Not all individuals have the same level of strength, some may be more resilient than others. Specifically, this pandemic period has revealed that employees have been looking for other jobs that they can feel more secure and protected. Before the pandemic crisis, having a secure job or performing a secure work have included different aspects of security. However, pandemic period has changed the job description and the requirements or the expectations of both employees and organizations.

Most sectors have been affected severely by the emergence of the pandemic. Some of them have taken the advantage by evaluating the current situation, but some of them have had difficulties to cope with and apply the new normal strategies into the business environment.

PROMOTING EMPLOYEE WELLBEING AND RESILIENCE IN WORKPLACES

Organizations and employees have the responsibility to increase happiness and resilience in the workplace. Individual strategies are as important as organizational strategies. As it is all known, sudden changes in social and work life due to the pandemic have affected employees physically, emotionally, and mentally. Remote/hybrid working models and digital transformation planned for the future for employees and organizations have accelerated and become a milestone for organizations. It is obvious that the increasing workload with digitalization, the new working environments causing social isolation, the widespread use of technological tools and the fact that employees are accessible from anywhere and at any time, such as the feeling of occupation of personal life and the fear of being unemployed have caused stress, fatigue, and negative feelings such as being alienated from work. It is important to maintain efficiency and performance while attempting to overcome the challenges. It is considered that happiness and resilience give employees flexibility to cope with stress, enable them to do their jobs with pleasure, to be connected to their jobs and to focus on their work. These all result in better performance and efficiency which are two important work attitudes. Therefore, it has become more important than ever for organizations and employees to protect psychological health, well-being, and resilience to keep up with this intense pressure and change. However, not only the pandemic, but also the economic and social events, which can be described as sudden crises, have revealed the necessity of protecting the resilience and well-being of the employees.

The answer to the question of whose responsibility it is to protect and increase the psychological resilience and well-being of employees is both the workplace and the employee. Along with organizational strategies, individual strategies of employees have an important place in the development of both happiness and resilience. Organizations should strategically be aligned with their leaders, organizational culture, values, social landscape of the workplace, job designs, management practices and resources to specifically support the mental health and well-being of their employees. Employees, on the other hand, need to consciously explore the psychological, emotional, and economic resources that are good for them, enable them to enjoy their work, be more flexible coping with the difficulties, and use their resources with awareness in the best way possible, and give them the strength to endure. Studies and researches on workplace and employee happiness[2]; positive organizational experiences with employee-oriented management and leadership practices, career opportunities, feedback and rewards, social relations in the workplace, job security, job designs, material/spiritual satisfaction of the job, job flexibility, work-life balance, job security, mental and physiological well-being show that employee happiness depends on many factors such as internal motivation sources such as autonomy, need for development, competence, relationship, finding meaning in work, purpose, psychological capital, emotional intelligence, passion and participation.

One of the important determinants of happiness is performing a meaningful job and living a meaningful life (Diener, & Biswas-Diener, 2011). In addition, meaning sources act as a buffer against the negativities experienced (Debats, 1999). In order for individuals to have meaningful and valuable experiences in their work, they need to discover the sources of meaning and/or present their work experiences that will enable their organizations to find their work more meaningful. It is one of the methods that make the employee find the job more meaningful by assigning tasks that will benefit others and serve a higher purpose than himself with a social mission, and clearly stating what purpose the work serves. Giving the employee the opportunity to learn new things, become an expert of the job, reveal the potential, increase self-awareness, taste the feeling of success, be appreciated, provide the employee with the opportunity to realize the employee's sense of meaning. Again, for some employees, financial gains such as gaining power, status and earning more money may also be meaningful. In addition to these financial gains, social rewards such as a sense of belonging to a community, knowing that their ideas are worth listening, caring and useful, and being busy with jobs that allow autonomy also help the employee to find meaning at work (Rosso, et al., 2010; Lips-Wiersman & Wright, 2012; Hansen et al., 2018). It should be noted that while meaning is a part of happiness, there is a strong connection between the two and similarities between their sources. It should also be noted that the source of meaning for each employee may be different from each other, therefore, practices specific to individual differences and preferences should be developed for employees to find their work meaningful.

Besides, social relations, support and connections are among the important factors affecting the happiness of employees. According to PWC's The COVID-19 Remote Working Experiment report, employees stated that if they continue to work remotely, the two most likely factors to affect their mental health will be a lack of social interaction and feeling disconnected from the office. The feeling of loneliness is a problem in this new way of working, and the absence of social relationships that reduce the effect of stress can lead to unhappiness (Issa & Jaleel, 2021). The existence and maintenance of positive social relations not only increases happiness, but also positively affects the productivity and creativity capacity of employees (Berman, et al., 2013). Therefore, this problem can be overcome to some extent by face-to-face meetings and social organizations that may take place at regular intervals, assigning tasks in a way that does not affect their social lives, establishing work teams where sharing is encouraged, the manager nurtures the mood of the employee through feedback by supporting the colleagues and manager.

Leadership and management practices are another important factor for the employees to be filled with mental and spiritual energy and to support their happiness. For happy employees, managers should express their gratitude, support benevolence, appreciate good work, and be forgiving, when necessary, by stating that mistakes are an opportunity to learn. In addition to the relationship and communication established due to work procedures, relationships based on sincerity and trust should be established, feedback should be given frequently, and the strengths of the employees should be supported (Cameron, 2012). Managers should be fair and objective in decisions and actions, employees should be given value they deserve, two-way communication should be supported, the interests of employees should be considered, they should be interested not only in the results but also in the way they were obtained, instructive, that is, ethical and virtuous behaviors should be exhibited (Nassif et al., 2021; Schwepker et al., 2021). One way to increase employee well-being in the workplace and beyond is the quality of working life. A safe and healthy working environment should be created for the employee, jobs where an employee can develop capacity, job security should be provided, adequate and fair compensation should be provided, workplace flexibility should be provided, and the employee should be hopeful and proactive about the future (Walton, 1974; Grote & Guest, 2017).

Guest (2017) listed HR practices designed to promote employee happiness, focusing on employee well-being rather than contribution as follows, hiring and selection, training/development, and investing in employees through mentoring and career support. The job should be attractive to the employee by giving jobs where the employee can challenge with autonomous job designs through mutual knowledge sharing and feedback, and where the employee can use his/her creativity and skills. A positive social and physical environment should be created for the employee by giving priority to employee safety, managing diversity, providing equal opportunities to everyone, never tolerating bullying and harassment, creating social interaction environments at the required level and optionally, giving high pay and fair collective rewards, and ensuring employment. Applications such as questionnaires, two-way communication, collective participation, where employees can convey their opinions, should be developed and employee voice should be supported. Employees should be included in organizational decision-making processes, empowered, assisted, and guided to complete their tasks, flexible and/or family-friendly work arrangements should be made, performance management should be development-oriented so that employees should be provided with the organizational support they need. In addition, activity-based happiness interventions that aim to express gratitude, perform acts of kindness, think optimistically, exercise, and spiritual activities such as yoga or mindfulness can be developed for employees (Le Blanc & Oerlemans, 2016).

Like wellbeing, resilience can be learned and developed, and resilience and wellbeing are interrelated. Better Up's survey of over 6,000 people during the pandemic provides important clues as to why resilience is important. According to the research, individuals with high resilience report 35% higher wellbeing and 31% higher productivity than those who are not. Also, resilience refers to coping with difficulties and stressors and adapting. For this reason, increasing the resilience of employees is perhaps more important than ever for organizations that try to maintain their own resilience, especially in unexpected crisis situations and flexible working periods.

One of the important elements to increase the resilience of the employees is to strengthen the psychological safety perception of the employees through the leader member exchange. Thus, employees can have the tendency to perceive to some extent a psychological exchange which can enhance followers' psychological assurance and provide cognitive strengths to adapt to the uncertainty (Liao et al., 2017; Rego et al., 2017). Bardoel et al. (2014) offered a series of recommendations based on the resilience and HRM literature that would be useful in increasing employee resilience: There should be social support mechanisms for employees and the employee should be encouraged to establish social relationships. Cognitive and emotional support is a powerful coping strategy where an individual can talk about the problem, get ideas in order to overcome a stressful situation or a negative life event (Folkman et. al, 1986).

It has been considered important to encourage leaders to provide supportive behaviors, leadership behavior and participation also need to be emphasized (Luthans, 2002). Also, employee assistance programs, development programs to increase resilience, flexible/hybrid working models if the employee demands, occupational health and safety practices, steps taken to overcome risk and crisis and management of diversity are some of the practices that HRM can implement to build resilience to employees (Bardoel, et al., 2014). People who believe that they have control over their own lives and the work they do, who are competent and have sufficient skills to do their job, that is, who have self-efficacy, experience less stress in their jobs and are more resilient (Ojo, et al., 2021).

Successful experiences and social persuasion are two important factors that influence one's belief that one is competent (Bandura, 1977). Therefore, it is important for managers to give their employees tasks that will challenge them but by doing so, they can experience a sense of accomplishment, and give frequent acknowledgment and appreciative feedback about how they are performing during work.

SOLUTIONS AND RECOMMENDATIONS

Building happy and resilient employees in order to grow and be sustainable require examining the psychological situations of the employees who have the potentiality to share and experience challenging times in the social and work environment. More cross-sectional or longitudinal studies should be conducted to be able to address the psychological needs and problems of the employees in order to build a strong connection with the organization.

FUTURE RESEARCH DIRECTIONS

Understanding the reasons of the employees may be considered as an essential step for the organizations to have a long survival period and gain sustainability. Besides, the importance of having more resilient employees in the organizations is one of the ways of organizational sustainability. However, understanding employee behavior, determining the reactions over stressful work environments, the harmony of working as a team can be other aspects which are needed to be examined to minimize the severe effects of the unexpected crisis that created new challenges for organizations. The survival and sustainability of the organizations are interrelated with survival of human workforce. Also, the digital technology automatically attempts to replace human workforce, thus these developments should be improved and applied in a balance not to cause a huge unemployment rate.

Organizations need more resilient employees in order to have the power to overcome the unexpected barriers of the future. These barriers can come from any source such as pandemic, natural disasters or even wars. Minimizing the effects of aforementioned reasons, organizations require psychologically resilient workforce to restart, replan and determine to apply the new rules within a short period of adaptation time. The relationship between sustainability and resilience needs to be examined for future studies since the main goal of the organizations is to be sustainable and survive for longer periods. A consensus on the definition of resilience highlights it as a trait or an outcome. However, the changing structure of the term "resilience" is needed to be understood clearly in order to differentiate with the other psychological terms (Fletcher and Sarkar, 2013). Resilience investigators emphasize that gender differences matter and affect the level of resilience (Boardman et al., 2008). In order to generalize the results for majority, more studies are required to examine the gender differences.

CONCLUSION

Covid-19 pandemic has caused many damages and adverse effects on individual and organizational life. It also has affected and still does affect specifically the employee candidates' job and career choices. Potential employee or employer candidates of the future keep in their minds and attempt avoiding working in the jobs which may have many risks of another pandemic crisis. However, this current reality does not make any changes of need for employment in any kind of job titles including healthcare industry.

While organizations and employees share some goals in common such as being sustainable, they may also share their expectations. Specifically, being aware of these expectations in order to meet the psychological needs can be the core of sustainability of the organizations. Within the rapid development of the digitalization or robot technology, there is still a growing need for human workforce. Organizational sustainability includes both skilled human workforce and digitalization. It is important to follow the latest technology, however, employees with high adaptation ability to changes also plays an essential role in order to apply the recent developments.

In the context of the unexpected events' occurrence such as Covid-19 pandemic, organizations have been affected as well as the employees from the first stay-at-home guidance. Even this first step has caused emotional changes performing daily activities. There have been many unanswered questions for employees or organizations. Besides, for some organizations and jobs, the risk of getting infected has been more potential compared to other jobs or people who work from home. Employees who work in the highly potential risk group within the organizations have experience more stressful time and even some of them have had the tendency to leave their jobs. Among the challenges of the pandemic, emergence of emotional experiences of both negative and positive, but mostly negative have made the coping strategies more necessary for survival.

ACKNOWLEDGMENT

This research received no specific grant from any funding agency in the public, commercial, or not-for-profit sectors.

REFERENCES

Achor, S. (2010). *The happiness advantage: How a positive brain fuels success in work and life*. Currency. Crown Business/Random House.

Atan, A., Ozgit, H., & Silman, F. (2021). Happiness at work and motivation for a sustainable workforce: Evidence from female hotel employees. *Sustainability*, *13*(14), 1–17.

Bandura, A. (1977). Self-efficacy: Toward a unifying theory of behavioral change. *Psychological Review*, *84*(2), 191–215.

Bardoel, E. A., Pettit, T. M., De Cieri, H., & McMillan, L. (2014). Employee resilience: An emerging challenge for HRM. *Asia Pacific Journal of Human Resources*, *52*(3), 279–297.

BelletC.De NeveJ. E.WardG. (2022). Does employee happiness have an impact on productivity? *Saïd Business School WP*, 1-38. Available at: https://ssrn.com/abstract=3470734

Berman, E. M., West, J. P., & Richter, M. N. Jr. (2002). Workplace relations: Friendship patterns and consequences (according to managers). *Public Administration Review*, *62*(2), 217–230.

BetterUp. (2021). *Five strategies to build workforce resilience*. https://grow.betterup.com/resources/five-strategies-to-build-workforce-resilience/?hsCtaTracking=aff5cfcb-e1b0-4062-a096-0910197538c0%7C26da8608-a596-4482-9062-7c6bb88d811b

Boardman, J. D., Blalock, C. L., & Button, T. M. (2008). Sex differences in the heritability of resilience. *Twin Research and Human Genetics*, *11*(1), 12–27.

Cameron, K. (2012). *Positive leadership: Strategies for extraordinary performance.* Berrett-Koehler Publishers.

Chua, S. E., Cheung, V., McAlonan, G. M., Cheung, C., Wong, J. W., Cheung, E. P., Chan, M. T., Wong, T. K., Choy, K. M., Chu, C. M., Lee, P. W., & Tsang, K. W. (2004). Stress and psychological impact on SARS patients during the outbreak. *Canadian Journal of Psychiatry*, *49*(6), 385–390.

Clifton, J., & Harter, J. (2021). *Wellbeing at work.* Simon and Schuster.

Cook, I. (2021, September 15). Who is driving the great resignation? *Harvard Business Review.* https://hbr.org/2021/09/who-is-driving-the-great-resignation

De Smet, A., Dowling, B., Mugayar-Baldocchi, M., & Schaninger, B. (2021, September 8). *How companies can turn the Great Resignation into the Great Attraction.* McKinsey & Company. https://www.mckinsey.com/businessfunctions/people-and-organizational-performance/our-insights/great-attrition-orgreat-attraction-the-choice-is-yours

Debats, D. L. (1999). Sources of meaning: An investigation of significant commitments in life. *Journal of Humanistic Psychology*, *39*(4), 30–57.

Deloitte. (2020, January). *Mental health and employers: Refreshing the case for investment.* Deloitte. https:// www2.deloitte.com/content/dam/Deloitte/uk/Documents/consultancy/deloitte-uk-mental-health-and-employers.pdf

Diener, E., & Biswas-Diener, R. (2011). *Happiness: Unlocking the mysteries of psychological wealth.* John Wiley & Sons.

Diener, E., Sandvik, E., & Pavot, W. (1991). Happiness is the frequency, not the intensity, of positive versus negative affect. In F. Strack, M. Argyle, & N. Schwarz (Eds.), *Subjective well-being: An interdisciplinary perspective.* Pergamon.

Duncan, D. L. (2020). What the COVID-19 pandemic tells us about the need to develop resilience in the nursing workforce. *Nursing Management*, *27*(3), 22–27.

Edmunds, L. D., & Pryce-Jones, J. (2008). Relationships between happiness, overtime, sick leave and intention to stay or leave. *Selection and Development Review*, *24*(1), 812.

Fisher, C. D. (2010). Happiness at work. *International Journal of Management Reviews*, *12*(4), 384–412.

Fletcher, D., & Sarkar, M. (2013). Psychological resilience: A review and critique of definitions, concepts, and theory. *European Psychologist*, *18*(1), 1–33.

Folkman, S., Lazarus, R. S., Dunkel-Schetter, C., DeLongis, A., & Gruen, R. J. (1986). Dynamics of a stressful encounter: Cognitive appraisal, coping, and encounter outcomes. *Journal of Personality and Social Psychology*, *50*, 992–1003.

Foster, K., Roche, M., Giandinoto, J., & Furness, T. (2020). Workplace stressors, psychological well-being, resilience, and caring behaviours of mental health nurses: A descriptive correlational study. *International Journal of Mental Health Nursing*, *29*(1), 56–68.

Future Workplace. (2021). *2021 HR sentiment survey: Five strategic priorities for the hybrid workplace.* https://futureworkplace.com/ebooks/2021-hr-sentiment-survey/

Gallup. (2022). *State of the global workplace: 2022 Report, The voice of the World's employees.* Gallup. https://www.gallup.com/workplace/349484/state-of-the-global-workplace-2022-report.aspx#ite-393218

Gilbert, D., Mckee, A., Spreitzer, G., & Amabile, T. (2017). *Happiness (HBR emotional intelligence series).* Harvard Business Review Press.

Grote, G., & Guest, D. (2017). The case for reinvigorating quality of working life research. *Human Relations, 70*(2), 149–167.

Guest, D. E. (2017). Human resource management and employee well-being: Towards a new analytic framework. *Human Resource Management Journal, 27*(1), 22–38.

Hansen, M. T., Amabile, T. M., Snook, S. A., & Craig, N. (2018). *Purpose, Meaning, and Passion (HBR emotional intelligence series).* Harvard Business Review Press.

Henry, P. (2021, November 19). *Explainer: What's driving 'the Great Resignation'?* World Economic Forum. https://www.weforum.org/agenda/2021/11/greatresignation-career-change-mental-health-covid/

Issa, H., & Jaleel, E. (2021). Social isolation and psychological wellbeing: Lessons from Covid-19. *Management Science Letters, 11*(2), 609–618.

Kahneman, D., & Krueger, A. B. (2006). Developments in the measurement of subjective well-being. *The Journal of Economic Perspectives, 20*, 3–24.

Khatri, P., & Gupta, P. (2019). Development and validation of employee wellbeing scale–a formative measurement model. *International Journal of Workplace Health Management, 12*(5), 352–368.

Kuntz, J. R., Näswall, K., & Malinen, S. (2016). Resilient employees in resilient organizations: Flourishing beyond adversity. *Industrial and Organizational Psychology: Perspectives on Science and Practice, 9*(2), 456–462.

Lama, D., & Cutler, H. C. (2008). *İş hayatında mutluluk sanatı* (M. Tayga, Trans.). Klan Yayınları.

Le Blanc, P. M., & Oerlemans, W. G. (2016). Amplition in the workplace: Building a sustainable workforce through individual positive psychological interventions. *Psychologist Papers, 37*(3), 185–191.

Liao, S., Hu, D., & Chung, Y.-C. (2017). LMX and Employee satisfaction: Mediating effect of psychological capital. *Leadership and Organization Development Journal, 38*(3), 433–449.

Lips-Wiersma, M., & Wright, S. (2012). Measuring the meaning of meaningful work: Development and validation of the Comprehensive Meaningful Work Scale (CMWS). *Group & Organization Management, 37*(5), 655–685.

Lund, S., Madgavkar, A., Manyika, J., Smit, S., Ellingrud, K., Meaney, M., & Robinson, O. (2021). *The future of work after COVID-19.* McKinsey Global Institute. https://www.mckinsey.com/featured-insights/future-of-work/the-future-of-workafter-covid-19

McKee, A. (2017). *How to Be happy at work: The power of purpose, hope, and friendship*. Harvard Business Press.

Monnot, M. J., & Beehr, T. A. (2014). Subjective well-being at work: Disentangling source effects of stress and support on enthusiasm, contentment, and meaningfulness. *Journal of Vocational Behavior*, *85*(2), 204–218.

Myerson, J., & Tidd, P. (2017). *Developing a practical framework for workplace design to affect employee wellbeing: A research study*. Gensler and the Helen Hamlyn Centre for Design at the Royal College of Art.

Nassif, A. G., Hackett, R. D., & Wang, G. (2021). Ethical, virtuous, and charismatic leadership: An examination of differential relationships with follower and leader outcomes. *Journal of Business Ethics*, *172*(3), 581–603.

Nassir, I. (2017). Happiness in the workplace underpins a sustainable business environment. *InBusiness*. https://www.thenationalnews.com/business/comment/happiness-in-the-workplace-underpins-a-sustainable-business-environment-1.683369

Ojo, A., Fawehinmi, O., & Yusliza, M. (2021). Examining the predictors of resilience and work engagement during COVID-19 pandemic. *Sustainability*, *13*(5), 2902–2923.

Pryce-Jones, J. (2010). *Happiness at work: Maximizing your psychological capital for success*. John Wiley & Sons.

Pryce-Jones, J., & Lindsay, J. (2014). What happiness at work is and how to use it. *Industrial and Commercial Training*, *46*(3), 130–134.

PWC-PricewaterhouseCoopers. (2022). *Redefining a post-pandemic world: Challenges in today's employee wellbeing and how to alleviate them*. https://www.pwc.com/mt/en/publications/humanresources/redefining-wellbeing-in-a-post-pandemic-world.html

REBA. (2020, July). *REBA / AXA PPP healthcare employee wellbeing research report*. https://reba.global/ reports/reba/axa-ppp-healthcare-employee-wellbeing-research-2020

Rego, A., Owens, B., & Leal, S. (2017). How leader humility helps teams to be humbler, psychologically stronger, and more effective: A moderated mediation model. *The Leadership Quarterly*, *28*, 639–658.

Rosso, B. D., Dekas, K. H., & Wrzesniewski, A. (2010). On the meaning of work: A theoretical integration and review. *Research in Organizational Behavior*, *30*, 91–127.

Royal Government of Bhutan. (2012). *The report of the high-level meeting on wellbeing and happiness: Defining a new economic paradigm*. The Permanent Mission of the Kingdom of Bhutan to the United Nations.

Ryff, C. D., & Keyes, C. L. M. (1995). The structure of psychological well-being revisited. *Journal of Personality and Social Psychology*, *69*(4), 719–727.

Ryff, C. D., & Singer, B. H. (2006). Best news yet on the six-factor model of well-being. *Social Science Research*, *35*(4), 1103–1119.

Salas-Vallina, A., & Alegre, J. (2021). Happiness at work: Developing a shorter measure. *Journal of Management & Organization*, *27*(3), 460–480.

Salas-Vallina, A., López-Cabrales, Á., Alegre, J., & Fernández, R. (2017). On the Road to Happiness at Work (HAW): Transformational Leadership and Organizational Learning Capability as Drivers of HAW in a Healthcare Context. *Personnel Review*, *46*(2), 314–338.

Schwepker, C. H., Valentine, S. R., Giacalone, R. A., & Promislo, M. (2021). Good barrels yield healthy apples: Organizational ethics as a mechanism for mitigating work-related stress and promoting employee well-being. *Journal of Business Ethics*, *174*(1), 143–159.

Singh, S., & Aggarwal, Y. (2018). Happiness at work scale: Construction and psychometric validation of a measure using mixed method approach. *Journal of Happiness Studies*, *19*(5), 1439–1463.

Sommovigo, V., Setti, I., & Argentero, P. (2019). The role of service providers' resilience in buffering the negative impact of customer incivility on service recovery performance. *Sustainability*, *11*(1), 1–22.

Thompson, A., & Bruk-Lee, V. (2021). Employee happiness: Why we should care. *Applied Research in Quality of Life*, *16*(4), 1419–1437.

Wald, J., Taylor, S., Asmundson, G. J., Jang, K. L., & Stapleton, J. (2006). *Literature review of concepts: Psychological resiliency*. Defence R&D Canada.

Walton, R. (1974). Improving the quality of working life. *Harvard Business Review*, *54*(3), 12–16.

Warr, P. (1999). Well-being and the workplace. In D. Kahneman, E. Diener, & N. Schwarz (Eds.), *Well-being: The foundations of hedonic psychology* (pp. 392–412). Russell Sage Foundation.

Warr, P. B. (2013). Jobs and Job-Holders: Two sources of Happiness and Unhappiness. In S. A. David, I. Boniwell, & A. C. Ayers (Eds.), *The Oxford Handbook of happiness* (pp. 733–750). Oxford University Press.

Wright, T. A., & Doherty, E. M. (1998). Organizational behavior 'rediscovers' the role of emotional well-being. *Journal of Organizational Behavior*, *19*, 481–485.

ENDNOTES

1. More than 90% of all people agree with the statement "a happy worker is a productive worker" (Fisher, 2003).
2. References for more detailed information: Warr, 1999; Page & Vella-Brodrick Achor, 2010; Diener & Biswas-Diener, 2011; Pryce-Jones & Lindsay, 2014; Mckee, 2017; Gilbert, D., Mckee, A., Spreitzer, G., Amabile, T. 2017; Clifton & Harter, 2021; Salas-Vallina, Alegre, & Fernández, 2017.

Chapter 4
Dynamics of Self-Belief to Fight Against Climate Change:
Evidence From European Social Survey

Cristina Raluca Gh. Popescu
https://orcid.org/0000-0002-5876-0550
University of Bucharest, Romania & The Bucharest University of Economic Studies, Romania

Esra Karapınar Kocağ
https://orcid.org/0000-0002-2239-0519
Gümüşhane University, Turkey

ABSTRACT

All prominent leaders, managers, researchers, and specialists worldwide position the positive and constructive contributions for Sustainable Development Goals (SDGs) in the centre of their activities and interests due to the power that the international community holds in reaching all SDG targets and achieving a global partnership for sustainable development (SD). The focal point of this study is represented by individuals' self-belief to fight against climate change and utilizes valuable data from the European Social Survey (ESS) Wave 10 in 2020 on two main areas: the impact that large numbers of people limiting their energy use might have on climate change and the causes of climate change which could be represented by natural processes, human activity, or both. The findings show that more than half of those individuals in the sample are taking bold and transformative steps towards a better future for all choosing sustainability, being more likely to have positive attitudes about individual efforts to control climate change, centering on reducing their energy consumption.

INTRODUCTION

This study on the novel and original theme describing the "Dynamics of Self-Belief to Fight against Climate Change: Evidence from European Social Survey" is part of the pivotal book entitled "Positive and Constructive Contributions for Sustainable Development Goals".

DOI: 10.4018/978-1-6684-7499-0.ch004

In this section represented by the "Introduction" to this study, the authors mention the importance of the topic chosen for the current analysis, based on the fact that the dynamics of individuals' self-belief to fight against climate change in order to successfully reach the Sustainable Development Goals (SDGs) represents a major concern these days for all interested individuals and, probably mainly, for reputed scholars, researchers, and professors worldwide. A first argument in this regard could rely on the fact that human nature is highly unpredictable and the decisions one takes most often affect not only the person itself but the entire population. A second argument in this matter could be that people have always relied on the power and the strength nature itself brought in their lives, since there is a strong bond between the environment and individuals. It should be added at this point that individuals depend on nature and its capacity to regenerate, bring resources, and influence, at a large scale, people's general health and state of mind, mental health, happiness, and all activities that take place. A third argument in this regard could constitute in the fact that people are the ones responsible for maintaining the biodiversity of our planet Earth and the health of the ecosystems, thus being able to find the necessary potential to continue their lives in a healthy and sustainable way in this environment. A fourth argument in this case could be represented by the fact that individuals' interest tend to differ from one moment to another, from one situation to another, which may lead to unfortunate and, in some cases, damaging activities and decisions that may lead to harming the environment, other living beings, and other people in a direct or and indirect manner. A fifth argument in this current matter could be represented by the fact that individuals' self-beliefs regarding the importance of achieving Sustainable Development Goals (SDGs), in general, and in fighting against climate change, in particular, might depend on several factors, such as, for example: the education level, the age level, the gender, the marital status, the involvement in a petition/claim, the capacity and desire to be social and get involved in social activities either with their close family or with their friends and colleagues, the health status and the mental state of mind, the trust in scientists and relevant studies, the political orientation, the satisfaction with life, the general happiness, the migrant statues, and the religiosity aspects. All in all, human activity influences the environment in which individuals live in far more than the natural processes might do. Besides all that, specialists might even argue that, in most regions and countries around the world, the natural processes have been severely affected by human activity, which led to real natural disasters that are still affecting the lives of the inhabitants of those areas.

In continuation, in this introductory section the authors point out the general perspective of the chapter, since it represents a decisive matter in both choosing the theme and arranging the format of this current work. On the one hand, the general perspective of the chapter is represented by acknowledging the importance of the Sustainable Development Goals (SDGs) in our lives as well as the power that is conferred to all people around the Globe when centring our activities and interests on these bold objectives and important targets meant to make our lives better and more secure. On the other hand, the general perspective of the chapter is represented by analysing and understanding the implications that climate change brought in the last decades in individuals' lives as well as the vital fight against climate change for which all people and entities should be held responsible.

Also, the authors considered extremely important to stress in the "Introduction" section the fact that, besides the theoretical aspects that ought to be emphasized at several stages, the focus should be as well on the statistical matters specific to such a scientific work, which are responsible for better positioning the book chapter, thus offering it more visibility and more reasons to support the achievement Sustainable Development Goals (SDGs), the targets promoted in the 2030 Agenda for Sustainable Development and the Paris Agreement, the fight against climate change, while taking decisive climate action. The authors of this book chapter ought to point out, at this stage, that this book chapter includes a consistent and valuable statistical analysis focused on individuals' self-belief to fight against climate change. In this matter, data from the European Social Survey (ESS) Wave 10 in 2020 was utilized. What is more, this cross-national survey proved to be extremely relevant for the current scientific work as well as for providing valuable insights on individuals' self-belief to fight against climate change, since it contains observations from ten European countries (namely, Bulgaria, Croatia, Czechia, Estonia, Finland, France, Hungary, Lithuania, Slovakia, and Slovenia), covering public attitudes, beliefs, and values of individuals within Europe.

The United Nations Environment Programme (UNEP) stressed the fact that climate change has become more and more dangerous for people and their current ways of lives while centring on the topic "Learn more about SDG 13: Take urgent action to combat climate change and its impacts" (United Nations Environment Programme (UNEP), 2022). Hence, this international organization pointed out that, for instance, "extreme weather events", such as "heat waves, droughts, floods and tropical cyclones", are highly responsible for accentuating the problems concerning the global water management situation, the agricultural production network, the world's food resources, the infrastructure of different regions and countries, and the health of people (United Nations Environment Programme (UNEP), 2022).

In the same line with the aforementioned aspects, The Global Goals international organization mentioned that the entire population was severely affected in the last decades by climate change, characterizing these days' situation concerning climate change as a "real and undeniable threat" to the existence of all living individuals at the global scale (The Global Goals, 2022). What is more, the results of climate change on our planet might prove to be catastrophic and might lead to irreversible damages unless real, resilient, robust, and sustainable measures are taken with the aid of the benefits and the opportunities provided by adhering to "climate commitments" as well as with the help of valuable results coming from different key domains, such as education, innovation, and research (The Global Goals, 2022).

Furthermore, according to the article on "Action on Climate and SDGs" published by the United Nations Framework Convention on Climate Change (UNFCCC) (2022), today climate change is believed to be probably the most accentuated and worrying "threat to Sustainable Development" (SD) ever encountered especially due to several notable characteristics, namely: first of all, climate change is spread at a global level; second of all, climate change has unprecedented impacts on day-to-day activities, life, health, well-being, ecosystems, and surroundings; third of all, although it represent a great threat to everybody, climate change affects individuals in a disproportionate manner, putting at risk especially "the poorest and the most vulnerable" categories of population; and fourth of all, climate change is expected to bring more damaging effects in our lives if the right, responsible, and sustainable actions are not taken as soon as possible (United Nations Framework Convention on Climate Change (UNFCCC), 2022).

Nevertheless, the United Nations Framework Convention on Climate Change (UNFCCC) emphasized in the documentation published recently the fact that taking action in order to stop the devastating effects of climate change on our planet represents a must on the long and challenging way of achieving all the Sustainable Development Goals (SDGs), describing the vital importance of uniting "our collective efforts" at all levels, namely: the civil society, the governments, the countries' leaders, the organizations, and the business representatives (United Nations Framework Convention on Climate Change (UNFCCC), 2022).

The main objectives of the chapter on the "Dynamics of Self-Belief to Fight against Climate Change: Evidence from European Social Survey", namely the three key objectives, are stated in the lines below, as follows:

Step 1: First of all, in this book chapter the authors intend to highlight the importance of the Sustainable Development Goals (SDGs) for today's generations as well as for the future generations to come. In this matter, key concepts were described and explained in this book chapter, with a particular accent on the impact of climate change on our daily lives and the measures that ought to be taken gradually in order to have the strongest approach possible on supporting the fight against climate change. These key concepts may be encountered in several sections of this book chapter, namely: the "Introduction" section, the "Background" section, and the "Key terms and definitions" section. Hence, the First General Objective (GO1) of this scientific work is represented by the authors' key focus on addressing the vital power of the Sustainable Development Goals (SDGs) for supporting life, health, well-being, and a sustainable future for all generations.

Step 2: Second of all, in this book chapter the authors intend to present individuals' self-belief to fight against climate change. Valuable data from the European Social Survey (ESS) Wave 10 in 2020 was utilized. Also, this cross-national survey has proven to be extremely relevant for the current scientific work as well as for providing valuable insights on individuals' self-belief to fight against climate change, since it contains observations from ten European countries (namely, Bulgaria, Croatia, Czechia, Estonia, Finland, France, Hungary, Lithuania, Slovakia, and Slovenia), while covering public attitudes, beliefs, and values of individuals within Europe. The sections that fit the description specific to this step are as follows: the "Data and empirical strategy" section and the "Findings of the empirical investigation" section. Thus, the Second General Objective (GO2) of this scientific work is represented by the authors' key focus on presenting the implications of the dual relationship that exists between climate change and the Sustainable Development Goals (SDGs) for supporting life, health, well-being, and a sustainable future for all generations.

Step 3: Third of all, in this book chapter the authors intend to emphasize the importance of reaching the aims displayed in the 2030 Agenda for Sustainable Development and the manner in which individuals might contribute in a consistent and coherent manner to supporting the fight against climate change at an international level. These points are made, in particular, in the following decisive sections, namely: "Solutions and recommendations" section, the "Future research directions" section, and "Conclusion" section. Also, the "References" section proves to be highly valuable to the entire book chapter, since it brings to light the most relevant and the most recent studies in the field, with a particular emphasis on dominant issues these days, as follows: the Sustainable Development Goals (SDGs), the 2030 Agenda for Sustainable Development, the Paris Agreement, climate change, climate action, the future of the developing and developed countries, the ability of individuals, of regions, and of countries to become more aware of the impact of climate change and the measures capable to climate action, resilience, sustainability, and sustainable development (SD). Hence, the Third General Objective (GO3) of this scientific work is represented by the authors' key focus on presenting the connections of the dual relationship that exists between climate change and the Sustainable Development Goals (SDGs) in order to preserve our natural beauties and heritage and ensure a sustainable future for all generations.

The next section is represented by the "Background" section which aims to provide broad and relevant definitions and discussions of the topic chosen for debate, and incorporate views of others (literature review) into the discussion to support and demonstrate the authors' position on the topic. This section should also be analysed together with the "Key terms and definitions" section, since these two important sections are interconnected and are meant to present highly valuable insights on the current topic.

BACKGROUND

The section is represented by the "Background" of this book chapter. The authors aim to provide at this stage broad and relevant definitions and discussions on the topic chosen for debate, namely "Dynamics of Self-Belief to Fight against Climate Change: Evidence from European Social Survey", and incorporate views of others (literature review) into the discussion to support and demonstrate the authors' position on the topic. Also, this section ought to also be analysed together with the "Key terms and definitions" section, since these two important sections are interrelated and are meant to present relevant insights on the current topic.

The Department of Economic and Social Affairs belonging to the United Nations (UN) (2022) developed over the years a great concern towards promoting both the importance of Sustainable Development (SD) and the necessity of achieving the Sustainable Development Goals (SDGs), which is shown in the document entitled "Do you know all 17 SDGs?" (United Nations (UN), 2022). In this matter, according to the United Nations (UN) specialists, the year 2015 proved to be a historic year for humanity due to the fact that several crucial agreements focused on the future of our planet and the necessity to take good care of the present and the future generations were signed, such as: the "Sendai Framework for Disaster Risk Reduction" (in March 2015); the "Addis Ababa Action Agenda on Financing for Development" (in July 2015); the document on the importance of "Transforming our world: the 2030 Agenda for Sustainable Development" with its 17 SDGs, the United Nations (UN) Sustainable Development Summit in New York (in September 2015); and the "Paris Agreement on Climate Change" (in December 2015) (United Nations (UN), 2022).

The Sustainable Development Goals (SDGs) are of crucial importance since they acknowledge the way in which human activity has changed life on this planet, taking into account both the advantages and the disadvantages that human activity has had over the years. In like manner, the Sustainable Development Goals (SDGs) shed a new light on the fragile nature of the world we live in and point out the importance of nourishing and preserving the strong bond that exists between individuals and the environment, since nature has been a defining part of our lives and of our activities. In addition, the success of the business environment has its roots in the way in which people are capable to act responsible towards nature, proving that by taking sustainable measures individuals act in the spirit of preserving life on Earth and supporting well-being, happiness, and health for all, at all ages.

Figure 1 entitled "Solutions Capable to Support the Achievement of the Sustainable Development Goals (SDGs) in the Post-COVID-19 Era" aims to tackle the most relevant issues according to the authors that might be considered as highly relevant in order to lead the individuals and the society to accomplish the Sustainable Development Goals (SDGs) in current times (see, in this matter, Figure 1. Solutions Capable to Support the Achievement of the Sustainable Development Goals (SDGs) in the Post-COVID-19 Era).

Among other pivotal aspects addressed, the Sustainable Development Goals (SDGs) rely on the case of finding solutions to climate change in order to be able to cope better with disasters at a wide level and to save precious human lives at an international scale (United Nations (UN), 2015a). According to the "Sendai Framework for Disaster Risk Reduction 2015–2030" (March 2015), over the last years disasters have affected "the well-being and safety of persons, communities and countries as a whole", threatening the global balance and endangering lives (United Nations (UN), 2015a, p.10). Hence, it appears that climate change puts in great risk mainly the vulnerable categories of population, namely: women, children, and elderly individuals (United Nations (UN), 2015a, p.10). What is more, climate

Figure 1. Solutions Capable to Support the Achievement of the Sustainable Development Goals (SDGs) in the Post-COVID-19 Era. Source: the authors, based on the sources highlighted in the references section of this book chapter

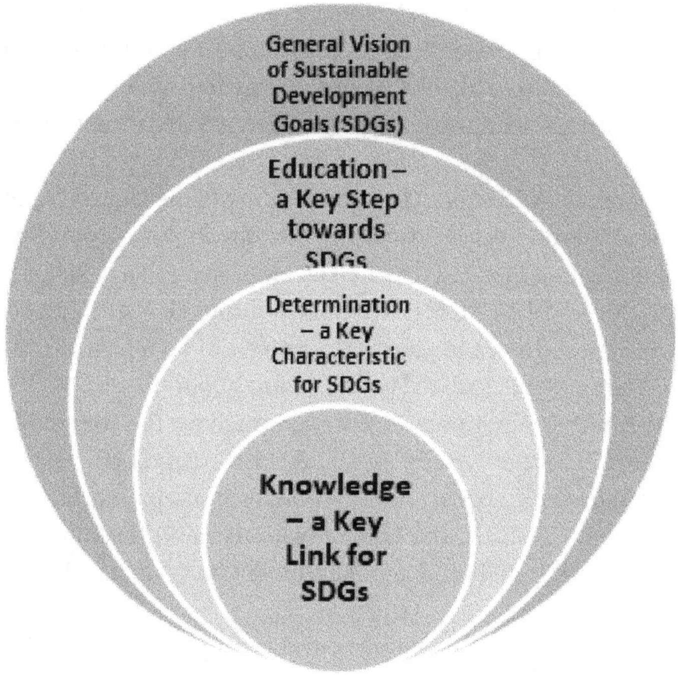

change – described "as one of the drivers of disaster risk", puts a new light on people's finances, showing that emerging and developing countries are more exposed to greater shocks as a result of disasters being "faced with increasing levels of possible hidden costs and challenges in order to meet financial and other obligations" (United Nations (UN), 2015a, pp.10-11).

Furthermore, based on the "Addis Ababa Action Agenda on Financing for Development" (July 2015), prominent world leaders and reputed governmental representatives highlighted the paramount necessity to cope with "the challenge of financing and creating an enabling environment at all levels for sustainable development in the spirit of global partnership and solidarity" (United Nations (UN), 2015b, p.1). In the same vein with the aforementioned ideas, the same Agenda mentioned the primary aim of the international meeting, namely the desideratum "to end poverty and hunger, and to achieve sustainable development in its three dimensions through promoting inclusive economic growth, protecting the environment, and promoting social inclusion" (United Nations (UN), 2015b, p.1). Also, even though at that time the officials stressed the fact that "economic activity and financing flows have increased substantially", besides the monetary instruments they also strongly depend and rely on the "advances in science, technology and innovation" which have increased over time "the potential to achieve our development goals" (United Nations (UN), 2015b, p.2). Although the Agenda pointed out that the financial and economic crisis is likely to subject the regions and the countries worldwide to great monetary instabilities and reveal the vulnerabilities that might exist in this type of system, there are also other major concerns that accompany the financial and economic risks, namely the "environmental degradation, climate change, and other environmental risks" which are believed to "threaten to undermine past successes and future prospects" (United Nations (UN), 2015b, p.2). While pointing out these environmental problems, the international leaders displayed among possible solutions the countries commitment to become more resilient in order to support development and sustainability, more dedicated in achieving the Sustainable Development Goals (SDGs), more concerned in supporting the environment and the resources to regenerate and to be preserved in order for people to be able to lead healthy and happy lives (United Nations (UN), 2015b, p.2). In this matter, "promoting inclusive and sustainable industrial development" represents a must in our society which should centre more on noteworthy challenges such as, for instance, "growth and jobs, resources and energy efficiency, pollution and climate change, knowledge-sharing, innovation and social inclusion" (United Nations (UN), 2015b, p.9). It can be seen, in this matter, that climate change and taking climate action profoundly depend on the existence of financial resources, using energy resources efficiently, taking care of the environment and treasuring the existing resources, while seeking new resources, new sources of energy, and finding solutions to promote in a better way development, science, innovation, and research for healthy, robust, resilient, and sustainable lifestyles (United Nations (UN), 2015b, p.9). The "Addis Ababa Action Agenda on Financing for Development" (July 2015) noted that humanity finds itself at a crucial moment in history in which "protecting our ecosystems for all" has become a prime necessity due to the commitment taken by leaders and governmental officials worldwide "to protect and preserve our planet and natural resources, our biodiversity and our climate" (United Nations (UN), 2015b, p.9). Hence, climate change (with worrying side effects in terms of death, desertification, degradation, flooding, other natural disasters, and pollution) has led, over the years, to the ecosystems' degradation threatening biodiversity and people's lives, which has determined the necessity of individuals and of entities to "avoid harmful activities" and start changing the behavioural patterns (United Nations (UN), 2015b, p.9).

Going even further, the document on the importance of "Transforming our world: the 2030 Agenda for Sustainable Development" with its 17 SDGs, presented at the United Nations (UN) Sustainable Development Summit in New York (September 2015), put a great accent on "people, planet and prosperity" (United Nations (UN), 2015c). First of all, while referring to people, the Agenda stressed the importance of leading lives with dignity and respect for nature, in the spirit of equality, since leading decent lives on Earth depends on the existence of a "healthy environment" (United Nations (UN), 2015c). Second of all, while mentioning the planet, the Agenda emphasized the fact that the damages created by climate change ought to be reversed and solutions ought to be found in order to stop our "planet from degradation", bringing into discussion several important solutions among which could be mentioned the following ones: finding reliable patterns of sustainable consumption and production both by individuals and entities; cherishing the planet's natural resources and learning how to make use of them more rationally and more sustainable both by individuals and entities; and taking care of "the present and future generations" by helping the environment and by bringing the benefits of innovation, research, and science into all the activities that take place (United Nations (UN), 2015c). Third of all, while addressing prosperity, the Agenda displayed the utmost importance "to ensure that all human beings can enjoy prosperous and fulfilling lives and that economic, social and technological progress occurs in harmony with nature" (United Nations (UN), 2015c). All in all, the 2030 Agenda for Sustainable Development successfully connected the three key points – namely the people, the planet and the lives led in prosperity but while being in harmony with nature, on the one hand, with the desire to lead lives in peace and, on the other hand, with the necessity to be part of a "Global Partnership for Sustainable Development" (United Nations (UN), 2015c).

Figure 2. Main Characteristics of the Sustainable Development Goals (SDGs) in the Post-COVID-19 Era. Source: the authors, based on the sources highlighted in the references section of this book chapter

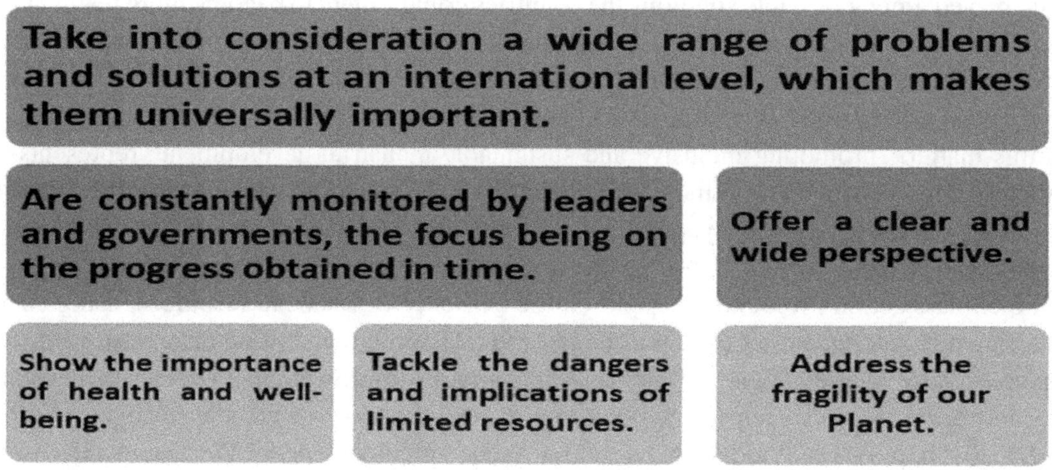

Figure 2 entitled "Main Characteristics of the Sustainable Development Goals (SDGs) in the Post-COVID-19 Era" aims to present the main traits of the Sustainable Development Goals (SDGs) in the current times (see, in this matter, Figure 2. Main Characteristics of the Sustainable Development Goals (SDGs) in the Post-COVID-19 Era).

The "Paris Agreement on Climate Change" (December 2015) highlighted, on the one hand, "the need for an effective and progressive response to the urgent threat of climate change on the basis of the best available scientific knowledge", in particular for "those that are particularly vulnerable to the adverse effects of climate change" and, on the other hand, the necessity of all individuals to have equal access to the benefits and the opportunities offered to them and to their countries by sustainable development (SD) and the "eradication of poverty" (United Nations (UN), 2015d). Also, the "Paris Agreement on Climate Change" noted that immediate action is required at a global level as an immediate result of climate change, since the food resources have been severely affected especially in the case of vulnerable groups of individuals, mentioning that the "fundamental priority" of this Agreement is represented by "safeguarding food security and ending hunger" (United Nations (UN), 2015d). In continuation, this Agreement pointed out that there are several implications that reside from climate change as follows: first of all, the implications refer to the human rights, since there are numerous vulnerable groups of individuals that require immediate assistance and help in order to be able to cope in a sustainable manner with the effects of climate change; second of all, the implications address the right to health for all individuals, which brings to the attention the case of " indigenous peoples, local communities, migrants, children, persons with disabilities and people in vulnerable situations"; third of all, the implications stress individuals' equal right to development which leads to the necessity to ensure this equality for vulnerable groups as well, such as women, children, the elderly people (United Nations (UN), 2015d).

The next section is represented by the "Data and empirical strategy" section which aims to present the case study that comes to support the theoretical background displayed so far in this book chapter. This section is believed to be vital to the development of this book chapter, since it brings to the attention relevant data from the European Social Survey (ESS) Wave 10 in 2020 (European Social Survey

European Research Infrastructure (ESS ERIC), 2022a; European Social Survey European Research Infrastructure (ESS ERIC), 2022b).

DATA AND EMPIRICAL STRATEGY

In the analysis of self-belief to fight against climate change, this chapter utilizes European Social Survey (ESS) Wave 10 in 2020 (European Social Survey European Research Infrastructure (ESS ERIC), 2022a; European Social Survey European Research Infrastructure (ESS ERIC), 2022b). This survey contains observations from ten European countries that are Bulgaria, Croatia, Czechia, Estonia, Finland, France, Hungary, Lithuania, Slovakia, and Slovenia. This cross-national survey covers public attitudes, beliefs, and values of individuals within Europe. Usually, ESS is done through face-to-face interviews, however, countries could use different approaches such as video interviews because of COVID-19 conditions (European Social Survey European Research Infrastructure (ESS ERIC)). Round 10 covers 18,060 individual observations in the beginning. Nevertheless, data analysis of this chapter has 5,603 observations due to the fact that dependent variable is only asked in a subgroup within those observations (European Social Survey European Research Infrastructure (ESS ERIC), 2022a; European Social Survey European Research Infrastructure (ESS ERIC), 2022b).

The survey question to be utilised as a dependent variable is "*Now imagine that large numbers of people limited their energy use. How likely do you think it is that this would reduce climate change?*". Ordered answers of this question is coded as follows:

- *1 Not at all likely*
- *2 Not very likely*
- *3 Likely*
- *4 Very likely*

Summary statistics both on the dependent variable and independent variables used in the empirical investigation of this chapter is given in Table 1 below. To explain individuals' attitudes reducing climate change, this investigation includes a wide range of independent variables. Along with a standard set of socio-demographic indicators such as education level, age level, gender, and marital status, indicators that may affect individual attitudes such as involvement in a petition recently, being social, subjective health, trusting scientists, political orientation, satisfaction with life, general happiness, migrant statues, and religiosity. These variables are expected to influence formation of attitudes on the sensitivity towards environmental issues, as well as some other issues. Age and education variables are given as number of years. Gender variable is coded as 1 if respondent is male. Rest of the independent variables are categorical or dichotomous as might be seen from the table.

A closer look at responses to the dependent variable of interest, it is seen that most of the survey participants (i.e., 45.73%) answer the question as they are thinking in a way that climate change is likely to be reduced if large numbers of people reduce their energy consumption. 10.33 per cent of the participants is even more positive on the power of individual preference, reporting it is very likely to reduce climate change if this occurs. However, nearly 37 per cent of them believe that this is not very likely, while 7.17 per cent reports that reducing climate change through reduction of individual energy use is not likely at all. Therefore, it can be said that more than half of those individuals in the sample

Table 1 (a). Summary statistics of the variables used in the analysis. Source: The authors, based on the references highlighted in this book chapter, with a particular emphasis on the European Social Survey European Research Infrastructure (ESS ERIC) (European Social Survey European Research Infrastructure (ESS ERIC), 2022a; European Social Survey European Research Infrastructure (ESS ERIC), 2022b)

Variable		Obs	Mean	Std. Dev.	Min	Max	Frequency	Percent
CC	Would limited energy use reduce climate change?							
	Not at all likely	5603	0.072	0.258	0	1	402	7.17
	Not very likely	5603	0.368	0.482	0	1	2,060	36.77
	Likely	5603	0.457	0.498	0	1	2,562	45.73
	Very likely	5603	0.103	0.304	0	1	579	10.33
Edu	Years of full-time education completed	5603	13.198	3.699	0	114		
Age	Age of respondent	5603	50.658	18.269	15	90		
Male	Gender							
	0	5603	0.543	0.498	0	1	3,045	54.35
	1	5603	0.457	0.498	0	1	2,558	45.65
Petition	Signed petition last 12 months							
	Yes	5603	0.172	0.377	0	1	962	17.17
	No	5603	0.828	0.377	0	1	4,641	82.83
Social	How often socially meet with friends, relatives or colleagues							
	Never	5603	0.021	0.142	0	1	115	2.05
Less than once a month		5603	0.122	0.328	0	1	685	12.03
Once a month		5603	0.113	0.317	0	1	635	11.33
Several times a month		5603	0.234	0.424	0	1	1,312	23.42
	Once a week		0.160	0.367	0	1	896	15.99
Several times a week		5603	0.228	0.420	0	1	1,278	22.81
	Every day	5603	0.122	0.327	0	1	682	12.17
Health	Subjective general health							
	Very good	5603	0.221	0.415	0	1	1,236	22.06
	Good	5603	0.422	0.494	0	1	2,363	42.17
	Fair	5603	0.278	0.448	0	1	1,559	27.82
	Bad	5603	0.068	0.251	0	1	379	6.76
	Very bad	5603	0.012	0.108	0	1	66	1.18

are more likely to have positive attitudes about individual efforts to control climate change (see, in this matter, Table 1 Summary statistics of the variables used in the analysis).

Considering the structure of the dependent variable used in the investigation, ordered probit model is utilised test the model as specified in Equation 1 below. Let CC_i be the outcome to be observed about individuals' attitudes towards whether reduction of energy use of people would reduce climate change by a survey respondent i. Through selecting among those categorical answers given in the questionnaire,

Table 1 (b). Summary statistics of the variables used in the analysis

Variable		Obs	Mean	Std. Dev.	Min	Max	Frequency	Percent
Migrant	Born in country							
	Yes	5603	0.948	0.223	0	1	5,309	94.75
	No	5603	0.052	0.223	0	1	294	5.25
Marital_S	Legal marital status							
Legally married		5603	0.467	0.499	0	1	2,614	46.65
In a legally registered civil union		5603	0.010	0.100	0	1	57	1.02
Legally separated		5603	0.030	0.171	0	1	168	3
Legally divorced/Civil union dissolved		5603	0.102	0.302	0	1	569	10.16
Widowed/Civil partner died		5603	0.096	0.295	0	1	539	9.62
None of these		5603	0.296	0.456	0	1	1,656	29.56
Trust	Trust in scientists							
	Untrusted	5603	0.184	0.388	0	1	1,033	18.44
	Trusted	5603	0.816	0.388	0	1	4,570	81.56
PP	Political placement							
	Right	5603	0.775	0.418	0	1	4,341	77.48
	Left	5603	0.225	0.418	0	1	1,262	22.52
Satisfaction	Satisfied with life as a whole							
	Unsatisfied	5603	0.238	0.426	0	1	1,332	23.77
	Satisfied	5603	0.762	0.426	0	1	4,271	76.23
Happiness								
	Unhappy	5603	0.200	0.400	0	1	1,120	19.99
	Happy	5603	0.800	0.400	0	1	4,483	80.01
Religiosity								
	Not religious	5603	0.624	0.485	0	1	3,494	62.36
	Religious	5603	0.376	0.485	0	1	2,109	37.64

this respondent individual will evaluate how likely to reduce climate change by limiting individual energy use. Selected category will approximate his or her personal evaluation. In this respect, the reported category might be interpreted as a measured level of self-belief to reduce climate change.

$$CC_i^* = {}^2{}_0D_i + {}^2{}_1O_i + \partial_c + \mu_i \quad (1)$$

where D_i covers individual *i*'s socio-demographic characteristics that are education level, age level, gender, and marital status. Other subjective individual judgements that are involvement in a petition recently, being social, subjective health, trusting scientists, political orientation, satisfaction with life, general happiness, migrant statues, and religiosity are denoted by *O*. Model specification also includes country specific factors that is shown as ∂_c in the equation. εi finally denotes a zero mean random error term to reflect unobserved factor related to individual feeling about reduction of climate change.

Table 1 (c). Summary statistics of the variables used in the analysis

Variable		Obs	Mean	Std. Dev.	Min	Max	Frequency	Percent
Country								
BG	Bulgaria	5603	0.152	0.359	0	1	851	15.19
CZ	Czechia	5603	0.130	0.336	0	1	727	12.98
EE	Estonia	5603	0.091	0.287	0	1	509	9.08
FI	Finland	5603	0.092	0.289	0	1	515	9.19
FR	France	5603	0.117	0.321	0	1	654	11.67
HR	Croatia	5603	0.087	0.282	0	1	489	8.73
HU	Hungary	5603	0.104	0.306	0	1	585	10.44
LT	Lithuania	5603	0.088	0.283	0	1	492	8.78
SI	Slovenia	5603	0.070	0.255	0	1	390	6.96
SK	Slovakia	5603	0.070	0.255	0	1	391	6.98

The next section displays the "Findings of the empirical investigation" and presents the most notable results of the study, which makes this section of vital importance to this book chapter.

FINDINGS OF THE EMPIRICAL INVESTIGATION

Findings of the empirical investigation that is based on an ordered probit model is presented in this section. Table 2 presents findings of the ordered probit model. Original coefficients obtained from ordered probit specification is presented in the first column. Due to the nature of this kind of models (i.e., ordered probit model), coefficients are not directly interpretable. Hence, marginal effects are calculated. Following columns of the table, in this respect, shows calculated marginal effects for each answer category that is used to interpret findings easier and meaningful. Since this is a probability of occurrence of an event among a set of options, the sum of coefficients in each answer category is equal to 1.

Original coefficients might only be useful to see if there exist a significant relationship, and in which way this relationship is. However, marginal effects provides a more precise information on the size of the effect. As shown in Table 2, there is statistically significant relationship between education level and attitudes towards climate change. Accordingly, one more year of education decreases the probability of reporting climate change is not at all likely to reduce through reduction of energy use of large number of people by 2 percentage points, and decreases the probability of reporting not very likely by 3 percentage points. However, it increases the probability of reporting likely by 3 percentage points, and very likely by 2 percentage points. This means when individuals get more education, they are more likely to think in a way that individual efforts of many would matter to reduce climate change. This relationship is just the opposite when considering age of respondents. That is to say, one more year of age lowers the probability of reporting very likely, and likely, while it increases the probability of reporting not at all likely, and not very likely. Therefore, it can be said that when individuals get older they are more likely to think that this kind of efforts will not reduce climate change. There is significant gender effect as well. More precisely, being male rather than female decreases the probability of reporting it is either likely or very likely, while it increases the probability of reporting not likely at all, and likely. Hence, this sample shows that males are more pessimist than females. It is also found that there is no significant effect of marital status as one socio-demographic indicator (see, in this matter, Table 2 Findings of Ordered Probit Model).

As mentioned earlier, this empirical investigation covers variety of independent variables that are likely to explain individuals' self-belief to reduce climate change, and they are represented by O in Equation 1. Some of them among those variables ends up significant relationship with the dependent variable. Those individuals who socially meet with friends, relatives or colleagues several times a month (rather than those who never meet) were found to be more likely to express that climate change is likely/very likely to be reduced by limited energy use of people. Coefficients of the category of people who meet several times a week are even larger, which means more social people are more likely to feel positive on fighting climate change through reduction of individual energy use. Even if the impact is only marginal, it was also found that those who report good and fair health (rather than very good health), natives (rather than migrants), religious, and satisfied with life in general are likely to feel positive. Finally trusting scientist, having a left ideology, and being happy increases the likelihood of reporting limited energy use is likely/very likely reduce climate change.

This chapter also provide an analysis of how those people who think that climate change is caused by human activity. For this purpose, a survey question, asking "*Do you think that climate change is caused by natural processes, human activity, or both?*" is used. This question originally has five answer categories as follows:

1. Entirely by natural processes
2. Mainly by natural processes
3. About equally by natural processes and human activity
4. Mainly by human activity
5. Entirely by human activity

For the purpose of this chapter, those people who think that climate change is mainly caused by human activity and entirely caused by human activity were subgrouped. Then, the analysis above is tested for this subgroup. Findings are presented in Table 3 below (see, in this matter, Table 3 Findings for subgroup (i.e. those who think climate change is caused by human activity)):

Finding for subgroup of people who think that climate change is mainly or entirely caused by human activity reveal similar structure for socio-demographic indicators such as education, age level, and gender although statistical significance varies. However, it should be noted that other indicators shows some differences. As one of them, variable social which present how social respondent is ends up very significant and larger coefficients. The coefficient is the largest for those who meet socially every day (in comparison with those who never meet) that is statistically significant at 1 per cent significance level. This means those social people who think climate change is caused by human activity are likely to report climate change might be reduced by reduction of individual energy use. Therefore, it might be thought that this group believes human being is responsible with this disaster, and human being then can fix this problem. Interestingly, health, migration status, satisfaction, happiness, and religiosity were found not statistically significant. Finally, trusting scientists is positive and statistically significant at 1 per cent significance level though magnitude is larger than the original specification.

The next sections are represented by the "Solutions and recommendations", "Future research directions", "Conclusion", "References", and "Key terms and definitions", which come to successfully present the

Table 2 (a). Findings of Ordered Probit Model. Source: The authors, based on the references highlighted in this book chapter, with a particular emphasis on the European Social Survey European Research Infrastructure (ESS ERIC) (European Social Survey European Research Infrastructure (ESS ERIC), 2022a; European Social Survey European Research Infrastructure (ESS ERIC), 2022b)

Variables	Original	Not at all likely	Not very likely	Likely	Very likely
Edu	0.014***	-0.002***	-0.003***	0.003***	0.002***
	(0.004)	(0.001)	(0.001)	(0.001)	(0.001)
Age	-0.003***	0.000***	0.001***	-0.001***	-0.001***
	(0.001)	(0.000)	(0.000)	(0.000)	(0.000)
Male	-0.142***	0.019***	0.035***	-0.030***	-0.024***
	(0.030)	(0.004)	(0.008)	(0.006)	(0.005)
Petition (Base Category: Yes)					
No	-0.011	0.002	0.003	-0.002	-0.002
	(0.041)	(0.005)	(0.010)	(0.008)	(0.007)
Social (Base category: Never)					
Less than once a month	0.145	-0.022	-0.034	0.034	0.022
	(0.111)	(0.018)	(0.025)	(0.027)	(0.016)
Once a month	0.141	-0.021	-0.033	0.033	0.021
	(0.113)	(0.018)	(0.025)	(0.027)	(0.016)
Several times a month	0.194*	-0.028	-0.046*	0.044*	0.030**
	(0.109)	(0.018)	(0.024)	(0.026)	(0.015)
Once a week	0.179	-0.026	-0.042*	0.041	0.028*
	(0.111)	(0.018)	(0.025)	(0.027)	(0.016)
Several times a week	0.217**	-0.031*	-0.052**	0.048*	0.034**
	(0.110)	(0.018)	(0.024)	(0.027)	(0.016)
Every day	0.153	-0.023	-0.036	0.035	0.023
	(0.115)	(0.019)	(0.026)	(0.028)	(0.016)
Health (Base category: Very good)					
Good	0.068*	-0.009	-0.016*	0.014	0.011*
	(0.041)	(0.006)	(0.010)	(0.009)	(0.007)
Fair	0.083*	-0.011*	-0.020*	0.017*	0.014*
	(0.048)	(0.007)	(0.012)	(0.010)	(0.008)
Bad	0.074	-0.010	-0.018	0.016	0.012
	(0.072)	(0.010)	(0.018)	(0.015)	(0.012)
Very bad	-0.030	0.004	0.007	-0.007	-0.005
	(0.144)	(0.021)	(0.034)	(0.033)	(0.022)
Migrant (Base category: Yes)					
No	0.109	-0.013*	-0.028	0.021*	0.020
	(0.067)	(0.008)	(0.017)	(0.012)	(0.013)
Marital_S (Base category: Legally married					
In a legally registered civil union	-0.163	0.024	0.038	-0.036	-0.026
	(0.150)	(0.024)	(0.033)	(0.036)	(0.021)
Legally separated	0.131	-0.016	-0.034	0.024	0.025
	(0.093)	(0.010)	(0.024)	(0.016)	(0.019)
Legally divorced/Civil union dissolved	-0.021	0.003	0.005	-0.004	-0.004
	(0.052)	(0.007)	(0.013)	(0.011)	(0.009)
Widowed/Civil partner died	-0.006	0.001	0.002	-0.001	-0.001
	(0.057)	(0.007)	(0.014)	(0.012)	(0.010)
None of these	-0.030	0.004	0.007	-0.006	-0.005
	(0.042)	(0.006)	(0.010)	(0.009)	(0.007)
Trust (Base category: Untrusted)					
Trusted	0.178***	-0.025***	-0.042***	0.039***	0.029***
	(0.042)	(0.006)	(0.010)	(0.010)	(0.006)

Table 2 (b). Findings of Ordered Probit Model

Variables	Original	Not at all likely	Not very likely	Likely	Very likely
PP (Base Category: Right)					
Left	0.139***	-0.017***	-0.035***	0.027***	0.025***
	(0.036)	(0.004)	(0.009)	(0.007)	(0.007)
Satisfaction (Base category: Unsatisfied)					
Satisfied	0.077*	-0.010*	-0.019*	0.016*	0.013*
	(0.043)	(0.006)	(0.011)	(0.010)	(0.007)
Happiness (Base category: Unhappy)					
Happy	0.113**	-0.015**	-0.028**	0.024**	0.019**
	(0.046)	(0.007)	(0.011)	(0.011)	(0.007)
Religiosity (Base category: Not religious)					
Religious	0.053*	-0.007*	-0.013	0.011*	0.009
	(0.032)	(0.004)	(0.008)	(0.007)	(0.006)
Observations	5,603	5,603	5,603	5,603	5,603
Pseudo R2	0.0296				
Standard errors in parentheses					
*** p<0.01, ** p<0.05, * p<0.1					

most relevant aspects that ought to be improved in this current situation, while focusing on new themes that could be part of future research directions meant to make even a more in-depth analysis than the present one, or bring new arguments besides the ones already pointed out in this current scientific work.

SOLUTIONS AND RECOMMENDATIONS

This section addresses the authors' solutions and recommendations in dealing with the aspects and the problems covered in the preceding sections.

First of all, in this matter, the authors would like to note the fact that this study on the novel and original theme describing the "Dynamics of Self-Belief to Fight against Climate Change: Evidence from European Social Survey", part of the pivotal book entitled "Positive and Constructive Contributions for Sustainable Development Goals", is intended to shed a new light on the importance of the Sustainable Development Goals (SDGs) for humankind. These Global Goals are pivotal to promoting health, happiness, and well-being, while empowering individuals to become more aware of the dangers brought by their activities in those situations in which individuals act with ought respecting the nature, the biodiversity, and the ecosystems.

Second of all, in the same line with the aspects highlighted above, the authors would like to mention that climate change represents probably one of the greatest dangers and one of the vital concerns which specialists have managed to point out throughout the Sustainable Development Goals (SDGs). In this case, taking climate action brings individuals much closer and offers them the possibility to act in a

Table 3 (a). Findings for subgroup (i.e., those who think climate change is caused by human activity). Source: The authors, based on the references highlighted in this book chapter, with a particular emphasis on the European Social Survey European Research Infrastructure (ESS ERIC) (European Social Survey European Research Infrastructure (ESS ERIC), 2022a; European Social Survey European Research Infrastructure (ESS ERIC), 2022b)

Variables	Original	Not at all likely	Not very likely	Likely	Very likely
Edu	0.011*	-0.001*	-0.003*	0.001*	0.002*
	(0.006)	(0.001)	(0.001)	(0.001)	(0.001)
Age	-0.003*	0.000*	0.001*	-0.000*	-0.001*
	(0.002)	(0.000)	(0.000)	(0.000)	(0.000)
Male	-0.122***	0.013***	0.031***	-0.017***	-0.027***
	(0.046)	(0.005)	(0.012)	(0.006)	(0.010)
Petition (Base Category: Yes)					
No	-0.034	0.003	0.009	-0.005	-0.008
	(0.058)	(0.006)	(0.015)	(0.007)	(0.013)
Social (Base category: Never)					
Less than once a month	0.472***	-0.068**	-0.111***	0.096**	0.083***
	(0.176)	(0.032)	(0.036)	(0.043)	(0.026)
Once a month	0.474***	-0.068**	-0.111***	0.096**	0.083***
	(0.176)	(0.032)	(0.036)	(0.043)	(0.026)
Several times a month	0.492***	-0.070**	-0.116***	0.099**	0.087***
	(0.170)	(0.032)	(0.034)	(0.043)	(0.023)
Once a week	0.443**	-0.065**	-0.103***	0.092**	0.076***
	(0.173)	(0.032)	(0.035)	(0.043)	(0.024)
Several times a week	0.449***	-0.065**	-0.105***	0.093**	0.077***
	(0.171)	(0.032)	(0.034)	(0.043)	(0.023)
Every day	0.511***	-0.072**	-0.121***	0.101**	0.092***
	(0.179)	(0.032)	(0.037)	(0.044)	(0.027)
Health (Base category: Very good)					
Good	0.008	-0.001	-0.002	0.001	0.002
	(0.060)	(0.006)	(0.015)	(0.008)	(0.013)
Fair	-0.002	0.000	0.001	-0.000	-0.000
	(0.073)	(0.007)	(0.019)	(0.010)	(0.016)
Bad	-0.022	0.002	0.006	-0.003	-0.005
	(0.112)	(0.012)	(0.029)	(0.016)	(0.025)
Very bad	-0.169	0.020	0.043	-0.028	-0.035
	(0.246)	(0.032)	(0.061)	(0.046)	(0.046)
Migrant (Base category: Yes)					
No	0.114	-0.011	-0.029	0.013	0.027
	(0.111)	(0.010)	(0.028)	(0.011)	(0.027)
Marital_S (Base category: Legally married)					
In a legally registered civil union	-0.330*	0.041	0.082**	-0.058	-0.065**
	(0.180)	(0.028)	(0.042)	(0.040)	(0.030)
Legally separated	0.244	-0.019*	-0.062	0.018***	0.063
	(0.156)	(0.010)	(0.039)	(0.006)	(0.044)
Legally divorced/Civil union dissolved	-0.093	0.010	0.024	-0.013	-0.021
	(0.078)	(0.009)	(0.020)	(0.012)	(0.017)
Widowed/Civil partner died	-0.014	0.001	0.004	-0.002	-0.003
	(0.095)	(0.009)	(0.024)	(0.012)	(0.022)
None of these	-0.083	0.009	0.021	-0.011	-0.019
	(0.063)	(0.007)	(0.016)	(0.009)	(0.014)
Trust (Base category: Untrusted)					
Trusted	0.208***	-0.024***	-0.053***	0.033***	0.043***
	(0.067)	(0.009)	(0.017)	(0.012)	(0.013)

Table 3 (b). Findings for subgroup (i.e., those who think climate change is caused by human activity)

Variables	Original	Not at all likely	Not very likely	Likely	Very likely
PP (Base Category: Right)					
Left	0.122**	-0.012**	-0.031**	0.015**	0.028**
	(0.054)	(0.005)	(0.014)	(0.006)	(0.013)
Satisfaction (Base category: Unsatisfied)					
Satisfied	0.055	-0.006	-0.014	0.008	0.012
	(0.071)	(0.008)	(0.018)	(0.010)	(0.015)
Happiness (Base category: Unhappy)					
Happy	0.102	-0.011	-0.026	0.015	0.022
	(0.075)	(0.009)	(0.019)	(0.012)	(0.016)
Religiosity (Base category: Not religious)					
Religious	0.055	-0.006	-0.014	0.007	0.012
	(0.049)	(0.005)	(0.013)	(0.006)	(0.011)
Observations	2,415	2,415	2,415	2,415	2,415
Pseudo R2	0.0250				
Standard errors in parentheses					
*** p<0.01, ** p<0.05, * p<0.1					

responsible and in a sustainable manner, displaying their altruism, their concern towards the vulnerable groups, and their care towards nature and preserving the harmony in which humans should live with nature.

There are several solutions and recommendations that ought to be taken into consideration in this particular case, among which the authors would like to mention the ones in the lines below.

Firstly, based on the results of the study displayed in this scientific research, individuals should learn to rediscover the benefits of nature and the importance of nature in their lives and in their daily activities. It seems that the age variable is extremely important when deciding whether or not nature plays an important role in our lives and, also, whether or not nature has the power to contribute to our health, happiness, and well-being. Since over the years individuals become more mature and more aware of the dangers that they might face, they also tend to reflect more on their habits and consumptions patterns, becoming more inclined to choose healthier, more sustainable lives, relying more on nature and the benefits that nature has to offer. Hence, one possible solution and recommendation is to present individuals from early stages of life the importance of nature, and the dangers brought by climate change, in order to raise responsible generations capable to support resilient lifestyles at the early stages.

Second of all, based on the results of the study displayed in this scientific research, individuals tend to have different visions concerning nature and the manner in which their activities affect the biodiversity and the ecosystems. This visions might be related to the type of group they are part of (weather it is a vulnerable one or not), on the financial possibilities that they have (in terms of access of education, the wage that they receive, the family possibilities, and so on), on the education they received and they have access to (the education received at early stages of life and the education received later on in school), on the culture they are part of and the country they reside, study, or work. Hence, another possible solution and recommendation is to find ways to make all individuals aware of the advantages and the benefits of acting in a sustainable manner at all times, with a deep focus on themselves and their families, but also on other individuals and the future generations.

Third of all, based on the results of the study displayed in this scientific research, individuals tend to become more inclined to care about their health, their happiness, and their well-being if they have access to education and to reliable sources of information. In this matter, it should be pointed out that the achievement of the Sustainable Development Goals (SDGs) relies on the level of education of individuals and on their possibilities to support through their activities and their actions nature. Hence, another possible solution and recommendation is to find ways to make all individuals aware of the importance of education at early stages of life and to support the access to education.

It seems that making individuals aware of the implications of climate change is highly difficult, especially in those cases in which taking actions in order to fight climate change might affect the day-to-day comfort individuals got used to over the years. This book chapter successfully managed to make connections between climate change and the use of energy (as seen through the results analysed and presented from European Social Survey European Research Infrastructure (ESS ERIC), 2022a; European Social Survey European Research Infrastructure (ESS ERIC), 2022b). Although all human activities rely on the use of energy one way or another, the achievement of the Sustainable Development Goals (SDGs) depends on the correct, proper and sustainable use of energy. Even though there are numerous cases in which individuals are unaware of the implications of energy consumption on their own health and nature itself, there are different constructive ways in which these people could be informed of these implications and could be helped to become more and more responsible and committed to helping the process of sustainability and supporting live of this planet for the current and for the future generations. Besides these aspects, the vulnerable groups of individuals ought to receive care, help, and additional guidance from authorities and from organizations in order to be able to contribute in turn to accomplishment of the Sustainable Development Goals (SDGs) and in order to be able to show their support to these causes.

The next section addresses possible future research directions which are derived from the aspects already tackled in this book chapter.

FUTURE RESEARCH DIRECTIONS

This section brings into discussion future and emerging trends and is intended to provide insight about the future of the book's theme from the perspective of the chapter focus, being keen on making viable suggestions on future research opportunities within the domain of the topic.

In this matter, one possible research direction due to be considered in the future could be represented by analysing and presenting other connections that might exist at a larger scale besides those between climate change, climate action, and the use of energy. For instance, possible connections could be made between individuals' behavioural patterns in terms of consumption, entities frameworks in terms of production, and the need to consider the implications of climate change on these activities, while taking robust climate action.

In addition, another possible research direction due to be considered in the future could be represented by analysing and presenting the benefits of green management and green marketing while displaying the dangers occurring inevitably from climate change and while centring on the benefits of the Sustainable Development Goals (SDGs) on life at a global scale.

The next section is represented by the "Conclusion", which aims to provide discussion of the overall coverage of the chapter and insert some vital concluding remarks for this current scientific work.

CONCLUSION

This section highlights the most important conclusions of this book chapter on the "Dynamics of Self-Belief to Fight against Climate Change: Evidence from European Social Survey".

First of all, humankind displays a great concern when it comes to supporting the Sustainable Development Goals (SDGs), since the aims targeted in this matter are intended to promote healthier ways of life based on the desire to become more prosperous and, in the same time, more sustainable. Hence, this book chapter brings to the attention the benefits that arise from becoming aware of the advantages that the Sustainable Development Goals (SDGs) bring both for people and for nature.

Second of all, humankind displays a great concern when it comes to addressing the implications of climate change, especially in the case of developing countries and vulnerable groups of individuals. Hence, this book chapter brings to light the possibilities that individuals have to become more sustainable and more responsible in their activities, which is, also, dependent on their financial level, education, and care for themselves, families, and other people.

Third of all, the results of the case study presented display that most of the survey participants (i.e., 45.73%) answer the question as they are thinking in a way that climate change is likely to be reduced if large numbers of people reduce their energy consumption, which leads to the conclusion that more than half of those individuals in the sample are more likely to have positive attitudes about individual efforts to control climate change (see, in this matter, the analysis concerning the data from the European Social Survey European Research Infrastructure (ESS ERIC), 2022a and the European Social Survey European Research Infrastructure (ESS ERIC), 2022b). In addition, the results for the sub group of people who think that climate change is mainly or entirely caused by human activity reveal similar structure for socio-demographic indicators such as education, age level, and gender although statistical significance varies (see, in this matter, the analysis concerning the data from the European Social Survey European Research Infrastructure (ESS ERIC), 2022a and the European Social Survey European Research Infrastructure (ESS ERIC), 2022b). Nevertheless, it should be noted that other indicators shows some differences (see, in this matter, the analysis concerning the data from the European Social Survey European Research Infrastructure (ESS ERIC), 2022a and the European Social Survey European Research Infrastructure (ESS ERIC), 2022b). In essence, this means those social people who think climate change is caused by human activity are likely to report climate change might be reduced by reduction of individual energy use, which it might be thought that this group believes human being is responsible with this disaster, and human being then can fix this problem (see, in this matter, the analysis concerning the data from the European Social Survey European Research Infrastructure (ESS ERIC), 2022a and the European Social Survey European Research Infrastructure (ESS ERIC), 2022b). In continuation, it ought to be stressed that health, migration status, satisfaction, happiness, and religiosity were found not statistically significant, while trusting scientists is positive and statistically significant at 1 per cent significance level though magnitude is larger than the original specification (see, in this matter, the analysis concerning the data from the European Social Survey European Research Infrastructure (ESS ERIC), 2022a and the European Social Survey European Research Infrastructure (ESS ERIC), 2022b).

These days context proved to be very demanding in terms of the organization and the reorganization of the society while compared to past situation, even though there are numerous similarities between present days and past time periods when it comes to situations such as: first of all, the need to preserve life and the requirement to support a balance between the society's needs and the Planet's limited resources; (Popescu, 2011); second of all, the necessity to address individuals' health in the same line with the necessity to foresee the future and respond to the next generations' needs (Popescu, 2012a; 2012b); and third of all, the impossibility to promptly respond to crisis situations, due to the lack of coherence in terms of social, economic, financial, and social international systems, which is justified in a way by the fact that it is always better to address the problems at a smaller scale, rather than at a larger scale, in order to be able to cope better with the issues and know more in-depth the reality of regions, and nations (Popescu, 2012a; 2013).

ACKNOWLEDGMENT

This research received no specific grant from any funding agency in the public, commercial, or not-for-profit sectors. Author Contributions: Conceptualization, C.R.G.P. (Cristina Raluca Gh. Popescu) and E.K.K. (Esra Karapınar Kocağ); methodology, C.R.G.P. and E.K.K.; software, C.R.G.P. and E.K.K.; validation, C.R.G.P. and E.K.K.; formal analysis, C.R.G.P. and E.K.K.; investigation, C.R.G.P. and E.K.K.; resources, C.R.G.P. and E.K.K.; data curation, C.R.G.P. and E.K.K.; writing—original draft preparation, C.R.G.P. and E.K.K.; writing—review and editing, C.R.G.P. and E.K.K.; visualization, C.R.G.P. and E.K.K.; supervision, C.R.G.P. and E.K.K.; project administration, C.R.G.P. and E.K.K.; funding acquisition, C.R.G.P. and E.K.K. All authors have equally contributed to the manuscript. All authors have read and agreed to the published version of the manuscript.

REFERENCES

European Social Survey European Research Infrastructure (ESS ERIC). (2022a). ESS20 - integrated file, edition 1.2 [Data set]. Sikt - Norwegian Agency for Shared Services in Education and Research. doi:10.21338/ESS10E01

European Social Survey European Research Infrastructure (ESS ERIC). (2022b). *ESS10 Data Documentation*. Sikt - Norwegian Agency for Shared Services in Education and Research. doi:10.21338/NSD-ESS10-2020

European Social Survey European Research Infrastructure (ESS ERIC). (2022c). *About the European Social Survey European Research Infrastructure (ESS ERIC)*. Retrieved August 15, 2022, from https://www.europeansocialsurvey.org/about/

Popescu, V. A., Popescu, G. N., & Popescu, C. R. G. (2011). "Liquid Assets" Or Turning Fine Wines In A Very Profitable Investment. *Crises After The Crisis: Inquiries From A National, European And Global Perspective, Vol. IV. 18th International Economic Conference on Crisis After the Crisis - Inquiries from a National European and Global Perspective.*

Popescu, V. A., Popescu, G. N., & Popescu, C. R. G. (2012a). Building a culture for innovation through competitive intelligence and accountability: case of Romania. *Innovation And Sustainable Competitive Advantage: From Regional Development To World Economies,* Vols. 1-5. *18th International-Business-Information-Management-Association Conference (IBIMA).*

Popescu, V. A., Popescu, G. N., & Popescu, C. R. G. (2012b). Knowledge And Knowledge Management - New Challenges And Future Perspectives. *EDULEARN12: 4th International Conference On Education And New Learning Technologies. Book Series: EDULEARN Proceedings. 4th International Conference on Education and New Learning Technologies (EDULEARN),* 1011-1019.

Popescu, V. A., Popescu, G. N., & Popescu, C. R. G. (2013). The Impact Of Higher Education On The Development Of Nowadays Society - A Case Study On Romania's Experience. *7th International Technology, Education And Development Conference (INTED2013). Book Series: INTED Proceedings. 7th International Technology, Education and Development Conference (INTED),* 4988-4996.

The Global Goals. (2022). *Climate Change: Take Urgent Action to Combat Climate Change and its Impacts.* Retrieved August 20, 2022, from https://www.globalgoals.org/goals/13-climate-action/

United Nations Environment Programme (UNEP). (2022). *Learn more about SDG 13: Take Urgent Action to Combat Climate Change and its Impacts.* Retrieved August 20, 2022, from https://www.unep.org/explore-topics/sustainable-development-goals/why-do-sustainable-development-goals-matter/goal-13

United Nations Framework Convention on Climate Change (UNFCCC). (2022). *Action on Climate and SDGs.* Retrieved August 20, 2022, https://unfccc.int/topics/action-on-climate-and-sdgs/action-on-climate-and-sdgs

United Nations (UN). (2015a). *Sendai Framework for Disaster Risk Reduction 2015–2030.* Retrieved August 20, 2022, from https://sustainabledevelopment.un.org/frameworks/sendaiframework and https://sustainabledevelopment.un.org/content/documents/2157sendaiframeworkfordrren.pdf

United Nations (UN). (2015b). *Addis Ababa Action Agenda of the Third International Conference on Financing for Development (Addis Ababa Action Agenda).* Retrieved August 20, 2022, from https://sustainabledevelopment.un.org/frameworks/addisababaactionagenda and https://sustainabledevelopment.un.org/content/documents/2051AAAA_Outcome.pdf

United Nations (UN). (2015c). *Transforming our world: the 2030 Agenda for Sustainable Development.* Retrieved August 20, 2022, from https://sdgs.un.org/2030agenda

United Nations (UN). (2015d). *Paris Agreement on Climate Change.* Retrieved August 20, 2022, from https://sdgs.un.org/frameworks/parisagreement

United Nations (UN). (2022). *Do you know all 17 SDGs?* Department of Economic and Social Affairs. Sustainable Development. Retrieved August 20, 2022, from https://sdgs.un.org/goals

KEY TERMS AND DEFINITIONS

Climate Action: Taking climate action has become a must these days, due to the prolonged and unprecedented challenges that climate change has on our planet; in this matter, the "Paris Agreement" brings to light the "development priorities" plan of world's leaders which relies on taking immediate measures to reduce the greenhouse gases, to create national and international legislation capable to cope with the effects of climate change and to support actions towards reducing its effects, to eradicate poverty, and to support sustainable development (SD) (United Nations (UN), 2015d; United Nations (UN), 2022).

Climate Change: These days, climate change seriously and irreversibly affected our lives and our communities, which led to the utmost necessity to find solutions capable to enhance the efforts of individuals and of entities worldwide to take climate action and become more responsible and more sustainable; in continuation, it ought to be pointed out that according to studies, climate change mainly affects developing countries, vulnerable groups, biodiversity and ecosystems (United Nations (UN), 2015d; United Nations (UN), 2022).

Climate Services and Decision-Making in Supporting Climate Action: Nowadays, climate services capable to support resilient, robust and wise decision-making in terms of sustainable climate action represent the most valuable solution especially in times of crisis; these services strongly depend on the advances that science has to offer which are interrelated with the powerful sustainable development (SD) plans designed through innovation, research, and common scientific knowledge and effort; the transfer of technology projects are vital to the development of nations at a global level, especially in the case of developing countries which have a lot to benefit from these exchanges of ideas, information, and knowledge (United Nations (UN), 2015d; United Nations (UN), 2022).

Development and Enhancement of Relevant Climate Action Plans and Strategies: According to reputed international specialists, the development and enhancement of relevant climate action plans and strategies come to support the success of all the 17 Sustainable Development Goals (SDGs), since all the actions taken by both individuals and entities have the capacity to help authorities prioritize the measures that ought to be taken in terms of assessing and addressing the climate change vulnerabilities and solutions; what is more, not only people are the ones vulnerable in the way of climate change, but also the biodiversity and the ecosystems; furthermore, the policies that address the case of climate change need to become a priority for all governments and for all nations in order to be able to support unanimously the "resilience of socioeconomic and ecological systems" as well as the "economic diversification and sustainable management of natural resources" (United Nations (UN), 2015d; United Nations (UN), 2022).

European Social Survey (ESS): Based on the information found on the official website of the European Social Survey (ESS), it ought to be mentioned that is a European Research Infrastructure Consortium known as ESS-ERIC (European Social Survey European Research Infrastructure (ESS ERIC), 2022c).

Global Economic Environment (GEE): The Global Economic Environment (GEE) is highly dependent on direct and indirect variables, since there is a very fragile equilibrium between the natural resources of our planet and the economic possibilities that nations possess; nevertheless, taking good care of the natural resources of Earth and finding ways to cope with different types of crisis (such as, for instance, the economic and financial crisis; the energy crisis; the natural resources crisis; different forms of crisis derived from epidemics and pandemics – the COVID-19 pandemic and crisis), since our great task is to preserve today's resources not solely for us, and our families, but also for the future generations.

Low Greenhouse Gas Emission Development Strategies: The Sustainable Development Goals (SDGs) as well as the "Paris Agreement" support the Low Greenhouse Gas Emission Development

Strategies which are intended to act as guidelines and frameworks for countries and regions worldwide in order to take differentiated and targeted action depending on the "national circumstances" surrounding the pollution levels; in this matter, authorities believe that this is a problem that can only be solved with common efforts, although it requires "differentiated responsibilities and respective capabilities" (United Nations (UN), 2015d; United Nations (UN), 2022).

Sustainable Development Goals (SDGs): The Sustainable Development Goals (SDGs) are supported by "The 2030 Agenda for Sustainable Development", adopted by all the United Nations Member States in 2015; these Global Goals highlight, on the one hand, the importance of life on planet Earth in accordance to the world leaders and the governmental officials' desire to enhance climate action while trying to cope with the immediate and imminent results of rapid climate change and, on the other hand, the necessity to find viable, robust, and long term solutions to become more prosperous, while living in peace and harmony with nature (United Nations (UN), 2022).

Chapter 5
Corporate Social Responsibility vs. Corporate Sustainability:
Different Concepts for a Common Goal

Javier Martínez Falcó
https://orcid.org/0000-0001-9004-5816
University of Alicante, Spain

Bartolomé Marco-Lajara
https://orcid.org/0000-0001-8811-9118
University of Alicante, Spain

Patrocinio Zaragoza-Saez
University of Alicante, Spain

ABSTRACT

The research is of great interest since it allows us to know the points of convergence and divergence between two of the concepts most used today to refer to the company's commitment to society and the environment in which it operates: corporate social responsibility (CSR) and corporate sustainability (CS). Through the narrative review conducted, the research shows that both concepts are converging to refer to the commitment of companies to economic, social, and environmental well-being. However, CS researchers consider that the three dimensions are interconnected, while CSR researchers do not seem to recognize this link. Furthermore, CSR is considered to have emerged to address social issues, while CS focused on environmental issues, given that CSR has its origins in the critique of neoclassical economic theory and CS in the environmental impact of organizations.

INTRODUCTION

This research presents the main proposals in the academic literature to address the study of social responsibility and sustainability in organizations. Through the review carried out, the study shows the

DOI: 10.4018/978-1-6684-7499-0.ch005

importance of social and environmental issues for companies, as well as the intensification of their study and relevance in recent decades.

Corporate Social Responsibility (CSR) is discussed at the international level and many initiatives have been developed to promote corporate behavior that goes beyond the simple generation of profits and incorporates social and environmental aspects into business strategy. Most of these initiatives have arisen in developed countries, with the aim of promoting certain behaviors on the part of multinational companies, which, although they may have operations in developing countries, their corporate policies are designed in their parent companies according to the needs and demands of their stakeholders in these markets.

The debate on the requirements of social responsibility has been framed by two competing views of the role of business in society: (1) the classical or market view and (2) the socio-economic or broader view. According to the first view, attributed to Friedman (2000), the only social responsibility of business is to maximize profits. Profit maximization is constrained by "the rules of the game", which requires compliance with laws and other social norms. Thus, "the rules of the game" identify the social responsibilities of the firm. According to Friedman (2000), firms must act in open and free competition without deception and fraud, according to the norms of society. Under this view, companies have to meet a responsibility that is demanded by society and nothing else. The socioeconomic view offers a broad consideration of social responsibility. According to this view, companies have obligations that go beyond the pursuit of profit and include protecting and improving society.

The socio-economic vision approach is related to how society believes companies should behave, and for this reason, it is a normative vision. Society identifies what companies are expected to do beyond making a profit, and this varies over time and is becoming more demanding. These are socially controversial demands and should not be confused with what is morally required. The reason society can make demands on companies is because companies operate with public consent and their purpose is to serve society. Because society expects companies to demonstrate genuine social responsibility, and stakeholders' expectations receive much public attention, there are prudent reasons for companies to take their social responsibility seriously.

Given the pervasiveness of social and environmental issues, definitions and key concepts of CSR and Corporate Sustainability (CS) have proliferated over the past decade, increasing uncertainty for managers. Ambiguous definitions and concepts can prevent managers from identifying CSR and CS objectives for their companies. The challenge is even greater for researchers, given that in order to produce reproducible results, it is important that well-defined, clearly delimited and commonly agreed upon constructs exist. Historically, research on social issues has been based on CSR and research on environmental issues on CS. However, in recent years, CSR - which includes social and environmental issues - has seen its boundaries blurred with other concepts. Although CSR and CS have evolved from different fronts, they are pushing towards a common future. Both share the same vision, which aims to balance economic responsibilities with social and environmental ones.

Organizations have become aware of the need to broaden their objectives beyond traditional economic issues (Marco-Lajara et al., 2021a; Marco-Lajara et al., 2021b; Marco-Lajara et al., 2021c; Marco-Lajara et al., 2022a; Marco-Lajara et al., 2022b; Marco-Lajara et al., 2022c; Marco-Lajara et al., 2022d; Marco-Lajara et al., 2022e; Marco-Lajara et al., 2022f; Marco-Lajara et al., 2022g; Marco-Lajara et al., 2022h; Marco-Lajara et al., 2022i; Marco-Lajara et al., 2022j; Marco-Lajara et al., 2022k; Marco-Lajara et al., 2022l; Marco-Lajara et al., 2022m; Marco-Lajara et al., 2022n; Marco-Lajara et al., 2022o; Seva-Larrosa et al., 2022). Thus, since the introduction of the concepts of CSR and CS, more and more managers are introducing social and environmental objectives into their decision-making process. On the one hand, CSR represents the voluntary commitment of companies to behave appropriately, fairly and responsibly with the environment in which they operate. On the other hand, CS refers to a business approach that takes into account economic, environmental and social issues in a balanced, holistic and long-term manner, for the benefit of current and future stakeholders. The common denominator of both concepts is the pursuit of social and environmental well-being through business activities. However, to what extent can the two concepts be assimilated? are they interchangeable? what similarities and differences exist between the two? The study attempts to address these research questions in order to bring clarity to the field of study.

To achieve the stated objective, after this brief introduction, Section 2 presents the set of steps to reach the stated objectives. Section 3 presents the main results. Section 4 presents the conclusions and, finally, Section 5 shows the limitations and future lines of research.

METHODOLOGY

In this research, a narrative literature review was conducted to analyze the similarities and differences between CSR and CS. The literature review is considered a detailed study that aims to gather information on a given topic through the analysis of published literature (Oliver, 2012).

The aim of the narrative review of the literature is to synthesize the fragmented knowledge of previous research on CSR and CS. The research, therefore, presents a descriptive scope, given that there are no hypotheses to be contrasted, but rather the information collected is described and given meaning. Furthermore, the present review follows more flexible and less restrictive procedures than systematic reviews (Ferrari, 2015). Therefore, the present review does not intend to generalize the results obtained to the population (Tranfield et al., 2003), but to offer an interpretation of the literature that allows for a better understanding of the field of study of CSR and CS. To conduct the literature review, the phases proposed by Wee & Banister (2016) were followed, which are: topic selection, source selection and reading, and topic writing. First, the selected topic is the analysis of the conceptualization of CSR and CS. Second, manuals, readings, books, books, chapters and articles focused on the evolution and conceptualization of CSR and CS were included for the research, excluding colloquium reports, seminars, doctoral dissertations and working papers. The time period of the publications covers the period from the beginnings of the concept of CSR in the 1950s to the present day, given that the aim of the research is to analyze all the conceptualization of CSR and CS. Likewise, the Scopus and Web of Science databases were used to select the publications, as they are prestigious databases that contain articles published in high-impact journals, which ensures that the information obtained is accurate and of high value, legitimizing reliable results. A total of 65 academic papers were reviewed and read in depth, this being the scientific production that allowed us to reflect on the concept of CSR and CS. Thirdly, once the article and sources had been selected and the publications had been read, the bibliographic review was drafted.

RESULTS

Several researchers consider CSR as the main pillar of CS (Sarvaiya & Wu, 2014). From this approach, CSR is conceived as the social aspect of the three-dimensional model under which the CS construct is built. In this sense, Ebner & Baumgartner (2006) consider that, while CS encompasses the economic, ecological and social dimensions, CSR only encompasses the latter. Similarly, Sharma & Rudd (2003) pointed out that CS scholars tend to focus on environmental issues, while those who study CSR focus on social and ethical issues. However, these authors argue that CS is a broad concept that incorporates social aspects, so that the term CS encompasses CSR.

Malovics et al. (2008) considered CSR as a means to achieve CS objectives, concluding that both external and internal CSR practices will lead to a higher level of CS. Therefore, some scholars consider CSR as a path leading to the achievement of CS as the ultimate goal (Moon, 2007; Hui, 2008; Porter, 2008). For their part, Guler & Crowther (2008) stated that CS is one of the three principles of CSR activity, together with accountability and transparency. In this regard, Long (2008) argued that CS is an important part of the broader CSR program.

In addition, there are other arguments put forward in the literature that have given rise to confusion among academics. On the one hand, Gallego (2006) explained that CSR was a tool for measuring CS in economic, social and environmental terms. On the other hand, Sottorrio & Sanchez (2008) used CSR as one of the indicators to measure CSR performance. Furthermore, it has been argued that CSR is one of the key factors in the evolution of CS and vice versa. For example, Wilson (2003) noted that CSR has contributed decisively to the development of CS. Zink (2005) noted that CSR should be promoted to balance social and environmental concerns, with CS being a precondition for achieving long-term sustainability. Dewangga et al. (2008) explored the relationship between CSR and CS, recommending that CSR guidelines should be integrated with CS guidelines. In the words of the authors: "CSR should eventually be transformed into a comprehensive framework for organizational sustainable development planning to proactively and effectively help organizations move towards a sustainable society. The majority of CSR and CSR experts surveyed agreed that CSR guidelines will eventually become part of overall CS guidelines" (p. 19).

Schwartz & Carroll (2008) conducted a comparative analysis of five competing concepts, including CSR, business ethics, stakeholder management, CS and corporate citizenship. The authors argued that there is some difficulty in understanding these concepts and relating them to each other. To integrate these five constructs, they developed the Value, Balance and Accountability (VBA) model, proposing that: "all organizations and individuals operating in a business context have a responsibility (CSR) as good citizens to contribute to the sustainable value of society (CS) and to appropriately balance stakeholder interests, including shareholders and/or moral standards, while demonstrating sufficient accountability" (p. 173).

On the other hand, Panapanaan et al. (2003) commented that "the overlaps of environmental and social issues cause many companies to assume that their CS program already encompasses CSR along with environmental management. However, this assumption is not clear and is an area of intense debate" (p. 139). In this sense, there is no consensus to discuss the overlap between the two constructs, given that scholars have established various relationships between CSR and CS, which, instead of providing clarity, have generated a complex web and a vague relationship between the two terms. In the following sections we attempt to shed light on this problem by identifying the similarities and differences between concepts identified in the literature.

Similarities Between Concepts

The term CS has been used as a synonym for other concepts, such as sustainable development and CSR (Van Marrewijk, 2003; Wilson, 2003; Moon, 2007). In fact, Ebner & Baumgartner (2006) stated that there was a tendency to define CSR similarly to CS, since, although historically CSR has been associated with social issues and CS with environmental aspects (Funk, 2003; Dewangga et al., 2008), the concepts are currently converging (Van Marrewijk, 2003; Montiel, 2008). In fact, several scholars consider the concepts identical in their research (Colbert et al., 2003; Marsiglia & Falautano, 2005; Meisinger, 2007; Dewangga et al., 2008; Ferns et al., 2008), even considering CS as the terminological evolution of CSR. In the words of Faragher (2008): "CSR is an old concept; the new buzzword is CS" (p. 1).

In this sense, Montiel (2008) pointed out that, due to the common purpose of CSR and CS, the two terms were converging: "in fact, the conceptualization of CSR that integrates the economic, social and environmental dimensions and the conceptualization of CS that includes the economic, social and environmental dimensions are very similar. Thus, both CSR and CS are aimed at balancing economic prosperity, social growth and environmental integrity" (p. 260).

Both CSR and CSR are considered voluntary activities, encompassing the environmental and social concerns of the organization (Van Marrewijk & Werre, 2003; Lo & Sheu, 2007). Van den Brink and Van der Woerd (2004) agree that there is confusion among companies regarding the application of the concepts of CSR and CSR. For this reason, they preferred to use the term Corporate Sustainability and Corporate Responsibility (CS-R), which is conceptualized in the European Framework for Corporate Sustainability (Van Marrewijk & Hardjono, 2003).

Additionally, the information provided by companies in relation to CSR and CS programs is similar. In fact, Diana (2006) stated that "the report formerly called corporate responsibility report is now called sustainability report" (p. 46). Even companies belonging to the Global Reporting Initiative overlap their social responsibility reports with sustainability reports (Montiel, 2008). In addition, some researchers have used the term SR-Sustainability report in their studies, which shows that they find no difference between concepts (Ferns et al., 2008).

Differences Between Concepts

A review of the literature reveals that, despite the overlap between the terms, there are certain points of divergence between them. Although, theoretically, both CSR and CS coincide in balancing economic, social and environmental issues, CSR is still considered a process of managing social issues with stakeholders, while CS is seen as a method for achieving ecological balance (Kleine & Hauff, 2009).

According to Montiel (2008), both CSR and CSR rest on the three-dimensional basis of economic, social and environmental aspects. However, there are three points of divergence. First, CS researchers consider that the three dimensions are interconnected, whereas CSR researchers do not seem to recognize this link. Secondly, CS tends to discuss the intrinsic value of organizations (value that an entity contributes by carrying out an activity, regardless of its benefit to humanity), whereas CSR tends to address "use value" (benefits to human beings) in greater depth. Thirdly, research on CSR is more closely linked to Stakeholder Theory, while most of the scientific production on CS is associated with RBV and Institutional Theory.

Similarly, Steurer et al. (2005) also noted several differences between the terms under study. On the one hand, they argue that CSR is based on stakeholder expectations, whereas CS is more dependent on societal interpretation. On the other hand, they consider CSR to be a short-term notion that addresses the needs of current stakeholders, while CS is a long-term concept that addresses the needs of future stakeholders. Furthermore, they argue that CSR originally emerged to address social issues, while CS focused on environmental issues, with CSR having its origins in the critique of neoclassical economic theory and CS in the environmental impact of organizations (Dentchev, 2009).

Likewise, although Van Marrewijk (2003) considered CSR and CS to be synonymous, the author argued that a fine line had to be drawn between the two concepts, for while CSR linked people and organizations through transparency, stakeholder dialogue and sustainability reporting, CS represented a principle of agency encompassing value creation, environmental management and human capital management. In fact, CSR is concerned with balancing economic, legal, ethical and social responsibility, while CS addresses ecological dependency and social impacts at the global level (Moon, 2007).

CONCLUSION

The research is of great relevance for academics focused on the analysis of CSR and/or CSR, since it clarifies the points of convergence and divergence between the two concepts, bringing clarity to the field of study.

On the one hand, the term CS has been used as a synonym for other concepts, such as sustainable development and CSR. In fact, there is a tendency to define CSR in a similar way to CS, since, although historically CSR has been associated with social issues and CS with environmental aspects, the concepts are now converging. Several academics consider the concepts to be identical in their research work, and even consider CSR to be the terminological evolution of CSR. Both CSR and CSR are considered voluntary activities, encompassing the environmental and social concerns of the organization. In addition, the information provided by companies regarding CSR and CSR programs is similar. In fact, companies belonging to the Global Reporting Initiative overlap their CSR reports with their sustainability reports. Moreover, some researchers have used the term SR-Sustainability reporting in their studies, which shows that they find no difference between concepts.

On the other hand, the literature review reveals that, despite the overlap between the terms, there are certain points of divergence between them. Although, theoretically, both CSR and CSR coincide in balancing economic, social and environmental issues, CSR is still considered a process of managing social issues with stakeholders, while CS is seen as a method for achieving ecological balance. Both CSR and CS are based on the three-dimensional foundation of economic, social and environmental aspects. However, there are five points of divergence. First, CS researchers consider the three dimensions to be interconnected, whereas CSR researchers do not seem to recognize this link. Secondly, CS tends to discuss the intrinsic value of organizations (value provided by an entity for carrying out an activity, regardless of its benefit to humanity), whereas CSR tends to address "use value" (benefits to human beings) in greater depth. Third, research on CSR is more closely linked to Stakeholder Theory, while most of the scientific production on CS is associated with RBV and Institutional Theory. Fourth, while CSR is based on stakeholder expectations, CS is more dependent on societal interpretation. Fifth, CSR is seen as a short-term notion that addresses the needs of current stakeholders, while CS is a long-term concept that addresses the needs of future stakeholders. Furthermore, CSR is considered to have emerged to address social issues, while CS focused on environmental issues, given that CSR has its origins in the critique of neoclassical economic theory and CS in the environmental impact of organizations.

FUTURE RESEARCH DIRECTIONS

Despite the important contributions of the study, it is important to point out that the research suffers from certain limitations. The fundamental limitation of the study is methodological in nature, given that narrative reviews are dominated by the subjective criteria of the authors and do not quantitatively synthesize the data found in the different publications. To overcome these limitations of narrative reviews, a systematic review of the concepts of CSR and CS is proposed as a line of future research, with the aim of increasing the reproducibility of the research and increasing the validity of the results obtained.

REFERENCES

Colbert, B., Wheeler, D., & Freeman, R. (2003). Focusing on value: Reconciling corporate social responsibility, stakeholder theory and sustainability in a network world. *Journal of General Management*, *28*(3), 1–28. doi:10.1177/030630700302800301

Dentchev, N. (2009). To what extent is business and society literature idealistic? *Business & Society*, *48*(1), 10–38. doi:10.1177/0007650307299222

Dewangga, A., Goldsmith, S., & Pegram, N. (2008). *Social responsibility guidelines & sustainable development: Integrating a common goal of a sustainable society* [Unpublished Masters dissertation]. Blekinge Institute of Technology, Karlaskrona, Sweden.

Dewangga, A., Goldsmith, S., & Pegram, N. (2008). *Social responsibility guidelines & sustainable development: Integrating a common goal of a sustainable society* [Unpublished Masters dissertation]. Blekinge Institute of Technology, Karlaskrona, Sweden.

Diana, T. (2006). Doing Business the Socially Responsible Way. *Business Credit*, *108*(6), 45–48.

Ebner, D., & Baumgartner, R. (2006). The relationship between sustainable development and corporate social responsibility. In Corporate responsibility research conference (Vol. 4, No. 5.9, p. 2006). Queens University.

Ferns, B., Emelianova, O., & Sethi, S. (2008). In his own words: The effectiveness of CEO as spokesperson on CSR-sustainability issues. *Corporate Reputation Review*, *11*(2), 116–129. doi:10.1057/crr.2008.11

Ferrari, R. (2015). Writing narrative style literature reviews. *Medical Writing*, *24*(4), 230–235. doi:10.1179/2047480615Z.000000000329

Friedman, M. (2007). The social responsibility of business is to increase its profits. In *Corporate ethics and corporate governance* (pp. 173–178). Springer. doi:10.1007/978-3-540-70818-6_14

Funk, K. (2003). Sustainability and performance. *MIT Sloan Management Review*, *44*(2), 65–70.

Gallego, I. (2006). The use of economic, social and environmental indicators as a measure of sustainable development in Spain. *Corporate Social Responsibility and Environmental Management*, *13*(2), 78–97. doi:10.1002/csr.94

Guler, A., & Crowther, D. (2008). Towards equitable sustainability. *Ivey Business Journal*, *72*(1), 1–7.

Hui, L. (2008). Combining faith and CSR: A paradigm of corporate sustainability. *International Journal of Social Economics*, *35*(6), 449–465. doi:10.1108/03068290810873429

Kleine, A., & Hauff, M. (2009). Sustainability-driven implementation of corporate social responsibility. *Journal of Business Ethics*, *85*(3), 517–533. doi:10.100710551-009-0212-z

Lo, S. F., & Sheu, H. J. (2007). Is corporate sustainability a value-increasing strategy for business? *Corporate Governance*, *15*(2), 345–358. doi:10.1111/j.1467-8683.2007.00565.x

Long, J. (2008). From Cocoa to CSR: Finding sustainability in a cup of hot chocolate. *Thunderbird International Business Review*, *50*(5), 315–320. doi:10.1002/tie.20215

Málovics, G., Csigéné, N. N., & Kraus, S. (2008). The role of corporate social responsibility in strong sustainability. *Journal of Socio-Economics*, *37*(3), 907–918. doi:10.1016/j.socec.2006.12.061

Marco-Lajara, B., Martínez-Falcó, J., Ruiz-Fernández, L., & Seva-Larrosa, P. (2022k). Evolución del pensamiento en la disciplina de dirección estratégica: la visión de la empresa basada en las capacidades dinámicas y en el conocimiento. [Evolution of thinking in the discipline of strategic management: the vision of the company based on dynamic capabilities and knowledge] In *Investigación y transferencia de las ciencias sociales frente a un mundo en crisis* [Social science research and transfer in the face of a world in crisis]. (pp. 1801–1826). Dykinson.

Marco-Lajara, B., Sánchez-García, E., Martínez-Falcó, J., & Poveda-Pareja, E. (2022l). Regional Specialization, Competitive Pressure, and Cooperation: The Cocktail for Innovation. *Energies*, *15*(15), 5346.

Marco-Lajara, B., Sánchez-García, E., Seva-Larrosa, P., & Martínez-Falcó, J. (2022m). Knowledge creation and diffusion inspecialized environments: What are the factors involved? In *Empresa, economía y derecho. Oportunidades ante un entorno global y disruptivo* [Business, economy and law. Opportunities in a global and disruptive environment]. (pp. 432–459). Dykinson.

Marco-Lajara, B., Seva-Larrosa, P., Martínez-Falcó, J., & García-Lillo, F. (2022i). Wine clusters and Protected Designations of Origin (PDOs) in Spain: An exploratory analysis. *Journal of Wine Research*, *33*(3), 1–22. doi:10.1080/09571264.2022.2110051

Marco-Lajara, B., Seva-Larrosa, P., Martinez-Falco, J., & Sanchez-Garcia, E. (2021a). How Has COVID- 19 Affected The Spanish Wine Industry? An Exploratory Analysis. *Natural Volatiles & Essential Oils Journal*, *8*(6), 2722–2731.

Marco-Lajara, B., Seva-Larrosa, P., Martínez-Falcó, J., & Sánchez-García, E. (2021j). El clúster vitivinícola de Jumilla: Entre la tradición y la modernidad [The Jumilla wine cluster: Between tradition and modernity]. In XLIII jornadas de viticultura y enología de la Tierra de Barros: III Congreso agroalimentario de Extremadura [XLIII Tierra de Barros Viticulture and Oenology Conference: III Agri-food Congress of Extremadura] (pp. 56-70). Centro Universitario Santa Ana.

Marco-Lajara, B., Seva-Larrosa, P., Ruiz-Fernandez, L., & Martinez-Falco, J. (2021b). The Effect of COVID- 19 on the Spanish Wine Industry. In *Impact of Global Issues on International Trade* (pp. 211–232). IGI Global., doi:10.4018/978-1-7998-8314-2.ch012

Marco-Lajara, B., Zaragoza-Saez, P., Martínez-Falcó, J., & Sánchez-García, E. (2022c). COVID-19 and Wine Tourism: A Story of Heartbreak. In Handbook of Research on SDGs for Economic Development, Social Development, and Environmental Protection (pp. 90-112). IGI Global.

Marco-Lajara, B., Zaragoza-Sáez, P., Falcó, J. M., & Millan-Tudela, L. A. (2022f). Corporate Social Responsibility: A Narrative Literature Review. *Frameworks for Sustainable Development Goals to Manage Economic, Social, and Environmental Shocks and Disasters*, 16-34.

Marco-Lajara, B., Zaragoza-Saez, P., & Martínez-Falcó, J. (2022e). Green Innovation: Balancing Economic Efficiency With Environmental Protection. In Frameworks for Sustainable Development Goals to Manage Economic, Social, and Environmental Shocks and Disasters (pp. 239-254). IGI Global.

Marco-Lajara, B., Zaragoza Sáez, P., & Martínez-Falcó, J. (2022n). Does Green Intellectual Capital Affect Green Performance? The Mediation of Green Innovation. *Telematique*, *21*(1), 4594–4602.

Marco-Lajara, B., Zaragoza-Saez, P., Martínez-Falcó, J., & Millan-Tudela, L. A. (2022b). Analysing the Relationship Between Green Intellectual Capital and the Achievement of the Sustainable Development Goals. In *Handbook of Research on Building Inclusive Global Knowledge Societies for Sustainable Development* (pp. 111–129). IGI Global. doi:10.4018/978-1-6684-5109-0.ch005

Marco-Lajara, B., Zaragoza-Sáez, P., Martínez-Falcó, J., & Ruiz-Fernández, L. (2022g). The Effect of Green Intellectual Capital on Green Performance in the Spanish Wine Industry: A Structural Equation Modeling Approach. *Complexity*, *2022*, 2022. doi:10.1155/2022/6024077

Marco-Lajara, B., Zaragoza-Sáez, P., Martínez-Falcó, J., & Sánchez-García, E. (2022a). Green Intellectual Capital in the Spanish Wine Industry. In Innovative Economic, Social, and Environmental Practices for Progressing Future Sustainability (pp. 102-120). IGI Global. doi:10.4018/978-1-7998-9590-9.ch006

Marco-Lajara, B., Zaragoza-Sáez, P., Martínez-Falcó, J., & Sánchez-García, E. (2022d). El capital intelectual verde como hoja de ruta para la sostenibilidad: El caso de bodegas Luzón [Green Intellectual Capital as a Roadmap for Sustainability:The case of Luzon Wineries]. *GeoGraphos: Revista Digital para Estudiantes de Geografía y Ciencias Sociales*, *13*(147), 137–146.

Marco-Lajara, B., Zaragoza-Sáez, P., Martínez-Falcó, J., & Sánchez-García, E. (2022o). Las rutas del vino de España: el impacto económico derivado de las visitas a bodegas y museos. [Spain's wine routes: the economic impact of visits to wineries and museums] In *Investigación y transferencia de las ciencias sociales frente a un mundo en crisis* [Social science research and transfer in the face of a world in crisis]. (pp. 1774–1800). Dykinson.

Marco-Lajara, B., Zaragoza-Sáez, P. C., Martínez-Falcó, J., & Sánchez-García, E. (2022h). Does green intellectual capital affect green innovation performance? Evidence from the Spanish wine industry. *British Food Journal*, ahead-of-print.

Marsiglia, E., & Falautano, I. (2005). Corporate social responsibility and sustainability challenges for a Bancassurance Company. *The Geneva Papers on Risk and Insurance. Issues and Practice*, *30*(3), 485–497. doi:10.1057/palgrave.gpp.2510040

Meisinger, S. (2007). HR's role in social responsibility and sustainability. *HRMagazine*, *52*(12), 8.

Montiel, I. (2008). Corporate social responsibility and corporate sustainability: Separate pasts, common futures. *Organization & Environment, 21*(3), 245–269. doi:10.1177/1086026608321329

Moon, J. (2007). The contribution of corporate social responsibility to sustainable development. *Sustainable Development, 15*(5), 296–306. doi:10.1002d.346

Oliver, P. (2012). *Succeeding with your literature review. A handbook for students.* McGraw-Hill, Open University Press.

Panapanaan, V., Linnanen, L., Karvonen, M., & Phan, V. (2003). Roadmapping corporate social responsibility in Finnish companies. *Journal of Business Ethics, 44*(2), 133–148. doi:10.1023/A:1023391530903

Porter, T. (2008). Managerial applications of corporate social responsibility and systems thinking for achieving sustainability outcomes. *Systems Research and Behavioral Science: The Official Journal of the International Federation for Systems Research, 25*(3), 397–411. doi:10.1002res.902

Sarvaiya, H., & Wu, M. (2014). An integrated approach for corporate social responsibility and corporate sustainability. *Asian Social Science, 10*(17), 57. doi:10.5539/ass.v10n17p57

Schwartz, M., & Carroll, A. (2008). Integrating and unifying competing and complementary frameworks: The search for a common core in the business and society field. *Business & Society, 47*(2), 148–186. doi:10.1177/0007650306297942

Seva-Larrosa, P., Martínez-Falcó, J., & Ruiz-Fernández, L. (2022). Analizando las principales variables empresariales en los clusters vinícolas españoles teniendo en cuenta la localización de las empresas y su pertenencia a una marca colectiva. [Analyzing the main business variables in Spanish wine clusters taking into account the location of the companies and their membership in a collective brand] In *Miradas sobre el emprendimiento ante la crisis del coronavirus* [Perspectives on entrepreneurship in the face of the coronavirus crisis]. (pp. 629–634). Dykinson.

Sharma, S., & Rudd, A. (2003). On the path to sustainability: Integrating social dimensions into the research and practice of environmental management. *Business Strategy and the Environment, 12*(4), 205–214. doi:10.1002/bse.366

Sotorrío, L. L., & Sánchez, J. L. F. (2008). Corporate social responsibility of the most highly reputed European and North American firms. *Journal of Business Ethics, 82*(2), 379–390. doi:10.100710551-008-9901-2

Steurer, R., Langer, M., Konrad, A., & Martinuzzi, A. (2005). Corporations, stakeholders and sustainable development I: A theoretical exploration of business-society relations. *Journal of Business Ethics, 61*(3), 263–281. doi:10.100710551-005-7054-0

Tranfield, D., Denyer, D., & Smart, P. (2003). Towards a methodology for developing evidence-informed management knowledge by means of systematic review. *British Journal of Management, 14*(3), 207–222. doi:10.1111/1467-8551.00375

Van Marrewijk, M. (2003). Concepts and definitions of CSR and corporate sustainability: Between agency and communion. *Journal of Business Ethics, 44*(2), 95–105. doi:10.1023/A:1023331212247

Van Marrewijk, M., & Hardjono, T. (2003). European corporate sustainability framework for managing complexity and corporate transformation. *Journal of Business Ethics*, *44*(2), 121–132. doi:10.1023/A:1023335414065

Van Marrewijk, M., & Werre, M. (2003). Multiple levels of corporate sustainability. *Journal of Business Ethics*, *44*(2), 107–119. doi:10.1023/A:1023383229086

Wee, B. V., & Banister, D. (2016). How to write a literature review paper? *Transport Reviews*, *36*(2), 278–288. doi:10.1080/01441647.2015.1065456

Wilson, M. (2003). Corporate sustainability: What is it and where does it come from? *Ivey Business Journal*, *67*(6), 1.

Zink, K. J. (2005). Stakeholder orientation and corporate social responsibility as a precondition for sustainability. *Total Quality Management & Business Excellence*, *16*(8-9), 1041–1052. doi:10.1080/14783360500163243

ADDITIONAL READING

Atkinson, G. (2000). Measuring corporate sustainability. *Journal of Environmental Planning and Management*, *43*(2), 235–252. doi:10.1080/09640560010694

Benn, S., Edwards, M., & Williams, T. (2014). *Organizational change for corporate sustainability*. Routledge. doi:10.4324/9781315819181

Herzig, C., & Schaltegger, S. (2006). Corporate sustainability reporting. An overview. *Sustainability Accounting and Reporting*, 301-324.

Meuer, J., Koelbel, J., & Hoffmann, V. H. (2020). On the nature of corporate sustainability. *Organization & Environment*, *33*(3), 319–341. doi:10.1177/1086026619850180

Montiel, I., & Delgado-Ceballos, J. (2014). Defining and measuring corporate sustainability: Are we there yet? *Organization & Environment*, *27*(2), 113–139. doi:10.1177/1086026614526413

Schaltegger, S., & Burritt, R. (2005). Corporate sustainability. *The International Yearbook of Environmental and Resource Economics*, *2006*, 185–222.

Taticchi, P., Carbone, P., & Albino, V. (2013). *Corporate sustainability*. Springer. doi:10.1007/978-3-642-37018-2

KEY TERMS AND DEFINITIONS

Corporate Social Responsibility: The responsibility that each organization has with the environment in which it operates and with the society of which it is a part.

Corporate Sustainability: It is a business approach that seeks to create long-term shareholder value by seizing opportunities and effectively managing the risks inherent in economic, environmental, and social development.

Narrative Review: It is a work that analyzes and discusses articles and reports, generally scientific and academic, published in or about an area of knowledge. Scientific reports may be of an empirical, theoretical, critical, analytical, or methodological nature.

Theory: A logical-deductive system consisting of a set of hypotheses, a field of application and some rules to draw consequences from the hypotheses.

Chapter 6
Data-Driven Behaviour Finance for Mutual Fund Investment Decision Making

Chabi Gupta
https://orcid.org/0000-0002-1927-4349
Christ University, India

ABSTRACT

When it comes to money and investing funds, the individual portfolio investor isn't always as logical as he feels he is, which is why there's a whole school of thought dedicated to explaining why people behave in irrational and weird ways. The primary objective of this research is to investigate the effects of five major behavioural biases on individual investor decisions in a metro city India, with a focus on mutual funds, as well as to examine how individuals make decisions to ensure that their investments generate greater returns for a better future. The statistical evidence shows that a variety of behavioural elements have a significant part in people' investment decision-making patterns, which has an impact on the population's economic situation. The purpose of this study is to illustrate how an individual's perspective, attitude, and conduct affect mutual fund investments.

INTRODUCTION

We are not always as sensible as we believe when it comes to money and investing, thus there is a whole school of study that explains our often-unusual financial behaviour. This assumption is at the heart of the idea, but academics who have questioned it have found evidence that rational action isn't always as common as we might think. Investors do not always operate in accordance with economic theory; however, in times of risk and uncertainty, people may utilize mental shortcuts to attain their goals. The assumption that individuals behave rationally and that the investing process considers all of the information that is available is the basis for a significant portion of economic theory.

Individuals strive to research the market before investing, but no one knows how successful they are. When managing their portfolios, investors often make a variety of mental blunders that have an effect

DOI: 10.4018/978-1-6684-7499-0.ch006

on the returns they perceive on their assets. Behavioral finance is the academic field that investigates the absence of objective decision-making that occurs in relation to investment (Carhart, M. 1997). Some managers of mutual funds have started looking for ways to make money off of quirks in the market due to the fact that irrational investing choices may lead to securities being priced incorrectly.

Because investors are continually seeking for methods to outperform the market, one question that arises is whether behavioral finance-oriented funds may be of assistance. The theory of finance tells us that investors make choices logically and rationally, considering all of the information at their disposal. In actuality, nothing of the kind takes place. When making judgments, investors often pick and choose which bits of information to pay attention to, and frequently base their choices on emotion rather than logic. The study of behavioral finance has uncovered several mistakes by investors influenced by cognitive biases. As a result, decision making is a complex process that necessitates the use of financial models to estimate the projected risk and return associated with a certain investment (Fama, E. 1970).

LITERATURE REVIEW

A study of individual investors was carried out by Shanmugham (2000) with the intention of discovering the kind of information sources that individual investors depend on. According to the results, economic, social, and psychological elements all play a role in the process of making investment choices. (Madhusudhan V. Jambodekar 1996) worked on the goals of determining the factors that investors consider most important when making investment choices pertaining to mutual funds and evaluating the path that investors believe mutual funds should take. The results of the survey indicated that respondents favoured income and open-ended plans over closed and growth plans. (Fama, E et al 1992) discussed about the security of capital and investor services, access to and use of news media, and other variables and prioritized their importance when deciding whether or not to invest in mutual funds. (Sujit Sikidar and Amrit Pal Singh 1996) researched more to learn about how people in the Northeast view equity and mutual fund investments. The tax advantages of mutual funds have led to their popularity among both wage earners and self-employed individuals, the survey found. The poll indicated that index funds were the most popular funds in that region, while the other fund was considered outdated. Syama Sunder (1998) surveyed the private sector mutual fund industry with an eye on acquiring a holistic understanding of a reputed fund's operations. The poll found that people in smaller cities at the time knew very little about mutual funds. It was also discussed how agents could catalyse the mutual fund culture, how open-ended options are far more popular than other schemes, and how the reputation of the asset management firm when investing in mutual funds is crucial. Asset management organisations need to develop and drive the consumer product distribution model, as stated by Shankar (1996), for the culture of mutual funds to thoroughly infiltrate society. To boost mutual funds' popularity, Raja Rajan (1997) emphasised the need of investor and product segmentation. The identification of behavioural opportunities may be accomplished by fund managers via the use of a variety of indicators. Metrics such as the price-to-earnings ratio and the price-to-book ratio are examples of metrics that may be used to identify equities that are either overbought or oversold. Opportunities to capitalise on may present themselves in the form of occurrences such as stock splits, which often lead to a rise in share price even though nothing substantive has changed with the firm. (Barber, B. and Odean, T. 2008) discussed that the financial markets 'know' the behaviour of investors is influenced by relative investment biases; as a result, they are shifting their attention away from logical price movements based on fundamentals that lie under the market's surface.

This also serves as the basis for the transactions that take place in the equity markets, which are based on the notion that two separate individuals may make independent investment choices about the same stock at the same time (Carhart, M. 1997).

Although one investor is more likely to sell the shares at that price, the other investor is inclined to purchase the stock at such price (Shleifer, A. 2000). Active investing and passive investing are the two basic investment techniques that investors may choose to use while investing in the stock markets. Investors may also opt to employ a combination of the two. The term "active investing" refers to the process of selecting stocks for a portfolio in an intentional manner, taking into consideration a variety of factors in addition to the fundamentals of individual companies. (Chan, L. et al 2002) discussed that tracking a benchmark index and modelling the portfolio after its make-up is an example of passive investment, which is contrasted with active investing. When a scheme is managed actively, the fund manager makes the decisions on the stocks to invest in and the amount of each stock that should be invested. On the other hand, when a scheme chooses to invest using a passive strategy, the fund manager is required to passively replicate the portfolio of underlying index it aims to replicate. This can be accomplished by purchasing or selling stocks that are included in an index in almost the same proportion as the index itself. As a result, investors may reduce the unsystematic risk that is associated with their investment plan by using passive investing. Investors using the passive investing method are required to use investment judgement to choose the appropriate underlying benchmark index.

RESEARCH METHODOLOGY

Bad performance is often the consequence of behaviorally biased investors making poor judgments about fund type and fees, trading frequency and timing, and other related factors. In addition, it seems that behavioral biases are tied to trend chasing, rather than the practice of logically inferring management competence from previous success. According to the findings of a factor analysis, prejudiced investors often correspond to certain stereotypes, which may be described as Poker players, Smart People, Overconfident Investors, Narrow Founders, and Experienced Individuals. (Black, F. 1986) advocated that behaviorally biased investors have a greater propensity to make bad choices regarding fund type and cost, trading frequency, and timing, all of which contribute to poor performance. This is because behavioral biases are caused by human psychology. In addition, it seems that trend chasing is tied to many behavioral biases, rather than just being a method of logically deducing management excellence from previous success. The discussion and conclusion of the study have been produced based on these and secondary relevant facts found in journals, news, and media, among other places. To overcome cognitive biases, the research used a questionnaire to collect responses from more than 680 portfolio investors living in a metropolitan area in Northern India. The results were used to develop techniques for investing in mutual funds.

OBSERVATIONS

Portfolio investors make a variety of mental errors that have an impact on the returns on their mutual fund investments. Because some irrational investment decisions lead to mispriced assets, some mutual fund managers have begun to profit off mutual fund investors' peculiarities. (Ekholm, A et al 2008)

Table 1. Respondents Profile

Size of the Portfolio	Age	Investing Experience in Mutual Funds	Average Percentage of Return on Investment
12% (Below 1 lakh)	15-20 years (16%)	Below 5 years (10%)	Losses (2%)
18% (1 -2 lakhs)	20-25 years (14%)	5-10 years (25%)	2-5% (25%)
10% (2-3 lakhs)	25-30 years (24%)	10-12 years (35%)	6-9% (15%)
16% (3-4 lakhs)	30-40 years (6%)	Over 12 years (30%)	10-13% (10%)
24% (5-10 lakhs)	40-60 years (20%)		14-17% (22%)
20% (Over 10 lakhs)	Over 60 years (20%)		Over 18% (26%)

advocated in their essay that theoretical finance advises us that investors make judgments based on all available data and without emotion. In fact, this does not occur. Investors frequently pick and choose which pieces of data they pay attention to, making judgments based on emotion rather than logic. Investors make a variety of mistakes, but these are five of the most common, according to behavioral finance.

1. Anchoring – A behavioural finance heuristic where the portfolio investor chooses a reference point or an 'anchor' for making future choices concerning that security. An example of this would be using a security's purchase price as an anchor. Because of this, individuals are more likely to judge the item's worth to be greater if the proposed sticker price is much more than usual. This may lead to a wrong portfolio decision in the long run.
2. Loss Aversion - This suggests that the anguish that comes with suffering a loss is greater than the joy that comes with making a profit. As a direct consequence of this, investors commonly demonstrate their unwillingness to accept a loss on an investment by making statements such as "I'll sell it when it gets back to where I purchased it." Under these conditions, investors could keep potentially risky assets for a longer period of time than they should, which might result in further financial losses.
3. Choice Paralysis - When one has to choose between possibilities that are difficult to compare, they experience decision paralysis. Simply put, decision paralysis occurs when portfolio investors have trouble deciding between actions A and B and end up taking action C or doing nothing at all. The more options they have, the more difficult it gets to choose one. Furthermore, as the complexity or importance of the problem grows, so does the quantity of energy required for analysis.
4. Confirmation Bias - This occurs when an individual decides to give more value to information that relates to him while giving less weightage to information that contradicts his perception. It is possible for an investor to listen to a report that suggests purchasing a stock that they already own and come to the conclusion that the information is accurate, while simultaneously ignoring a report that recommends selling the stock; this may lead to an imbalance in the accepted facts.
5. Herd Mentality - This is sometimes referred to as "following the mob." Because it is more comfortable and easier to rationalise, portfolio investors may tend to follow the crowd's lead. When everyone is purchasing equities, like in a 'market bubble', it's simpler to conclude that everyone is making the right decision. Instead of understanding that tech companies were highly expensive, investors continued to buy out of fear of missing out on future gains.

Table 2. Descriptive Statistics for Investment Values

Anchoring Effect	Mean	Std Deviation	Std Error
>200,000	17.29	3.518	0.283
Rs 200,000-400,000	16.57	3.232	0.303
Rs 400,000-600,000	16.16	3.543	0.47
Rs 600,000-800,000	16.35	3.445	0.601
Rs 800,000-10,00,000	17.26	4.198	0.783
More than 10 lakhs	15.32	5.433	0.738
Total	16.8	3.872	0.187

Table 3. Descriptive Statistics for Investment Values

Loss Aversion	Mean	Std Deviation	Std Error
>200,000	15.71	3.778	0.303
Rs 200,000-400,000	16.16	3.145	0.304
Rs 400,000-600,000	16.88	3.356	0.594
Rs 600,000-800,000	15.06	3.309	0.634
Rs 800,000-10,00,000	16.2	4.198	0.783
More than 10 lakhs	17.06	5.433	0.736
Total	16.62	3.872	0.187

Table 4. Descriptive Statistics for Investment Values

Choice Paralysis	Mean	Std Deviation	Std Error
>200,000	16.71	3.778	0.303
Rs 200,000-400,000	16.16	3.145	0.304
Rs 400,000-600,000	15.75	3.356	0.564
Rs 600,000-800,000	15.31	3.309	0.63
Rs 800,000-10,00,000	16.64	4.198	0.783
More than 10 lakhs	16.44	5.433	0.765
Total	15.89	3.872	0.134

ANALYSIS

There was observed a significant link between the behavioural biases. The detected biases were significantly positively correlated with one another, which was also the case with other biases.

Mutual fund investors accepted the awareness of behavioural finance and various cognitive biases that may interfere with rational decision making especially during times of crisis or financial stress. A

Table 5. Descriptive Statistics for Investment Values

Confirmation Bias	Mean	Std Deviation	Std Error
>200,000	16.9	3.778	0.304
Rs 200,000-400,000	17.88	3.221	0.564
Rs 400,000-600,000	15.72	3.456	0.342
Rs 600,000-800,000	15.31	3.145	0.98
Rs 800,000-10,00,000	16.64	3.356	0.783
More than 10 lakhs	16.78	3.309	0.765
Total	17.22	4.198	0.156

Table 6. Descriptive Statistics for Investment Values

Herd Mentality	Mean	Std Deviation	Std Error
>200,000	16.31	3.432	0.311
Rs 200,000-400,000	17.64	3.229	0.544
Rs 400,000-600,000	15.78	3.478	0.322
Rs 600,000-800,000	16.23	4.122	0.45
Rs 800,000-10,00,000	17.21	3.145	0.871
More than 10 lakhs	16.22	3.356	0.328
Total	17.34	3.309	0.178

variety of indicators can be used by fund managers to spot behavioural opportunities. Price-to-earnings and price-to-book ratios, for example, might indicate if a security is overbought or oversold. Stock splits, which frequently result in a stock price rebound even though nothing about the company has changed, can give exploitable possibilities.

Contrarian strategies, which look for companies who's worth the manager believes is not fully recognised by the public, are examples of behavioural finance. Momentum funds strive to take advantage of the fact that investors like to acquire stocks with an upward price trend. As a result, mutual fund managers can simply forecast market patterns. We have observed that sophisticated investors i.e., those who are better informed, have higher incomes, are older, and have more experience, tend to invest better. These investors hold a high proportion of funds for a longer duration, do not sell merely on a whim,

Table 7. Descriptive Statistics for Correlation Analysis

	Anchoring	Loss Aversion	Choice Paralysis	Confirmation Bias	Herd Mentality
Anchoring	1	0.293	0.354	0.431	0.437
Loss Aversion	0.354	1	0.476	0.47	0.471
Choice Paralysis	0.26	0.556	1	0.376	0.354
Confirmation Bias	0.106	0.456	0.563	1	0.312
Herd Mentality	0.108	0.367	0.355	0.358	1

avoid funds with high charges and expenses, compare funds across all levels and enjoy relatively good returns in the long run. However, investors who have strong behavioural biases or who do not give heed to firm-specific or contextual news are less prone to hold mutual funds for long or choose the mutual funds for the wrong reasons. This is because investors with strong behavioural biases are less likely to be receptive to news about firms. When they do buy mutual funds, they often have a tendency to make poor decisions on the timing of their purchases and sales often ending up investing in high-expense funds and active funds over index funds. The fact that prejudiced investors are more prone to pursue fund performance lends credence to the assumption that trend chasing does not represent rational fund selection choices; nevertheless, our findings put doubt on this notion.

CONCLUSION

Investment in various enterprises has become complicated in the current changing economic landscape, as people have committed enormous sums of money even when there is a small chance that the company will be lucrative. The majority of investors have realistic expectations and seek to maximise their utility. (Elton, E. et al 1996) Behavioural economists, on the other hand, claim that markets are inefficient, especially in the short run, and that people do not make rational judgments to maximise profits based on their active study. Humans are prone to a variety of behavioural oddities that are incompatible with wealth maximising principles, leading to irrational behaviour. In any industry, understanding consumer impression is critical. The players would benefit much from a thorough understanding of perception and possible cognitive biases. In the current scenario, it is critical to determine mutual fund investors' personal needs, as well as their preferences for mutual fund schemes and their performance evaluation. Therefore, this idea for research germinated.

The road ahead will entail making more and more people aware of cognitive biases prevalent while investing in mutual funds. We suggest such people with limited financial knowledge about investments must rely on index funds for returns. These funds have less expense ratio and over time tend to give excellent returns. Typically, people who are less averse to risk invest in mutual funds rather than stocks, so it is but expected that these investors will be affected by their and others behaviour near them. Biases exist and especially in Indian scenario where investments are affected by social biases, mental errors, behaviour biases etc even a lunar eclipse can bring about a change in buying and selling patterns of investors. So, for a country like India, any study about biases should be propagated and investors made aware of their existence.

REFERENCES

Agrawal, G., & Jain, M. (2013). Investor's Preference towards Mutual Fund in comparison to other Investment Avenues. *Journal of Indian Research*, *1*(4), 115–131.

Barber, B., & Odean, T. (2008). All that glitters: The effect of attention and news on the buying behavior of individual and institutional investors. *Review of Financial Studies*, *21*(2), 785–818. doi:10.1093/rfs/hhm079

Black, F. (1986). Noise. *The Journal of Finance*, *41*(3), 529–543. doi:10.1111/j.1540-6261.1986.tb04513.x

Carhart, M. (1997). On persistence in mutual fund performance. *The Journal of Finance*, *52*(1), 57–82. doi:10.1111/j.1540-6261.1997.tb03808.x

Chan, L., Chen, H., & Lakonishok, J. (2002). On mutual fund investment styles. *Review of Financial Studies*, *15*(5), 1407–1437. doi:10.1093/rfs/15.5.1407

Ekholm, A., & Pasternack, D. (2008). Overconfidence and investor size. *European Financial Management*, *14*(1), 82–98.

Elton, E., Gruber, M., & Blake, C. (1996). Survivorship bias and mutual fund performance. *Review of Financial Studies*, *9*(4), 1097–1120. doi:10.1093/rfs/9.4.1097

Fama, E. (1970). Efficient capital markets: A review of theory and empirical work. *The Journal of Finance*, *25*(2), 383–417. doi:10.2307/2325486

Fama, E., & French, K. (1992). The cross-section of expected stock returns. *The Journal of Finance*, *47*(2), 427–465. doi:10.1111/j.1540-6261.1992.tb04398.x

Rajarajan, V. (2003). Investors' demographics and risk bearing capacity. *Finance India*, *17*(2), 565.

Shanmugham, R. (2000). Factors influencing investment decisions. In Indian Capital Markets–Trends and Dimensions. Tata McGraw-Hill Publishing Company Limited.

Shleifer, A. (2000). *Inefficient markets: An introduction to behavioural finance*. OUP. doi:10.1093/0198292279.001.0001

Sikidar, S. (1996). Equity and Mutual Funds—A Behavioural Study. *Management of Financial Services*, 136.

Vadakkepatt, G., Shankar, V., & Varadarajan, R. (2021). Should firms invest more in marketing or R&D to maintain sales leadership? An empirical analysis of sales leader firms. *Journal of the Academy of Marketing Science*, *49*(6), 1088–1108. doi:10.100711747-021-00774-2

Vyas, R. (2012). Mutual fund investor's behaviour and perception in Indore city. *Researchers World*, *3*(3), 67.

Chapter 7
Theoretical Perspectives on Corporate Social Responsibility: A Narrative Review

Javier Martínez Falcó
https://orcid.org/0000-0001-9004-5816
University of Alicante, Spain

Bartolomé Marco-Lajara
https://orcid.org/0000-0001-8811-9118
University of Alicante, Spain

Patrocinio Zaragoza-Saez
University of Alicante, Spain

ABSTRACT

The research aims to analyze the different theoretical perspectives under which corporate social responsibility (CSR) has been analyzed. Based on the narrative review conducted, five motivations have been identified that drive the implementation of CSR practices: (1) the alignment of interests between agents and principal, (2) the satisfaction of stakeholder demands, (3) compliance with the institutional context, (4) obtaining a competitive advantage, and (5) maintaining congruence between the objectives of society and the objectives of the organization. These objectives are not mutually exclusive, but complementary. Thus, the reason why organizations develop CSR practices can be an accumulation of the five factors mentioned above.

INTRODUCTION

It is understood that the adoption of Corporate Social Responsibility (CSR) criteria in business management entails the formalization of policies and management systems in the economic, social and environmental fields; also, informative transparency with respect to the results achieved in these fields;

DOI: 10.4018/978-1-6684-7499-0.ch007

and, finally, external scrutiny of the same. In this sense, it is said that organizations exercise their social responsibility when they pay attention to the expectations that the different stakeholders have regarding their behavior, with the ultimate purpose of contributing to a socially and environmentally sustainable and economically viable development (Lindgreen & Swaen, 2010; Velte, 2021).

By stakeholders, interested parties, or participants, we usually mean, in a broad sense, any individual, group or organization that can affect or may be affected by the company's activities; in a narrower version, the identifiable and relevant individuals, groups or entities on which the firm depends for its survival (Baxi & Ray, 2012). The CSR management model proposes that the articulation of the expectations of the various stakeholders involved in the business activity results in better anticipation of risks and, ultimately, in the stable creation of shareholder value (Okafor et al., 2021). The adoption of the CSR philosophy by companies begins with the adoption of formal policies and management systems in the economic, social and environmental fields, transparency of information on the results achieved in these fields and, finally, external scrutiny of the results (Ye et al., 2020).

CSR seems to be gaining international importance. Its observance by companies conditions access to certain segments of the capital market and tends to influence the market value of shares. This is evidenced by the involvement of organizations such as the European Union (EU), the United Nations (UN) and the Organization for Economic Cooperation and Development (OECD), and the perception on the part of large institutional investors that CSR is a good indicator of the quality of corporate management and governance practices. In recent times, the debate on CSR has moved into the realm of public policy, especially the role to be played by public authorities in promoting the CSR philosophy. Many governments in the advanced economies have adopted formal policies for disseminating the corporate culture of CSR, on the understanding that it can favor the competitive advantages of companies in certain markets, channel their activities in emerging or developing countries, or provide access to certain segments of the capital market (Singh & Misra, 2021).

To a certain extent, the CSR philosophy is understood to be opposed to the philosophy of creating shareholder value, advocated by Friedman, as the ultimate goal of business activity (Sánchez-Torné et al., 2020). This conception of creating shareholder value is reductionist in comparison with the philosophy underlying the concept of CSR (stakeholder value), which sees the company as an organization called upon to play an active role in shaping society, whose mission should be to create value for stakeholders beyond the shareholder. This philosophy goes further: the creation of value for the various stakeholders results in greater value creation for the shareholder. Following the impact of the pathogen on all economic sectors worldwide, CSR and the fulfillment of the Sustainable Development Goals (SDGs) by organizations is becoming increasingly necessary to achieve economic, social and environmental well-being (Marco-Lajara et al., 2021a; Marco-Lajara et al., 2021b; Marco-Lajara et al., 2021c; Marco-Lajara et al., 2022a; Marco-Lajara et al., 2022b; Marco-Lajara et al., 2022c; Marco-Lajara et al., 2022d; Marco-Lajara et al., 2022e; Marco-Lajara et al., 2022f; Marco-Lajara et al., 2022g; Marco-Lajara et al., 2022h; Marco-Lajara et al., 2022i; Marco-Lajara et al., 2022j; Marco-Lajara et al., 2022k; Marco-Lajara et al., 2022l; Marco-Lajara et al., 2022m; Marco-Lajara et al., 2022n; Marco-Lajara et al., 2022o; Seva-Larrosa et al., 2022). The aim of this research is to find out under what theoretical perspectives CSR has been analyzed, given that its study has received little attention in academic literature. In this way, the study allows us to learn about the different arguments that exist to justify the implementation of CSR.

To achieve this objective, after this brief introduction, Section 2 presents the methodology followed in the study. Section 3 presents the results of the narrative review. Section 4 presents the main conclusions and, finally, Section 5 presents the limitations of the study, as well as future lines of research.

METHODOLOGY

In the present research, a narrative bibliographic review was carried out in order to analyze the theories under which CSR had been analyzed. The literature review is considered a detailed study that aims to gather information on a given topic through the analysis of published literature (Oliver, 2012).

The aim of the narrative review of the literature is to synthesize the fragmented knowledge of previous research on CSR. The research, therefore, presents a descriptive scope, given that there are no hypotheses to be contrasted, but rather the information collected is described and given meaning. Furthermore, the present review follows more flexible and less restrictive procedures than systematic reviews (Ferrari, 2015). Therefore, the present review does not intend to generalize the results obtained to the population (Tranfield et al., 2003), but to offer an interpretation of the literature that allows for a better understanding of the field of study of CSR. To conduct the literature review, the phases proposed by Wee & Banister (2016) were followed, which are: topic selection, source selection and reading, and topic writing. First, the selected topic is the theories that have addressed CSR. Second, manuals, readings, books, books, chapters and articles focused on the evolution and conceptualization of CSR were included for the research, excluding colloquium reports, seminars, doctoral dissertations and working papers. The time period of the publications covers the period from the beginnings of the concept of CSR in the 1950s to the present day, given that the aim of the research is to analyze all the perspectives under which CSR has been studied. Likewise, the Scopus and Web of Science databases were used to select the publications, as they are prestigious databases that contain articles published in high-impact journals, which ensures that the information obtained is accurate and of high value, legitimizing reliable results. A total of 75 academic papers were reviewed and read in depth, this being the scientific production that allowed us to reflect on the evolution of the perspectives under which CSR has been analyzed Thirdly, once the article and sources had been selected and the publications had been read, the bibliographic review was drafted.

RESULTS

Theoretical perspectives on CSR show how this construct has been observed and interpreted by scholars over time. The five predominant theoretical approaches in the academic literature on CSR are discussed below: Agency Theory, Stakeholder Theory, Institutional Theory, Resource and Capabilities Theory and Legitimacy Theory.

Agency Theory

Agency Theory analyzes the relationship between "principals" (individuals or organizations that employ another party to perform a specific job) and "agents" (those who perform that job). Following the seminal study by Berle & Means (1932), Agency Theory has traditionally been applied to the relationship between owners and managers of large firms (Eisenhardt, 1989).

Agency Theory addresses the "agency problem", which can arise as a result of a conflict of interest between principals, and how such a problem can be overcome through different governance mechanisms (Spence & Zeckhauser, 1971; Jensen & Meckling, 1976; Amihud & Lev, 1981; Eisenhardt, 1985).

With regard to CSR, Friedman (1962) was undoubtedly one of the first precursors of the Agency Theory by arguing that CSR represented selfish behavior by managers (agents) whose pursuit of social and environmental objectives ended up harming shareholders (principals) by generating lower corporate profit. Authors such as Galaskiewicz (1985), Atkinson & Galaskiewicz (1988) and Wright & Ferris (1997) subsequently made explicit applications of Agency Theory in relation to CSR, thus reinforcing Friedman's thesis. Atkinson & Galaskiewicz (1988) confirmed that ownership and corporate philanthropy were negatively related, since the higher the percentage of shares held by the CEO, the more profits he or she earned and, consequently, the less the firm contributed to philanthropic causes. On the contrary, several recent research studies carried out under this theory consider that CSR favors financial and non-financial performance (Berrone & Gómez-Mejía, 2009; Bear et al., 2010; Oh et al., 2011). As an example, Oh et al. (2011) found that large institutional shareholders and long-term oriented foreign investors supported companies' CSR initiatives, denoting that these investors preferred to invest in responsible companies to avoid financial risks.

The main limitation of Agency Theory is that it can only provide a partial explanation of CSR. As Eisenhardt (1989, p. 71) states, "agency theory presents a partial view of the world which, while valid, also ignores much of the complexity of organizations". Consequently, this theory can be more appropriately applied in conjunction with other theoretical perspectives to provide a holistic picture of individual-level phenomena and their interactions with other levels of analysis.

Stakeholder Theory

Stakeholders are interest groups that can help or harm the development of business activity (Freeman, 1984). Stakeholder Theory predicts that corporate actions are the direct result of pressures from different stakeholders, related to dependence on power (Freeman & Reed, 1983; Clarkson, 1995; Jawahar & McLaughlin, 2001) or claim to legitimacy (Hill and Jones, 1992; Langtry, 1994). Bringing these different factors together into a single model of stakeholder identification and relevance, Mitchel et al. (1997) proposed that the impact of stakeholders on organizations depended on three attributes: power (related to the stakeholder's ability to impose its will on others), legitimacy (related to the rights of stakeholders to use their power in the face of claims made on the firm), and urgency (the degree to which stakeholder claims demand immediate attention).

Studies from the stakeholder perspective have provided abundant empirical evidence on the impact of stakeholders on CSR strategies and how their pressures influence CSR-related activities (Brammer & Millington, 2004; Lamberti & Lettieri, 2009; Surroca et al., 2013). Studies have investigated, among other topics, the influence of stakeholder pressures on environmental policies and strategies (Christmann, 2004; Darnall et al., 2010), environmental disclosure (Roberts, 1992; Neu et al., 1998; Elijido-Tenet al., 2010) and corporate philanthropy (Brammer & Millington, 2003, 2004; Moir & Taffler, 2004). Likewise, a significant portion of studies has also focused on the relationship between CSR and organizational performance or financial performance of firms, both from a conceptual perspective (Miles & Covin, 2000; Schuler & Cording, 2006; Barnett, 2007, 2014) and from an empirical perspective (Wang & Choi, 2013; Oikonomou et al., 2014). While some empirical results point to an inconclusive or even negative relationship between CSR and organizational performance (Moore, 2001; Hoepneret al., 2014; Jia & Zhang, 2014), others demonstrate a positive relationship (Ruf et al., 2001; Brammer & Millington, 2004; Wang & Choi, 2013; Mellahi et al., 2016). In general, these studies start from the premise that investors and other key stakeholders reward companies that are responsive to their concerns.

Institutional Theory

Institutional Theory suggests that firms need to comply with the social norms of a given business environment because they cannot survive without a certain level of external social approval (legitimacy) (Meyer & Rowan, 1977; DiMaggio & Powell, 1983). This theory encompasses different intellectual traditions and approaches, which can be divided into three (Hotho & Pedersen, 2012). First, the economic approach has addressed the regulatory role of institutions underpinning economic activity (Davis & North, 1971; North, 1990). Second, the sociological approach has addressed the role of legitimacy in institutions (DiMaggio & Powell, 1983; Scott, 2001). Third, the comparative institutional approach, which overlaps with the first two approaches, has analyzed the differences between institutional arrangements and firm competitiveness (Whitley, 1999; Hall & Soskice, 2001; Wood et al., 2014).

Institutional Theory has been widely applied to CSR (Jennings & Zandbergen, 1995; Doh & Guay, 2006; Campbell, 2007; Matten & Moon, 2008). On the one hand, numerous studies have identified institutional factors that influence or shape responsible behavior, management, environmental practices or social and environmental disclosure. On the other hand, the CSR literature has also explored "institutional isomorphism", i.e., the idea that firms' strategies and practices resemble a defined institutional environment, as organizations in a given sector and territory face similar institutional pressures. This literature has investigated CSR strategies and practices among firms with similar attributes within the institutional context of countries (Doh & Guay, 2006; Holder-Webb & Cohen, 2012; Fransen, 2013) and that of local communities (Marquis et al., 2007). From a comparative perspective, Institutional Theory also helps to explain differences in the nature of CSR depending on the local context of firms (Matten & Moon, 2008; Sison, 2009; Xu & Yang, 2010; Jamali & Neville, 2011). For example, studies have shown significant differences between the United States and Europe in the impact of national institutional context on CSR (Doh & Guay, 2006; Matten & Moon, 2008; Sison, 2009; Avetisyan & Ferrary, 2013).

There are three mechanisms through which institutional isomorphism is generated: the coercive mechanism, the normative mechanism and the mimetic mechanism. The mimetic mechanism is the result of the voluntary impulse to imitate the CSR practices of other competitors in order to achieve an acceptable standard (Amran & Siti-Nabiha, 2009). The normative mechanism occurs when imitation of CSR strategy is considered a necessity to be within the institutional framework, such as guidelines from professional bodies and academic centers. The coercive mechanism, on the other hand, refers to the imitation of CSR practices by force, persuasion or invitation to sign an agreement. This occurs when an organization is dependent on another and cannot stand on its own. Therefore, the main objective of the Institutional Theory is the institutionalization of behavior, since, according to this approach, institutions can influence the behavior of organizations in the same sector by establishing acceptable and recognized standards, norms, specifications or modes of operation within industries (Kang & Moon, 2012).

Resource and Capabilities Theory

The intellectual origins of Resource Based View (RBV) date back to the pioneering work of Penrose (1959) (Rugman & Verbeke, 2002; Lockett & Thompson, 2004). The author conceives of the heterogeneity of resources and capabilities of organizations as the main source of sustainable competitive advantage, in contrast to the earlier emphasis in the discipline of strategic management on the adaptation of firms to the external environment. Accepting the general premise that firm-specific resources can lead toward gaining competitive advantage, RBV focuses on determining how firms can acquire greater profitability through the possession of valuable, rare and inimitable resources (Wernerfelt, 1984; Barney 1991, 1997; Kraaijenbrink et al. 2010). Barney (1997) introduced the Valuable, Rare, Imperfectly Imitable and Non-substitutable (VRIN) framework to help understand a firm's competitive advantage by posing a series of questions about whether a firm's resources were valuable, rare, costly to imitate, and exploited by the organization. Sustainable competitive advantage thus arises when firms have resources that combine all four attributes.

Research related to CSR under the RBV approach proposes that capabilities related to CSR investment can lead to economic benefits for firms (Hart, 1995; Russo & Fouts, 1997; McWilliams & Siegel; 2011). CSR can be justified as an investment that enables the firm to differentiate itself from its competitors and improve organizational performance. Therefore, CSR helps to understand the proactive strategies of companies in developing and using internal capabilities related to social and environmental issues to obtain economic benefits. Such capabilities may include, among others, green innovations (Chen et al., 2006), stakeholder management and strategic proactivity (Torugsa et al., 2012) or sustainability leadership (Lourenço et al., 2014).

Several studies have applied RBV to CSR empirically, mostly focusing on testing the statistical relationship between social/environmental performance and ecological performance (Russo & Fouts, 1997; Menguc et al., 2010; Ben Brik et al., 2011) or applying the VRIN framework (Peters et al., 2011) to find out whether social and environmental capabilities can improve organizational performance.

However, such research is ambiguous in demonstrating whether CSR enables sustainable competitive advantages over competitors. Some studies have suggested that CSR-related capabilities can generate competitive advantages for firms (Chen et al., 2006; Lourenço et al., 2014). In contrast, other research conducted from the RBV perspective (McWilliams & Siegel, 2011; Frynas, 2015) suggests that while CSR can generate business advantages for the firm, it is unlikely to generate sustainable competitive advantage, because in contrast to, for example, the firm's intangible assets (Boddewyn & Brewer, 1994) or technological resources and capabilities (Huang et al., 2015), CSR activities are visible and rivals can imitate them.

Legitimacy Theory

Suchman (1995, p. 574) defines legitimacy as "a generalized perception or assumption that an entity's actions are desirable, appropriate, or fitting with some socially constructed system of norms, values, beliefs, and definitions." Deegan & Unerman (2011) state that Legitimacy Theory is based on the notion that there is a "social contract" between an organization and the society in which it operates. Therefore, companies try to legitimize their corporate actions by carrying out CSR activities and, in this way, guarantee their existence. According to this theory, companies are inseparable from society and have no inherent right to exist: they only exist to the extent that society confers legitimacy on them. Therefore, firms must continually legitimize their activities to maintain congruence between the objectives of society and those of the organization (Dowling & Pfeffer, 1975; Preston & Post, 1975; Lindblom, 1983; Ashford & Gibbs, 1990; Deegan, 2002).

Legitimacy has to do with two main concepts: the perception of stakeholders and the effectiveness of the communication channels used by the company. The Theory of Legitimacy requires organizations to continuously check whether their survival is serving the satisfaction of the needs of the different stakeholders (Mobus, 2005), since it is the community that determines the usefulness of organizations based on the congruence between what they expect and what they obtain from them. Likewise, communication is essential in the Theory of Legitimacy, since the dissemination of CSR initiatives is a source of creation and protection of organizational legitimacy. In fact, Patten (1992) observed that there was a positive relationship between the dissemination of CSR initiatives and organizational legitimacy. Later, Deegan & Rankin (1997) and Brown & Deegan, (1998) reaffirmed these findings. In the same vein, Campbell (2000) noted that the disclosure of CSR initiatives decreased the legitimacy gap between how an organization is perceived and how it wants to be perceived. By way of conclusion, Table 1 shows the theoretical perspectives that have addressed the study of CSR.

Table 1. Main theoretical perspectives on CSR. Source: own elaboration

Theoretical Perspectives	Basic assumption	Main reasons related to CSR
Agency Theory	Managers, as agents, have different incentives and objectives than their principals.	CSR is driven by alignment between agents and principals.
Stakeholders Theory	Companies are affected by the actions of stakeholders and must therefore address their interests.	CSR is governed by the organization's relationships with its stakeholders.
Institutional Theory	The survival and growth of companies depend on the acquisition of legitimacy in institutional environments.	CSR is driven by different institutional contexts.
Resource and Capabilities Theory	Differences in performance between companies are influenced by company-specific resources and capabilities.	CSR acts as a specialized skill or capability to gain a competitive advantage.
Legitimacy Theory	Companies operate on the basis of a social contract with society and their survival and growth depend on legitimacy.	CSR acts to maintain congruence between the objectives of society and the objectives of the organization.

CONCLUSION

This research is of great relevance for both CSR academics and professionals who are thinking of implementing these practices in their companies, given that, through the research, it is possible to understand the motivations that justify the need for companies to behave fairly with the society and the environment in which they operate.

Through the narrative review carried out, a total of five theories under which CSR has been analyzed were identified: the Agency Theory, the Stakeholder Theory, the Institutional Theory, the Resources and Capabilities Theory and the Legitimacy Theory. First, Agency Theory addresses the "agency problem", which can arise as a result of a conflict of interest among principals, and how this problem can be overcome through different governance mechanisms. Under such an approach CSR is conceived as a mechanism to align interests between agents and principals.

Secondly, according to stakeholder theory, companies are affected by the actions of their stakeholders and must therefore attend to their interests. CSR, therefore, is governed by the organization's relations with its stakeholders. Third, Institutional Theory suggests that firms need to comply with the social norms of a given business environment because they cannot survive without a certain level of external social approval (legitimacy). This theory encompasses different intellectual traditions and approaches. On the one hand, numerous studies have identified institutional factors that influence or shape responsible behavior, management, environmental practices or social and environmental disclosure. On the other hand, the CSR literature has also explored "institutional isomorphism", i.e. the idea that corporate strategies and practices resemble a defined institutional environment, since organizations in a given sector and territory face similar institutional pressures. Under this approach, CSR is driven by different institutional contexts.

Fourth, the intellectual origins of Resource and Capability Theory, in turn, can be traced back to the pioneering work of Penrose (1959). The author conceives the heterogeneity of resources and capabilities of organizations as the main source of sustainable competitive advantage, in contrast to the earlier emphasis in the discipline of Strategic Management on the adaptation of firms to the external environment. Accepting the general premise that firm-specific resources can lead toward gaining competitive advantage, RBV focuses on determining how firms can acquire greater profitability through the possession of valuable, rare and inimitable resources. Research related to CSR under the RBV approach proposes that capabilities related to CSR investment can lead to economic benefits for firms. CSR can be justified as an investment that enables the firm to differentiate itself from its competitors and improve organizational performance. Therefore, RBV helps to understand the proactive strategies of companies in developing and using internal capabilities related to social and environmental issues to obtain economic benefits.

Finally, the Legitimacy Theory is based on the notion that there is a "social contract" between an organization and the society in which it operates. Therefore, companies try to legitimize their corporate actions by carrying out CSR activities and, in this way, guarantee their existence. According to this theory, companies are inseparable from society and do not have an inherent right to exist: they only exist to the extent that society confers legitimacy on them. Therefore, based on the study conducted, five motivations can be identified that drive the implementation of CSR practices: (1) alignment of interests between agents and principal, (2) satisfying stakeholder demands, (3) complying with the institutional context, (4) gaining a competitive advantage and (5) maintaining congruence between the objectives of society and the objectives of the organization. These are not mutually exclusive, but complementary. Thus, the reason why organizations develop CSR practices may be an accumulation of the five factors mentioned above.

FUTURE RESEARCH DIRECTIONS

Despite the important contributions of the study, it is important to point out that the research suffers from certain limitations. The fundamental limitation of the study is methodological in nature, given that narrative reviews are dominated by the subjective criteria of the authors and do not quantitatively synthesize the data found in the different publications. To overcome these limitations of narrative reviews, a systematic review of the theoretical perspectives of CSR over time is proposed as a future line of research with the aim of increasing the reproducibility of the research and increasing the validity of the results obtained.

REFERENCES

Amihud, Y., & Lev, B. (1981). Risk reduction as a managerial motive for conglomerate mergers. *The Bell Journal of Economics*, *12*(2), 605–616. doi:10.2307/3003575

Amran, A., & Siti-Nabiha, A. (2009). Corporate social reporting in Malaysia: A case of mimicking the West or succumbing to local pressure. *Social Responsibility Journal, 5*(3), 358–375. doi:10.1108/17471110910977285

Ashford, B., & Gibbs, B. (1990). The double-edge of organizational legitimation. *Organization Science, 1*(2), 177–194. doi:10.1287/orsc.1.2.177

Atkinson, L., & Galaskiewicz, J. (1988). Stock ownership and company contributions to charity. *Administrative Science Quarterly, 33*(1), 82–100. doi:10.2307/2392856

Avetisyan, E., & Ferrary, M. (2013). 'Dynamics of stakeholders' implications in the institutionalization of the CSR field in France and in the United States. *Journal of Business Ethics, 115*(1), 115–133. doi:10.100710551-012-1386-3

Barnett, M. (2007). Stakeholder influence capacity and the variability of financial returns to corporate social responsibility. *Academy of Management Review, 32*(3), 794–816. doi:10.5465/amr.2007.25275520

Barnett, M. (2014). Why stakeholders ignore firm misconduct: A cognitive view. *Journal of Management, 40*(3), 676–702. doi:10.1177/0149206311433854

Barney, J. (1991). Firm resources and sustained competitive advantage. *Journal of Management, 17*(1), 99–120. doi:10.1177/014920639101700108

Barney, J. (1997). *Gaining and Sustaining a Competitive Advantage*. Addison Wesley.

Baxi, C. V., & Ray, R. S. (2012). *Corporate social responsibility*. Vikas Publishing House.

Bear, S., Rahman, N., & Post, C. (2010). The impact of board diversity and gender composition on corporate social responsibility and firm reputation. *Journal of Business Ethics, 97*(2), 207–221. doi:10.100710551-010-0505-2

Ben Brik, A., Rettab, B., & Mellahi, K. (2011). Market orientation, corporate social responsibility, and business performance. *Journal of Business Ethics, 99*(3), 307–324. doi:10.100710551-010-0658-z

Berle, A., & Means, G. (1932). *The Modern Corporation and Private Property*. Macmillan.

Berrone, P., & Gomez-Mejia, L. (2009). Environmental performance and executive compensation: An integrated agency-institutional perspective. *Academy of Management Journal, 52*(1), 103–126. doi:10.5465/amj.2009.36461950

Boddewyn, J., & Brewer, T. (1994). International business political behavior: New theoretical directions. *Academy of Management Review, 19*(1), 119–143. doi:10.5465/amr.1994.9410122010

Brammer, S., & Millington, A. (2003). The effect of stakeholder preferences, organizational structure and industry type on corporate community involvement. *Journal of Business Ethics, 45*(3), 213–226. doi:10.1023/A:1024151528646

Brammer, S., & Millington, A. (2004). The development of corporate charitable contributions in the UK: A stakeholder analysis. *Journal of Management Studies, 41*(8), 1411–1434. doi:10.1111/j.1467-6486.2004.00480.x

Brown, N., & Deegan, C. (1998). The public disclosure of environmental performance information—A dual test of media agenda setting theory and legitimacy theory. *Accounting and Business Research*, *29*(1), 21–41. doi:10.1080/00014788.1998.9729564

Campbell, D. (2000). Legitimacy theory or managerial reality construction? Corporate social disclosure in Marks and Spencer Plc corporate reports, 1969-1997. *Accounting Forum*, *24*(1), 80–100. doi:10.1111/1467-6303.00030

Campbell, J. (2007). Why would corporations behave in socially responsible ways? An institutional theory of corporate social responsibility. *Academy of Management Review*, *32*(3), 946–967. doi:10.5465/amr.2007.25275684

Chen, Y., Lai, S., & Wen, C. (2006). The influence of green innovation performance on corporate advantage in Taiwan. *Journal of Business Ethics*, *67*(4), 331–339. doi:10.100710551-006-9025-5

Christmann, P. (2004). Multinational companies and the natural environment: Determinants of global environmental policy standardization. *Academy of Management Journal*, *47*(5), 747–760. doi:10.2307/20159616

Clarkson, M. (1995). A stakeholder framework for analyzing and evaluating corporate social performance. *Academy of Management Review*, *20*(1), 92–117. doi:10.2307/258888

Darnall, N., Henriques, I., & Sadorsky, P. (2010). Adopting proactive environmental strategy: The influence of stakeholders and firm size. *Journal of Management Studies*, *47*(6), 1072–1094. doi:10.1111/j.1467-6486.2009.00873.x

Davis, L., & North, D. (1971). *Institutional Change and American Economic Growth*. Cambridge University Press. doi:10.1017/CBO9780511561078

Deegan, C. (2002). Introduction - The legitimising effect of social and environmental disclosures - a theoretical foundation. *Accounting, Auditing & Accountability Journal*, *15*(3), 282–311. doi:10.1108/09513570210435852

Deegan, C., Rankin, M., & Tobin, J. (2002). An examination of the corporate social and environmental disclosures of BHP from 1983-1997: A test of legitimacy theory. *Accounting, Auditing & Accountability Journal*, *15*(3), 312–343. doi:10.1108/09513570210435861

Deegan, C., & Unerman, J. (2011). *Financial accounting theory* (2nd ed.). McGraw-Hill.

DiMaggio, P., & Powell, W. (1983). The iron cage revisited: Institutional isomorphism and collective rationality in organizational fields. *American Sociological Review*, *48*(2), 147–160. doi:10.2307/2095101

Doh, J., & Guay, T. (2006). Corporate social responsibility, public policy, and NGO activism in Europe and the United States: An institutional stakeholder perspective. *Journal of Management Studies*, *43*(1), 47–73. doi:10.1111/j.1467-6486.2006.00582.x

Dowling, J., & Pfeffer, J. (1975). Organizational legitimacy: Social values and organizational behavior. *Pacific Sociological Review*, *18*(1), 122–136. doi:10.2307/1388226

Eisenhardt, K. (1985). Control: Organizational and economic approaches. *Management Science, 31*(2), 134–149. doi:10.1287/mnsc.31.2.134

Eisenhardt, K. (1989). Agency theory: An assessment and review. *Academy of Management Review, 14*(1), 57–74. doi:10.2307/258191

Elijido-Ten, E., Kloot, L., & Clarkson, P. (2010). Extending the application of stakeholder influence strategies to environmental disclosures. *Accounting, Auditing & Accountability Journal, 23*(8), 1032–1059. doi:10.1108/09513571011092547

Ferrari, R. (2015). Writing narrative style literature reviews. *Medical Writing, 24*(4), 230–235. doi:10.1179/2047480615Z.000000000329

Fransen, L. (2013). The embeddedness of responsible business practice: Exploring the interaction between national-institutional environments and corporate social responsibility. *Journal of Business Ethics, 115*(2), 213–227. doi:10.100710551-012-1395-2

Freeman, R. (1984). *Strategic Management - A Stakeholder Approach*. Pitman.

Freeman, R., & Reed, D. (1983). Stockholders and stakeholders: A new perspective on corporate governance. *California Management Review, 25*(3), 88–106. doi:10.2307/41165018

Friedman, M. (1962). *Capitalism and freedom*. University of Chicago Press.

Frynas, J. (2015). Strategic CSR, value creation and competitive advantage. In T. C. Lawton & T. S. Rajwani (Eds.), *The Routledge Companion to Non- Market Strategy: 245-262*. Routledge.

Galaskiewicz, J. (1985). *Social Organization of an Urban Grants Economy: A Study of Business Philanthropy and Nonprofit Organizations*. Academic Press.

Hall, P., & Soskice, D. (2001). *Varieties of Capitalism: The Institutional Basis of Competitive Advantage*. Oxford University Press. doi:10.1093/0199247757.001.0001

Hart, S. (1995). A natural resource-based view of the firm. *Academy of Management Review, 20*(4), 986–1014. doi:10.5465/amr.1995.9512280033

Hill, C., & Jones, T. (1992). Stakeholder agency theory. *Journal of Management Studies, 29*(2), 131–154. doi:10.1111/j.1467-6486.1992.tb00657.x

Hoepner, A., Aguiar, T., & Majithia, R. (2014). The level of compliance with the international code of marketing of breast-milk substitutes: Does it matter to stock markets? *Journal of Business Ethics, 119*(3), 329–348. doi:10.100710551-013-1625-2

Holder-Webb, L., & Cohen, J. (2012). The cut and paste society: Isomorphism in codes of ethics. *Journal of Business Ethics, 107*(4), 485–509. doi:10.100710551-011-1060-1

Hotho, J., & Pedersen, T. (2012). Beyond the rules of the game: three institutional approaches and how they matter for international business. In M. Demirbag & G. Wood (Eds.), *Handbook of Institutional Approaches to International Business*. Edward Elgar. doi:10.4337/9781849807692.00016

Huang, K., Dyerson, R., Wu, L., & Harindranath, G. (2015). From temporary competitive advantage to sustainable competitive advantage. *British Journal of Management*, *26*(4), 617–636. doi:10.1111/1467-8551.12104

Jamali, D., & Neville, B. (2011). Convergence versus divergence of CSR in developing countries: An embedded multi-layered institutional lens. *Journal of Business Ethics*, *102*(4), 599–621. doi:10.100710551-011-0830-0

Jawahar, I., & McLaughlin, G. (2001). Toward a descriptive stakeholder theory: An organizational life cycle approach. *Academy of Management Review*, *26*(3), 397–414. doi:10.2307/259184

Jennings, P., & Zandbergen, P. (1995). Ecologically sustainable organizations: An institutional approach. *Academy of Management Review*, *20*(4), 1015–1052. doi:10.5465/amr.1995.9512280034

Jensen, M., & Meckling, W. (1976). Theory of the firm: Managerial behavior, agency costs, and ownership structure. *Journal of Financial Economics*, *3*(4), 305–360. doi:10.1016/0304-405X(76)90026-X

Jia, M., & Zhang, Z. (2014). How does the stock market value corporate social performance? When behavioral theories interact with stakeholder theory. *Journal of Management Studies*, *51*(7), 1118–1152. doi:10.1111/joms.12090

Kang, N., & Moon, J. (2012). Institutional complementarity between corporate governance and corporate social responsibility: A comparative institutional analysis of three capitalisms. *Socio-economic Review*, *10*(1), 85–108. doi:10.1093er/mwr025

Kraaijenbrink, J., Spender, J., & Groen, A. (2010). The resource-based view: A review and assessment of its critiques. *Journal of Management*, *36*(1), 349–372. doi:10.1177/0149206309350775

Lamberti, L., & Lettieri, E. (2009). CSR practices and corporate strategy: Evidence from a longitudinal case study. *Journal of Business Ethics*, *87*(2), 153–168. doi:10.100710551-008-9876-z

Langtry, B. (1994). Stakeholders and the moral responsibilities of business. *Business Ethics Quarterly*, *4*(4), 431–443. doi:10.2307/3857342

Lindblom, C. (1983). *The concept of organizational legitimacy and its implications for corporate social responsibility disclosure*. Working Paper. American Accounting Association Public Interest Section.

Lindgreen, A., & Swaen, V. (2010). Corporate social responsibility. *International Journal of Management Reviews*, *12*(1), 1–7. doi:10.1111/j.1468-2370.2009.00277.x

Lockett, A., & Thompson, S. (2004). Edith Penrose's contributions to the resource-based view: An alternative perspective. *Journal of Management Studies*, *41*(1), 193–203. doi:10.1111/j.1467-6486.2004.00428.x

Lourenço, I., Callen, J., Branco, M., & Curto, J. (2014). The value relevance of reputation for sustainability leadership. *Journal of Business Ethics*, *119*(1), 17–28. doi:10.100710551-012-1617-7

Marco-Lajara, B., Martínez-Falcó, J., Ruiz-Fernández, L., & Seva-Larrosa, P. (2022k). Evolución del pensamiento en la disciplina de dirección estratégica: la visión de la empresa basada en las capacidades dinámicas y en el conocimiento. [Evolution of thinking in the discipline of strategic management: the vision of the company based on dynamic capabilities and knowledge] In *Investigación y transferencia de las ciencias sociales frente a un mundo en crisis* [Social science research and transfer in the face of a world in crisis]. (pp. 1801–1826). Dykinson.

Marco-Lajara, B., Sánchez-García, E., Martínez-Falcó, J., & Poveda-Pareja, E. (2022l). Regional Specialization, Competitive Pressure, and Cooperation: The Cocktail for Innovation. *Energies*, *15*(15), 5346.

Marco-Lajara, B., Sánchez-García, E., Seva-Larrosa, P., & Martínez-Falcó, J. (2022m). Knowledge creation and diffusion inspecialized environments: What are the factors involved? In *Empresa, economía y derecho. Oportunidades ante un entorno global y disruptivo* [Business, economy and law. Opportunities in a global and disruptive environment]. (pp. 432–459). Dykinson.

Marco-Lajara, B., Seva-Larrosa, P., Martínez-Falcó, J., & García-Lillo, F. (2022i). Wine clusters and Protected Designations of Origin (PDOs) in Spain: An exploratory analysis. *Journal of Wine Research*, *33*(3), 1–22. doi:10.1080/09571264.2022.2110051

Marco-Lajara, B., Seva-Larrosa, P., Martinez-Falco, J., & Sanchez-Garcia, E. (2021a). How Has COVID- 19 Affected The Spanish Wine Industry? An Exploratory Analysis. *Natural Volatiles & Essential Oils Journal*, *8*(6), 2722–2731.

Marco-Lajara, B., Seva-Larrosa, P., Martínez-Falcó, J., & Sánchez-García, E. (2021j). El clúster vitivinícola de Jumilla: Entre la tradición y la modernidad [The Jumilla wine cluster: Between tradition and modernity]. In XLIII jornadas de viticultura y enología de la Tierra de Barros: III Congreso agroalimentario de Extremadura [XLIII Tierra de Barros Viticulture and Oenology Conference: III Agri-food Congress of Extremadura] (pp. 56-70). Centro Universitario Santa Ana.

Marco-Lajara, B., Seva-Larrosa, P., Ruiz-Fernandez, L., & Martinez-Falco, J. (2021b). The Effect of COVID- 19 on the Spanish Wine Industry. In *Impact of Global Issues on International Trade* (pp. 211–232). IGI Global. doi:10.4018/978-1-7998-8314-2.ch012

Marco-Lajara, B., Zaragoza-Saez, P., Martínez-Falcó, J., & Sánchez-García, E. (2022c). COVID-19 and Wine Tourism: A Story of Heartbreak. In Handbook of Research on SDGs for Economic Development, Social Development, and Environmental Protection (pp. 90-112). IGI Global.

Marco-Lajara, B., Zaragoza-Sáez, P., Falcó, J. M., & Millan-Tudela, L. A. (2022f). Corporate Social Responsibility: A Narrative Literature Review. *Frameworks for Sustainable Development Goals to Manage Economic, Social, and Environmental Shocks and Disasters*, 16-34.

Marco-Lajara, B., Zaragoza-Saez, P., & Martínez-Falcó, J. (2022e). Green Innovation: Balancing Economic Efficiency With Environmental Protection. In Frameworks for Sustainable Development Goals to Manage Economic, Social, and Environmental Shocks and Disasters (pp. 239-254). IGI Global.

Marco-Lajara, B., Zaragoza Sáez, P., & Martínez-Falcó, J. (2022n). Does Green Intellectual Capital Affect Green Performance? The Mediation of Green Innovation. *Telematique*, *21*(1), 4594–4602.

Marco-Lajara, B., Zaragoza-Saez, P., Martínez-Falcó, J., & Millan-Tudela, L. A. (2022b). Analysing the Relationship Between Green Intellectual Capital and the Achievement of the Sustainable Development Goals. In *Handbook of Research on Building Inclusive Global Knowledge Societies for Sustainable Development* (pp. 111–129). IGI Global. doi:10.4018/978-1-6684-5109-0.ch005

Marco-Lajara, B., Zaragoza-Sáez, P., Martínez-Falcó, J., & Ruiz-Fernández, L. (2022g). The Effect of Green Intellectual Capital on Green Performance in the Spanish Wine Industry: A Structural Equation Modeling Approach. *Complexity, 2022*, 2022. doi:10.1155/2022/6024077

Marco-Lajara, B., Zaragoza-Sáez, P., Martínez-Falcó, J., & Sánchez-García, E. (2022a). Green Intellectual Capital in the Spanish Wine Industry. In Innovative Economic, Social, and Environmental Practices for Progressing Future Sustainability (pp. 102-120). IGI Global. doi:10.4018/978-1-7998-9590-9.ch006

Marco-Lajara, B., Zaragoza-Sáez, P., Martínez-Falcó, J., & Sánchez-García, E. (2022d). El capital intelectual verde como hoja de ruta para la sostenibilidad: El caso de bodegas Luzón. *GeoGraphos: Revista Digital para Estudiantes de Geografía y Ciencias Sociales, 13*(147), 137–146.

Marco-Lajara, B., Zaragoza-Sáez, P., Martínez-Falcó, J., & Sánchez-García, E. (2022o). Las rutas del vino de España: el impacto económico derivado de las visitas a bodegas y museos. [Spain's wine routes: the economic impact of visits to wineries and museums] In *Investigación y transferencia de las ciencias sociales frente a un mundo en crisis* [Social science research and transfer in the face of a world in crisis]. (pp. 1774–1800). Dykinson.

Marco-Lajara, B., Zaragoza-Sáez, P. C., Martínez-Falcó, J., & Sánchez-García, E. (2022h). Does green intellectual capital affect green innovation performance? Evidence from the Spanish wine industry. *British Food Journal*, ahead-of-print.

Marquis, C., Glynn, M., & Davis, G. (2007). Community isomorphism and corporate social action. *Academy of Management Review, 32*(3), 925–945. doi:10.5465/amr.2007.25275683

Matten, D., & Moon, J. (2008). "Implicit" and "explicit" CSR: A conceptual framework for a comparative understanding of corporate social responsibility. *Academy of Management Review, 330*(2), 404–424. doi:10.5465/amr.2008.31193458

McWilliams, A., & Siegel, D. (2011). Creating and capturing value: Strategic corporate social responsibility, resource-based theory, and sustainable competitive advantage. *Journal of Management, 37*(5), 1480–1495. doi:10.1177/0149206310385696

Mellahi, K., Frynas, J., Sun, P., & Siegel, D. (2016). A review of the nonmarket strategy literature: Towards a multi-theoretical integration. *Journal of Management, 42*(1), 143–173. doi:10.1177/0149206315617241

Menguc, B., Auh, S., & Ozanne, L. (2010). The interactive effect of internal and external factors on a proactive environmental strategy and its influence on a firm's performance. *Journal of Business Ethics, 94*(2), 279–298. doi:10.100710551-009-0264-0

Meyer, J., & Rowan, B. (1977). Institutionalized organizations: Formal structure as myth and ceremony. *American Journal of Sociology, 83*(2), 340–363. doi:10.1086/226550

Miles, M., & Covin, J. (2000). Environmental marketing: A source of reputational, competitive, and financial advantage. *Journal of Business Ethics, 23*(3), 299–311. doi:10.1023/A:1006214509281

Mitchell, R., Agle, B., & Wood, D. (1997). Toward a theory of stakeholder identification and salience. *Academy of Management Review, 22*(4), 853–886. doi:10.2307/259247

Mobus, J. (2005). Mandatory environmental disclosures in a legitimacy theory context. *Accounting, Auditing & Accountability Journal, 18*(4), 492–517. doi:10.1108/09513570510609333

Moir, L., & Taffler, R. (2004). Does corporate philanthropy exist? Business giving to the arts in the U.K. *Journal of Business Ethics, 54*(2), 149–161. doi:10.100710551-004-1777-1

Moore, G. (2001). Corporate social and financial performance: An investigation in the U.K. supermarket industry. *Journal of Business Ethics, 34*(4), 299–315. doi:10.1023/A:1012537016969

Neu, D., Warsame, H., & Pedwell, K. (1998). Managing public impressions: Environmental disclosures in annual reports. *Accounting, Organizations and Society, 23*(3), 265–282. doi:10.1016/S0361-3682(97)00008-1

North, D. (1990). *Institutions, Institutional Change and Economic Performance*. Cambridge University Press. doi:10.1017/CBO9780511808678

Oh, W., Chang, Y., & Martynov, A. (2011). The effect of ownership structure on corporate social responsibility: Empirical evidence from Korea. *Journal of Business Ethics, 104*(2), 283–297. doi:10.100710551-011-0912-z

Oikonomou, I., Brooks, C., & Pavelin, S. (2014). The financial effects of uniform and mixed corporate social performance. *Journal of Management Studies, 51*(6), 898–925. doi:10.1111/joms.12064

Okafor, A., Adeleye, B. N., & Adusei, M. (2021). Corporate social responsibility and financial performance: Evidence from US tech firms. *Journal of Cleaner Production, 292*, 126078. doi:10.1016/j.jclepro.2021.126078

Oliver, P. (2012). *Succeeding with your literature review. A handbook for students*. McGraw-Hill, Open University Press.

Patten, D. (1992). Intra-industry environmental disclosures in response to the Alaskan oil spill: A note on legitimacy theory. *Accounting, Organizations and Society, 17*(5), 471–475. doi:10.1016/0361-3682(92)90042-Q

Peters, M., Siller, L., & Matzler, K. (2011). The resource-based and the market-based approaches to cultural tourism in Alpine destinations. *Journal of Sustainable Tourism, 19*(7), 877–893. doi:10.1080/09669582.2010.547198

Preston, L., & Post, J. (1975). *Private Management and Public Policy*. Prentice-Hall.

Roberts, R. (1992). Determinants of corporate social responsibility disclosure: An application of stakeholder theory. *Accounting, Organizations and Society, 17*(6), 595–612. doi:10.1016/0361-3682(92)90015-K

Ruf, B., Muralidhar, K., Brown, R., Janney, J., & Paul, K. (2001). An empirical investigation of the relationship between change in corporate social performance and financial performance: A stakeholder theory perspective. *Journal of Business Ethics*, *32*(2), 143–156. doi:10.1023/A:1010786912118

Rugman, A., & Verbeke, A. (2002). Edith Penrose's contribution to the resource-based view of strategic management. *Strategic Management Journal*, *23*(8), 769–780. doi:10.1002mj.240

Russo, M., & Fouts, P. (1997). A resource-based perspective on corporate environmental performance and profitability. *Academy of Management Journal*, *40*(3), 534–559.

Sánchez-Torné, I., Morán-Álvarez, J. C., & Pérez-López, J. A. (2020). The importance of corporate social responsibility in achieving high corporate reputation. *Corporate Social Responsibility and Environmental Management*, *27*(6), 2692–2700. doi:10.1002/csr.1993

Schuler, D., & Cording, M. (2006). A corporate social performance-corporate financial performance behavioral model for consumers. *Academy of Management Review*, *31*(3), 540–558. doi:10.5465/amr.2006.21318916

Scott, R. (2001). *Institutions and Organizations*. Sage Publications.

Seva-Larrosa, P., Martínez-Falcó, J., & Ruiz-Fernández, L. (2022). Analizando las principales variables empresariales en los clusters vinícolas españoles teniendo en cuenta la localización de las empresas y su pertenencia a una marca colectiva. [Analyzing the main business variables in Spanish wine clusters taking into account the location of the companies and their membership in a collective brand] In *Miradas sobre el emprendimiento ante la crisis del coronavirus* [Perspectives on entrepreneurship in the face of the coronavirus crisis]. (pp. 629–634). Dykinson.

Singh, K., & Misra, M. (2021). Linking corporate social responsibility (CSR) and organizational performance: The moderating effect of corporate reputation. *European Research on Management and Business Economics*, *27*(1), 100139. doi:10.1016/j.iedeen.2020.100139

Sison, A. (2009). From CSR to corporate citizenship: Anglo-American and continental European perspectives. *Journal of Business Ethics*, *89*(3), 235–246. doi:10.100710551-010-0395-3

Spence, A., & Zeckhauser, R. (1971). Insurance, information, and individual action. *The American Economic Review*, *61*(2), 380–387.

Suchman, M. (1995). Managing legitimacy: Strategic and institutional approaches. *Academy of Management Review*, *20*(3), 571–610. doi:10.2307/258788

Surroca, J., Tribo, J., & Zahra, S. (2013). Stakeholder pressure on MNEs and the transfer of socially irresponsible practices to subsidiaries. *Academy of Management Journal*, *56*(2), 549–572. doi:10.5465/amj.2010.0962

Torugsa, N., O'Donohue, W., & Hecker, R. (2012). Capabilities, proactive CSR and financial performance in SMEs: Empirical evidence from an Australian manufacturing industry sector. *Journal of Business Ethics*, *109*(4), 483–500. doi:10.100710551-011-1141-1

Tranfield, D., Denyer, D., & Smart, P. (2003). Towards a methodology for developing evidence-informed management knowledge by means of systematic review. *British Journal of Management, 14*(3), 207–222. doi:10.1111/1467-8551.00375

Wang, H., & Choi, J. (2013). A new look at the corporate social-financial performance relationship: The moderating roles of temporal and interdomain consistency in corporate social performance. *Journal of Management, 39*(2), 416–441. doi:10.1177/0149206310375850

Wee, B. V., & Banister, D. (2016). How to write a literature review paper? *Transport Reviews, 36*(2), 278–288. doi:10.1080/01441647.2015.1065456

Wernerfelt, B. (1984). A resource-based view of the firm. *Strategic Management Journal, 5*(2), 171–180. doi:10.1002mj.4250050207

Whitley, R. (1999). *Divergent Capitalisms: The Social Structuring and Change of Business Systems.* Oxford University Press.

Wood, G., Dibben, P., & Ogden, S. (2014). Comparative capitalism without capitalism, and production without workers: The limits and possibilities of contemporary institutional analysis. *International Journal of Management Reviews, 16*(4), 384–396. doi:10.1111/ijmr.12025

Wright, P., & Ferris, S. (1997). Agency conflict and corporate strategy: The effect of divestment on corporate value. *Strategic Management Journal, 18*(1), 77–83. doi:10.1002/(SICI)1097-0266(199701)18:1<77::AID-SMJ810>3.0.CO;2-R

Xu, S., & Yang, R. (2010). Indigenous characteristics of Chinese corporate social responsibility conceptual paradigm. *Journal of Business Ethics, 93*(2), 321–333. doi:10.100710551-009-0224-8

Ye, N., Kueh, T. B., Hou, L., Liu, Y., & Yu, H. (2020). A bibliometric analysis of corporate social responsibility in sustainable development. *Journal of Cleaner Production, 272*, 122679. doi:10.1016/j.jclepro.2020.122679

ADDITIONAL READING

Barnett, M. L., Henriques, I., & Husted, B. W. (2020). Beyond good intentions: Designing CSR initiatives for greater social impact. *Journal of Management, 46*(6), 937–964. doi:10.1177/0149206319900539

Gillan, S. L., Koch, A., & Starks, L. T. (2021). Firms and social responsibility: A review of ESG and CSR research in corporate finance. *Journal of Corporate Finance, 66*, 101889. doi:10.1016/j.jcorpfin.2021.101889

Mao, Y., He, J., Morrison, A. M., & Andres Coca-Stefaniak, J. (2021). Effects of tourism CSR on employee psychological capital in the COVID-19 crisis: From the perspective of conservation of resources theory. *Current Issues in Tourism, 24*(19), 2716–2734. doi:10.1080/13683500.2020.1770706

Shahzad, M., Qu, Y., Javed, S. A., Zafar, A. U., & Rehman, S. U. (2020). Relation of environment sustainability to CSR and green innovation: A case of Pakistani manufacturing industry. *Journal of Cleaner Production*, *253*, 119938. doi:10.1016/j.jclepro.2019.119938

KEY TERMS AND DEFINITIONS

Corporate Social Responsibility: The responsibility that each organization has with the environment in which it operates and with the society of which it is a part.

Narrative Review: It is a work that analyzes and discusses articles and reports, generally scientific and academic, published in or about an area of knowledge. Scientific reports may be of an empirical, theoretical, critical, analytical, or methodological nature.

Philanthropy: Love for the human species and for all that concerns humanity, expressed in selfless help to others.

Stakeholders: A group of persons organized around a common interest, in order to act jointly in defense of the same.

Theory: A logical-deductive system consisting of a set of hypotheses, a field of application and some rules to draw consequences from the hypotheses.

Chapter 8
Digital Transformation Impact on Organizations' Culture and Employees' Motivation:
Shaping the "New Normal" and Addressing Sustainable Development Goals

Cristina Raluca Gh. Popescu
https://orcid.org/0000-0002-5876-0550
University of Bucharest, Romania & The Bucharest University of Economic Studies, Romania

Arturo Luque González
https://orcid.org/0000-0002-4872-891X
Universidad Técnica de Manabí, Ecuador & Observatorio Euromediterráneo de Espacio Público, Universidad Rey Juan Carlos, Spain

ABSTRACT

In the digital age, the COVID-19 pandemic and the COVID-19 crisis uncovered entities' pressing top-priority to reimagine and to reinvent themselves, thus embracing the unrivalled benefits and the unmatched opportunities offered by digital transformation. Hence, the advantages revealed by digital transformation helped shape the "new normal" and addressed the Sustainable Development Goals (SDGs) beyond compare, bringing inimitable changes and challenges to organizational culture and employee motivation. On the one hand, the aim of this novel and original study is to highlight the importance of digital transformation for all, now and for the future generations, thus ensuring better and more complex ways to communicate and to connect. On the other hand, the objective of this up-to-date and eye-opening chapter is to display the trends that come to fuel digital transformation in order to create new business processes and develop new cultural paths, thus accentuating customers' experiences, diversifying market requirements, and intensifying the need for better organizational security.

DOI: 10.4018/978-1-6684-7499-0.ch008

INTRODUCTION

The United Nations Environment Programme (UNEP) pointed out in document addressing the topic of "Digital Transformation (DT)" (2022) the potential that digital technology and digital products display in our society in terms of accelerating innovation, fostering development, and supporting sustainability (United Nations Environment Programme (UNEP), 2022a). In the same vein with the aforementioned ideas, the United Nations Environment Programme (UNEP) highlighted the importance of connecting the advantages of the new technologies with three "key action areas – climate, nature and pollution", being able in this way to find the right solutions capable to ensure the success of the Sustainable Development Goals (SDGs) for all individuals and for all nations, during present days and in the future (United Nations Environment Programme (UNEP), 2022a). Hence, the United Nations Environment Programme (UNEP) brought to the attention impressive figures capable to show the immense potential that the digital transformation brought in terms of turning the Sustainable Development Goals (SDGs) closer to reality than ever before, as follows: first of all, according to specialists, digital transformation has the capacity to reduce "Carbon dioxide emissions by at least 20%"; second of all, according to specialists, digital transformation has the possibility to reduce "the use of natural resources in products by 90%"; and third of all, according to specialists, digital transformation has the power to reduce waste and detoxify "supply chains by a factor of 10-100X" (United Nations Environment Programme (UNEP), 2022a).

Even though themes such as digital transformation, organizational change, organizational culture, employees' motivation, and Sustainable Development Goals (SDGs) are approached by specialists at a constant level, there are always new angles to the same problems that are waiting to be presented and improved solutions to the same challenges that are waiting to be uncovered. Besides this, the vast nature of studies that address these topics, creates room for new analysis, debates, and discussions, since these are very demanding times as a result of the COVID-19 pandemic and the COVID-19 crisis as well as of individuals and entities normal reluctance to everything that is new, bold, and out of the ordinary patterns with which humanity got used to until that very moment.

The novel and the original book chapter entitled "Digital Transformation Impact on Organizations' Culture and Employees' Motivation: Shaping the "New Normal" and Addressing Sustainable Development Goals" is part of the up-to-date trends and ingenious themes due to be unravelled in the new book entitled "Positive and Constructive Contributions for Sustainable Development Goals".

The main purpose of this highly challenging book chapter is to present the implications of digital transformation in a knowledge society profoundly dominated by the necessity to have fast access to information, in the new form imposed by the pressure to which both the COVID-19 pandemic and the COVID-19 crisis have subjected both the individuals and the entities worldwide. In this matter, the authors asked themselves the following key question (main research question MRQ): "Which are the dominant changes brought in our society by digital transformation as a result of the COVID-19 pandemic and the COVID-19 crisis?" (MRQ)

In continuation, several additional secondary research questions (SRQs) arise, due to the complex nature of digital transformation. These secondary research questions (SRQs) are displayed by the authors in the lines below, as follows:

Step 1: First of all, besides the main purpose already mentioned above, this book chapter seeks to present the theoretical background (the literature review, the most relevant studies) that constitutes the foundation of the concept "digital transformation", which turned out to be one of the most demanding ones in the society individuals currently live in, in particular, due to its complex nature. In general lines, the theoretical background (the literature review, the most relevant studies) tackle several aspects surrounding the concept "digital transformation", namely: offering complex definitions and displaying possible meanings of this term; stating the role and the importance of digital transformation in the Digital Age; bringing examples of ways in which digital transformation in the Digital Age helps the achievement of the Sustainable Development Goals (SDGs). Under these circumstances, the authors asked themselves the following complex secondary question (first secondary research question SRQ1): "What does digital transformation represent in our knowledge society in terms of concept, role, and importance?" (SRQ1)

Step 2: Second of all, this book chapter intends to shed a new light on the manner in which individuals and organizations chose to embrace digital transformation, since it is common knowledge that everything that is new and more demanding in an activity, task, or problem generates, in most cases, reluctance and scepticism at a first glance. In this matter, the authors' intention is to acknowledge in this book chapter both the advantages and the disadvantages of digital transformation, as well as both the opportunities and the threats of digital transformation. Nevertheless, the authors will focus in this current scientific work on the benefits of digital transformation as well as on the advantages of digital transformation, since they strongly believe the following issues: on the one hand, that advancement without change is not realistic in a world continually willing to brake new grounds, grow faster and more powerful; and, also, on the other hand, that the United Nations' (UN) desiderate to achieve the Sustainable Development Goals (SDGs) is not feasible without the involvement of substantial inputs derived from development, education, information, innovation, intellectual capital (IC), knowledge, research, and transfer of technology through common international commitment and global projects. Hence, the authors asked themselves the following complex secondary question (second secondary research question SRQ2): "Which are the principal benefits and opportunities offered by digital transformation due to facilitate the accomplishment of the targets tackled by the Sustainable Development Goals (SDGs)?" (SRQ2)

This current section represented by the "Introduction" which is responsible for describing the importance of the topic chosen for the analysis as well as the objectives targeted for exploration, is followed by the "Background" section which intends to present the literature review on the theme, focusing on tackling the most relevant notions. In addition, the "Main focus of the chapter" makes an in-depth analysis on the digital transformation impact on organizations' culture and employees' motivation, bringing to the attention the implications of shaping the "New Normal" and addressing the Sustainable Development Goals (SDGs) have for the society as a result of the COVID-19 pandemic and the COVID-19 crisis. The sections that come to follow are: the "Discussion and synthesis of results", which presents the main findings of the authors,; the "Solutions and recommendations", which show the manner in which digital transformation, organizational change, organizational culture, employees' motivation, and Sustainable Development Goals (SDGs) interrelate and bring benefits to both individuals and entities; the "Future research directions", which tackle potential areas due to be explored in the near future starting from the results, the solutions, and the recommendations presented in this book chapter; the "Conclusion", which offers a new and a broad perspective on the opportunities as well as the threats that the digitalization process brought to the entities; the "References", which address the most recent studies in the filed in order to be able to cover, in the best way possible, the topic under analysis; and the "Key terms and definitions", which come to support the "Background" section, pointing out to the most relevant concepts that make this current book chapter so different and so special.

BACKGROUND

The background section of this book chapter centres on the theoretical background (the literature review, the most relevant studies) that constitute the foundation of the concept "digital transformation", in order to provide to this current scientific work on "Digital Transformation Impact on Organizations' Culture and Employees' Motivation: Shaping the "New Normal" and Addressing Sustainable Development Goals" the opportunity to paint the adequate picture that concepts such as business, knowledge, human resources (HR), innovation, intangible assets (IA), intellectual capital (IC), Sustainable Development Goals (SDGs), Digitalization, Global Economic Environment (GEE), organizational culture, and COVID-19, ought to bring to the new book entitled "Positive and Constructive Contributions for Sustainable Development Goals".

This section provides responses to the authors following complex secondary question (first secondary research question SRQ1): "What does digital transformation represent in our knowledge society in terms of concept, role, and importance?" (SRQ1)

The first concept due to be analysed is "digital revolution", based on the fact that the United Nations Environment Assembly of the United Nations Environment Programme (UNEP) considers this notion crucial both for people and for the planet, being strongly responsible for the well-being and for the future of the humankind (United Nations Environment Programme (UNEP), 2021). The document entitled "For people and planet: the United Nations Environment Programme strategy for 2022–2025 to tackle climate change, loss of nature and pollution" provides a wide presentation of "digital revolution", on the one hand, regarding it "as a strategic asset for more inclusive, transparent and innovative outcomes" and, on the other hand, considering it a requirement to which both individuals and entities must learn to adapt in order to cope better with "environmental goals and commitments under international agreements" (United Nations Environment Programme (UNEP), 2021, p.5). The digital revolution started, according to specialists, long before the COVID-19 pandemic and the COVID-19 crisis and could represent the catalysts for the promoting and for fostering the Sustainable Development Goals (SDGs) – as acknowledged, "the digital revolution helps deliver, not hinder, the environmental dimension of the 2030 Agenda" (United Nations Environment Programme (UNEP), 2021, p.8).

In addition, the second concept due to be analysed is "digital transformation(s)", with the specific argument that by "accelerating systemic interventions that engage the financial and economic actors with an impact on the environment, while leveraging the power of digital technologies, to scale up environmental sustainability" the representatives of the United Nations Environment Programme (UNEP) believe that great success will be achieved with the Sustainable Development Goals (SDGs) (United Nations Environment Programme (UNEP), 2021, pp.5-6). In this matter, the digital transformation(s) require access to the best instruments, techniques, and technologies capable to enhance performance and productivity, making sure that the environment is well protected and individuals are not subjected to harm (Popescu, 2020a, 2020b).

Moving forward, the third concept due to be presented is "organization culture", which is responsible for reflecting the values of entities and pointing out the way in which the entities are capable to leave their positive and constructive mark in the society, supporting well-being and sustainability (United Nations Environment Programme (UNEP), 2022b). At an ideal level, the culture of organizations should embrace the environmental and the sustainability norms, aligning to the prerequisites of the new global digital economy as well as to the Sustainable Development Goals (SDGs), learning to support the "sustainable digital ecosystem for the Planet", healthier consumer behaviours and responsible markets, and strengthening "digital literacy, innovation" and good governance (United Nations Environment Programme (UNEP), 2022b).

Another key concept – the fourth one on our valuable list of notions due to be considered for a thorough analysis, that ought to be brought into discussion is "employees' motivation". There are numerous ways capable to motivate the employees, but the Digital Age tends to bring new challenges and to impose new changes for individuals and for organizations which might turn out to be difficult to cope with under certain circumstances (United Nations Environment Programme (UNEP), 2022c). In this matter, an in-depth study on "The digital age: Implications of automation, digitisation and platforms for work and employment, Challenges and prospects in the EU series", belonging to the Publications Office of the European Union, in Luxembourg, mentions "that digitalisation in EU establishments coincides with innovation, internationalisation and job creation" (Eurofound, 2021, p.1). Hence, individuals should be determined to embrace the benefits of the digital age, mainly due to the new possibilities in terms of employment, with the specific mention that "digital technologies are reaching a high level of sophistication and affordability, and are therefore becoming more and more central to work management systems", offering individuals the opportunity to expend their job interests but, in the same time, showing that they ought to become more prepared in order to be able to cope with the new techniques and technologies that arise at a rapid scale (Eurofound, 2021, p.1). A highly interesting exploratory study entitled "Public Employee Motivation in EU Central and Federal Public Administrations. An Exploratory Approach", stress the fact that the knowledge society brought severe changes in the employees' perception towards their job and the motivations that accompany the job requirements, as follows: motivation accompanies all human activities, is subjective, and may become subject to interpretation, since individuals constantly find themselves in changing and demanding situations (Directorate General for Administration and Public Employment and Department for International Relations and Communication, 2021, pp.4-5); the employees belonging to the public sector are more inclined to perform their work based on altruistic and intrinsic reasons, while compared to the employees belonging to the private sector (Directorate General for Administration and Public Employment and Department for International Relations and Communication, 2021, pp.7-8); the employees' well-being is vital in order to ensure harmony and unity at work, and preserving a healthy working environment should be the responsibility of all the managers and all the employees alike (Directorate General for Administration and Public Employment and Department for International Relations and Communication, 2021, pp.12-17); the long term success of any organization depends on the satisfaction that employees feel, and a good manner to keep the employees satisfied in the Digital Era is to find solutions to make them feel important, needed, and up-to-date with the latest technologies specific to their job requirements (Directorate General for Administration and Public Employment and Department for International Relations and Communication, 2021, pp.12-16); and, also, digitalization and artificial intelligence – which are responsible for creating digital transformation(s) in our society, should facilitate the implementation of those methods that can aid our society become better, more centred on doing good, and more inclined to act sustainably (Directorate General for Administration and Public Employment and Department for International Relations and Communication, 2021, p.5) (see, in this matter, Figure 1. Acting Responsibly in Achievement of the Sustainable Development Goals (SDGs) in the Digital Era).

In the end, the fifth concept that needs to be brought to the attention is represented by the Sustainable Development Goals (SDGs). According to the Eurostat study on "Sustainable development in the European Union: Monitoring report on progress towards the SDGs in an EU context", Sustainable Development (SD) is positioned by specialists for several years by now "at the heart of European policy-making",

Figure 1. Acting Responsibly in Achievement of the Sustainable Development Goals (SDGs) in the Digital Era. Source: the authors, based on the sources highlighted in the references section of this book chapter

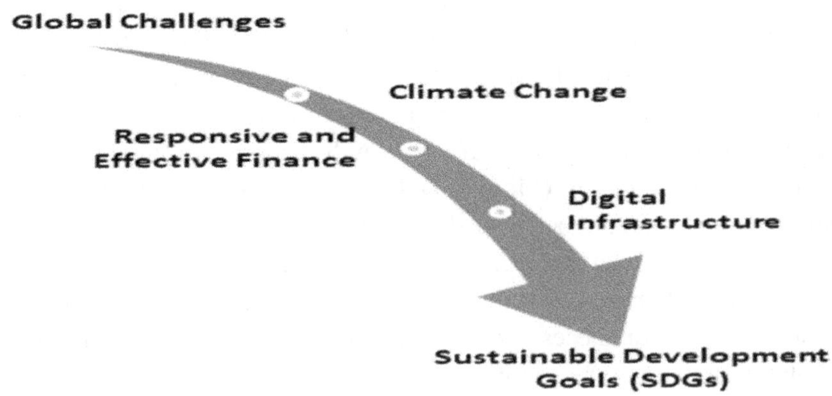

as follows: first of all, Sustainable Development (SD) may be encountered in renown European Treaties, being responsible for showing the individuals and the organizations the urgent necessity to create a constructive approach on the Sustainable Development Goals (SDGs), with accent on responsible actions concerning the well-being of people and the heath of the planet (Eurostat, 2021, p.9);: first of all, Sustainable Development (SD) may be discovered at the core of numerous "key projects, sectorial policies and initiatives" that seek to turn into reality the Sustainable Development Goals (SDGs), with great concern towards the future of the next generations, their capacity to enjoy life in a responsible manner and their need to be part of healthy ecosystems (Eurostat, 2021, p.9); third of all, Sustainable Development (SD) may be seen as an integrating part of all progress reports that address the Sustainable Development Goals (SDGs), since sustainability provides a different path towards the achievement of several international targets that address no poverty, good heath, well-being, happiness, prosperity, peace, sustainable cities, and responsible ways of consumption and of production (Eurostat, 2021, pp.10-12).

The next section is represented by the "Main focus of the chapter". In this section the authors provide an in-depth analysis on the place of digital transformation in our knowledge society based on the key implications derived from its role and importance. Also, in this section the authors offer numerous examples of good practices in terms of the implications of digital transformation that are intended to connect the benefits of digitalization with the Sustainable Development Goals (SDGs).

MAIN FOCUS OF THE CHAPTER

This current section represented by the "Main focus of the chapter" has the purpose of offering answers to the authors following complex secondary question (second secondary research question SRQ2): "Which are the principal benefits and opportunities offered by digital transformation due to facilitate the accomplishment of the targets tackled by the Sustainable Development Goals (SDGs)?" (SRQ2).

In the section "Scenario Thinking: A Glimpse into the Future of Digital Transformation in the EU", the issue number nine part of Monitor Deloitte encourages individuals to embrace the newest trends that have occurred in the society as part of the digital transformations and the digital revolution, stating that this is a global phenomenon that is currently happening, creating a new reality that can only be accepted as such, even though its effects are not yet known at their full extent in the political and in the economic areas (Monitor Deloitte, 2019, pp.4-5). What is more, the same document notes several key questions that specialists need to find answers to, such as, for instance: Which will be the future of technological developments?; Who will be responsible for driving these technological developments?; How can be the digital space be governed by laws, regulations, in order to better protect individuals and society?; and, with reference to Artificial Intelligence (AI), How will the interaction between human beings and machines will look like on the long term? (Monitor Deloitte, 2019, pp.4-5). Furthermore, in the same vein with the aforementioned aspects, reference is made to "alternative worlds", presenting different interesting and challenging scenarios for development, such as: "Scenario 1: EUtopia"; "Scenario 2: EUsed"; "Scenario 3: EUSSR"; and "Scenario 4: EUniformity" (Monitor Deloitte, 2019, pp.4-5; Deloitte, 2022).

Specialists worldwide show the necessity of connecting the benefits of the digital transformations and the digital revolution with the opportunities found in the Sustainable Development Goals (SDGs), as follows: first of all, by linking these two concepts, numerous opportunities arise at all levels and in all domains, which facilitates individuals' access to better and more sustainable lives, in accordance with the newest and more sophisticated trends in the field (Digital Europe, 2022); and second of all, by connecting these two notions, unlimited chances to have "a stronger digital industrial Europe" will come to life, since the digital transformations, the digital revolution and the Sustainable Development Goals (SDGs) could become the main advantages of the society these days, targeting healthy and prosperous lives, sustainable development and economic growth, and sustainable wealth (Digital Europe, 2022).

According to the "European Investment Bank (EIB) Investment Survey", besides the alarming side-effects of the coronavirus crisis, there were several opportunities that were offered both to people and to society as a result of the events surrounding this unprecedented situation, namely: first of all, the coronavirus crisis offered the opportunity to enhance the digital transformation of countries worldwide, bringing, one way or another, individuals and entities closer and forcing them to cooperate in order to survive (European Investment Bank (EIB), 2022); second of all, the coronavirus crisis showed the fact through innovation and research the implementation of digital technologies can be accelerated, thus offering a wider range of advantages to lead prosperous lives than ever before in the history of mankind (European Investment Bank (EIB), 2022); third of all, the coronavirus crisis offered a new perspective regarding the benefits of digital technologies, namely the fact that with the aid of them businesses can become more productive and grow faster, depending on their willingness to support invitation and accelerate digitalisation (European Investment Bank (EIB), 2022); and fourth of all, the coronavirus crisis demonstrated that the disruptions encountered in the society may either continue to lead to the digital divide in Europe, in particular, and in the world, in general, thus generating "a digital dilemma" or may determine individuals to act more responsible and more sustainable, promoting better and more assiduous the Sustainable Development Goals (SDGs) (European Investment Bank (EIB), 2022) (see, in this matter, Figure 2. Cybersecurity Governance and the Sustainable Development Goals (SDGs) in the Digital Era – Facing the Challenges of the New Strategic Business Priorities).

The members of the European Commission presented in their most recent reports valuable statistical data on the growth potential of Europe as a result of the implementation of the newest digital transformations. In this matter, the members of the European Commission feel there is a tremendous growth potential at the level of all European countries, pointing out to the best practices that should be followed by all Member States in terms of implementing the newest digital transformations, since organizations that foster these technologies seem to perform ten times better than the their competitors (European

Figure 2. Cybersecurity Governance and the Sustainable Development Goals (SDGs) in the Digital Era – Facing the Challenges of the New Strategic Business Priorities. Source: the authors, based on the sources highlighted in the references section of this book chapter

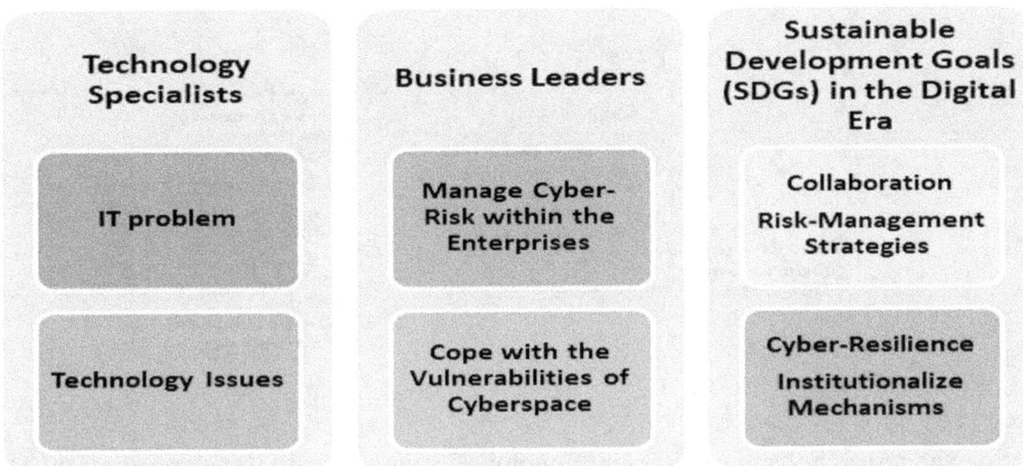

Commission, 2022, p.3). Additionally, the digital single market ought to receive continuous support to accelerate economic growth, since the job creation process could depend on this aid and the cost of administrating the businesses could be significantly lowered (European Commission, 2022, p.3). Also, the internet economy is in change with changing the lives of individuals in all areas, mainly targeting the manner in which individuals communicate, live, work, and play (European Commission, 2022, p.3).

Moreover, the Organization for Economic Cooperation and Development (OECD) points out that the international co-operation in the Digital Era is necessary in order to help the development of the digital economy since it offers timeless perspectives in terms of becoming more sustainably developed, taking international initiatives at a multilateral level, and exploring the possibility to build a regional digital market with unique characterises (Organization for Economic Cooperation and Development (OECD), 2020a) (see, in this matter, Figure 3. Focusing on Responsible and Secure Innovation in the Digital Era).

Furthermore, the Digital Era has visible implications on the education system, affecting the educational processes in terms of the learning and the evaluation process (Organization for Economic Cooperation and Development (OECD), 2020b). In this matter, the Organization for Economic Cooperation and Development (OECD) displayed a great concern, in particular, for the case of education at early stages of life, in the context in which digital transformations are responsible for making young individuals better prepared for the future, offering them the possibility to become more skilful in terms of the new digital technologies (Organization for Economic Cooperation and Development (OECD), 2020b). Nevertheless, specialists determined that individuals are more likely to feel the inequalities that exist in the society through the advancement of digitalization, since the education system had to adapt lately to the growing need to learn and be evaluated on-line, to communicate on-line, and be part of on-line different activities and common tasks (Organization for Economic Cooperation and Development (OECD), 2020b).

Another area of interest while addressing the implications of the Digital Era is represented by countries' health system, which relies on robust heath system management and unlimited benefits offered

Figure 3. Focusing on Responsible and Secure Innovation in the Digital Era. Source: the authors, based on the sources highlighted in the references section of this book chapter

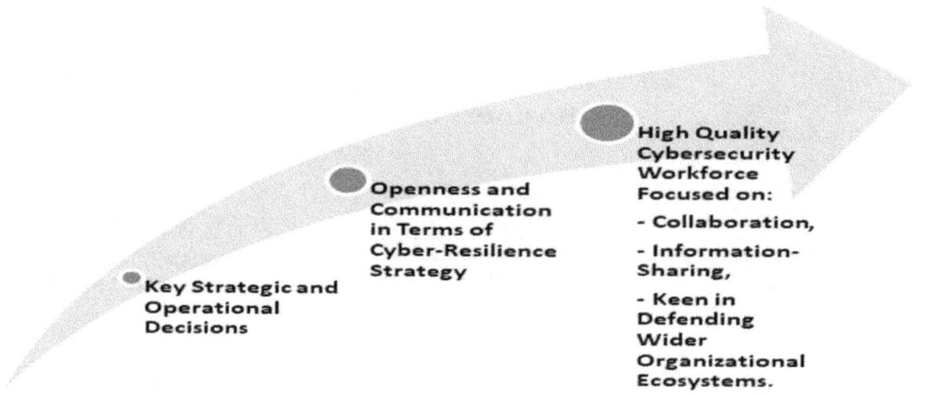

by innovation and research (Organization for Economic Cooperation and Development (OECD), 2022; Luque & Herrero-García, 2019; Luque, 2021).

All in all, the Digital Era has brought through its digital transformations important changes in our society, shedding a new light on our economies, education and health systems, public and private services, and business world.

Nowadays, digital transformation depends on the market's capacity to attract new technology and reflects the clients' availability to cope with the most recent techniques and instruments that technology has to offer (International Business Machines Corporation (IBM), 2022). Even though digital transformation shows individuals' and businesses' capacity to adapt in a specific rhythm to novel technology, it is highly important to see the links between the way in which technology fuels development centring on the employees experiences, perceptions and satisfaction, based on the principle known as "digital-first customer" (International Business Machines Corporation (IBM), 2022).

Also, digital transformation implicates generating core changes at the level of businesses, in order to create more effective and more efficient business processes, thus enabling sustainable development (SD) as well as creating new values capable to support better employees' needs and producers' requirements (Accenture, 2022).

The World Economic Forum (WEF) mentioned in the "Digital Transformation Initiative (DTI)" which was launched in the year 2015 the fact that the impact of digitalization on individuals activities, on the businesses and on the society will become more and more substantial over the next years based on specialists belief that technologies will offer, in time, to our society new opportunities to act and to think in a more sustainable manner, seeking abundance, well-being, and prosperity (World Economic Forum (WEF), 2022a). In this matter, there are several aspects of crucial importance due to be considered, as follows (World Economic Forum (WEF), 2022a):

- **Digital Transformation (DT):** Represents an optimum solution to cope better with the requirements of the new techniques and technologies, based on people's necessity to unlock important levels of abundance and prosperity (World Economic Forum (WEF), 2022a).
    - It has the capacity to offer advantages for individuals, businesses, and society by:

        - Offering new perspectives in terms of providing efficient work.
        - Showing new opportunities in terms of using technology and specific instruments (machines), rather than depending on physical labour.
        - Fostering sustainability for a better future for all, in accordance with the desideratum to preserve nature and life on Earth.
    - It brings new challenges in terms of developing and learning opportunities and requirements, thus determining businesses to grow at a faster pace and individuals to become more inclined to perfect themselves, be more educated, and become more skilful.
- **Digital Consumption (DC):** These days, it has become very difficult for businesses to keep up with consumers' expectations, since the benefits of digitalization have determined individuals to have more sophisticated tastes (World Economic Forum (WEF), 2022b). In this matter, entities have to constantly adapt their products to the desires of their clients and find solutions to attract more customers in order to cope with the growing competition on the marketplace (World Economic Forum (WEF), 2022b).
- **Digital Value (DV):** In continuation, the concept of "Digital Value (DV)" comes to support the two notions analysed in the lines above by supporting individuals' needs of adapting to the knowledge society, based on the fact that possessing a certain value is extremely important in all areas, especially when it comes to information, intellectual assets (IA), intellectual capital (IC), and intellectual property (IP) (World Economic Forum (WEF), 2022c). In other words, providing digital value (DV) means offering security in terms of a better future for all and implicates explaining the benefits of digitalization to people in order to become connected to the real needs of the society we live in these days (World Economic Forum (WEF), 2022c).

Digital transformation (DT) also implicates helping businesses to move forward by creating superior goods and by offering better services to the customers, since digitalization determined individuals to become more selective when it comes to their purchasing expectations and values (Oracle, 2022). In this matter, some well-known international companies recommend several areas in order to generate value with the aid of digital transformation (DT), namely: (a) by having a certain value and accompany it with a specific strategy; (b) by being the adept of a specific organizational culture capable to embrace specific values that are reflected in an adequate manner in the strategy declared; (c) by trying to see the unique qualities and the great potential offered by digitalization in the Digital Era; and (d) by trying to create new capabilities, competencies, and skills that have the power to reflect the benefits and the advantages of digitalization (Microsoft, 2022).

DISCUSSION AND SYNTHESIS OF RESULTS

The discussion and synthesis of results section of this book chapter presents the most important findings regarding the theme chosen for examination by the authors.

In this matter, the authors would like to point out the fact that measuring well-being in the digital age is of great importance and starts from understanding that change is inevitable and should be embraced based on the benefits and the advantages that it has to offer.

What is more, the authors would like to stress the fact that without policies capable to regulate all the domains affected by the digital age, our society will enter little by little in collapse. Hence, the risks specific to the digital age should be acknowledged and thoroughly documented, in order to help businesses address better the markets' openness and to aid individuals cope with innovation and embrace new technologies.

Hence, even though there are numerous advantages when it comes to addressing digital transformation (DT), digital consumption (DC), and digital value (DV), there are also several risks and threats that ought to be considered, as follows (Deloitte, 2018; Hametner, 2022):

- One possible risk might be represented by the rapid pace with which technologies are advancing these days, which might generate inequalities in terms of individuals and businesses capacity to accept and embrace novel techniques and technologies (Deloitte, 2018; Hametner, 2022).
- Another possible risk might be represented by the fact that the traditional IT is easier to cope with and to manage, while the new technologies represented, for instance, by the robots, the internet of things (IoT), the artificial intelligence (AI), cloud computing, predictive analytics and blockchain are much more difficult to understand and require the assistance of specialized personnel (Deloitte, 2018).
- Also, another possible risk might be represented by the cybercrime and the risks that might be encountered around data privacy; both being very difficult to handle in today's globalized economy (Deloitte, 2018).

All in all, the World Economic Forum (WEF) pointed out in the article published recently on "The digital transformation of logistics: Threat and opportunity" the fact that technological advancement is necessary for the development of businesses all around the globe, but the benefits should always be measured in comparison to the risks, since the focus should be on the environment and on the people's right to live in decent and healthy conditions (World Economic Forum (WEF), 2022d). What is more, digital transformation (DT), digital consumption (DC), and digital value (DV) are accompanied by digital innovations (DI), which is connected with logistics – that might be highly developed when it comes to referring to the biggest and the best established players in a certain domain, but which might turn out to be at risk if the reference is to less known and reputed companies in that field (World Economic Forum (WEF), 2022d). Furthermore, automation and digitalization enhance productivity when it comes to referring to certain domains, such as, for instance to the manufacturing firms that depend on the power brought by the "new technological revolution" (World Economic Forum (WEF), 2022e; 2022g).

SOLUTIONS AND RECOMMENDATIONS

The solutions and recommendations section of this book chapter offers a new perspective on the digital transformation impact on organizations' culture and employees' motivation, based on the individuals and society's necessity of shaping the "New Normal" and addressing the Sustainable Development Goals (SDGs), thus becoming more inclined to work towards the accomplishment of positive and constructive contributions for Sustainable Development Goals (SDGs).

First of all, one solution and recommendation would be to promote in an equal manner both the benefits and the risks that accompany the digital transformation of our society, offering a vital set of rules due to be followed by individuals and by entities in order to unleash the potential of the new technologies in a safe manner.

Second of all, another solution and recommendation would be to accentuate the investments in education, research, and innovation through all means possible (projects, transfer of technology), since intellectual capital (IC) plays a vital role, as an intangible asset (IA), in all the fields and in all the parts of our economy and society.

FUTURE RESEARCH DIRECTIONS

The future research directions are numerous due to the fact that the topic currently chosen is very powerful and tends to offer great perspectives of analysis and research.

One possible future research direction could be represented by linking the acceleration of investments in education, research, and innovation with the benefits of accomplishing the Sustainable Development Goals (SDGs) with the aid of digitalization.

Another possible future research direction could be represented by connecting the Sustainable Development Goals (SDGs) to Artificial Intelligence (AI), exploring, in particular, the doubts and the possible myths that accompany these vital concepts in our society.

CONCLUSION

In conclusion, innovation policies in the digital age are vital in a society striving to develop sustainably and to help individuals learn how to live healthy and prosperous.

Also, the digital age might lead to a digital divide – probably with great and irreversible consequences on all our lives and activities, unless the right measures are taken and the necessary support is provided to individuals and entities, in order to avoid the accentuation of inequalities in our society.

In continuation, the digital age should implicate, in turn, learning to become more flexible in terms of embracing new technologies – considering and avoiding the risks brought by the Digital Era, since innovation is the key to sustainability, to individuals' well-being, and to the success of the Sustainable Development Goals (SDGs).

ACKNOWLEDGMENT

This research received no specific grant from any funding agency in the public, commercial, or not-for-profit sectors. Author Contributions: Conceptualization, C.R.G.P. (Cristina Raluca Gh. Popescu) and A.L.G. (Arturo Luque González); methodology, C.R.G.P. and A.L.G.; software, C.R.G.P. and A.L.G.; validation, C.R.G.P. and A.L.G.; formal analysis, C.R.G.P. and A.L.G.; investigation, C.R.G.P. and A.L.G.; resources, C.R.G.P. and A.L.G.; data curation, C.R.G.P. and A.L.G.; writing—original draft preparation, C.R.G.P. and A.L.G.; writing—review and editing, C.R.G.P. and A.L.G.; visualization, C.R.G.P. and A.L.G.; supervision, C.R.G.P. and A.L.G.; project administration, C.R.G.P. and A.L.G.; funding acquisition, C.R.G.P. and A.L.G. All authors have equally contributed to the manuscript. All authors have read and agreed to the published version of the manuscript.

REFERENCES

Accenture. (2022). *Technology. Digital transformation. Understand digital transformation and how our insights can help drive business value*. Retrieved September 27, 2022, from https://www.accenture.com/us-en/insights/digital-transformation-index

Deloitte. (2018). *Managing Risk in Digital Transformation*. Retrieved September 27, 2022, from https://www2.deloitte.com/content/dam/Deloitte/za/Documents/risk/za_managing_risk_in_digital_transformation_112018.pdf

Deloitte. (2022). *Future of Digital Transformation in the European Union 2035*. Retrieved August 20, 2022, from https://www2.deloitte.com/de/de/pages/strategy/articles/future-of-digital-transformation-eu-2035.html

Digital Europe. (2022). *A stronger digital industrial Europe - Digital Transformation as its Focus*. Retrieved August 20, 2022, from https://www.digitaleurope.org/policies/a-stronger-digital-industrial-europe-digital-transformation-as-its-focus/

Directorate General for Administration and Public Employment and Department for International Relations and Communication. (2021). *Public Employee Motivation in EU Central and Federal Public Administrations. An Exploratory Approach*. Retrieved August 20, 2022, from https://www.eupan.eu/wp-content/uploads/2021/10/Motivation_study_2021.pdf

Eurofound. (2021). *The digital age: Implications of automation, digitisation and platforms for work and employment, Challenges and prospects in the EU series*. Publications Office of the European Union, Luxembourg. Retrieved August 20, 2022, from https://euagenda.eu/upload/publications/ef21007en.pdf

European Commission. (2022). *Digital Transformation of European Industry and Enterprises: Report and Recommendations of the Strategic Policy Forum on Digital Entrepreneurship*. Retrieved August 20, 2022, from http://www.eurasiancommission.org/ru/act/dmi/workgroup/materials/Pages/%D0%9F%D1%80%D0%BE%D0%BC%D1%8B%D1%88%D0%BB%D0%B5%D0%BD%D0%BD%D0%BE%D1%81%D1%82%D1%8C/%D0%95%D0%A1_%D0%A6%D0%B8%D1%84%D1%80%D0%BE%D0%B2%D0%B0%D1%8F%20%D1%82%D1%80%D0%B0%D0%BD%D1%81%D1%84%D0%BE%D1%80%D0%BC%D0%B0%D1%86%D0%B8%D1%8F%20%D0%BF%D1%80%D0%BE%D0%BC%D1%8B%D1%88%D0%BB%D0%B5%D0%BD%D0%BD%D0%BE%D1%81%D1%82%D0%B8_2016.pdf

European Investment Bank (EIB). (2022). *Digitalisation in Europe 2021-2022: Evidence from the EIB Investment Survey*. Retrieved August 20, 2022, from https://www.eib.org/attachments/publications/digitalisation_in_europe_2021_2022_en.pdf doi:10.2867/091152

Eurostat. (2021). *Sustainable development in the European Union: Monitoring report on progress towards the SDGs in an EU context*. European Union. Retrieved August 20, 2022, from https://ec.europa.eu/eurostat/documents/3217494/12878705/KS-03-21-096-EN-N.pdf doi:10.2785/636600

González, A. L., Alkorta, A. B., & Salcedo, J. L. (2022). The Social and Solidarity Economics, Public Policies, and Non-Monetary Economic Practices: The Case of Associative Firms in Loja, Ecuador. In J. Saiz-Alvarez (Ed.), *Handbook of Research on Emerging Business Models and the New World Economic Order* (pp. 242–266). IGI Global. doi:10.4018/978-1-7998-7689-2.ch012

Hametner, M. (2022). Economics without ecology: How the SDGs fail to align socioeconomic development with environmental sustainability. *Ecological Economics*, *199*, 107490. doi:10.1016/j.ecolecon.2022.107490

International Business Machines Corporation (IBM). (2022). *What is digital transformation?* Retrieved September 27, 2022, from https://www.ibm.com/topics/digital-transformation

Luque, A. (2021). Practicality, support or premeditated calculation in the digital age: The case of Ecuador. *Revista Venezolana De Gerencia, 26*(6), 29-46. https://www.produccioncientificaluz.org/index.php/rvg/article/view/37135 doi:10.52080/rvgluz.26.e6.3

Luque, A., & Herrero-García, N. (2019). How corporate social (ir)responsibility in the textile sector is defined, and its impact on ethical sustainability: An analysis of 133 concepts. *Corporate Social Responsibility and Environmental Management*, *26*(6), 1–22. doi:10.1002/csr.1747

Microsoft. (2022). *Focus on four areas to unlock value*. Retrieved September 20, 2022, from https://www.microsoft.com/en-us/industry/digital-transformation

Monitor Deloitte. (2019). *Digital Transformation in the EU 2035. A Glimpse into the Future*. Center for the Long View. Retrieved August 20, 2022, from https://www2.deloitte.com/content/dam/Deloitte/de/Documents/strategy/deloitte-future-of-digital-transformation-eu-2035.pdf

Oracle. (2022). *What is Digital Transformation?* Retrieved September 20, 2022, from https://www.oracle.com/cloud/digital-transformation/

Organization for Economic Cooperation and Development (OECD). (2019a). *Measuring the Digital Transformation. A Roadmap for the Future*. Retrieved August 20, 2022, from https://www.oecd-ilibrary.org/science-and-technology/measuring-the-digital-transformation_97dc0edb-en

Organization for Economic Cooperation and Development (OECD). (2019b). *Characterising innovation in the digital age*. Retrieved August 20, 2022, from https://www.oecd-ilibrary.org/science-and-technology/digital-innovation_2f5d36df-en

Organization for Economic Cooperation and Development (OECD). (2020a). *Chapter 5: The role of international co-operation in the digital age*. Retrieved August 20, 2022, from https://www.oecd-ilibrary.org/docserver/7d3929e1-en.pdf?expires=1663745432&id=id&accname=guest&checksum=4792067EFB409431E5D8B29BBABACC6B

Organization for Economic Cooperation and Development (OECD). (2020b). *Education in the Digital Age: Healthy and Happy Children*. Retrieved August 20, 2022, from https://www.oecd-ilibrary.org/sites/1209166a-en/index.html?itemId=/content/publication/1209166a-en

Organization for Economic Cooperation and Development (OECD). (2021). *OECD Report on Public Communication. The Global Context and the Way Forward*. Retrieved August 20, 2022, from https://www.oecd-ilibrary.org/governance/oecd-report-on-public-communication_f68023c0-en

Organization for Economic Cooperation and Development (OECD). (2022). *Health Data Governance for the Digital Age. Implementing the OECD Recommendation on Health Data Governance.* Retrieved August 20, 2022, from https://www.oecd-ilibrary.org/social-issues-migration-health/health-data-governance-for-the-digital-age_68b60796-en

Popescu, C. R. G. (2020a). Developing a Model for Entrepreneurship Competencies: Innovation, Knowledge Management, and Intellectual Capital – Success Competences for Building Inclusive Entrepreneurship and Organizational Performance. In J. Šebestová (Ed.), *Developing Entrepreneurial Competencies for Start-Ups and Small Business* (pp. 1–22). IGI Global. doi:10.4018/978-1-7998-2714-6.ch001

Popescu, C. R. G. (2020b). Analyzing the Impact of Green Marketing Strategies on the Financial and Non-Financial Performance of Organizations: The Intellectual Capital Factor. In V. Naidoo & R. Verma (Eds.), *Green Marketing as a Positive Driver Toward Business Sustainability* (pp. 186–218). IGI Global. doi:10.4018/978-1-5225-9558-8.ch008

United Nations Environment Programme (UNEP). (2021). *For people and planet: the United Nations Environment Programme strategy for 2022–2025 to tackle climate change, loss of nature and pollution.* United Nations Environment Assembly of the United Nations Environment Programme. Retrieved August 20, 2022, from https://wedocs.unep.org/bitstream/handle/20.500.11822/35162/Doc3%20Reve1%20EnglishK2100501.pdf?sequence=1&isAllowed=y

United Nations Environment Programme (UNEP). (2022a). *Digital Transformation.* Retrieved August 20, 2022, from https://www.unep.org/explore-topics/technology/what-we-do/digital-transformation

United Nations Environment Programme (UNEP). (2022b). *What is UNEP's ambition?* Retrieved August 20, 2022, from https://www.unep.org/explore-topics/technology/what-we-do/digital-transformation/what-uneps-ambition

United Nations Environment Programme (UNEP). (2022c). *Digital Transformation: Becoming an Innovative, Agile and Collaborative Organization, Fit for Purpose in the Digital Age - 2022 Version 1.0.* Retrieved August 20, 2022, from https://www.unep.org/resources/policy-and-strategy/digital-transformation-becoming-innovative-agile-and-collaborative

World Economic Forum (WEF). (2022a). *Digital Transformation Initiative (DTI).* Retrieved September 20, 2022, from https://reports.weforum.org/digital-transformation/

World Economic Forum (WEF). (2022b). *Digital Consumption.* Retrieved September 20, 2022, from https://reports.weforum.org/digital-transformation/digital-consumption/

World Economic Forum (WEF). (2022c). *Introducing Digital Value to Society.* Retrieved September 20, 2022, from https://reports.weforum.org/digital-transformation/unlocking-trapped-value/?doing_wp_cron=1664281325.0679690837860107421875

World Economic Forum (WEF). (2022d). *The digital transformation of logistics: Threat and opportunity.* Retrieved September 20, 2022, from https://reports.weforum.org/digital-transformation/the-digital-transformation-of-logistics-threat-and-opportunity/

World Economic Forum (WEF). (2022e). *The Digital Transformation Of Business. Automation can empower workers and enhance productivity. Here's how.* Retrieved September 20, 2022, from https://www.weforum.org/agenda/2022/09/how-to-transform-your-company-with-lean-augmentation-regardless-of-size/

World Economic Forum (WEF). (2022f). *Infrastructure. Digital public infrastructure can help solve global challenges. This is how to implement it.* Retrieved September 20, 2022, from https://www.weforum.org/agenda/2022/09/6-first-principles-for-making-digital-public-infrastructure-impactful/

World Economic Forum (WEF). (2022g). *Cybersecurity. Cybersecurity: 5 ways to make your business more cyber secure.* Retrieved September 20, 2022, from https://www.weforum.org/agenda/2022/09/cybersecurity-business-cyber-secure/

KEY TERMS AND DEFINITIONS

Digital Infrastructure: The global challenges have determined leaders and governments worldwide to pay a particular attention to the digital infrastructure (DI) development, since there are many vital aspects to be considered in this regard, such as: (a) the climate change implicates finding solutions capable to offer effective and responsible answers when it comes to public finance management, since countries have to focus on helping the ecosystems regenerate (World Economic Forum (WEF), 2022f); and (b) the climate change implicates finding solutions capable to offer effective and responsible answers when it comes to inclusive digital infrastructure (DI), since besides seeking modern digital systems, the focus should be on creating inclusive solutions aiming to support innovation with care for nature and global communities (World Economic Forum (WEF), 2022f).

Economic Globalization: "This is a phenomenon in expansion that causes profound changes on the world stage. It revolves around trade, the flow of investment, financial capital, division of labour and specialization. The concept is not limited only to economic variables since its effects extend to individuals, society to the state. Developing countries are experiencing stagnation in the face of their inability to cope with globalization, which is compounded by poor management of their financial markets, leading to an increase in the income inequality gap. Economic globalization brings with it the mobilization of goods and capital, reduces distance between borders and energizes international trade with some alterations to sovereignty" (González et al., 2022).

Empowerment as a Result of the New Technological Revolution: The Digital Age implicates collaborative business processes and practices, and businesses increase in growth and productivity depends on entities capacity to motivate individuals to work more and become more dedicated to the goals of the companies; since people are very difficult to manage due to the particular nature of human beings, the New Technological Revolution offered companies the opportunity to use machines instead of individuals in certain areas, which gave employees the chance to leave the routine activities to specific technologies and focus on other tasks that tend to fulfil better expectations (World Economic Forum (WEF), 2022e).

Innovation in the Digital Age: Innovation represents the key for development, yet the development should be done sustainably in order to generate well-being and prosperity during present times as well as in the future; the digital age placed innovation among its top priorities, due to the fact that the advancement of the new technologies depend on investments in research activities (Organization for Economic Cooperation and Development (OECD), 2019b).

Resilience: "Transformations within a complex system related to the capacity for self-organization while maintaining internal structure, together with the ability to create adaptive responses, generate knowledge, experience, and learning. Resilience and sustainability are directly related to changes within societies, economies, and the human system as a whole. The transformation of systems is inevitable since it allows systems to strengthen" (González et al., 2022).

Sustainability: These days, sustainability refers to numerous areas being given uncountable definitions, but when it comes to addressing digital transformation it embodies the instruments and the technologies' capacity to create an adequate environment that should reflect care for employees, comfortable working environment, circular economy, water conservation systems, smart workstations, and systems development in accordance to nature (World Economic Forum (WEF), 2022e).

Sustainable Development Goals (SDGs): The great concern of leaders, managers, and researchers towards reaching the Sustainable Development Goals (SDGs) represents the result of the society's need to cope better with its challenges, especially in the new context generated by the COVID-19 pandemic and the COVID-19 crisis (Organization for Economic Cooperation and Development (OECD), 2021).

Well-Being in the Digital Age: The digital age has promoted the importance of individuals and entities to communicate, yet at all times the target of these forms of connectivity tend to address healthier ways to learn, live, work, and play; even though the digital age has brought an enormous potential to become more closer to one another, individuals should become more aware of the dangers of the digital age and should learn to cope better with the existing treats, focusing on healthy ways of living, their well-being, and sustainability in terms of the development of the society (Organization for Economic Cooperation and Development (OECD), 2019a).

Chapter 9
Corporate Social Responsibility: A Comprehensive Analysis

Javier Martínez Falcó
https://orcid.org/0000-0001-9004-5816
University of Alicante, Spain

Bartolomé Marco-Lajara
https://orcid.org/0000-0001-8811-9118
University of Alicante, Spain

Patrocinio Zaragoza-Sáez
University of Alicante, Spain

ABSTRACT

Corporate social responsibility (CSR) refers to a business approach that takes into account economic, environmental, and social issues in a balanced, holistic, and long-term manner for the benefit of current and future stakeholders. However, when did the term emerge? How has it evolved since its inception? Under what theoretical perspectives has it been approached? Through a narrative review of the literature, the research addresses these research questions to bring clarity to the field of study. The results of the research show that the term emerged in the 1950s, having evolved to include the economic, social, and environmental dimensions and that there are five motivations that drive its implementation: (1) alignment of interests between agents and principal, (2) satisfaction of stakeholder demands, (3) compliance with the institutional context, (4) obtaining a competitive advantage, and (5) maintaining congruence between the objectives of society and the objectives of the organization.

INTRODUCTION

Corporate Social Responsibility (CSR) refers to the voluntary commitment of the organization to behave fairly and appropriately with the environment in which it operates (Velte, 2021). Therefore, organiza-

DOI: 10.4018/978-1-6684-7499-0.ch009

tions exercise their economic, social and environmental responsibility when they meet the demands of the different stakeholders involved in the operation of the organization (Lindgreen & Swaen, 2010).

There are ten main reasons why organizations implement CSR programs: (1) to improve corporate image and reputation, (2) to prevent risks, (3) to attract and retain talent, (4) to improve the working environment and productivity, (5) to foster innovation, (6) to improve energy efficiency, (7) to bring advantages in attracting financing, (8) to increase consumer and customer loyalty, (9) to facilitate obtaining awards and recognition, and (10) to place the company in the preference for public contracting and bidding.

We are currently experiencing what experts refer to as the reputation economy. In markets where everything is copied, intangibles - brand and reputation - have become fundamental variables for differentiation. Reputation building has also been transformed in recent times. The company is still the main actor, but no longer the only one (Flammer & Luo, 2017). Today, the contributions and interactions of customers, employees, suppliers and other stakeholders play an essential role, which is why CSR plays a key role (Chernev & Blair, 2015).

CSR is also a very effective instrument to reduce the potential risks associated with the activities carried out by companies (Baxi & Ray, 2012). The creation of codes of ethics and conduct, the establishment of responsible standards in the selection of suppliers or the incorporation of environmental or human rights considerations throughout the value chain significantly reduce the likelihood of companies engaging in malpractice (Birch, 2017). By strengthening the control of a company's operations, it can minimize conflicts with the communities in which it operates, reduce complaints and legal proceedings, improve relations with customers, employees, trade unions, public administrations and other stakeholders, and drastically reduce the possibility of suffering risks such as negative publicity or boycotts of its products or services (Okafor et al., 2021).

Millennials will make up the bulk of the workforce of the future. According to forecasts, they will account for 75% of the workforce by 2023 (Ye et al., 2020). For millennials, work is not a burden, but an area of enjoyment and fulfilment. When they value a job, the economic factor loses weight to variables such as its suitability for their life project. They seek to join causes, prefer companies that are committed to society and the environment, and value environments that promote multiculturalism and diversity. In this scenario, CSR helps to design and offer innovative and attractive proposals for this new profile of 21st century workers (Duanmu et al., 2021). In addition to attracting and retaining talent, a good CSR strategy has very positive effects on the degree of satisfaction and commitment of employees to the company. The implementation of corporate volunteering programs offers many advantages. It improves employees' motivation, skills and self-esteem; it fosters pride in being part of the company and reinforces employees' involvement and commitment to the company. Proper diversity management has a positive impact on productivity and competitiveness, which increases the likelihood of finding more innovative and robust solutions (Glavas, 2016).

CSR encourages the development of innovative products and services. Dialogue with the different stakeholders, together with the search for solutions linked to sustainability and social impact objectives, encourages the development of innovative products that allow access to new market segments (Jeje, 2017). Moreover, the environmental objectives assumed by companies within the framework of their CSR actions usually include energy efficiency measures, recycling and other initiatives to reduce the consumption of natural resources (Shiu et al., 2017).

Responsible behavior implies the implementation of good governance, ethical and transparent practices that have a favorable impact on their credibility in the markets and improve their access to financing (Tiba et al., 2019). In addition to tax advantages, responsible companies reduce the risk of contingencies, thus offering an added value that increases the value of their shares and reinforces the confidence of real and potential investors (Kim et al., 2021). Consumers admire companies that value their employees, develop social projects, care for the environment and invest in anti-corruption efforts. Social responsibility is therefore an essential factor in ensuring consumer loyalty. This is a growing trend, taking into account the new consumer habits of the coming generations.

CSR seems to be gaining international importance. Its observance by companies conditions access to certain segments of the capital market and tends to influence the market value of shares. This is evidenced by the involvement of organizations such as the European Union (EU), the United Nations (UN) and the Organization for Economic Cooperation and Development (OECD), and the perception on the part of large institutional investors that CSR is a good indicator of the quality of corporate management and governance practices. In recent times, the debate on CSR has moved into the realm of public policy, especially the role to be played by public authorities in promoting the CSR philosophy. Many governments in the advanced economies have adopted formal policies for disseminating the corporate culture of CSR, on the understanding that it can favor the competitive advantages of companies in certain markets, channel their activities in emerging or developing countries, or provide access to certain segments of the capital market (Singh & Misra, 2021).

To a certain extent, the CSR philosophy is understood to be opposed to the philosophy of creating shareholder value, advocated by Friedman, as the ultimate goal of business activity (Sánchez-Torné et al., 2020). This conception of creating shareholder value is reductionist in comparison with the philosophy underlying the concept of CSR (stakeholder value), which sees the company as an organization called upon to play an active role in shaping society, whose mission should be to create value for stakeholders beyond the shareholder. This philosophy goes further: the creation of value for the various stakeholders results in greater value creation for the shareholder. Following the impact of the pathogen on all economic sectors worldwide, CSR and the fulfillment of the Sustainable Development Goals (SDGs) by organizations is becoming increasingly necessary to achieve economic, social and environmental well-being (Marco-Lajara et al., 2021a; Marco-Lajara et al., 2021b; Marco-Lajara et al., 2021c; Marco-Lajara et al., 2022a; Marco-Lajara et al., 2022b; Marco-Lajara et al., 2022c; Marco-Lajara et al., 2022d; Marco-Lajara et al., 2022e; Marco-Lajara et al., 2022f; Marco-Lajara et al., 2022g; Marco-Lajara et al., 2022h; Marco-Lajara et al., 2022i; Marco-Lajara et al., 2022j; Marco-Lajara et al., 2022k; Marco-Lajara et al., 2022l; Marco-Lajara et al., 2022m; Marco-Lajara et al., 2022n; Marco-Lajara et al., 2022o; Seva-Larrosa et al., 2022). The aim of this research is to learn about the historical evolution, conceptualisation and theoretical perspectives CSR has been analysed, given that its study has received little attention in the academic literature. In this way, the study provides insight into the beginnings and evolution of the discipline, the different ways in which CSR has been conceptualised, as well as the different arguments that exist to justify its implementation.

To achieve this objective, after this brief introduction, Section 2 presents the methodology followed in the study. Section 3 presents the results of the narrative review. Section 4 presents the main conclusions and, finally, Section 5 presents the limitations of the study, as well as future lines of research.

METHODOLOGY

In this research, a narrative literature review was carried out to analyze the historical evolution, conceptualization and theories under which CSR has been analyzed. The literature review is considered a detailed study that aims to gather information on a given topic through the analysis of published literature (Oliver, 2012).

The aim of the narrative review of the literature is to synthesize the fragmented knowledge of previous research on CSR. The research, therefore, presents a descriptive scope, given that there are no hypotheses to be contrasted, but rather the information collected is described and given meaning. Furthermore, the present review follows more flexible and less restrictive procedures than systematic reviews (Ferrari, 2015). Therefore, the present review does not intend to generalize the results obtained to the population (Tranfield et al., 2003), but to offer an interpretation of the literature that allows for a better understanding of the field of study of CSR. To conduct the literature review, the phases proposed by Wee & Banister (2016) were followed, which are: topic selection, source selection and reading, and topic writing. First, the selected topic is related to three axes: (1) historical evolution, (2) conceptualization and (3) theories that have addressed CSR. Second, manuals, readings, books, books, chapters and articles focused on the evolution and conceptualization of CSR were included for the research, excluding colloquium reports, seminars, doctoral dissertations and working papers. The time period of the publications covers the period from the beginnings of the concept of CSR in the 1950s to the present day, given that the aim of the research is to analyze all the perspectives under which CSR has been studied. Likewise, the Scopus and Web of Science databases were used to select the publications, as they are prestigious databases that contain articles published in high-impact journals, which ensures that the information obtained is accurate and of high value, legitimizing reliable results. A total of 115 academic papers were reviewed and read in depth, this is the scientific production that allowed us to reflect on the historical and conceptual evolution under which CSR has been analyzed. Thirdly, once the article and sources had been selected and the publications had been read, the bibliographic review was drafted.

RESULTS

Historical Evolution of CSR

Today's prevailing belief that companies should take responsibility for the society and the territory in which they operate is not new, as such convictions can be found several centuries ago (Carroll, 2008). However, it was not until the 1950s that the identification of the social responsibilities that organizations should have been first addressed in the academic literature, which is understood as the birth of the modern construct of CSR.

The post-World War II period is seen as a time of adaptation and changing attitudes towards the CSR debate, as well as a period characterized by few corporate actions that went beyond philanthropic activities (Carroll, 2008). The change in attitude towards corporate behavior came from the author Bowen (1953), who believed that the large corporations of the time concentrated a great deal of power, as their actions had a great impact on society. Consequently, according to this author, it was necessary to change the decision-making process of organizations to include considerations of the impact of their activities on society. Following Bowen's (1953) contribution, other authors addressed business behavior and its effect on the social context of the time. For example, in the book *Corporation Giving in a Free Society*, Eells (1956) argues that the large corporations of the time were not living up to their social responsibility. Similarly, in *A Moral Philosophy for Management*, Selekman (1959) explores the evolution of corporate moral responsibility as a response to the labor expectations of the time.

During the 1960s, academic contributions sought to respond to the problems and desires of the new society that was flourishing. In this regard, Davis (1960) argued that the social, economic and political changes of the time put added pressure on businessmen to re-examine their role in society and their social responsibility. He argued that organizations needed to take responsibility for the environment in which they operated, highlighting the positive relationship of social responsibility to the economic profitability of business (Davis, 1960; Carroll, 1999). Other influential authors of the time such as Frederick (1960), McGuire (1963) or Walton (1967) defended the same claims.

It is important to note that, although most authors began to take a position in favor of CSR, there were others who were skeptical of the concept. In particular Friedman (1962) considered that companies should limit themselves to profit maximization. Friedman (1970) elaborated on his position in the article. The social responsibility of business is to increase its profits, in which he considers CSR activities to be an inappropriate use of company resources as they result, according to the author, in an unjustified waste of money for the general social interest. In Friedman's (1962) words, "few trends could so thoroughly undermine the very foundations of our free society as the acceptance by businessmen of a social responsibility other than to make as much money for their shareholders as possible" (p. 1).

The 1970s saw the creation of some of the most relevant companies in terms of social responsibility, such as the Body Shop, founded in 1976 in the United Kingdom, and Ben and Jerry's, founded in 1978 in the United States. Whether in response to new social expectations, a new regulatory framework or their competitive strategies, the companies described above were two notable examples of organizations that began to formalize and integrate policies that addressed the social and public issues of an era characterized, according to Carroll (2015, p. 88), by "corporate social responsibility management". This led to the term CSR becoming increasingly popular, resulting in its indistinct use in various contexts (Votaw, 1973; Sethi, 1975).

The ambiguous use of the term CSR during the 1970s created uncertainty about its definition. In order to address this problem, in the late 1970s, Carroll (1979) proposed the first unified definition of CSR, defining it as the set of "economic, legal, ethical and discretionary expectations that society has of organizations at a given point in time" (p. 500). Although Carroll's (1979) approach to CSR corresponded to the debate on corporate behavior at the time, its relevance lies in the fact that his definition built on the work of other scholars to provide a clear and concise conceptualization that could be applicable in any context, unlike previous definitions (Frederick, 1960; Friedman, 1962; McGuire, 1963; Walton, 1967; Davis, 1973). Another relevant contribution of Carroll's (1979) conceptualization is that it does not consider ecological and social objectives as mutually exclusive trade-offs, but as an integral part of the business framework of social responsibility (Lee, 2008).

During the 1980s, the Reagan and Thatcher administrations introduced a new liberal doctrine characterized by reduced fiscal pressures on corporations (Feldstein, 2013; Wankel, 2008). As the role of governments in regulating corporate behavior was reduced, managers had to respond to different interest groups that continued to expect companies to meet the social expectations of the time. In particular, the reduction of the regulatory framework led scholars to consider business ethics and the operationalization of CSR as an appropriate response to various stakeholders involved in the organization, such as shareholders, employees and consumers (Carroll, 2008; Wankel, 2008). Social concerns were also on the rise during the decade, as seen through a series of events reflecting the international community's approach to sustainable development and, to some extent, to corporate behavior. The most relevant of these were: the creation of the European Commission's Directorate-General for Environment (1981), the creation of the World Commission on Environment and Development chaired by Norwegian Prime Minister GroHarlem Brundtland (1983), the Chernobyl nuclear disaster (1986), the publication of the Brundtland Commission's report Our Common Future (1987) defining sustainable development, the creation of the United Nations and the establishment of the European Commission, the adoption by the United Nations of the Montreal Protocol (1987) and the creation of the Intergovernmental Panel on Climate Change (1988).

Although these events were not directly related to CSR and therefore did not directly influence the evolution of the concept, they reflect a growing awareness of the international community for environmental protection and sustainable development. Indeed, for Carroll (2008), society's most relevant concerns and expectations about corporate behavior during the 1980s revolved around "environmental pollution, employment discrimination, consumer abuses, employee health and safety, quality of working life, deterioration of urban life, and questionable/abusive practices of multinational corporations" (p. 36).

The 1990s were no exception to the growing interest in CSR and, indeed, it was during this decade that the concept gained appeal as a result of the international focus on sustainable development at the time along with the globalization process that was taking place (Agudelo et al., 2019). As Carroll (2015) argues, during the 1990s the globalization process increased the operations of multinational corporations in countries with weak regulatory frameworks. For these global corporations, the incorporation of CSR represented a series of new opportunities that were accompanied by global competition, increased reputational risk due to increased global visibility, as well as conflicting pressures, demands and expectations from home and host countries (Carroll, 2015).

Many multinational companies understood that being socially responsible could balance the challenges and opportunities of the globalization process they were experiencing. As a result, the institutionalization of CSR became stronger (Carroll, 2015). The most notable example of its institutionalization was the founding in 1992 of the Business for Social Responsibility (BSR) association, which initially included 51 companies with the vision of becoming a "force for positive social change, a force that preserves and restores natural resources, ensures human dignity and justice, and operates transparently" (Business for Social Responsibility, 2000). Another key contribution to the debate on corporate behavior was the concept of the Triple Bottom Line (TBL), as it conceived for the first time a sustainability framework for balancing the social, environmental and economic impact of organizations (Elkington, 1998). The TBL concept became popular in the late 1990s as a comprehensive approach to achieve sustainability, being relevant in the CSR debate, since, under such an approach, companies should have a balanced social and environmental performance along with their economic objectives (Agudelo et al., 2019).

The globalization process of the 1990s increased the global reach of multinational companies, increasing their concern for competitiveness, reputation, global visibility and stakeholder network (Carroll, 2015). This led to the generation of new alternative theoretical perspectives to CSR, such as Stakeholder Theory (Freeman, 1994), corporate social performance (Swanson, 1995) and corporate citizenship (Carroll, 1998). The introduction of these new perspectives created uncertainty regarding the definition of CSR to the extent that the concept ended up having "unclear boundaries and debatable legitimacy" (Lantos, 2001, p. 1). In fact, in the late 1990s there was no globally accepted definition of CSR (Lantos, 2001).

The 2000s saw important contributions to the concept of CSR. In the early years of the 21st century, Smith (2001) argued that business policies had changed in response to the public interest, allowing for a positive impact on the environment in which organizations operated. This meant that the scope of social responsibility included a broader set of stakeholders, establishing a new definition of CSR. In the words of Smith (2001), CSR refers to "a company's obligations to its stakeholders, i.e. the people affected by business policies and practices. These obligations go beyond legal requirements and the company's duties to its shareholders. The fulfilment of these obligations aims to minimize any harm and maximize the long-term beneficial impact of the company on society" (p. 142).

Underlying the definition of CSR proposed by Smith (2001) was the idea that such socially responsible practices should be part of the strategic perspective of organizations in order to meet their long-term obligations. Similarly, Lantos (2001) asserted that during the 21st century, society would demand that companies include social issues in their strategies. In fact, Lantos (2001) drew on Smith's (2001) definition to include strategic considerations in his own definition of CSR, concluding that "CSR implied the obligation arising from the implicit social contract between business and society to meet the needs and wants of society over the long term, optimizing the positive effects and minimizing the negative effects of their actions on society" (p. 9). Furthermore, Lantos (2001) explained that CSR could become a strategic activity when it was part of the company's management plans to generate profits, as companies engaged in activities that could be understood as socially responsible only if they translated into economic benefits. On the other hand, Freeman (2001) and Friedman & Miles (2002) made further contributions to Stakeholder Theory in the early 2000s, reinforcing the belief that companies should be managed for the benefit of a broader set of stakeholders. Thus, while Freeman (2001) argued that firms had responsibilities to suppliers, consumers, employees, shareholders and the local community, Friedman & Miles (2002) argued that the relationship between firms and their stakeholders was dynamic, having different levels of influence on the firm. Thus, Freeman (2001) and Friedman & Miles (2002) contributed to the evolution of CSR by reinforcing the belief that companies were accountable to an increasingly broad set of stakeholders.

Van Marrewijk (2003) introduced the concept of Corporate Sustainability (CS) as a new perspective for understanding CSR. Van Marrewijk (2003) explained this new approach as a strategic response to new business challenges which, he argued, were the result of the evolving roles and responsibilities of each sector in society. For Van Marrewijk (2003), companies responded to their challenges by adopting different levels of integration of CSR into the company structure. The holistic interpretation provided by Van Marrewijk (2003) implied the full integration of CSR under the sustainability approach, understanding that companies had a new role within society and, consequently, had to make strategic decisions to adapt to the environment, transforming CSR "from a minimal commitment to become a strategic necessity" (Werther & Chandler, 2005, p. 319).

Later, Porter & Kramer (2006) argued that firms could gain competitive advantage through the creation of shared value. This term was conceived by these authors as a necessary step in the evolution of firms, defining it as the "operational policies and practices that enhance a firm's competitiveness and at the same time improve the economic and social conditions of the communities in which it operates" (p. 2). For Porter & Kramer (2006), a company should look inward to determine the social impact of its value chain and identify the positive and negative effect of its activities on society, focusing on those of greatest strategic value. The company then had to focus externally to understand the influence of its social context on its productivity and the execution of its business strategy. In this way, the work of these authors provided a new understanding of CSR by representing a way to maximize the interdependence between business and society through a strategic approach rather than a narrow focus on a set of objectives.

While not directly contributing to the concept of CSR, Porter & Kramer (2011) called for a shift in business strategies to focus on the generation of shared value as a primary objective. This new theoretical approach was embodied in what Trapp (2012) called the third generation of CSR, which he defined as the moment when companies reflect their concern for social and global issues in their activities, even when some of these concerns may not be directly linked to their core business. In the mid-2010s, Carroll (2015) revisited his work on CSR to complement his 1999 and 2010 literature review (Carroll, 1999; Carroll & Shabana, 2010) by analyzing the competing and complementary concepts that have become part of the modern business vocabulary. Carroll (2015) reviewed the concepts of stakeholder engagement and management, business ethics, corporate citizenship, CS and shared value creation, concluding that they were all interrelated and overlapping with the concept of CSR. In particular, Carroll (2015) points out that all these concepts have been incorporated into CSR and, as a consequence, CSR has to be taken as a reference point and centerpiece of the socially responsible business movement.

In addition, 2015 saw the launch of the United Nations 2030 Agenda for Sustainable Development, articulated under seventeen Sustainable Development Goals (SDGs), which represents a "shared vision of humanity and a social contract between world leaders and people" (Ban, 2015). Although the SDGs do not represent any obligations for the private sector, countries that adopt them must create specific policies and regulations that translate into pressures for companies to implement new business practices or improve their current practices (Agudelo et al., 2019; Marco-Lajara et al., 2022a). This is particularly relevant given that the Sustainable Development Goals (SDGs) cover a wide range of areas, from climate change to eradicating poverty and hunger, as well as promoting innovation and sustainable consumption. Thus, since their emergence, the academic literature has tended to address the application of CSR and its impact on specific SDG performance areas (Chuang & Huang, 2016; Benites-Lazaro & Mello-Théry, 2017; Kao et al., 2018).

Definition and Characteristics of CSR

Since the 1950s, various definitions of CSR have been put forward by academics as well as national and international institutions. Table 1 shows a selection of the most prominent definitions over the last seven decades, identifying which dimension of CSR each definition focuses on.

As can be seen, there is no consensus on the definition of CSR, since, from the 1950s to the present day, various authors and definitions have contributed to defining the concept. However, there are a number of characteristics that recur in the definitions that have been proposed.

Firstly, authors such as Eilbert & Parket (1973), Jones (1980), Van Marrewijk (2003), Cuervo (2009), the CSR Observatory (2014) and Sarkar & Searcy (2016) argue that CSR is voluntary for companies. Its conception as a voluntary practice is closely linked to the idea of going beyond strict compliance with legal requirements put forward by Waldam et al. (2006) and the Expert Forum on Corporate Social Responsibility (2007). Davis (1973, p. 313) clearly reflects this idea when he states that "social responsibility begins where the law ends". Similarly, in the words of Manne & Wallich (1972, p. 40) "when the company has social objectives imposed by law, the company does not exercise its responsibility when it implements them".

Likewise, while Walton (1967), Van Marrewijk (2003), Hopkins (2004), Castillo (2009), Cuervo (2009) and the European Commission (2011) highlight the close relationship that the company must maintain with its stakeholders, David & Blosmstrom (1966) and Waldman et al. (2006) focus on satisfying the needs and expectations of the different stakeholders. Along the same lines, Jones (1980), Cuesta

Table 1. Definitions of CSR

Author	Definition	Dimensions
Bowen (1953, p. 6)	"The obligation of business people to follow those policies, make those decisions, or pursue those courses of action that are desirable in terms of the goals and values of our society."	Social
Davis (1960, p. 70)	"Decisions and actions taken by employers for reasons, at least partially, beyond the economic or technical interests of the company."	Social
Frederick (1960, p. 60)	"It means that entrepreneurs must oversee the operation of an economic system that meets the expectations of the public. This means, in turn, that the means of economic production must be employed in such a way that production and distribution improve overall socio-economic welfare."	Social, Economic
McGuire (1963, p. 144)	"It assumes that a company not only has economic and legal obligations, but also has certain responsibilities to society that go beyond economic and legal obligations."	Social
Davis & Blomstrom (1966, p. 12)	"Social responsibility refers to a person's obligation to consider the effects of his or her decisions and actions on the social system as a whole. Entrepreneurs apply Social Responsibility when they consider the needs and interests of third parties that may be affected by the actions of the business. In doing so, they look beyond the economic and technical interests of the company."	Social
Walton (1967, p. 18)	"CSR recognizes the depth of relationships between business and society and realizes that these relationships must be taken into account by senior management as business and related groups pursue their respective objectives."	Social
Manne & Wallich (1972, p. 40)	"The company is, to some extent, a free agent to implement its CSR. When the company has social objectives imposed by law, the company does not exercise responsibility when it implements them."	Social
Eilbert & Parket (1973, p. 7)	"Perhaps the best way to understand social responsibility is to think of it as good neighborliness. The concept encompasses two phases. On the one hand, it means not doing things that spoil the neighborhood. On the other, it should be expressed as the voluntary acceptance of an obligation to help solve neighborhood problems. Businesses have an active role to play in solving social problems such as racial discrimination, pollution, transport or urban decay."	Social, Environmental
Eells & Walton (1974, p. 247)	"It represents a concern for the needs and goals of society, which go beyond the purely economic. Since the business system as it exists today can only survive with the effective functioning of a free society, CSR represents a general concern with the role of business in supporting and improving the social order".	Social
Sethi (1975, p. 62)	"It involves taking corporate behavior to the level where it is congruent with the prevailing social norms, values and performance expectations of society."	Social
Fitch (1976, p. 38)	"The serious attempt to solve social problems caused in whole or in part by business."	Social
Carroll (1979, p. 500)	"It encompasses the economic, legal, ethical and discretionary expectations that society has of companies at a given point in time."	Social, Economic
Jones (1980, p. 60)	"The idea that companies have an obligation to the groups that make up society, beyond shareholders and beyond what is established by law and contract. Two facets of this definition are critical. First, that the obligation must be voluntarily adopted; behavior influenced by the coercive forces of law or union contracts is not voluntary. Second, the obligation extends beyond the duty to shareholders to other social groups such as customers, employees, suppliers and surrounding communities."	Social
Hopkins (1998)	CSR is concerned with dealing with the company's stakeholders in an ethical or socially responsible manner. Stakeholders exist both inside and outside the company. Therefore, socially responsible behavior will enhance the human development of stakeholders both inside and outside the company.	Social
Carroll (1999, p. 43)	"A socially responsible company must generate profit, comply with the law, be ethical and be a good corporate citizen."	Social, Economic
Khoury, Rostami & Turnbull (1999)	CSR is the company's overall relationship with all its stakeholders. These include customers, employees, communities, owners/ investors, government, suppliers and competitors. Elements of social responsibility include community investment, employee relations, job creation and retention, environmental protection and financial performance.	Social, Economic, Environmental
Business for Social Responsibility (2000)	Making business decisions linked to ethical values, compliance with legal requirements and respect for people, communities and the environment.	Social Economic
Comisión Europea (2001, p. 7)	"The voluntary integration, by companies, of social and environmental concerns into their business operations and their relations with their stakeholders."	Social, Environmental
Marsden (2001)	CSR refers to the basic behavior of companies and their responsibility for their overall impact on the societies in which they operate. CSR is not an optional extra or an act of philanthropy. A socially responsible company is one that runs a profitable business that considers all the positive and negative environmental, social and economic effects it has on society.	Social, Economic, Environmental
Mohr et al. (2001, p. 47)	"The company's commitment to minimize or eliminate any detrimental effects and to maximize its beneficial impact on society in the long term."	Social
Van Marrewijk (2003)	In general, CS and CSR refer to corporate activities, voluntary by definition, that demonstrate the inclusion of social and environmental concerns in business operations and stakeholder interactions.	Social, Economic, Environmental
Cuesta & Valor (2003, p. 7)	"The set of obligations and commitments, legal and ethical, national and international, with stakeholders, which are derived from the impacts that the activity and operations of organizations produce in the social, labor, environmental and human rights spheres. Therefore, CSR affects the very management of organizations, both in their productive and commercial activities and in their relations with stakeholders."	Social, Economic, Environmental
Smith (2003, p. 2)	"The company's obligations to society or, more specifically, to its stakeholders."	Social
Hopkins (2004, p. 1)	"It refers to treating the company's stakeholders in an ethical or responsible manner. Ethical or responsible treatment of its stakeholders means acting in a way that is accepted by society. Social includes economic responsibility. There are stakeholders internal and external to the company - the environment is a stakeholder. The aim of corporate social responsibility in its broadest sense is to create ever higher standards of living, while preserving the profitability of the company, for people inside and outside the company."	Social, Economic, Environmental
Maignan & Ferrell (2004)	"It designates the duty to meet or improve stakeholder standards by defining desirable business behaviors."	Social
García-Marzá (2004, p. 187)	"It defines the set of actions, decisions and policies that make up the company's response to the demands and requirements of its corresponding interest groups."	Social
McWilliams, Siegel & Wright (2006)	A situation in which a company goes beyond the requirements imposed on it and includes in its activities actions that create a social good.	Social
Waldman et al. (2006, p. 824)	"Actions by the company that meet the needs or objectives of an identifiable stakeholder group, or a broader social group (...) Actions that go beyond the immediate legal requirements of the company. Shareholders or other owners are included as constituting a stakeholder group relevant to CSR, along with broader stakeholders."	Social
Foro de Expertos sobre RSE (2007, p. 7)	"It is, in addition to strict compliance with current legal obligations, the voluntary integration in its governance and management, in its strategy, policies and procedures, of the social, labor, environmental and human rights concerns that arise from the relationship and transparent dialogue with its stakeholders, thus taking responsibility for the consequences and impacts that derive from its actions."	Social, Environmental

continued on following page

Table 1. Continued

Author	Definition	Dimensions
Kotler & Lee (2007)	The company's commitment to enhancing the well-being of society through independent business practices and the use of company resources.	Social
Carroll (2008)	CSR refers to companies' commitments to pursue strategies, make decisions or follow lines of activity that are in line with society's values and expectations.	Social
Castillo (2009, p. 226)	"It is a fundamental component of the organization and involves concern for ethics, people, community and the environment, within the context of the company's operations and decision-making process. It encompasses all the actions and policies that are part of a corporation's normal operations, and includes an internal dimension, focused on employee relations and management practices, and an external dimension, directed at the environment and the commitment to contribute to the economic and social development of the community. Its practice generates a series of connections or linkages that lead to relationships and thus interactions and dialogue between the company and all its stakeholders."	Social, Economic, Environmental
Cuervo (2009, p. 51)	"It implies that companies voluntarily incorporate social and environmental criteria into economic activities and stakeholder relations."	Social, Environmental
Ismail (2009)	The concept that business organizations consider the public interest by taking responsibility for the impact of their activities on customers, suppliers, employees, shareholders, communities and other stakeholders, as well as the environment.	Social, Environmental
Hediger (2010)	Programs in which companies not only seek to increase their profits, but also contribute to the well-being of stakeholders.	Social
Comisión Europea (2011, p. 6)	"The responsibility of business for its impact on society. To fully embrace their social responsibility, companies should implement, in close collaboration with stakeholders, a process to integrate social, environmental and ethical concerns, respect for human rights and consumer concerns into their business operations and core strategy."	Social, Environmental
Aguinis & Glavas (2012)	Context-specific organizational actions and policies that consider stakeholder expectations and the triple bottom line (economic, social and environmental).	Social, Economic, Environmental
Fontaine (2013)	The ongoing commitment of companies to behave appropriately, fairly and responsibly and to contribute to economic development by improving the lives of workers and their families, as well as the local community and society as a whole.	Social, Economic
Observatorio de RSC (2014, p. 5)	"It involves mandatory compliance with national and international social, labor, environmental and human rights legislation, as well as any other voluntary action that the company wishes to undertake to improve the quality of life of its employees, the communities in which it operates and society as a whole."	Social, Environmental
Sheehy (2015, p. 639).	"A socio-political movement that generates private self-regulatory initiatives, incorporating public and private international law standards that seek to ameliorate and mitigate social harms and promote the public good by industry organizations."	Social
Sarkar & Searcy (2016)	CSR implies that companies should voluntarily assume their social responsibility to be ethical in all their activities and consider the impact of their actions on their stakeholders, while contributing to global sustainability.	Social, Economic, Environmental
Monfort & Villagra (2016)	It is a strategy aligned with the company's corporate values to share with the environment.	Social
Ayala del Pino (2021, p. 7)	"CSR is, in addition to strict compliance with legal obligations, the voluntary integration of CSR concerns into its governance and management, strategy, policies and procedures. legal obligations, the voluntary integration into its governance and management, strategy, policies and procedures of the social, labor, environmental and human rights concerns that arise from the relationship and social, labor, environmental and human rights concerns that arise from the relationship and transparent dialogue with its stakeholders, thus taking responsibility for the consequences and impacts of its actions."	Social, Economic, Environmental

& Valor (2003), Smith (2003), García-Marzá (2004) and Corredera & González (2011) conceive CSR practices as a commitment and obligation that the company has towards its stakeholders. On the other hand, other authors highlight in their definitions those actions that transcend the economic interests of the organization (Davis, 1960; Davis & Bomstrom, 1966; Eells & Walton, 1974), since the underlying idea is to integrate social and environmental concerns in the activities carried out by the organization (European Commission, 2001; Cuesta & Valor, 2003; Van Marrewijk, 2003; Ismail, 2009; Corredera & González; 2011; Aguinis & Glavas, 2012; Observatorio de RSC, 2014).

The responsibility of organizations to mitigate the negative externalities generated by their activity is another common denominator when defining CSR (Fitch, 1976; Mohr et al., 2001; Cuesta and Valor, 2003; Expert Forum on Corporate Social Responsibility, 2007; European Commission, 2011; CSR Observatory, 2014). As Eilbert & Parket (1973, p. 7) point out very clearly, organizations "should not do things that spoil the neighborhood". By way of conclusion, Table 2 sets out the main characteristics of the term CSR derived from the definitions analyzed.

Theoretical Perspectives

Theoretical perspectives on CSR show how this construct has been observed and interpreted by scholars over time. The five predominant theoretical approaches in the academic literature on CSR are discussed

Table 2. Main characteristics of CSR. Source: own elaboration

There is no standardized definition of CSR
Voluntary practice
Management of negative externalities
Stakeholder orientation
Alignment of social, environmental and economic responsibilities
Beyond philanthropy

below: Agency Theory, Stakeholder Theory, Institutional Theory, Resource and Capabilities Theory and Legitimacy Theory.

Agency Theory analyzes the relationship between "principals" (individuals or organizations that employ another party to perform a specific job) and "agents" (those who perform that job). Following the seminal study by Berle & Means (1932), Agency Theory has traditionally been applied to the relationship between owners and managers of large firms (Eisenhardt, 1989).

Agency Theory addresses the "agency problem", which can arise as a result of a conflict of interest between principals, and how such a problem can be overcome through different governance mechanisms (Spence & Zeckhauser, 1971; Jensen & Meckling, 1976; Amihud & Lev, 1981; Eisenhardt, 1985).

With regard to CSR, Friedman (1962) was undoubtedly one of the first precursors of the Agency Theory by arguing that CSR represented selfish behavior by managers (agents) whose pursuit of social and environmental objectives ended up harming shareholders (principals) by generating lower corporate profit. Authors such as Galaskiewicz (1985), Atkinson & Galaskiewicz (1988) and Wright & Ferris (1997) subsequently made explicit applications of Agency Theory in relation to CSR, thus reinforcing Friedman's thesis. Atkinson & Galaskiewicz (1988) confirmed that ownership and corporate philanthropy were negatively related, since the higher the percentage of shares held by the CEO, the more profits he or she earned and, consequently, the less the firm contributed to philanthropic causes. On the contrary, several recent research studies carried out under this theory consider that CSR favors financial and non-financial performance (Berrone & Gómez-Mejía, 2009; Bear et al., 2010; Oh et al., 2011). As an example, Oh et al. (2011) found that large institutional shareholders and long-term oriented foreign investors supported companies' CSR initiatives, denoting that these investors preferred to invest in responsible companies to avoid financial risks.

The main limitation of Agency Theory is that it can only provide a partial explanation of CSR. As Eisenhardt (1989, p. 71) states, "agency theory presents a partial view of the world which, while valid, also ignores much of the complexity of organizations". Consequently, this theory can be more appropriately applied in conjunction with other theoretical perspectives to provide a holistic picture of individual-level phenomena and their interactions with other levels of analysis.

Stakeholders are interest groups that can help or harm the development of business activity (Freeman, 1984). Stakeholder Theory predicts that corporate actions are the direct result of pressures from different stakeholders, related to dependence on power (Freeman & Reed, 1983; Clarkson, 1995; Jawahar & McLaughlin, 2001) or claim to legitimacy (Hill and Jones, 1992; Langtry, 1994). Bringing these different factors together into a single model of stakeholder identification and relevance, Mitchel et al. (1997) proposed that the impact of stakeholders on organizations depended on three attributes: power (related to the stakeholder's ability to impose its will on others), legitimacy (related to the rights of stakeholders to use their power in the face of claims made on the firm), and urgency (the degree to which stakeholder claims demand immediate attention).

Studies from the stakeholder perspective have provided abundant empirical evidence on the impact of stakeholders on CSR strategies and how their pressures influence CSR-related activities (Brammer & Millington, 2004; Lamberti & Lettieri, 2009; Surroca et al., 2013). Studies have investigated, among other topics, the influence of stakeholder pressures on environmental policies and strategies (Christmann, 2004; Darnall et al., 2010), environmental disclosure (Roberts, 1992; Neu et al., 1998; Elijido-Tenet al., 2010) and corporate philanthropy (Brammer & Millington, 2003, 2004; Moir & Taffler, 2004). Likewise, a significant portion of studies has also focused on the relationship between CSR and organizational performance or financial performance of firms, both from a conceptual perspective (Miles & Covin, 2000; Schuler & Cording, 2006; Barnett, 2007, 2014) and from an empirical perspective (Wang & Choi, 2013; Oikonomou et al., 2014). While some empirical results point to an inconclusive or even negative relationship between CSR and organizational performance (Moore, 2001; Hoepneret al., 2014; Jia & Zhang, 2014), others demonstrate a positive relationship (Ruf et al., 2001; Brammer & Millington, 2004; Wang & Choi, 2013; Mellahi et al., 2016). In general, these studies start from the premise that investors and other key stakeholders reward companies that are responsive to their concerns.

Institutional Theory suggests that firms need to comply with the social norms of a given business environment because they cannot survive without a certain level of external social approval (legitimacy) (Meyer & Rowan, 1977; DiMaggio & Powell, 1983). This theory encompasses different intellectual traditions and approaches, which can be divided into three (Hotho & Pedersen, 2012). First, the economic approach has addressed the regulatory role of institutions underpinning economic activity (Davis & North, 1971; North, 1990). Second, the sociological approach has addressed the role of legitimacy in institutions (DiMaggio & Powell, 1983; Scott, 2001). Third, the comparative institutional approach, which overlaps with the first two approaches, has analyzed the differences between institutional arrangements and firm competitiveness (Whitley, 1999; Hall & Soskice, 2001; Wood et al., 2014).

Institutional Theory has been widely applied to CSR (Jennings & Zandbergen, 1995; Doh & Guay, 2006; Campbell, 2007; Matten & Moon, 2008). On the one hand, numerous studies have identified institutional factors that influence or shape responsible behavior, management, environmental practices or social and environmental disclosure. On the other hand, the CSR literature has also explored "institutional isomorphism", i.e., the idea that firms' strategies and practices resemble a defined institutional environment, as organizations in a given sector and territory face similar institutional pressures. This literature has investigated CSR strategies and practices among firms with similar attributes within the institutional context of countries (Doh & Guay, 2006; Holder-Webb & Cohen, 2012; Fransen, 2013) and that of local communities (Marquis et al., 2007). From a comparative perspective, Institutional Theory also helps to explain differences in the nature of CSR depending on the local context of firms (Matten & Moon, 2008; Sison, 2009; Xu & Yang, 2010; Jamali & Neville, 2011). For example, studies have shown significant differences between the United States and Europe in the impact of national institutional context on CSR (Doh & Guay, 2006; Matten & Moon, 2008; Sison, 2009; Avetisyan & Ferrary, 2013).

There are three mechanisms through which institutional isomorphism is generated: the coercive mechanism, the normative mechanism and the mimetic mechanism. The mimetic mechanism is the result of the voluntary impulse to imitate the CSR practices of other competitors in order to achieve an acceptable standard (Amran & Siti-Nabiha, 2009). The normative mechanism occurs when imitation of CSR strategy is considered a necessity to be within the institutional framework, such as guidelines from professional bodies and academic centers. The coercive mechanism, on the other hand, refers to the imitation of CSR practices by force, persuasion or invitation to sign an agreement. This occurs when an organization is dependent on another and cannot stand on its own. Therefore, the main objective of the Institutional Theory is the institutionalization of behavior, since, according to this approach, institutions can influence the behavior of organizations in the same sector by establishing acceptable and recognized standards, norms, specifications or modes of operation within industries (Kang & Moon, 2012).

The intellectual origins of Resource Based View (RBV) date back to the pioneering work of Penrose (1959) (Rugman & Verbeke, 2002; Lockett & Thompson, 2004). The author conceives of the heterogeneity of resources and capabilities of organizations as the main source of sustainable competitive advantage, in contrast to the earlier emphasis in the discipline of strategic management on the adaptation of firms to the external environment. Accepting the general premise that firm-specific resources can lead toward gaining competitive advantage, RBV focuses on determining how firms can acquire greater profitability through the possession of valuable, rare and inimitable resources (Wernerfelt, 1984; Barney 1991, 1997; Kraaijenbrink et al. 2010). Barney (1997) introduced the Valuable, Rare, Imperfectly Imitable and Non-substitutable (VRIN) framework to help understand a firm's competitive advantage by posing a series of questions about whether a firm's resources were valuable, rare, costly to imitate, and exploited by the organization. Sustainable competitive advantage thus arises when firms have resources that combine all four attributes.

Research related to CSR under the RBV approach proposes that capabilities related to CSR investment can lead to economic benefits for firms (Hart, 1995; Russo & Fouts, 1997; McWilliams & Siegel; 2011). CSR can be justified as an investment that enables the firm to differentiate itself from its competitors and improve organizational performance. Therefore, CSR helps to understand the proactive strategies of companies in developing and using internal capabilities related to social and environmental issues to obtain economic benefits. Such capabilities may include, among others, green innovations (Chen et al., 2006), stakeholder management and strategic proactivity (Torugsa et al., 2012) or sustainability leadership (Lourenço et al., 2014).

Several studies have applied RBV to CSR empirically, mostly focusing on testing the statistical relationship between social/environmental performance and ecological performance (Russo & Fouts, 1997; Menguc et al., 2010; Ben Brik et al., 2011) or applying the VRIN framework (Peters et al., 2011) to find out whether social and environmental capabilities can improve organizational performance.

However, such research is ambiguous in demonstrating whether CSR enables sustainable competitive advantages over competitors. Some studies have suggested that CSR-related capabilities can generate competitive advantages for firms (Chen et al., 2006; Lourenço et al., 2014). In contrast, other research conducted from the RBV perspective (McWilliams & Siegel, 2011; Frynas, 2015) suggests that while CSR can generate business advantages for the firm, it is unlikely to generate sustainable competitive advantage, because in contrast to, for example, the firm's intangible assets (Boddewyn & Brewer, 1994) or technological resources and capabilities (Huang et al., 2015), CSR activities are visible and rivals can imitate them.

Suchman (1995, p. 574) defines legitimacy as "a generalized perception or assumption that an entity's actions are desirable, appropriate, or fitting with some socially constructed system of norms, values, beliefs, and definitions." Deegan & Unerman (2011) state that Legitimacy Theory is based on the notion that there is a "social contract" between an organization and the society in which it operates. Therefore, companies try to legitimize their corporate actions by carrying out CSR activities and, in this way, guarantee their existence. According to this theory, companies are inseparable from society and have no inherent right to exist: they only exist to the extent that society confers legitimacy on them.

Therefore, firms must continually legitimize their activities to maintain congruence between the objectives of society and those of the organization (Dowling & Pfeffer, 1975; Preston & Post, 1975; Lindblom, 1983; Ashford & Gibbs, 1990; Deegan, 2002).

Legitimacy has to do with two main concepts: the perception of stakeholders and the effectiveness of the communication channels used by the company. The Theory of Legitimacy requires organizations to continuously check whether their survival is serving the satisfaction of the needs of the different stakeholders (Mobus, 2005), since it is the community that determines the usefulness of organizations based on the congruence between what they expect and what they obtain from them. Likewise, communication is essential in the Theory of Legitimacy, since the dissemination of CSR initiatives is a source of creation and protection of organizational legitimacy. In fact, Patten (1992) observed that there was a positive relationship between the dissemination of CSR initiatives and organizational legitimacy. Later, Deegan & Rankin (1997) and Brown & Deegan, (1998) reaffirmed these findings. In the same vein, Campbell (2000) noted that the disclosure of CSR initiatives decreased the legitimacy gap between how an organization is perceived and how it wants to be perceived. By way of conclusion, Table 3 shows the theoretical perspectives that have addressed the study of CSR.

Table 3. Main theoretical perspectives on CSR. Source: own elaboration

Theoretical Perspectives	Basic assumption	Main reasons related to CSR
Agency Theory	Managers, as agents, have different incentives and objectives than their principals.	CSR is driven by alignment between agents and principals.
Stakeholders Theory	Companies are affected by the actions of stakeholders and must therefore address their interests.	CSR is governed by the organization's relationships with its stakeholders.
Institutional Theory	The survival and growth of companies depend on the acquisition of legitimacy in institutional environments.	CSR is driven by different institutional contexts.
Resource and Capabilities Theory	Differences in performance between companies are influenced by company-specific resources and capabilities.	CSR acts as a specialized skill or capability to gain a competitive advantage.
Legitimacy Theory	Companies operate on the basis of a social contract with society and their survival and growth depend on legitimacy.	CSR acts to maintain congruence between the objectives of society and the objectives of the organization.

CONCLUSION

This research is of great relevance for both CSR academics and professionals who are thinking of implementing these practices in their companies, given that, through the research, it is possible to understand the motivations that justify the need for companies to behave fairly with the society and the environment in which they operate.

The results of the study show that it was not until the 1950s that the identification of the social responsibilities that organizations should have was first addressed in the academic literature, which is understood to be the birth of the modern construct of CSR. During the 1960s, academic contributions sought to respond to the problems and desires of the new society that was flourishing. A number of academics argued that the social, economic and political changes occurring at the time represented added pressure for businessmen to reexamine their role in society and their social responsibility.

The 1970s saw the creation of some of the most relevant companies in terms of social responsibility, which began to formalize and integrate policies that addressed the social and public issues of the era. This led to the term CSR becoming increasingly popular, giving rise to its indistinct use in various contexts. During the 1980s, the Reagan and Thatcher administrations introduced a new liberal doctrine characterized by the reduction of fiscal pressures on corporations. Thus, as the role of governments in regulating corporate behavior was reduced, managers had to respond to different interest groups that continued to expect companies to meet the social expectations of the time. In particular, the reduction of the regulatory framework led scholars to consider business ethics and the operationalization of CSR as an appropriate response to the various stakeholders involved in the organization, such as shareholders, employees and consumers. In addition, during the decade, social concerns were on the rise, as seen through a series of events that reflect the international community's approach to sustainable development and, to a certain extent, to corporate behavior.

The 1990s were no exception to the growing interest in CSR and, in fact, it was during this decade that the concept gained appeal as a result of the international focus on sustainable development at the time together with the process of globalization that was taking place. Indeed, during that decade the globalization process increased the operations of multinational corporations in countries with weak regulatory frameworks. For these global corporations, the incorporation of CSR represented a series of new opportunities that were accompanied by global competition, increased reputational risk due to increased global visibility, as well as conflicting pressures, demands and expectations from home and host countries. The 2000s saw important contributions to the concept of CSR. The scientific output of the time argued that business policies had changed in response to the public interest, making it possible to generate a positive impact on the environment in which organizations operated. This meant that the scope of social responsibility included a broader set of stakeholders.

In the mid-2010s, Carroll (2015) revisited his work on CSR to complement his 1999 and 2010 literature review by analyzing the competing and complementary concepts that have become part of the modern business vocabulary. Carroll (2015) reviewed the concepts of stakeholder engagement and management, business ethics, corporate citizenship, CS and shared value creation, concluding that they were all interrelated and overlapping with the concept of CSR, noting that all of these concepts had been incorporated into CSR and, as a consequence, such term is to be taken as a reference point and centerpiece of the socially responsible business movement. Additionally, 2015 saw the launch of the 2030 Agenda by the United Nations for Sustainable Development, articulated under seventeen SDGs (Marco-Lajara et al., 2021a; Marco-Lajara et al., 2021b; Marco-Lajara et al., 2022a; Marco-Lajara et al., 2022b, Marco-Lajara et al., 2022c).Thus, although the SDGs do not represent any obligation for the private sector, the countries that adopt them must create specific policies and regulations that translate into pressures for companies to implement new business practices or improve their current practices. This is especially relevant considering that the SDGs cover a wide range of areas, from climate change to the eradication of poverty and hunger, as well as the promotion of innovation and sustainable consumption. Thus, since their emergence, academic publications have tended to address the application of CSR and its impact on specific areas of SDG performance.

Based on a review of the literature on the concept of CSR, it is possible to state that: (1) there is no standardized definition of CSR, with the consequent problems that this entails, (2) it is a voluntary practice, (3) it implies the management of negative externalities, (4) it involves orienting practices to meet the needs of different stakeholders, (3) practices must align social, environmental and economic responsibilities, and (4) they must go beyond philanthropy.

Moreover, through the narrative review carried out, a total of five theories under which CSR has been analyzed were identified: the Agency Theory, the Stakeholder Theory, the Institutional Theory, the Resources and Capabilities Theory and the Legitimacy Theory. First, Agency Theory addresses the "agency problem", which can arise as a result of a conflict of interest among principals, and how this problem can be overcome through different governance mechanisms. Under such an approach CSR is conceived as a mechanism to align interests between agents and principals.

Secondly, according to stakeholder theory, companies are affected by the actions of their stakeholders and must therefore attend to their interests. CSR, therefore, is governed by the organization's relations with its stakeholders. Third, Institutional Theory suggests that firms need to comply with the social norms of a given business environment because they cannot survive without a certain level of external social approval (legitimacy). This theory encompasses different intellectual traditions and approaches. On the one hand, numerous studies have identified institutional factors that influence or shape responsible behavior, management, environmental practices or social and environmental disclosure. On the other hand, the CSR literature has also explored "institutional isomorphism", i.e. the idea that corporate strategies and practices resemble a defined institutional environment, since organizations in a given sector and territory face similar institutional pressures. Under this approach, CSR is driven by different institutional contexts.

Fourth, the intellectual origins of Resource and Capability Theory, in turn, can be traced back to the pioneering work of Penrose (1959). The author conceives the heterogeneity of resources and capabilities of organizations as the main source of sustainable competitive advantage, in contrast to the earlier emphasis in the discipline of Strategic Management on the adaptation of firms to the external environment. Accepting the general premise that firm-specific resources can lead toward gaining competitive advantage, RBV focuses on determining how firms can acquire greater profitability through the possession of valuable, rare and inimitable resources. Research related to CSR under the RBV approach proposes that capabilities related to CSR investment can lead to economic benefits for firms. CSR can be justified as an investment that enables the firm to differentiate itself from its competitors and improve organizational performance. Therefore, RBV helps to understand the proactive strategies of companies in developing and using internal capabilities related to social and environmental issues to obtain economic benefits.

Finally, the Legitimacy Theory is based on the notion that there is a "social contract" between an organization and the society in which it operates. Therefore, companies try to legitimize their corporate actions by carrying out CSR activities and, in this way, guarantee their existence. According to this theory, companies are inseparable from society and do not have an inherent right to exist: they only exist to the extent that society confers legitimacy on them. Therefore, based on the study conducted, five motivations can be identified that drive the implementation of CSR practices: (1) alignment of interests between agents and principal, (2) satisfying stakeholder demands, (3) complying with the institutional context, (4) gaining a competitive advantage and (5) maintaining congruence between the objectives of society and the objectives of the organization. These are not mutually exclusive, but complementary. Thus, the reason why organizations develop CSR practices may be an accumulation of the five factors mentioned above.

FUTURE RESEARCH DIRECTIONS

Despite the important contributions of the study, it is important to point out that the research suffers from certain limitations. The fundamental limitation of the study is methodological in nature, given that narrative reviews are dominated by the subjective criteria of the authors and do not quantitatively synthesize the data found in the different publications. To overcome these limitations of narrative reviews, a systematic review of the theoretical perspectives of CSR over time is proposed as a future line of research with the aim of increasing the reproducibility of the research and increasing the validity of the results obtained.

REFERENCES

Agudelo, M., Jóhannsdóttir, L., & Davídsdóttir, B. (2019). A literature review of the history and evolution of corporate social responsibility. *International Journal of Corporate Social Responsibility*, *4*(1), 1–23. doi:10.118640991-018-0039-y

Aguinis, H., & Glavas, A. (2012). What we know and don't know about corporate social responsibility: A review and research agenda. *Journal of Management*, *38*(4), 932–968. doi:10.1177/0149206311436079

Amihud, Y., & Lev, B. (1981). Risk reduction as a managerial motive for conglomerate mergers. *The Bell Journal of Economics*, *12*(2), 605–616. doi:10.2307/3003575

Amran, A., & Siti-Nabiha, A. (2009). Corporate social reporting in Malaysia: A case of mimicking the West or succumbing to local pressure. *Social Responsibility Journal*, *5*(3), 358–375. doi:10.1108/17471110910977285

Ashford, B., & Gibbs, B. (1990). The double-edge of organizational legitimation. *Organization Science*, *1*(2), 177–194. doi:10.1287/orsc.1.2.177

Atkinson, L., & Galaskiewicz, J. (1988). Stock ownership and company contributions to charity. *Administrative Science Quarterly*, *33*(1), 82–100. doi:10.2307/2392856

Avetisyan, E., & Ferrary, M. (2013). 'Dynamics of stakeholders' implications in the institutionalization of the CSR field in France and in the United States. *Journal of Business Ethics*, *115*(1), 115–133. doi:10.100710551-012-1386-3

Ayala del Pino, C. (2021). La responsabilidad social corporativa: Concepto, ámbito de aplicación, grupos de interés y objetivos [Corporate social responsibility: concept, scope of application, stakeholders and objectives]. *Anuario Jurídico y Económico Escurialense*, *54*(54), 173–198. doi:10.54571/ajee.462

Ban, K. (2015). *Launch of new sustainable development agenda to guide development actions for the next 15 years.* Disponible en: https://sustainabledevelopment. un.org/?page=view&nr=1021&type=230&menu=2059

Barnett, M. (2007). Stakeholder influence capacity and the variability of financial returns to corporate social responsibility. *Academy of Management Review*, *32*(3), 794–816. doi:10.5465/amr.2007.25275520

Barnett, M. (2014). Why stakeholders ignore firm misconduct: A cognitive view. *Journal of Management, 40*(3), 676–702. doi:10.1177/0149206311433854

Barney, J. (1991). Firm resources and sustained competitive advantage. *Journal of Management, 17*(1), 99–120. doi:10.1177/014920639101700108

Barney, J. (1997). *Gaining and Sustaining a Competitive Advantage*. Addison Wesley.

Baxi, C. V., & Ray, R. S. (2012). *Corporate social responsibility*. Vikas Publishing House.

Bear, S., Rahman, N., & Post, C. (2010). The impact of board diversity and gender composition on corporate social responsibility and firm reputation. *Journal of Business Ethics, 97*(2), 207–221. doi:10.100710551-010-0505-2

Ben Brik, A., Rettab, B., & Mellahi, K. (2011). Market orientation, corporate social responsibility, and business performance. *Journal of Business Ethics, 99*(3), 307–324. doi:10.100710551-010-0658-z

Benites-Lazaro, L., & Mello-Théry, N. (2017). CSR as a legitimatizing tool in carbon market: Evidence from Latin America's clean development mechanism. *Journal of Cleaner Production, 149*, 218–226. doi:10.1016/j.jclepro.2017.02.095

Berle, A., & Means, G. (1932). *The Modern Corporation and Private Property*. Macmillan.

Berrone, P., & Gomez-Mejia, L. (2009). Environmental performance and executive compensation: An integrated agency-institutional perspective. *Academy of Management Journal, 52*(1), 103–126. doi:10.5465/amj.2009.36461950

Boddewyn, J., & Brewer, T. (1994). International business political behavior: New theoretical directions. *Academy of Management Review, 19*(1), 119–143. doi:10.5465/amr.1994.9410122010

Bowen, H. (1953). *Social responsibilities of the businessman*. University of Iowa Press.

Brammer, S., & Millington, A. (2003). The effect of stakeholder preferences, organizational structure and industry type on corporate community involvement. *Journal of Business Ethics, 45*(3), 213–226. doi:10.1023/A:1024151528646

Brammer, S., & Millington, A. (2004). The development of corporate charitable contributions in the UK: A stakeholder analysis. *Journal of Management Studies, 41*(8), 1411–1434. doi:10.1111/j.1467-6486.2004.00480.x

Brown, N., & Deegan, C. (1998). The public disclosure of environmental performance information—A dual test of media agenda setting theory and legitimacy theory. *Accounting and Business Research, 29*(1), 21–41. doi:10.1080/00014788.1998.9729564

Business for Social Responsibility. (2000). *Introduction to Corporate Social Responsibility*. Disponible en: http://www.khbo.be/~lodew/Cursussen/4eingenieurCL/The%20Global%20Business%20Responsibility%20Resource%20Center.doc

Campbell, D. (2000). Legitimacy theory or managerial reality construction? Corporate social disclosure in Marks and Spencer Plc corporate reports, 1969-1997. *Accounting Forum, 24*(1), 80–100. doi:10.1111/1467-6303.00030

Campbell, J. (2007). Why would corporations behave in socially responsible ways? An institutional theory of corporate social responsibility. *Academy of Management Review*, *32*(3), 946–967. doi:10.5465/amr.2007.25275684

Carroll, A. (1991). The Pyramid of CSR: Toward the Moral Management of Organizational Stakeholders. *Business Horizons*, *34*(4), 39–48. doi:10.1016/0007-6813(91)90005-G

Carroll, A. (1998). The four faces of corporate citizenship. *Business and Society Review*, *100*(1), 1–7. doi:10.1111/0045-3609.00008

Carroll, A. (1999). Corporate social responsibility. *Business & Society*, *38*(3), 268–295. doi:10.1177/000765039903800303

Carroll, A. (2008). A history of corporate social responsibility: concepts and practices. In A. M. Andrew Crane, D. Matten, J. Moon, & D. Siegel (Eds.), *The Oxford handbook of corporate social responsibility* (pp. 19–46). Oxford University Press. doi:10.1093/oxfordhb/9780199211593.003.0002

Carroll, A. (2015). Corporate social responsibility: The centerpiece of competing and complementary frameworks. *Organizational Dynamics*, *44*(2), 87–96. doi:10.1016/j.orgdyn.2015.02.002

Carroll, A., & Shabana, K. (2010). The business case for corporate social responsibility: A review of concepts, research and practice. *International Journal of Management Reviews*, *12*(1), 85–105. doi:10.1111/j.1468-2370.2009.00275.x

Carroll, A. B. (1979). A three-dimensional conceptual model of corporate performance. *Academy of Management Review*, *4*(4), 497–505. doi:10.2307/257850

Castillo, A. (2009). *Relaciones Públicas. Teoría e historia*. Editorial UOC.

Chen, Y., Lai, S., & Wen, C. (2006). The influence of green innovation performance on corporate advantage in Taiwan. *Journal of Business Ethics*, *67*(4), 331–339. doi:10.100710551-006-9025-5

Christmann, P. (2004). Multinational companies and the natural environment: Determinants of global environmental policy standardization. *Academy of Management Journal*, *47*(5), 747–760. doi:10.2307/20159616

Chuang, S., & Huang, S. (2016). The effect of environmental corporate social responsibility on environmental performance and business competitiveness: The mediation of green information technology capital. *Journal of Business Ethics*, *150*(4), 991–1009. doi:10.100710551-016-3167-x

Clarkson, M. (1995). A stakeholder framework for analyzing and evaluating corporate social performance. *Academy of Management Review*, *20*(1), 92–117. doi:10.2307/258888

Comisión Europea. (2001). *Libro Verde de la Comisión Europea para Fomentar un Marco Europeo para la Responsabilidad Social de las Empresas* [European Commission Green Paper on Promoting a European Framework for Corporate Social Responsibility]. Author.

Comisión Europea. (2011). Estrategia renovada de la UE para 2011-2014 sobre la responsabilidad social de las empresas [Renewed EU Corporate Social Responsibility Strategy 2011-2014]. Author.

Cuervo, A. (2009). Corporate social responsibility, corporate governance and stakeholders (Corporate social responsibility, corporate governance and stakeholders.). In *Responsabilidad social: una reflexión global sobre la RSE* (pp. 51–61). Pretince Hall.

Cuesta, M., & Valor, C. (2003). Responsabilidad social de la empresa: concepto, medición y desarrollo en España [Corporate social responsibility: concept, measurement and development in Spain]. *Boletín Económico De ICE. Información Comercial Española, 2755*, 7–20.

Darnall, N., Henriques, I., & Sadorsky, P. (2010). Adopting proactive environmental strategy: The influence of stakeholders and firm size. *Journal of Management Studies, 47*(6), 1072–1094. doi:10.1111/j.1467-6486.2009.00873.x

Davis, K. (1960). Can business afford to ignore social responsibilities? *California Management Review, 2*(3), 70–76. doi:10.2307/41166246

Davis, K. (1973). The case for and against business assumption of social responsibilities. *Academy of Management Journal, 16*(2), 312–322.

Davis, K., & Blomstrom, R. (1966). *Business and its environment*. McGraw-Hill.

Davis, L., & North, D. (1971). *Institutional Change and American Economic Growth*. Cambridge University Press. doi:10.1017/CBO9780511561078

Deegan, C. (2002). Introduction - The legitimising effect of social and environmental disclosures - a theoretical foundation. *Accounting, Auditing & Accountability Journal, 15*(3), 282–311. doi:10.1108/09513570210435852

Deegan, C., Rankin, M., & Tobin, J. (2002). An examination of the corporate social and environmental disclosures of BHP from 1983-1997: A test of legitimacy theory. *Accounting, Auditing & Accountability Journal, 15*(3), 312–343. doi:10.1108/09513570210435861

Deegan, C., & Unerman, J. (2011). *Financial accounting theory* (2nd ed.). McGraw-Hill.

DiMaggio, P., & Powell, W. (1983). The iron cage revisited: Institutional isomorphism and collective rationality in organizational fields. *American Sociological Review, 48*(2), 147–160. doi:10.2307/2095101

Doh, J., & Guay, T. (2006). Corporate social responsibility, public policy, and NGO activism in Europe and the United States: An institutional stakeholder perspective. *Journal of Management Studies, 43*(1), 47–73. doi:10.1111/j.1467-6486.2006.00582.x

Dowling, J., & Pfeffer, J. (1975). Organizational legitimacy: Social values and organizational behavior. *Pacific Sociological Review, 18*(1), 122–136. doi:10.2307/1388226

Eells, R. (1956). *Corporation giving in a free society*. Harper.

Eells, R., & Walton, C. (1974). Conceptual Foundations of Business. Richard D. Irwin.

Eilbert, H., & Parket, I. R. (1973). The current status of corporate social responsibility. *Business Horizons, 16*, 5–14.

Eisenhardt, K. (1985). Control: Organizational and economic approaches. *Management Science, 31*(2), 134–149. doi:10.1287/mnsc.31.2.134

Eisenhardt, K. (1989). Agency theory: An assessment and review. *Academy of Management Review, 14*(1), 57–74. doi:10.2307/258191

Elijido-Ten, E., Kloot, L., & Clarkson, P. (2010). Extending the application of stakeholder influence strategies to environmental disclosures. *Accounting, Auditing & Accountability Journal, 23*(8), 1032–1059. doi:10.1108/09513571011092547

Elkington, J. (1998). Partnerships from cannibals with forks: The triple bottom line of 21st-century business. *Environmental Quality Management, 8*(1), 37–51. doi:10.1002/tqem.3310080106

Feldstein, M. (2013). *The Reagan-Thatcher revolution.* Disponible en: https://www.dw.com/en/the-reagan-thatcher-revolution/a-16732731

Ferrari, R. (2015). Writing narrative style literature reviews. *Medical Writing, 24*(4), 230–235. doi:10.1179/2047480615Z.000000000329

Fitch, H. (1976). Achieving corporate social responsibility. *Academy of Management Review, 1*(1), 38–46. doi:10.5465/amr.1976.4408754

Fontaine, M. (2013). Corporate social responsibility and sustainability: The new bottom line? *International Journal of Business and Social Science, 4*(4), 1–10.

Foro de Expertos en Responsabilidad Social de las Empresas. (2007). *Informe del foro de expertos en responsabilidad social de las empresas* [Report of the forum of experts in corporate social responsibility]. Established on March 17, 2005 at the initiative of the Ministry of Labor and Social Affairs. Concluded on July 12, 2007.

Fransen, L. (2013). The embeddedness of responsible business practice: Exploring the interaction between national-institutional environments and corporate social responsibility. *Journal of Business Ethics, 115*(2), 213–227. doi:10.100710551-012-1395-2

Frederick, W. (1960). The growing concern over business responsibility. *California Management Review, 2*(4), 54–61. doi:10.2307/41165405

Freeman, R. (1984). *Strategic Management - A Stakeholder Approach.* Pitman.

Freeman, R. (2001). A stakeholder theory of the modern corporation. *Perspectives in Business Ethics, 3*, 144.

Freeman, R., & Reed, D. (1983). Stockholders and stakeholders: A new perspective on corporate governance. *California Management Review, 25*(3), 88–106. doi:10.2307/41165018

Friedman, A., & Miles, S. (2002). Developing stakeholder theory. *Journal of Management Studies, 39*(1), 1–21. doi:10.1111/1467-6486.00280

Friedman, M. (1962). *Capitalism and freedom.* University of Chicago Press.

Friedman, M. (1970). The social responsibility of business is to increase its profits. *The New York Times Magazine*.

Frynas, J. (2015). Strategic CSR, value creation and competitive advantage. In T. C. Lawton & T. S. Rajwani (Eds.), *The Routledge Companion to Non- Market Strategy*. Routledge.

Galaskiewicz, J. (1985). *Social Organization of an Urban Grants Economy: A Study of Business Philanthropy and Nonprofit Organizations*. Academic Press.

García-Marzá, D. (2004). *Ética empresarial. Del diálogo a la confianza (Business ethics. From dialogue to trust)*. Trotta.

Hall, P., & Soskice, D. (2001). *Varieties of Capitalism: The Institutional Basis of Competitive Advantage*. Oxford University Press. doi:10.1093/0199247757.001.0001

Hart, S. (1995). A natural resource-based view of the firm. *Academy of Management Review*, *20*(4), 986–1014. doi:10.5465/amr.1995.9512280033

Hediger, W. (2010). Welfare and capital-theoretic foundations of corporate social responsibility and corporate sustainability. *Journal of Socio-Economics*, *39*(4), 518–526. doi:10.1016/j.socec.2010.02.001

Hill, C., & Jones, T. (1992). Stakeholder agency theory. *Journal of Management Studies*, *29*(2), 131–154. doi:10.1111/j.1467-6486.1992.tb00657.x

Hoepner, A., Aguiar, T., & Majithia, R. (2014). The level of compliance with the international code of marketing of breast-milk substitutes: Does it matter to stock markets? *Journal of Business Ethics*, *119*(3), 329–348. doi:10.100710551-013-1625-2

Holder-Webb, L., & Cohen, J. (2012). The cut and paste society: Isomorphism in codes of ethics. *Journal of Business Ethics*, *107*(4), 485–509. doi:10.100710551-011-1060-1

Hopkins, M. (1998). *The Planetary Bargain: Corporate Social Responsibility Comes of Age*. Macmillan.

Hopkins, M. (2004). *The Planetary Bargain. Corporate Social Responsibility Matters*. Routledge.

Hotho, J., & Pedersen, T. (2012). Beyond the rules of the game: three institutional approaches and how they matter for international business. In M. Demirbag & G. Wood (Eds.), *Handbook of Institutional Approaches to International Business*. Edward Elgar. doi:10.4337/9781849807692.00016

Huang, K., Dyerson, R., Wu, L., & Harindranath, G. (2015). From temporary competitive advantage to sustainable competitive advantage. *British Journal of Management*, *26*(4), 617–636. doi:10.1111/1467-8551.12104

Ismail, M. (2009). Corporate social responsibility and its role in community development: An international perspective. *Journal of International Social Research*, *2*(9), 1–12.

Jamali, D., & Neville, B. (2011). Convergence versus divergence of CSR in developing countries: An embedded multi-layered institutional lens. *Journal of Business Ethics*, *102*(4), 599–621. doi:10.100710551-011-0830-0

Jawahar, I., & McLaughlin, G. (2001). Toward a descriptive stakeholder theory: An organizational life cycle approach. *Academy of Management Review*, *26*(3), 397–414. doi:10.2307/259184

Jennings, P., & Zandbergen, P. (1995). Ecologically sustainable organizations: An institutional approach. *Academy of Management Review*, *20*(4), 1015–1052. doi:10.5465/amr.1995.9512280034

Jensen, M., & Meckling, W. (1976). Theory of the firm: Managerial behavior, agency costs, and ownership structure. *Journal of Financial Economics*, *3*(4), 305–360. doi:10.1016/0304-405X(76)90026-X

Jia, M., & Zhang, Z. (2014). How does the stock market value corporate social performance? When behavioral theories interact with stakeholder theory. *Journal of Management Studies*, *51*(7), 1118–1152. doi:10.1111/joms.12090

Jones, T. (1980). Corporate social responsibility revisited, redefined. *California Management Review*, *22*(3), 59–67. doi:10.2307/41164877

Kang, N., & Moon, J. (2012). Institutional complementarity between corporate governance and corporate social responsibility: A comparative institutional analysis of three capitalisms. *Socio-economic Review*, *10*(1), 85–108. doi:10.1093er/mwr025

Kao, E., Yeh, C., Wang, L., & Fung, H. (2018). The relationship between CSR and performance: Evidence in China. *Pacific-Basin Finance Journal*, *51*, 155–170. doi:10.1016/j.pacfin.2018.04.006

Khoury, G., Rostami, J., & Turnbull, J. (1999). *Corporate Social Responsibility: Turning Words into Action*. Conference Board of Canada.

Kotler, P., & Lee, N. (2007). *Corporate Social Responsibility: doing the most good for your company and your case*. John Wiley & Sons.

Kraaijenbrink, J., Spender, J., & Groen, A. (2010). The resource-based view: A review and assessment of its critiques. *Journal of Management*, *36*(1), 349–372. doi:10.1177/0149206309350775

Lamberti, L., & Lettieri, E. (2009). CSR practices and corporate strategy: Evidence from a longitudinal case study. *Journal of Business Ethics*, *87*(2), 153–168. doi:10.100710551-008-9876-z

Langtry, B. (1994). Stakeholders and the moral responsibilities of business. *Business Ethics Quarterly*, *4*(4), 431–443. doi:10.2307/3857342

Lantos, G. (2001). The boundaries of strategic corporate social responsibility. *Journal of Consumer Marketing*, *18*(7), 595–632. doi:10.1108/07363760110410281

Lee, M. (2008). A review of the theories of corporate social responsibility: Its evolutionary path and the road ahead. *International Journal of Management Reviews*, *10*(1), 53–73. doi:10.1111/j.1468-2370.2007.00226.x

Lindblom, C. (1983). *The concept of organizational legitimacy and its implications for corporate social responsibility disclosure*. Working Paper. American Accounting Association Public Interest Section.

Lindgreen, A., & Swaen, V. (2010). Corporate social responsibility. *International Journal of Management Reviews*, *12*(1), 1–7. doi:10.1111/j.1468-2370.2009.00277.x

Lockett, A., & Thompson, S. (2004). Edith Penrose's contributions to the resource-based view: An alternative perspective. *Journal of Management Studies, 41*(1), 193–203. doi:10.1111/j.1467-6486.2004.00428.x

Lourenço, I., Callen, J., Branco, M., & Curto, J. (2014). The value relevance of reputation for sustainability leadership. *Journal of Business Ethics, 119*(1), 17–28. doi:10.100710551-012-1617-7

Maignan, I., & Ferrell, O. (2004). Corporate social responsibility and marketing: An integrative framework. *Journal of the Academy of Marketing Science, 32*(1), 3–19. doi:10.1177/0092070303258971

Manne, H., & Wallich, H. (1972). *The Modern Corporation and Social Responsibility*. American Enterprise Institute for Public Policy Research.

Marco-Lajara, B., Martínez-Falcó, J., Ruiz-Fernández, L., & Seva-Larrosa, P. (2022k). Evolución del pensamiento en la disciplina de dirección estratégica: la visión de la empresa basada en las capacidades dinámicas y en el conocimiento. [Evolution of thinking in the discipline of strategic management: the vision of the company based on dynamic capabilities and knowledge] In *Investigación y transferencia de las ciencias sociales frente a un mundo en crisis* [Social science research and transfer in the face of a world in crisis]. (pp. 1801–1826). Dykinson.

Marco-Lajara, B., Sánchez-García, E., Martínez-Falcó, J., & Poveda-Pareja, E. (2022l). Regional Specialization, Competitive Pressure, and Cooperation: The Cocktail for Innovation. *Energies, 15*(15), 5346.

Marco-Lajara, B., Sánchez-García, E., Seva-Larrosa, P., & Martínez-Falcó, J. (2022m). Knowledge creation and diffusion inspecialized environments: What are the factors involved? In *Empresa, economía y derecho. Oportunidades ante un entorno global y disruptivo* [Business, economy and law. Opportunities in a global and disruptive environment]. (pp. 432–459). Dykinson.

Marco-Lajara, B., Seva-Larrosa, P., Martínez-Falcó, J., & García-Lillo, F. (2022i). Wine clusters and Protected Designations of Origin (PDOs) in Spain: An exploratory analysis. *Journal of Wine Research, 33*(3), 1–22. doi:10.1080/09571264.2022.2110051

Marco-Lajara, B., Seva-Larrosa, P., Martinez-Falco, J., & Sanchez-Garcia, E. (2021a). How Has COVID- 19 Affected The Spanish Wine Industry? An Exploratory Analysis. *Natural Volatiles & Essential Oils Journal, 8*(6), 2722–2731.

Marco-Lajara, B., Seva-Larrosa, P., Martínez-Falcó, J., & Sánchez-García, E. (2021j). El clúster vitivinícola de Jumilla: Entre la tradición y la modernidad [The Jumilla wine cluster: Between tradition and modernity]. In XLIII jornadas de viticultura y enología de la Tierra de Barros: III Congreso agroalimentario de Extremadura [XLIII Tierra de Barros Viticulture and Oenology Conference: III Agri-food Congress of Extremadura] (pp. 56-70). Centro Universitario Santa Ana.

Marco-Lajara, B., Seva-Larrosa, P., Ruiz-Fernandez, L., & Martinez-Falco, J. (2021b). The Effect of COVID- 19 on the Spanish Wine Industry. In *Impact of Global Issues on International Trade* (pp. 211–232). IGI Global. doi:10.4018/978-1-7998-8314-2.ch012

Marco-Lajara, B., Zaragoza-Saez, P., Falcó, J. M., & Millan-Tudela, L. A. (2022a). Analysing the Relationship Between Green Intellectual Capital and the Achievement of the Sustainable Development Goals. In *Handbook of Research on Building Inclusive Global Knowledge Societies for Sustainable Development* (pp. 111–129). IGI Global. doi:10.4018/978-1-6684-5109-0.ch005

Marco-Lajara, B., Zaragoza-Sáez, P., Falcó, J. M., & Millan-Tudela, L. A. (2022f). Corporate Social Responsibility: A Narrative Literature Review. *Frameworks for Sustainable Development Goals to Manage Economic, Social, and Environmental Shocks and Disasters*, 16-34.

Marco-Lajara, B., Zaragoza-Saez, P., Falcó, J. M., & Sánchez-García, E. (2022b). COVID-19 and Wine Tourism: A Story of Heartbreak. In Handbook of Research on SDGs for Economic Development, Social Development, and Environmental Protection (pp. 90-112). IGI Global.

Marco-Lajara, B., Zaragoza-Saez, P., & Martínez-Falcó, J. (2022e). Green Innovation: Balancing Economic Efficiency With Environmental Protection. In Frameworks for Sustainable Development Goals to Manage Economic, Social, and Environmental Shocks and Disasters (pp. 239-254). IGI Global.

Marco-Lajara, B., Zaragoza Sáez, P., & Martínez-Falcó, J. (2022n). Does Green Intellectual Capital Affect Green Performance? The Mediation of Green Innovation. *Telematique*, *21*(1), 4594–4602.

Marco-Lajara, B., Zaragoza-Sáez, P., Martínez-Falcó, J., & Ruiz-Fernández, L. (2022g). The Effect of Green Intellectual Capital on Green Performance in the Spanish Wine Industry: A Structural Equation Modeling Approach. *Complexity*, *2022*, 2022. doi:10.1155/2022/6024077

Marco-Lajara, B., Zaragoza-Sáez, P., Martínez-Falcó, J., & Sánchez-García, E. (2022c). Green Intellectual Capital in the Spanish Wine Industry. In Innovative Economic, Social, and Environmental Practices for Progressing Future Sustainability (pp. 102-120). IGI Global. doi:10.4018/978-1-7998-9590-9.ch006

Marco-Lajara, B., Zaragoza-Sáez, P., Martínez-Falcó, J., & Sánchez-García, E. (2022d). El capital intelectual verde como hoja de ruta para la sostenibilidad: El caso de bodegas Luzón [Green intellectual capital as a roadmap for sustainability: the case of bodegas Luzón]. *GeoGraphos: Revista Digital para Estudiantes de Geografía y Ciencias Sociales*, *13*(147), 137–146.

Marco-Lajara, B., Zaragoza-Sáez, P., Martínez-Falcó, J., & Sánchez-García, E. (2022o). Las rutas del vino de España: el impacto económico derivado de las visitas a bodegas y museos. [Spain's wine routes: the economic impact of visits to wineries and museums] In *Investigación y transferencia de las ciencias sociales frente a un mundo en crisis* [Social science research and transfer in the face of a world in crisis]. (pp. 1774–1800). Dykinson.

Marco-Lajara, B., Zaragoza-Sáez, P. C., Martínez-Falcó, J., & Sánchez-García, E. (2022h). Does green intellectual capital affect green innovation performance? Evidence from the Spanish wine industry. *British Food Journal*, ahead-of-print.

Marquis, C., Glynn, M., & Davis, G. (2007). Community isomorphism and corporate social action. *Academy of Management Review*, *32*(3), 925–945. doi:10.5465/amr.2007.25275683

Marsden, C. (2001). *The Role of Public Authorities in Corporate Social Responsibility*. http://www.alter.be/socialresponsibility/ people/marchri/en/displayPerson

Matten, D., & Moon, J. (2008). "Implicit" and "explicit" CSR: A conceptual framework for a comparative understanding of corporate social responsibility. *Academy of Management Review*, *330*(2), 404–424. doi:10.5465/amr.2008.31193458

McGuire, J. (1963). *Business and society*. McGraw-hill.

McWilliams, A., & Siegel, D. (2011). Creating and capturing value: Strategic corporate social responsibility, resource-based theory, and sustainable competitive advantage. *Journal of Management, 37*(5), 1480–1495. doi:10.1177/0149206310385696

McWilliams, A., Siegel, D., & Wright, P. (2006). Corporate social responsibility: Strategic implications. *Journal of Management Studies, 43*(1), 1–18. doi:10.1111/j.1467-6486.2006.00580.x

Mellahi, K., Frynas, J., Sun, P., & Siegel, D. (2016). A review of the nonmarket strategy literature: Towards a multi-theoretical integration. *Journal of Management, 42*(1), 143–173. doi:10.1177/0149206315617241

Menguc, B., Auh, S., & Ozanne, L. (2010). The interactive effect of internal and external factors on a proactive environmental strategy and its influence on a firm's performance. *Journal of Business Ethics, 94*(2), 279–298. doi:10.100710551-009-0264-0

Meyer, J., & Rowan, B. (1977). Institutionalized organizations: Formal structure as myth and ceremony. *American Journal of Sociology, 83*(2), 340–363. doi:10.1086/226550

Miles, M., & Covin, J. (2000). Environmental marketing: A source of reputational, competitive, and financial advantage. *Journal of Business Ethics, 23*(3), 299–311. doi:10.1023/A:1006214509281

Mitchell, R., Agle, B., & Wood, D. (1997). Toward a theory of stakeholder identification and salience. *Academy of Management Review, 22*(4), 853–886. doi:10.2307/259247

Mobus, J. (2005). Mandatory environmental disclosures in a legitimacy theory context. *Accounting, Auditing & Accountability Journal, 18*(4), 492–517. doi:10.1108/09513570510609333

Mohr, L., Webb, D., & Harris, K. (2001). Do consumers expect companies to be socially responsible? The impact of corporate social responsibility on buying behavior. *The Journal of Consumer Affairs, 35*(1), 45–72. doi:10.1111/j.1745-6606.2001.tb00102.x

Moir, L., & Taffler, R. (2004). Does corporate philanthropy exist? Business giving to the arts in the U.K. *Journal of Business Ethics, 54*(2), 149–161. doi:10.100710551-004-1777-1

Monfort, A., & Villagra, N. (2016). Corporate Social Responsibility and Corporate Foundations in Building Responsible Brands. *El Profesional de la Información, 25*(5), 767–777. doi:10.3145/epi.2016.sep.07

Moore, G. (2001). Corporate social and financial performance: An investigation in the U.K. supermarket industry. *Journal of Business Ethics, 34*(4), 299–315. doi:10.1023/A:1012537016969

Neu, D., Warsame, H., & Pedwell, K. (1998). Managing public impressions: Environmental disclosures in annual reports. *Accounting, Organizations and Society, 23*(3), 265–282. doi:10.1016/S0361-3682(97)00008-1

North, D. (1990). *Institutions, Institutional Change and Economic Performance*. Cambridge University Press. doi:10.1017/CBO9780511808678

Observatorio de RSC. (2014). *Introducción a la Responsabilidad Social Corporativa* [Introduction to Corporate Social Responsibility]. Observatorio de RSC.

Oh, W., Chang, Y., & Martynov, A. (2011). The effect of ownership structure on corporate social responsibility: Empirical evidence from Korea. *Journal of Business Ethics, 104*(2), 283–297. doi:10.100710551-011-0912-z

Oikonomou, I., Brooks, C., & Pavelin, S. (2014). The financial effects of uniform and mixed corporate social performance. *Journal of Management Studies, 51*(6), 898–925. doi:10.1111/joms.12064

Okafor, A., Adeleye, B. N., & Adusei, M. (2021). Corporate social responsibility and financial performance: Evidence from US tech firms. *Journal of Cleaner Production, 292*, 126078. doi:10.1016/j.jclepro.2021.126078

Oliver, P. (2012). *Succeeding with your literature review. A handbook for students*. McGraw-Hill, Open University Press.

Patten, D. (1992). Intra-industry environmental disclosures in response to the Alaskan oil spill: A note on legitimacy theory. *Accounting, Organizations and Society, 17*(5), 471–475. doi:10.1016/0361-3682(92)90042-Q

Peters, M., Siller, L., & Matzler, K. (2011). The resource-based and the market-based approaches to cultural tourism in Alpine destinations. *Journal of Sustainable Tourism, 19*(7), 877–893. doi:10.1080/09669582.2010.547198

Porter, M., & Kramer, M. (2006). Strategy & Society. *Harvard Business Review, 84*(12), 1–16. PMID:17183795

Preston, L., & Post, J. (1975). *Private Management and Public Policy*. Prentice-Hall.

Roberts, R. (1992). Determinants of corporate social responsibility disclosure: An application of stakeholder theory. *Accounting, Organizations and Society, 17*(6), 595–612. doi:10.1016/0361-3682(92)90015-K

Ruf, B., Muralidhar, K., Brown, R., Janney, J., & Paul, K. (2001). An empirical investigation of the relationship between change in corporate social performance and financial performance: A stakeholder theory perspective. *Journal of Business Ethics, 32*(2), 143–156. doi:10.1023/A:1010786912118

Rugman, A., & Verbeke, A. (2002). Edith Penrose's contribution to the resource-based view of strategic management. *Strategic Management Journal, 23*(8), 769–780. doi:10.1002mj.240

Russo, M., & Fouts, P. (1997). A resource-based perspective on corporate environmental performance and profitability. *Academy of Management Journal, 40*(3), 534–559.

Sánchez-Torné, I., Morán-Álvarez, J. C., & Pérez-López, J. A. (2020). The importance of corporate social responsibility in achieving high corporate reputation. *Corporate Social Responsibility and Environmental Management, 27*(6), 2692–2700. doi:10.1002/csr.1993

Sarkar, S., & Searcy, C. (2016). Zeitgeist or chameleon? A quantitative analysis of CSR definitions. *Journal of Cleaner Production, 135*, 1423–1435. doi:10.1016/j.jclepro.2016.06.157

Schuler, D., & Cording, M. (2006). A corporate social performance-corporate financial performance behavioral model for consumers. *Academy of Management Review, 31*(3), 540–558. doi:10.5465/amr.2006.21318916

Scott, R. (2001). *Institutions and Organizations*. Sage Publications.

Selekman, B. (1959). *A moral philosophy for management*. McGraw-Hill.

Sethi, S. (1975). Dimensions of corporate social performance: An analytical framework. *California Management Review*, *17*(3), 58–64. doi:10.2307/41162149

Seva-Larrosa, P., Martínez-Falcó, J., & Ruiz-Fernández, L. (2022). Analizando las principales variables empresariales en los clusters vinícolas españoles teniendo en cuenta la localización de las empresas y su pertenencia a una marca colectiva. [Analyzing the main business variables in Spanish wine clusters taking into account the location of the companies and their membership in a collective brand] In *Miradas sobre el emprendimiento ante la crisis del coronavirus* [Perspectives on entrepreneurship in the face of the coronavirus crisis]. (pp. 629–634). Dykinson.

Sheehy, B. (2015). Defining CSR: Problems and solutions. *Journal of Business Ethics*, *131*(3), 625–648. doi:10.100710551-014-2281-x

Singh, K., & Misra, M. (2021). Linking corporate social responsibility (CSR) and organizational performance: The moderating effect of corporate reputation. *European Research on Management and Business Economics*, *27*(1), 100139. doi:10.1016/j.iedeen.2020.100139

Sison, A. (2009). From CSR to corporate citizenship: Anglo-American and continental European perspectives. *Journal of Business Ethics*, *89*(3), 235–246. doi:10.100710551-010-0395-3

Smith, N. (2001). Changes in corporate practices in response to public interest advocacy and actions. In Handbook of Marketing and Society. Sage.

Smith, N. (2003). Corporate social responsibility: Whether or how? *California Management Review*, *45*(4), 52–76. doi:10.2307/41166188

Spence, A., & Zeckhauser, R. (1971). Insurance, information, and individual action. *The American Economic Review*, *61*(2), 380–387.

Suchman, M. (1995). Managing legitimacy: Strategic and institutional approaches. *Academy of Management Review*, *20*(3), 571–610. doi:10.2307/258788

Surroca, J., Tribo, J., & Zahra, S. (2013). Stakeholder pressure on MNEs and the transfer of socially irresponsible practices to subsidiaries. *Academy of Management Journal*, *56*(2), 549–572. doi:10.5465/amj.2010.0962

Swanson, D. (1995). Addressing a theoretical problem by reorienting the corporate social performance model. *Academy of Management Review*, *20*(1), 43–64. doi:10.2307/258886

Torugsa, N., O'Donohue, W., & Hecker, R. (2012). Capabilities, proactive CSR and financial performance in SMEs: Empirical evidence from an Australian manufacturing industry sector. *Journal of Business Ethics*, *109*(4), 483–500. doi:10.100710551-011-1141-1

Tranfield, D., Denyer, D., & Smart, P. (2003). Towards a methodology for developing evidence-informed management knowledge by means of systematic review. *British Journal of Management*, *14*(3), 207–222. doi:10.1111/1467-8551.00375

Trapp, N. (2012). Corporation as climate ambassador: Transcending business sector boundaries in a Swedish CSR campaign. *Public Relations Review, 38*(3), 458–465. doi:10.1016/j.pubrev.2012.03.004

Van Marrewijk, M. (2003). Concepts and definitions of CSR and corporate sustainability: Between agency and communion. *Journal of Business Ethics, 44*(2), 95–105. doi:10.1023/A:1023331212247

Votaw, D. (1973). Genius becomes rare: A comment on the doctrine of social responsibility Pt. II. *California Management Review, 15*(3), 5–19. doi:10.2307/41164435

Waldman, D., Luque, M., Washburn, N., & House, R. (2006). Cultural and leadership predictors of corporate social responsibility values of top management: A GLOBE study of 15 countries. *Journal of International Business Studies, 37*(6), 823–837. doi:10.1057/palgrave.jibs.8400230

Walton, C. (1967). *Corporate social responsibilities.* Wadsworth Publishing Company.

Wang, H., & Choi, J. (2013). A new look at the corporate social-financial performance relationship: The moderating roles of temporal and interdomain consistency in corporate social performance. *Journal of Management, 39*(2), 416–441. doi:10.1177/0149206310375850

Wankel, C. (2008). *21st century management: a reference handbook.* SAGE Publications. doi:10.4135/9781412954006

Wee, B. V., & Banister, D. (2016). How to write a literature review paper? *Transport Reviews, 36*(2), 278–288. doi:10.1080/01441647.2015.1065456

Wernerfelt, B. (1984). A resource-based view of the firm. *Strategic Management Journal, 5*(2), 171–180. doi:10.1002mj.4250050207

Werther, W. Jr, & Chandler, D. (2005). Strategic corporate social responsibility as global brand insurance. *Business Horizons, 48*(4), 317–324. doi:10.1016/j.bushor.2004.11.009

Whitley, R. (1999). *Divergent Capitalisms: The Social Structuring and Change of Business Systems.* Oxford University Press.

Wood, G., Dibben, P., & Ogden, S. (2014). Comparative capitalism without capitalism, and production without workers: The limits and possibilities of contemporary institutional analysis. *International Journal of Management Reviews, 16*(4), 384–396. doi:10.1111/ijmr.12025

Wright, P., & Ferris, S. (1997). Agency conflict and corporate strategy: The effect of divestment on corporate value. *Strategic Management Journal, 18*(1), 77–83. doi:10.1002/(SICI)1097-0266(199701)18:1<77::AID-SMJ810>3.0.CO;2-R

Xu, S., & Yang, R. (2010). Indigenous characteristics of Chinese corporate social responsibility conceptual paradigm. *Journal of Business Ethics, 93*(2), 321–333. doi:10.100710551-009-0224-8

Ye, N., Kueh, T. B., Hou, L., Liu, Y., & Yu, H. (2020). A bibliometric analysis of corporate social responsibility in sustainable development. *Journal of Cleaner Production, 272*, 122679. doi:10.1016/j.jclepro.2020.122679

ADDITIONAL READING

Barnett, M. L., Henriques, I., & Husted, B. W. (2020). Beyond good intentions: Designing CSR initiatives for greater social impact. *Journal of Management, 46*(6), 937–964. doi:10.1177/0149206319900539

Gillan, S. L., Koch, A., & Starks, L. T. (2021). Firms and social responsibility: A review of ESG and CSR research in corporate finance. *Journal of Corporate Finance, 66*, 101889. doi:10.1016/j.jcorpfin.2021.101889

Mao, Y., He, J., Morrison, A. M., & Andres Coca-Stefaniak, J. (2021). Effects of tourism CSR on employee psychological capital in the COVID-19 crisis: From the perspective of conservation of resources theory. *Current Issues in Tourism, 24*(19), 2716–2734. doi:10.1080/13683500.2020.1770706

Shahzad, M., Qu, Y., Javed, S. A., Zafar, A. U., & Rehman, S. U. (2020). Relation of environment sustainability to CSR and green innovation: A case of Pakistani manufacturing industry. *Journal of Cleaner Production, 253*, 119938. doi:10.1016/j.jclepro.2019.119938

KEY TERMS AND DEFINITIONS

Corporate Social Responsibility: The responsibility that each organization has with the environment in which it operates and with the society of which it is a part.

Corporate Sustainability: A business management approach that seeks to generate organizational value, as it generates societal value.

Narrative Review: It is a work that analyzes and discusses articles and reports, generally scientific and academic, published in or about an area of knowledge. Scientific reports may be of an empirical, theoretical, critical, analytical, or methodological nature.

Philanthropy: Love for the human species and for all that concerns humanity, expressed in selfless help to others.

Stakeholders: A group of persons organized around a common interest, in order to act jointly in defense of the same.

Sustainability: It refers to the balance of a species with the resources of its environment.

Sustainable Development Goals: There are 17 interconnected global goals designed to be a blueprint for achieving a better and more sustainable future for all.

Theory: A logical-deductive system consisting of a set of hypotheses, a field of application and some rules to draw consequences from the hypotheses.

Chapter 10
Achieving the Sustainable Development Goals:
A Case Study of the Ministry of Chittagong Hill Tracts Affairs, Bangladesh

Parimal Roy
https://orcid.org/0000-0002-0461-2587
Universiti Malaya, Malaysia

Haris Abd Wahab
Universiti Malaya, Malaysia

Mashitah Hamidi
Universiti Malaya, Malaysia

ABSTRACT

This chapter addresses the following questions: What are the organizational gaps in achieving the SDGs indicators in the hilly ethnic groups, and how are they looking forward to sustainable development? This chapter also shows the organizational structure and its challenges concerning coping with SDGs and unfolding the links within ministries in Bangladesh. The Sustainable Development Goals are a burning issue worldwide, and they have significant consequences on economic growth as well as on public administration, either sound or immoral management. The Ministry of Chittagong Hill Tracts Affairs (MoCHTA) is mandated to ameliorate and ensure social safety and security in the life settings of the different ethnic people in the Chittagong Hill Tracts (CHT) area after signing an accord on 2nd December 1997. Methodologically, it is a neoliberalism study, and the authors conducted this chapter based on secondary data analyzed and reviewed, such as Ministry's APA, Citizen Charter, project or development activities, reports, and interviews with senior bureaucrats and ethnic leaders.

DOI: 10.4018/978-1-6684-7499-0.ch010

INTRODUCTION

Historically after the liberation of Bangladesh in 1971, confrontation of 11 ethnic groups started armed movements pressing the government for their self-determination or self-identity (Chakma & Maitrot, 2016; Mohsin, 2001, 2002; Tripura, 2016). These armed groups make the whole hilly area, consisting of three districts—Bandarban, Khagrachari, and Rangamati, political unrest. After the emergence of Independence, the Government of Bangladesh took several interventions- assimilation of nationalism, acculturation, settler colonialization, and militarization—to control and advance these ethnic groups in the hill tract area (Tripura, 2018, 2020). However, when all the ways became painstaking, the government thought of alternatives for avoiding the path of armed conflicts and finding a political solution, for a congenial backdrop for establishing peace in the Chottogram Hill Tracts area within the jurisdiction of the constitution and keeping the sovereignty of Bangladesh (Roy et al.,2022). An accord (Chittagong hill tracts accord) was signed between National Committee on Chittagong Hill Tracts Affairs and the Parbatya Chattagram Jana-Samhati Samiti on 2nd December 1997(www.mochta.gov.bd). After the signing of this treaty, the unstable situation in the CHT came to an end in Text. Consequently, the Ministry of Chittagram Hill Tracts Affairs (MoCHTA) emerged on 15th July 1998 to lead the hilly land and people's Development and security-oriented interventions; we can align with SDGs—11(Sustainable communities) and SDGs 16 (Peace, Justice, and Strong Institutions).

The Chittagong Hill Tracts is the eastern gateway to Bengal. The area covers 13,294 square kilometers, eleven ethnic groups, and is consisted of three districts: Bandarban, Khagrachari, and Rangamati (unicef.org/bangladesh/2019). Diverse cultures, versatile people, mountainous terrain, and potential resources make it a genuinely magnificent nature. However, the ethnic conflict here is a black spot on a beautiful face. Eleven hilly ethnic groups and diversified cultures and nature like mountains, hills, forests, rivers, lakes, and the diverse number of flora and fauna with outstanding natural beauty make up its ecological wealth. In and around the Chittagong Hill Tracts provides essential environmental services that contribute to economic Development, environmental protection, Sustainability, and human well-being. Indeed, the area covers about 40% forest area in Bangladesh.

The SDGs are supposed to provide a framework, targets, and indicators that GoB can adopt or implement into their national development agendas to move towards a more sustainable development path by 2030. So, this is a great opportunity and a vast responsibility for the ministry to align and track one's own country's progress with Sustainable Development Goals. What follows, though, is the obligation to order priorities and modify goals and objectives in response to regional difficulties and the available skills and resources. Every ministry has its priorities and planning methodology(mochta.gov.bd). Knowledge, capability, and institutional strategies are needed to integrate SDGs into the development process to balance national interests with the interests of sustainable development Goals on a global scale. The procedure will be time-consuming and demand technologies that can not only perform the reviews but also evaluate the efficiency of these processes and continuously update the user on progress. In order to identify, plan, and implement SDGs while keeping in mind how goals and targets are related, it is crucial to have a framework like this in place. It will also be crucial to consider for ministry's role.

SALIENT FEATURES OF THE MOCHTA

The Ministry got one secretariat, a Minster from a hilly area, and ethnic groups led. The secretariat consists of different wings and branches. Under this Ministry have some affiliated offices such as —

1. Chottogram Hill Tracts Regional Council
2. Chottogram Hill Tracts Development Board
3. Refugee Rehabilitation Task Force
4. Rangamati Hill Tracts District Council (Rangamati)
5. Bandarban Hill Tracts District Council (Bandarban)
6. Khagrachhari Hill Tracts District Council (Khagrachhari)

Figure 1. The CHT Area in Bangladesh

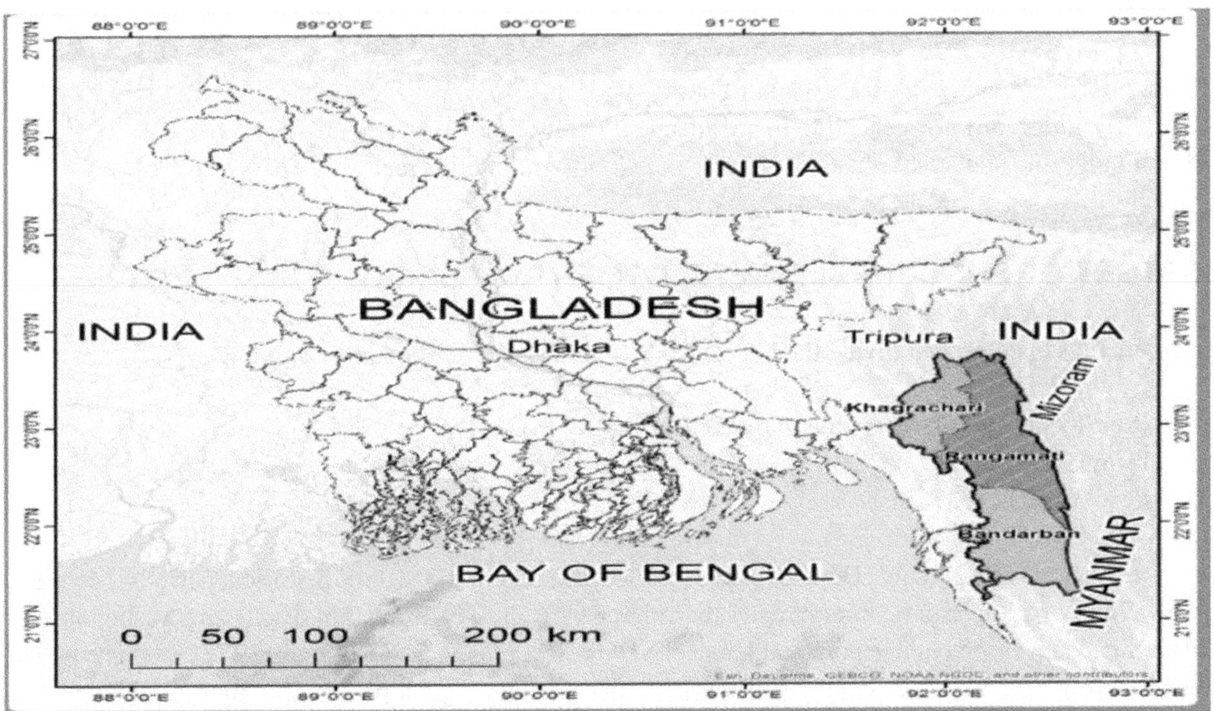

Source: ICIMOD, 2016, Pg.2

KEY RULES OF BUSINESS OF MoCHTA

The Ministry has a rule of business to operate the development and administration activities within its jurisdiction. The salient features of the rules of business that are the most related to SDGs and Ethnic issues are in following —

1. Advisory Support to Chottogram Hill Tracts local governments in selected issues.

2. Coordination among concerned ministries and departments.
3. Secretarial support for all council and working committees related to Chottogram Hill Tracts.
4. Advisory support, monitoring, and implementation to Government and different committees.
5. Preparation of planning and development activities for government and the Chittagong Hill Tracts.
6. Implementation of works in accordance with the customary laws of Chittagong Hill Tracts Upazila council, Municipality, Union council, village council, and other local government.
7. Coordination among all concerned government agencies to protect the environment and geological aspects of Chittagong Hill Tracts.
8. Development work for the betterment of the Tribal and non-tribal people of Chottogram Hill Tracts' economic, educational, cultural, social, language, religious, and indigenous activities.
9. Running and coordinating relief and rehabilitation work during the disaster in the Chittagong Hill Tracts.
10. Monitoring work of NGO activities in the Chittagong Hill Tracts.
11. Administration of Chottogram Hill Tracts Development Board.
12. Chottogram Hill Tracts related issues of the International Centre for integrated mountain Development (ICIMOD).
13. Liaison among the Ministries and issues.
14. Preparation of Laws related to the Ministry of Chottogram Hill Tracts.
15. Inquiry and statistical issues of Ministry of Chottogram Hill Tracts.

HISTORY OF SUSTAINABLE DEVELOPMENT: A GLANCE

In a general sense, we can divide the history of Sustainable Development into three parts —

1. Pre-Stockholm (Covering the until WCED — 1972).
2. From Stockholm to WCED (1972 —1978)
3. Post WCED (1987—1997).

The concept of Sustainable Development is categorized in the above three historical periods (Mebratu, year p.96). Nevertheless, we cannot deny the role of the "Club of Rome" in discussing Sustainable or Sustainable Development in a practical sense of SDGs discourse (Meadows et al., 1972). In this context, we can throw a light upon an equitably brief of history when the 'great powers' put then-dominant ideas into practice and, in mind, opened the way to 'Development' (Benjaminsen, 2021; Sen, 2009; Pissani, 2006).

Western belief in 'Development' has ancient roots "the end of the last century, with a long history already behind it, European colonization branched out in quite different forms according to the metropolis's pace and interests (Grober, 2007; Rist, 2014).

Victor Hugo informs us, "Men's destiny lies in the South. The moment has come to make Europe realize that it has Africa alongside it. In the nineteenth century, the White man civilized a black man; Europe civilized the rest of the world in the twentieth century. It was a fashion to make a new Africa amenable to civilization – that is the problem. This story is very relevant to the case of the Santal community in Bangladesh to make them Bangali by British East India Company, later the Independent State with the collaboration of global strategies like SDGs (Debnath, 2020,2012,2010; Tripura, 2020,2018,2016)

Nevertheless, in the immediate post-world war period, the most critical concerns seemed to be in the North rather than the South. First, there was the reconstruction of ruined Europe. On 5 June 1947, the Marshall Plan was launched to help the European economy and to provide America's colossal production capacity with the markets it needed for post-war conversion. However, there was also a looming breach between the wartime allies. Stalin's claims in Europe as Poland (1947), Romania (1948), Czechoslovakia (1948), and Hungary (1949) became 'people's democracies' – not forgetting the civil war in Greece between 1946 and 1949. By 1948, the Soviets were blockading berlin, and the Cold War called for serious preventive measures that led to the creation of NATO. The major powerful states were thus mainly preoccupied with events transforming European political relations. Concomitant, the changes in the South tended to be pushed into the background. In this hardly auspicious context, however, the concept of 'Development' entered the arena.

From 1949 onwards, often without realizing it, more than two billion inhabitants of the planet found themselves changing their name, being 'officially' regarded as they appeared in the eyes of others, called upon to deepen their Westernization by repudiating their own identity. No longer African, Latin American, or Asian. They were now simply 'underdeveloped.' Those who headed the independent state accepted this new 'definition.' Because it was a way of asserting their claim to benefit from the 'aid' that was supposed to lead to 'Development .'For the colonized, it was a way of affirming the legal equality that was refused. It looked as if they had everything to gain – respectability and prosperity.

Nevertheless, their right to self-determination had been acquired in exchange for a right to self-definition. In gaining political Independence, they forfeited their identity and economic autonomy. They were now forced to travel the 'development path' mapped out for them by others. Whereas the world of colonization had been seen mainly as a political space to encompass ever larger empires, the 'Development age' was the period when economic space spread everywhere, with the raising of GDP as the number one imperative (Barkat, 2016; Paul, 2008, p.79).

Colonization is now one of the highest activities of societies that have reached an advanced stage of civilization. A society colonizes when it reaches a high degree of maturity and strength; it procreates, protects, places in good conditions for Development, and leads on to virility. This new society has emerged from its entrails. Colonization is one of the most complex and delicate phenomena in social physiology; the merit of colonizing people is to place the young society it has brought forth. It is distressing that the East-India company did not motivate the local people in this sub-continent while they ruled over almost two hundreds year (1757-1947) even though their policy was divided and ruled the Indian people to prolong their power; moreover, they exploited Indian economy, and people labor to increase the GDP of the British empire. We see these scenarios in independent Bangladesh; Government did not ratify the UNDRIP-2007 and ILO convention 169 to strengthen the internal colonization in the job market (elope the quota system for ethnic communities), decreasing the Capability framework (Sen, 2009); for instance, Phulbari coal mine, Gobindoganj Police -Santal clash, violate human rights (Two Santals taken poisonous in daylight in front of people as protesting the injustice) and after all 'self-determination' (see the table 2 &3) as who are they (Hasan, 2020; ILO C169; UNDRIP, 2007)?

In the reports of Meadows et al. (1972) – "Sustainable Development had two objectives and proposed sustainability to depict the limits of growth as- sustainable without sudden and uncontrolled collapse; and capable of satisfying the basic requirements of all its people (Grober, 2007, p.6)." Environmental conservation is one of the critical global concerns that 'The Club of Rome,' a non-profit, unofficial group of versatile scholars, seeks to explore critically. In 1968, they established the Club of Rome in Rome, Italy's Accademia di Lincei. Current and former heads of State and government, UN administrators,

Table 1. Year-based SDGs Interventions. Source: Authors' compilation

Year	Organizations/ Individuals	Activities
1968	Club of Rome	Established
1972	Club of Rome	A report on 'The Limits to Growth ' indicated the Growth & environmental limitations.
1980	IUCN, WWF/ UNEP	They tried to fix up a world conservation strategy 'living resources conservation for sustainable Development. They gave priority of the Sustainability of natural protection.
1981	Brown	He elevated the concept of Sustainability within environmental discourse.
1983	WCED	It prioritized the concept of Human & Environment
1987	WCED	It used Sustainable Development in its naming Brundtland report mentioning our Common Future. This report emphasized Environment & Development.
1992	United Nations	UN conference on Environment & Development (Earth Summit or Rio Declaration) declared Agenda 21 to achieve global Development. Human Development was highlighted by dephasing poverty.
2002	UN	Follow up Agenda 21 – Poverty alleviation
2005	UN	Declared on MDGs (10 Goals)
2015	UN	Declared SDGs (17 Goals)

senior politicians and government officials, diplomats, scientists, economists, and business executives worldwide comprise this group. The release of the Club of Rome's inaugural report, The Limits to Growth (Meadows et al.,1972), significantly boosted public awareness of Environmental protection. Further, this report became a hive to make sense of Sustainable Development. Now we can see the evolutionary trend of SDGs in the following table.

SDGs are the hot cake for all politicians, policymakers, bureaucrats, professionals, students, businesspeople, and academic researchers. In that case, the salient features of Sustainable Development we may offer from Yetunde Jeje (2006) like following—

1. It is a worldview concept
2. It is characterized as expressionist
3. Multi-constructed or as a social construct concept.
4. It is a political act of power
5. Local to a global concept (Jeje, 2006)

METHODS

This study centers on secondary data with an extensive literature review of versatile books, journals, papers, treaties, and concerned websites. The first author interviewed ethnic leaders, senior bureaucrats, ministry officers of Bangladesh to understand their views, and a limited number of retired senior civil servants of Bangladesh. Furthermore, we also reviewed relevant literature, such as UNDRIP-2007 and ILO convention-169. This paper was under the project *"Achieving Sustainable Goals: Analyzing Organizational GAP."* The Rector of Bangladesh Public Administration Training Centre (BPATC) had taken the initiative to analyze the ministry's progress. The first author was responsible for analyzing the performance of the Chittagong Hill Tracts Affairs Ministry (Rahman et al., 2022). For almost one year (2018-2019), this project was running, and the center organized a series of workshops and presentations among the faculty members. It was a brainstorming activity to analyze the organizational GAP in BPATC. The First author was one of the team members to generate the report on SDGs based on "Organizational GAP (Rahman et al.,2022)."

THEORETICAL APPROACH AND CONCEPTUAL FRAMEWORK

What a theory in research is! It is a philosophical guideline to study people in a particular community. The 'Capability Approach (CA) is the philosophical methodology in this paper. This research will follow the post-positivism paradigm and secondary method to collect the data from the research field. Interviews and brainstorming workshops are the primary tools to catch up on the data from the target people while staying with this Project for almost one year as a faculty member.

'Capability Approach'- based on the collective ethnic data and identity; those peoples need a strong place to strengthen their social capabilities in a community. The identified aspect of social capabilities includes-

- Effective
- Accountability
- Inclusiveness

SDGs: SUSTAIN THE QUALITY OF LIFE IN THE COMMUNITY

The following section will explain why the Capability Approach (hereafter CA) contributes to the ethnic people's well-being that SDGs want to ensure in CHTA by its ministry. Let us quote first a definition of CA "A functioning is an achievement, whereas a capability is the ability to achieve. Functionings are, in a sense, more directly related to living conditions since they *are* different aspects of living conditions. Capabilities, in contrast, are notions of freedom, in the positive sense: what real opportunities you have regarding the life you may lead" (Sen,1987, p.36).

The CA adopts a holistic view of Development, highlighting the multiple dimensions of sustainable Development as the growth of people's well-being, including social, cultural, and political spheres. Amartya Sen emphasizes the material aspects of Development, the significance of a minority people's cultural diversity, traditional knowledge, and worldview. The CA involves an in-depth understanding of the diversity of ways ethnic peoples' perspectives on Development might augment lives.

'Capability approach' can bring about Community Development through Customary Law. Sen (2009) thinks that a " Rational theory of history is required to know the customary law linked with community development (p; 143)'. Rationality, Theory, and History are the three core words to understand the eleven ethnic community's traditional organization. Community Development and Customary law two words are concomitantly involved with the following structure as follows:

Figure 2. Sustainable relationship amid three concepts; Source: researcher's compilation

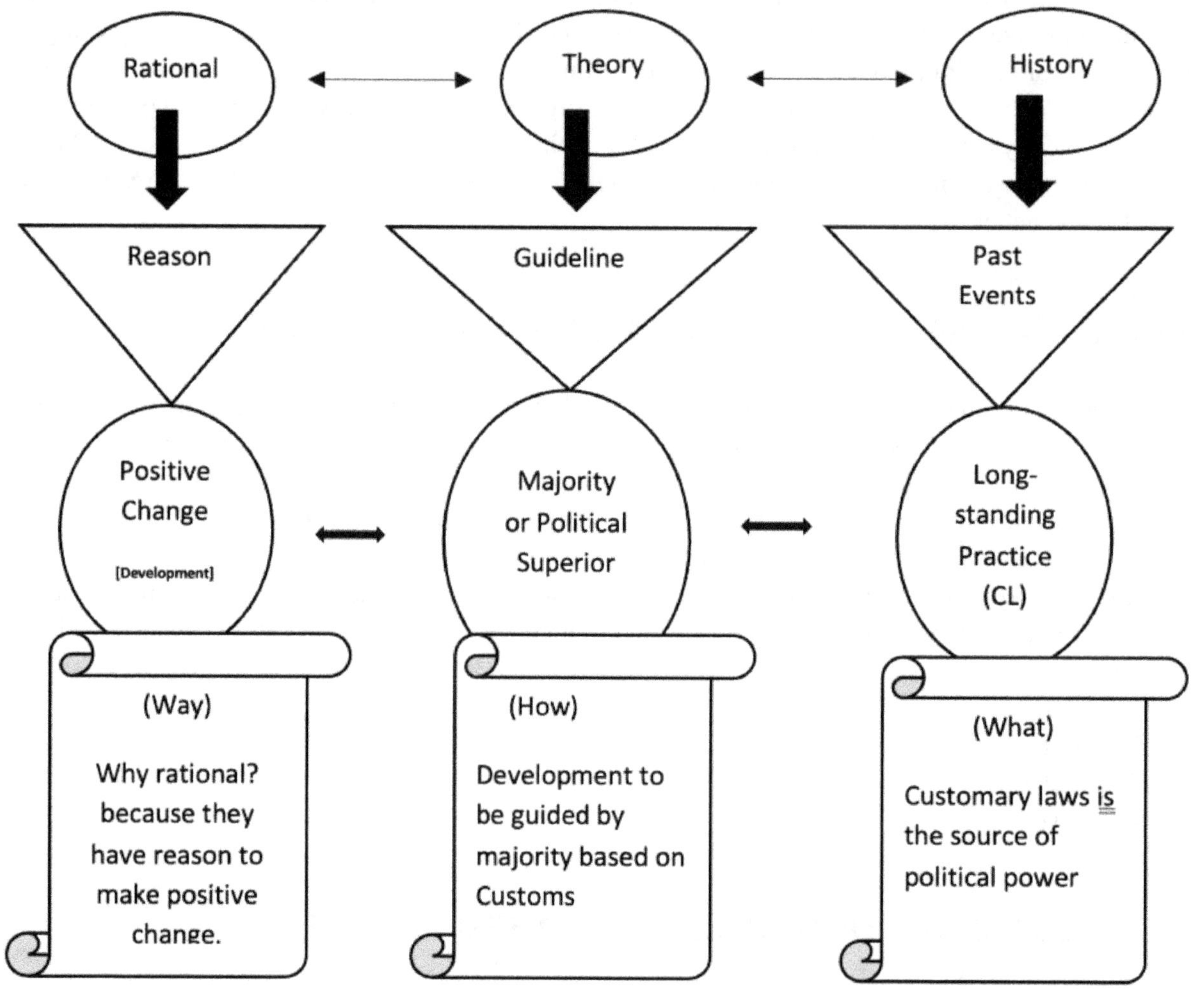

CA focuses on directly monitoring people's well-being (i.e., Indicators of quality of life) and moves away from considering development programs through measuring inputs or means. Amartya Sen acknowledges that value judgment about development priorities has to be performed by individuals and society themselves; and made precise by the theoretical framework (Shaife & Kilby, 2003; Sen, 1999).

CA focuses on minority [ethnic] peoples in that the process plays a crucial role in Development. So, Sen emphasizes the concept of capabilities which represents the potential or opportunities of a person to achieve esteemed functioning (Shafie & Kilby,2003). *Effective, Accountability, and Inclusiveness* are the conceptual framework that aid in this research. Understanding the MoCHTA performance and the transition in civil administration is now hit cake in Bangladesh to uplifting the country by 2040 in Development highway.

To understand the MoCHTA activities, we have used in this study — Effective, Inclusiveness, and Accountability concepts. Effective means are properly utilizing resources under the ministry's control, including ensuring accountability. According to ILO convention -169 and UNDRIP-2007, Inclusiveness is the key factor in empowering the ethnic group. When the ministry is formed to look after the small ethnic groups according to the peace accord in 1997 between the Government of Bangladesh and the hilly ethnic groups, then to inclusiveness of them in a decision is a matter of knowing the progress of SDGs achieved in this territory.

However, Amartya Sen's capability theory has been used to analyze our data from different sources. Because Amartya Sen believed that the small ethnic groups would be controlled by the majority while preserving their rights. Furthermore, if it has been disturbed, then humanity will suffer severely. Therefore, we have to focus on increasing the capacity of minority ethnic groups and how they can increase it. SDGs works on it to ameliorate their life according to SDGs-11 and SDGs-16.

CUSTOMARY LAW TO SDGs THEN COMMUNITY DEVELOPMENT

This chapter needs to understand the various aspects of the marginalization causes of the ethnic community in the light of either history or colonial context. Otherwise, injustice may occur on the accurate information of today's exploitation, inferiority, deprivation, and disgrace of this community's customary practice. Twentieth-century's 'Social justice' theory did not improve their quality of life, but rather the state and colonial governance system pushed them into an existential denial crisis (Debnath, 2010; Jahan, 2020).

As a forwarded way of this, Amartya Sen (2009) suggested that the state should take responsibility and protect the rights of the minority community by increasing their Capability. He argued in favour of political and moral philosophy to increase the Capability of the minority community peoples.

From an anthropological view, despite all the ethnic features of the Santal community, they are struggling for a separate identity in society. Long before, ethnographer William Hunter (1876, 1878) coined that the Santal society was suppressed and oppressed by Aryans, and since the Santal are non-Aryan (pp. 145-146). This process persisted during the British Company period from 1757 to 1947. Consequently, we see participation in different rebellions and movements. The continuation of today's conflict with the state force results from conflict.

Later in the Pakistan period (1947-1971) and post-Independence 1971, no government did justice to the ethnic peoples (Debnath, 2010; Tripura, 2016, 2018). That is why today's ethnic communities feel isolated from the state and have memories of the historical link with the pre-Aryan society since they had affluence. We can refer to James J. Novak (1993).

"All Bangladeshi people have a two-tiered mind. One is reflected in the mainstream Hindu-Muslim-Buddhist-Christian mind. They draw ancestral traits based on the belief in the moon, sun and village gods. Another one they feel the history of animism is their ancestral [Indigenous] (p.142)."

Amartya Sen (2009, 1999) negates Rawlsian Social justice, and it does not work for minority communities. He also showed a logic that ethnic people are a minority group that we can prove according to the census 2011(today's ethnic groups in Bangladesh as an example) for three reasons,

First, Social Justice has universal traits that cannot include and determine ethnic features; second, social justice depends on individualized perspectives; third, Amartya Sen thinks they need first exist, then

justice [for example, Santal as minority people]. Because they should have the right to self-management (ILO, 1989 / C 169; UNDRIP,2007) and 'self-determination' (UNDRIP,2007).

In light of the Capability theory (Sen, 1987, 1993), how will the community's rights come or be determined, and how will it affect the Development? In this context, Amartya Sen (2009,1999) thinks that the majority of people will rule the community or society as a condition, and that is, the ruler will protect the rights and ensure security. The Santal people's rights are always guided by their social norms and faith, which is customary law. Because the fundamental elements of the rights of minority people are social norms and faith (Mayali and Mousseron, eds, 2018; Saussine and Murphy, eds, 2007), and both are parts of customary law. Since the social norms and faith are unique and differ from place to place, community to community, these customary laws vary in different communities and areas. Since we already proved mathematically that the Santal people are the minority as ethnic (Roy et al.,2023 forthcoming), Social justice theory is not pertinent reasons are mentioned just a few lines before. Customary law can comply with 'Freedom and Choice' (Sen, 1999) with the community for upholding the Capabilities (Basu and Kanbur eds.,2009; Benjaminsen & Svarsted, 2021). For sustainable community development (SDGs-11), therefore, one may think of ethnic people. Hence, this chapter takes the customary law as the fundamental rights of that community, consisting of social norms and faith in alliance with international legal guidelines like UNDRIP-2007 and ILO-1989/169.

A contemporary example is Germany; in 2006, the Bangladesh government wanted to begin a coal power generating company in the Phulbari sub-district of Dinajpur to expand energy output – even though this would violate the customary rules of the local ethnic group. As a consequence, they (Santal) fight against state troops (Faruque, 2018), a few fatalities, and several hospitalizations; not to mention that initial government investment is still in a dormant condition (see,laboratoiredesfrondeurs.organd,www.minesandcommunities.org/Action/press1199.htm). However, the above discussion we can present in figure - 3

Most rulers will maintain the customary laws of the ethnic community with the help of state law (Orebech et al., 2005). Consequently, both the communities will directly benefit from sustainable Development through making the communal solidarities that are a connectedness between majority and minority instead of tension.

According to the 'Capability Aapproach (CA),' interrelationships are presented in figure 3; to consider in the organizational context. In other words, without political involvement, these relational functions will not sustain in community development. Furthermore, for that reason, we need to understand that the government's political ideology and historical knowledge of customary law go hand in hand. As explained before, the traditional law comes from social norms and faith. Customary law influences the political ideology to make state law. That is, political ideology is determined by customary law, which then became state law (Roy, 1911). However, the conflict is born when the state law denies the customary law after getting the mandate. Such denial politics cause disasters in the community and spread out over the country, interrupting the continuation of Development in the state. Santal's confrontation with the state force held at Gobindaganj in 2011 is an excellent example of development hurdles to community development (Chowdhury & Jhuma, 2014).

The customary law guides the community's culture. It follows the community's history to share "we" feelings as a part of the community. Such type of community feelings protects them from any hurdle. So that any inconvenience does not disturb them in their community life, they believe in longstanding practices as a series of past events- customary law.

Figure 3. Interrelationship between Customary law and State law. Source: Compiled by researchers

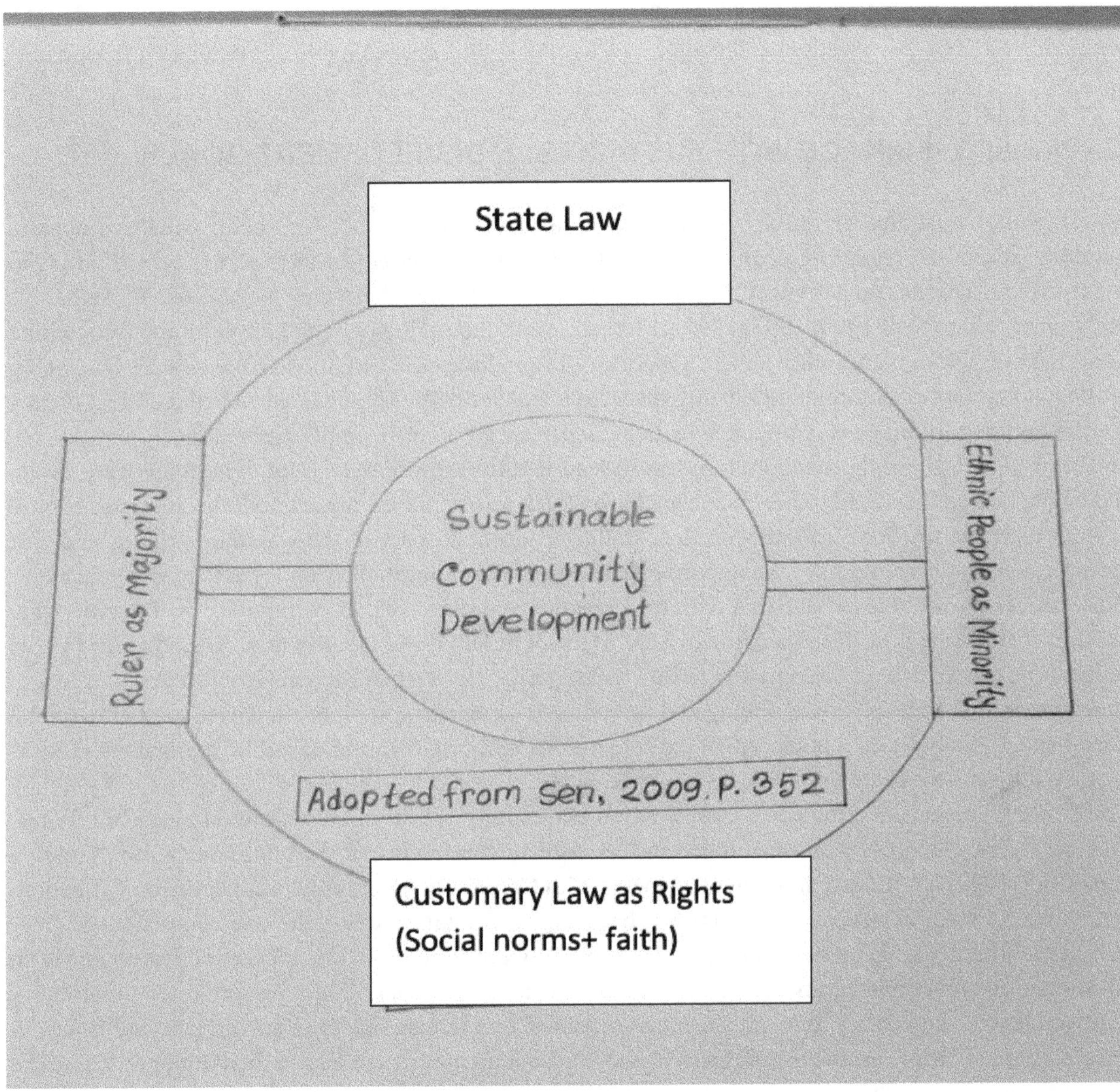

So, community bondage has to consider the customary law of that community; prior to using the Capability Approach - "[it] fits directly into the understanding of justice [freedom, choice, and quality of life] in terms of human lives and freedoms (Sen, 2009, p.xi)."

The state legislation protects the mainstream population and other minor ethnic groups, including educational and economic interests. These constitutional provisions have elevated the state's prominence for Indigenous community development. Santal is a minor ethnic group. It suggests that a happy state-santal community nexus offers maximal development advantages for the latter. Customary law can be a way to achieve this connection. The santal community suffers when these two are at odds. As a result, Amartya Sen (Basu & Kanbur, 2009) introduced notions to assure "quality of life," which may be achieved by providing the minority population "Capabilities" authority. To do so, Capabilities must be involved in a state's battle. S. L. Doshi (1990) suggests that the legislation will accommodate them. The community will choose freedom and choice as a human right for sustainable communal Development.

'CAPABILITY' LINKAGE WITH SUSTAINABLE DEVELOPMENT GOALS

How does the Capability Approach relate to well-being and Development? Well-being and Development should be discussed regarding people's capabilities to function based on their actual opportunities to undertake the actions and activities they want to engage in and be whom they want to be. These beings and doings, which Sen (1990, 1993, 1999) calls achieved functioning or actual opportunities, constitute what makes a life or community values. Opportunities include choosing customary or state law, being healthy, being part of a community, being respected, and so forth. The distinction between real opportunities and opportunities is to realize how much a person feels' well' in the community.

People should have the freedom (ability) to lead the kind of life they want, what they want to do, and be the person they want to be. Once they have effectively achieved these freedoms, they can choose to work on those freedoms in line with their traditions or the history of the way they want to live. For example, everyone should have the opportunity to be part of a community and practice customary law. However, they should also have this option to practice state law. Santal community will decide what satisfies them [that is utility according to Sen] in the community. In other words, Amartya Sen (1993) called it the preservation of minority rights by the majority. Here Amartya Sen (1999) refers to freedom which forms two concepts - 'well-being and Advantages.' Furthermore, it is often used to refer to (neo-) liberal economic policies that prioritize the free market and privatization of public companies. That is another subject here is not applicable to discuss.

The figure reveals that the person, family, and community are all interconnected to lead life. Wherever we start Development, it must touch the individual, the family, or the community life. Amartya Sen (1993, 1999) has judged these three elements with Capability. Capability is constituted of 'freedom and choice.' Freedom has two elements-well-being and advantage. Again, the one component of freedom is well-being, which means how much a person's well of being is in a community. Another is an advantage- the real opportunity for a person is to compare with others. So, a person in the community has two choices: customary law and state law to control or exercise power to solve the social issues in the community. However, they do not have freedom. That creates a problem in the community, and the research will work on that matter.

Nevertheless, they were not free to choose one in front of the research people. When we impose rules and regulations against their choice upon the ethnic community, this process affects the whole community; it becomes agitated community people. So, Development is barred or socially or economically disturbed when the community is in a predicament. So, to sustain the community and Development, we should ensure the community is stable and secure by preserving their rights.

Both ethnic groups and the CA emphasize sustainable Development's social, cultural, and political components as extensions of well-being. This study intends to assess the capabilities approach to sustainable human Development for community stability. Capacities are expanded in Amartya Sen's capability approach. There are various ways to improve one's talents. This study will look at how individuals, families, and communities exercise power to build a sustainable community. According to

Figure 4. Conceptual framework relationship between Capability and Community, Source: adopted idea from Sen, 1999

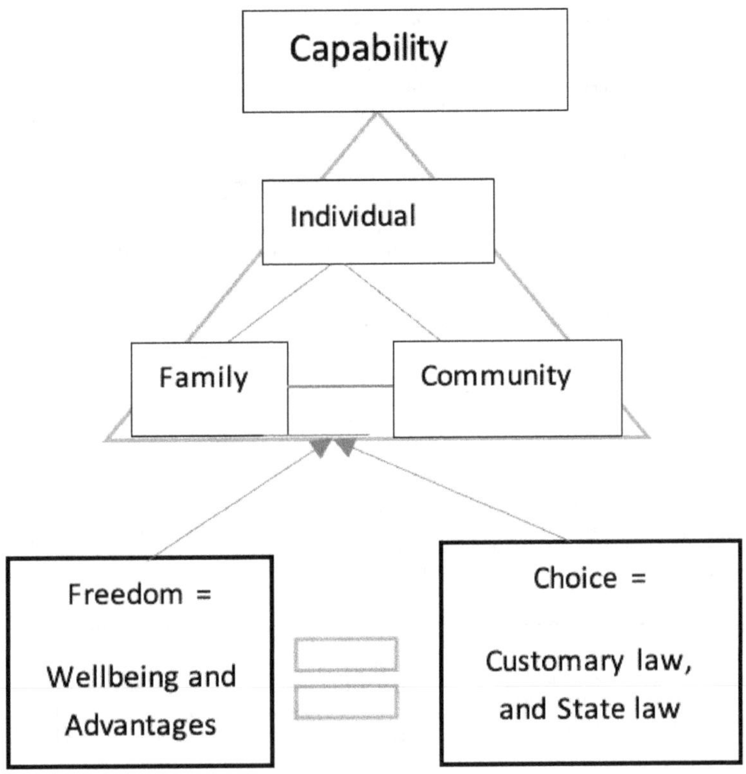

Amartya Sen, this comprehensive framework for measuring human well-being may be combined with other social theories and applied to varied geographical and cultural settings.

ACHIEVING SDGS: ORGANIZATIONAL GAP OF MOCHTA

SDGs has 17 Goals and 169 targets, but in the case of the Ministry of Chittagong Hill Tracts Affairs, we have selected only SDGs 11 (sustainable cities and communities) and SDGs -16 (Peace, Justice, and Strong Institutions) to explore the administrative cavities in Bangladesh. We have overlooked the overlapping Goals, targets, and mandates due to space limitations.

To implement the SDGs, the Civil Society Organization (CSO) has an important role, but in the case of MoCHTA, we did not get any clear-cut direction of their involvement in implementing the SDGs in the CHT area; also, it is SDGs achieving Gap of its; whether it very needs to their participation. However, Citizen's Platform for SDGs, Bangladesh has disclosed a table of CSO involvement levels that is in the following —

Table 2. Organizational Gap in SDGs under the MoCHTA. Source: Authors' compilation from different sources

Rules of Business	Goals & Target	Actions	GAPs
Matters relating to the administration of the Chittagong Hill Tracts Affairs.	16.5 Substantially reduce corruption and bribery in all their forms. 16.6 Develop effective, accountable, and transparent institutions at all levels. 16.7 Ensure responsive, inclusive, participatory, and representative decision-making at all levels.	-26 laws formulation; 12 customary laws are amended; as well as ten regional & district laws are amended under a project. -105 elected local government members are trained up on ICT under a project. -NIS implementing -Implementing GRS --Annual development plan meeting	- the land dispute has been going on for 23 years (The Daily Prothom Alo dated 8.9.22).
Coordination of all related matters with concerned Ministries / Divisions.	16.7 Ensure responsive, inclusive, participatory, and representative decision-making at all levels.	-Implementing Citizen Charter -Arranged training; 414 trainees from 2017-2018 -Set up the IT section & it is functioning.	- How much root level involvement in the development planning of ethnic people in CHT related is not clear to all. -
Counseling. Monitoring and, where required, implementing all relevant decisions of the government and the committees.	16.6 Develop effective, accountable, and transparent institutions at all levels.	-Established NIS monitoring framework. -The citizen Charter is published in field-level offices and H/Q as well as on the website.	-GRS data are not available
Formulating plans and programs, including a development action plan in respect of Chittagong Hill Tracts areas.	16.5 Substantially reduce corruption and bribery in all their forms. 16.6 Develop effective, accountable, and transparent institutions at all levels.	-Signed peace accord-1997 -Established e-nothi / online monitoring systems. -Formulated CHT development board law-2014.	-Ethnic leaders always claim that the accord of 1997 is not implemented properly. And different groups clash even clash with the state force we see in the newspaper.
Dealing with matters relating to Chittagong Hill Tracts Regional Council and Hill District Councils of Chittagong Hill Tracts areas.	16.5 Substantially reduce corruption and bribery in all their forms. 16.6 Develop effective, accountable, and transparent institutions at all levels.	-CHT Regional Council Law-2013 and District council-1989. -CHT Development Board -2014 -CHT land-conflict resolution law-2001,	-Land- conflict resolution is still a matter of Development in CHT areas.
Undertake socio-economic development programs, education, culture, social custom, manner, language, religion, rites, and practices and maintain the originality of tribal and non-tribal people of Chittagong Hill Tracts areas.	11.4 Strengthen efforts to protect and safeguard the world's cultural and natural heritage		-Cultural & natural heritage is maintained by national laws and rules, not customary laws even not formulated under this ministry. -Lack of Customary laws promotional activities. -Lack of Community Guidelines.
Matters relating to enacting all laws on subjects allotted to this ministry.	16.3 Promote the rule of law at the national and international levels and ensure equal access to justice for all.	-CHT Regional council Law-1998 -CHT development Board Law- 2014 -CHT land – conflict resolution Law-2001 -Peace accord - 1997 -Chittagong Hill Tracts Development Board -2014. -Implementing Peace accord-97 -CHT Zilla Parishad Law - 1989 -CHT Forest Transit regulations-1973 -CHT Fund Regulation- 1937. -Working with ICIMOD	-Did not ratify UNDRIP-2007 -Did not ratify ILO-169 - land dispute resolution commission is still now inactive.
Inquiries and statistics on subjects allotted to the ministry.	16.10 Ensure public access to information and protect fundamental freedoms in accordance with national legislation and international agreements.	-Established Citizen Chatter. -Exist web portal -Providing online service -Refugee Task Forces formed	-Public perception and satisfaction are still not disclosed regarding these.

Table 3. Civil Society participation level in SDGs. Source: Citizen's Platform for SDGs Bangladesh (www.bdplatform4sdgs.net)

SDGs	**More involved**	**Less involved**
11 SUSTAINABLE CITIES AND COMMUNITIES	-Affordable housing and basic services -Disaster deaths -Access to safe and green public spaces	-Affordable, safe transport system -Sustainable urbanization -Safeguarding the world's cultural and natural heritage
16 PEACE, JUSTICE AND STRONG INSTITUTIONS	-Violence-related deaths -Trafficking and violence against children -The rule of law and justice for all -Corruption and bribery -Accountable and transparent institutions -Inclusive and participatory decision making -Access to information	-Illicit financial and arm flows -Birth registration

CHT AREA'S ETHNIC GROUPS: REFERENCE TO UNDRIP-2007 AND ILO CONVENTION 169

UNDRIP-2007 and ILO-169 are effective strategies for conveying minorities into mainstreaming and ensuring human rights, SDGs 11 and 16. However, the Government of Bangladesh has not ratified the agreements, whether the SDGs would have straightforward dealings if the treaties were ratified.

The salient features are prioritized in the discussion on how these features are associated with the unregulated rights of the ethnic communities (table 3). As a point of referral and severing them to assuming human rights, UNDRIP and ILO believe that achieving or ensuring these significant features will ensure the SDGs of the Small Ethnic Community (SEGs). We can consider both treaties to contemplate the relationships between UNDRIP, ILO, and SDGs to foster human rights situations.

The agreement stipulates that the ethnic community can be given self-determination if these are achieved with the help of triparty relationships (www.ilo.org). This means that to ensure self-determination, it is now important to verify the mentioned features in the UNDRIP guidelines in the context of the ethnic people and Bangladesh (Chowdhury, eds, 2014). Whether the rights described under UNDRIP—2007, ILO are primarily enjoyed by the people of the ethnic community living in the eastern hill of Bangladesh? We can see those rights in the following table, and in determining yes or no, the information obtained from the common law (The Permanent Settlement Regulation -1793; The State Acquisition and Tenancy Act -1950; The Enemy Property Act-1965; The Acquisition of Immovable Property Act-1982; The Vested Property Act-1974; Biodiversity Act, 2017; Education Policy 2010), news published in newspapers (https://www.parbattanews.com;prothomalo.com;dailystar.net), articles(Debnath, 2020;

Sarker et al.,2014,2016; Shafie & Kilby, 2003), and books (Tripura, 2020; Barkat, 2016; Chowdhury, ed., 2014) have been used.

Table 4. Status of UNDRIP-2007 Rights assuming the S. Source: Authors' compilation

Rights/Dignity As of UNDRIP-2007 and ILO-169	Right Enjoying Status			Authors' Comment(s)
	Yes	No	Remarks	
Self-determination		✓		*i*. No Status is higher than yes. *ii*. we notified Limited Practice. In this backdrop, we have the opportunity to work with UNDRIP-2007 to lead the Sustainable SEGs Development in Bangladesh.
Self-Control		✓		
Political	✓		Limited	
Legal		✓		
Nationality	✓			
Fully Participation		✓		
Voting	✓			
Physical & mental Integrity			Not Defined	
Collective rights in freedom		✓		
An effective mechanism for prevention		✓		
Customary Rights & Practice	✓		Moderate	
Own Language Practice	✓		Limited	
Social dignity		✓		
Social security		✓	Limited	
Traditionally own land/ Common Property Resources / Common Resouces Pool.		✓		
Cultural institutions	✓		Moderate	
Social equity		✓		

LIMITATIONS OF THE MINISTRY TO ACHIEVING SDGs IN THE CHT AREA

It is misleading data or lack of data aggregation always disruption Development. In the case of MoCHTA, there is no complete data aggregation strategy to implement SDGs. Instead, they have to depend on the statistical bureau. It denounces the dependable result. However, we may refer to three limitations regarding SDGs of this mandate—

- *No tracking own implementation strategy*
- *No sensitizing interventions for policymakers*
- *No exchange of information programs.*

RECOMMENDATIONS: LOOKING FOR A FRAMEWORK TO ACHIEVING SDGs

Short-Term Integrated Approach

In the suggested framework for advancing the SDGs' implementation. The structure's principal parts are:

- Making financial and technical resources available for effective and accountable governance for strong institutions (SDGs-16).
- Pay attention to infrastructure, the environment, health, education, and human resources as significant forces behind economic Development;
- emphasizing the customary laws to settle land issues as a fundamental need for life settings.

Long-Term Integrated Approach

The SDGs localization level should determine a methodology to understand the linkages between mandates of line ministries and/or sector governance within the country. This determining level should be flexible, austere, and adaptive to national variations by targeting SDGs11 and 16 at the most appropriate level. In this connection, we can recommend ratifying UNDRIP -2007 and ILO-169 purposively to localize the SDGs to focus on local capacity development, building ownership, and responsibility. The cost of localizing, however, is still not addressed. Nevertheless, the Success of SDGs implementation depends on each country being responsible for their own economic and social Development. That is why our long-term recommendation is --

The Government should take the initiatives to ratify the UNDRIP-2007 and ILO convention 169 for comprehensive Development in the CHT area.

ACKNOWLEDGMENT

The first author received perfect financial support before working on this paper from Bangladesh Public Administration Training Centre (BPATC), Savar.

REFERENCES

Barkat, A. (2016). *Political economy of unpeopling of indigenous peoples: The case of Bangladesh.* Mukto Buddhi Prokasana.

Benjaminsen, T. A., & Svarstad, H. (2021). *Political ecology: A critical engagement with global environmental issues.* Springer Nature. doi:10.1007/978-3-030-56036-2

Besra, L. (2014). *A Critical Review of Democracy and Governance Challenges in Bangladesh with special refences to a human rights-based approach for the Development of marginalized indigenous people* [PhD thesis]. Flinders of Institute of Public Policy Management.

Chakma & Maitrot. (2016). *Working paper on how Ethnic Minorities became poor and stay poor in Bangladesh: A Qualitative enquiry*. EEP/Shiree.

Debnath, M. K. (2010). *Living on the Edge: The predicament of a rural indigenous Santal community in Bangladesh* [Doctoral dissertation].

Debnath, M. K. (2012). The invisible agenda: Civilising mission or missionizing civilization. *International Journal of Human Rights, 16*(3), 461–473. doi:10.1080/13642987.2011.572550

Debnath. (2020). A community under siege: exclusionary education policies and indigenous Santals in the Bangladeshi context. *Third World Quarterly, 41*(3), 453-469.

Du Pisani, J. A. (2006). Sustainable Development–historical roots of the concept. *Environmental Sciences, 3*(2), 83–96. doi:10.1080/15693430600688831

Grober, U. (2007). *Deep roots-a conceptual history of 'sustainable development'*. Academic Press.

Hasan, M. M. (2020). *Mining Conflict, Indigenous Peoples and Environmental Justice: The Case of Phulbari Coal Project in Bangladesh* [PhD Thesis]. https://www.ilo.org/wcmsp5/groups/public/---ed_norm/normes/documents/publication/wcms_205225.pdf

Jahan, F. (2020). *The issue of identity: state denial, local controversies and everyday resistance among the Santal in Bangladesh* [PhD Thesis]. Hale University.

Jeje, Y. (2006). *Southern Alberta Landscapes: Meeting the Challenges Ahead: Export Coefficients for Total Phosphorus, Total Nitrogen and Total Suspended Solids in the Southern Alberta Region: A Review of Literature*. Alberta Environment.

Meadows, D. H., Meadows, D. L., Randers, J., & Behrens, W. W. (2018). The limits to growth. In *Green planet blues* (pp. 25–29). Routledge. doi:10.4324/9780429493744-3

Mohsin, A. (2001). *The state of "minority" rights in Bangladesh*. International Centre for Ethnic Studies.

Mohsin, A. (2002). *The Politics of Nationalism: The Case of the Chittagong Hill Tracts Bangladesh* (2nd ed.). The University Press Limited.

Novak, J. J. (1993). Bangladesh: Reflections on the water. Indiana University Press.

Orebech, P., Bosselman, F., Bjarup, J., Callies, D., Chanock, M., & Petersen, H. (2005). *The role of customary law in sustainable development*. Cambridge University Press.

Parris, T. M., & Kates, R. W. (2003). Characterizing and measuring sustainable Development. *Annual Review of Environment and Resources, 28*(1), 559–586. doi:10.1146/annurev.energy.28.050302.105551

Paul, B. D. (2008). A history of the concept of sustainable Development: Literature review. The Annals of the University of Oradea. *Economic Sciences Series, 17*(2), 576–580.

Rahman, M. M. (2020). *Organizational gap analysis in achieving SDGs in Bangladesh*. Academic Press.

Rist, G. (2014). *The history of Development: from western origins to global faith*. Bloomsbury Publishing.

Roy, P., Chowdhury, J. S., Abd Wahab, H., & Saad, R. B. M. (2022). Ethnic Tension of the Bangladeshi Santal: A CDA of the Constitutional Provision. In Handbook of Research on Ethnic, Racial, and Religious Conflicts and Their Impact on State and Social Security (pp. 208-226). IGI Global. doi:10.4018/978-1-7998-8911-3.ch013

Roy, P. K., Hamidi, M., & Roy, S. (2022). Internet as a Field: An Analysis of the Santal Online Communities. In *Practices, Challenges, and Prospects of Digital Ethnography as a Multidisciplinary Method* (pp. 124–137). IGI Global. doi:10.4018/978-1-6684-4190-9.ch009

Sarker, M. A. R., Khan, N. A., & Musarrat, K. M. (2016). Livelihood and vulnerability of the Santals community in Bangladesh. *The Malaysian Journal of Social Administration*, *12*(1), 38–55. doi:10.22452/mjsa.vol12no1.2

Sen, A. (2009). *The Idea of Justice*. Allan Lane Penguin Books.

Shafie, H., & Kilby, P. (2003). *Including the excluded: ethnic inequality and Development in Northwest Bangladesh*. Academic Press.

Sneddon, C., Howarth, R. B., & Norgaard, R. B. (2006). Sustainable Development in a post-Brundtland world. *Ecological Economics*, *57*(2), 253–268. doi:10.1016/j.ecolecon.2005.04.013

Soeftestad, L. T. (1994). *Workshop on participatory development*. Academic Press.

Soeftestad, L. T. (2004). Biodiversity conservation, communication and language–is English a solution, a problem or both? *Policy Matters*, *13*, 281–283.

Tripura, J. (2016). Reflection of the Santal Rebellion and the Situations of the Indigenous Peoples of Bangladesh. *Unread Voice*.

Tripura, P. (2018). *Prantikotar Khaad Theke Mohaakashe*. Samhati Publication.

Tripura, P. (2020). *Colonial Shadow in Bangladesh*. Bangla Books. www.mochta.gov.bd

ADDITIONAL READING

Ali, A. (1998). *Santals of Bangladesh*. Institute of Social Research & Applied Anthropology.

Ali, M. (2002). *Dinajpurer Adivasi*. Adivasi Academy.

Bodding, P. O. (1925). *Studies in Santal Medicine and Connected Folklore: The Santals and Disease*. Royal Asiatic Society of Bengal.

Day, A. (2015). An Ancient History: Ethnographic Study of the Santhal. *International Journal of Novel Research in Humanity and Social Sciences*, *2*(4), 31–38.

Erueti, A. (2017). The Politics Of International Indigenous Rights. *University of Toronto Law Journal*, *67*(4), 569–595. doi:10.3138/utlj.67.5

Erueti, A. (2022). *The UN Declaration on the Rights of Indigenous Peoples: A New Interpretative Approach*. Oxford University Press. doi:10.1093/oso/9780190068301.001.0001

Gilbert, J. (2017). Indigenous Peoples, Human Rights, and Cultural Heritage: Towards a Right to Cultural Integrity. In A. Xanthaki, S. Valkonen, L. Heinämäki, & P. Nuorgam (Eds.), *Indigenous Peoples' Cultural Heritage: Rights, Debates, Challenges* (pp. 20–38). Brill.

Hossain, K. T. (2000). *The Santals of Bangladesh: an ethnic minority in transition*. Works Shop Paper of ENBS.

Kukutai, T., & Taylor, J. (2016). *Indigenous data sovereignty: Toward an agenda*. ANU press. doi:10.22459/CAEPR38.11.2016

Rafi, M. (2017). *Small ethnic groups of Bangladesh: a mapping exercise*. Panjeree Publications.

Roy, P., Chowdhury, J. S., Abd Wahab, H., Saad, M. R. B., & Parahakaran, S. (2021). Christianity, COVID-19, and marginal people of Bangladesh: An experience from the Santal Community. In Handbook of Research on the Impact of COVID-19 on Marginalized Populations and Support for the Future (pp. 65-82). IGI Global.

KEY TERMS AND DEFINITIONS

CHT Area: This belongs to the three districts of Bangladesh as peninsular like Bandarban, Rangamati, and Khagrachari. There is a debate about their territorial land, culture, and political rule.

Development: When the community feels the positive change to smooth their life without making their traditions devasted is called Development in the Santal community.

Ethnic Groups: There have fifty Ethnic groups, according to the Government of Bangladesh. Among those, eleven ethnic groups are living in the CHT area. The ethnic communities are Chakma, Marma, Tripura, Tanchangya, Lusai, Pankho, Bawm, Mro, Khyang, Khumi, and Chak.

Sustainable: Whatever we have in the Text regarding the meaning of Sustainable, we understand that it is the nurturing of nature based on community-based guidelines. So, the Santal community says they have Customary law to protect nature with love and humanity, called Sustainability.

Chapter 11
Social Management of Pharma Products for Sustainable Development

Meghmala S. Waghmode
https://orcid.org/0000-0002-5635-134X
Department of Microbiology, Annasaheb Magar Mahavidyalaya, Pune, India

Aparna Baban Gunjal
Dr. D.Y. Patil Arts, Commerce, and Science College, Pune, India

Neha N. Patil
https://orcid.org/0000-0003-1228-6475
Department of Microbiology, Annasaheb Magar Mahavidyalaya, Pune, India

ABSTRACT

Social aspects, management, and development are important in all the industries including the pharmaceutical industries. Sustainability management is necessary to be followed even in pharmaceutical industries, and there are many measures or pharmaceutical management practices that will help to achieve social management of pharma products. The chapter will cover the effective pharma products management through proper disposal of medicines and their use by sustainable approach.

INTRODUCTION

The pharmaceutical products include drugs, capsules, medicines, tablets, additives, etc. In the pharmaceutical industries, the processing and manufacturing of these products take place. There has to be a proper balanced and sustainable approach for this. This is very necessary also from the environmental related aspects to avoid pollution and other hazards. The social management is essential in the pharmaceutical industries during the processing and manufacturing of pharma products. The proper measure to be followed in these industries is the need of the hour. The term 'sustainability' is related with the

DOI: 10.4018/978-1-6684-7499-0.ch011

good health of human beings, safety at work place, various rights, quality of work, etc. (Bom et al., 2019; Moldan et al., 2012). The pharmaceutical industries have attracted many people globally. The production of new drugs, medicines, etc. involves Research and Development (R & D) in pharmaceutical industries (Garnier, 2008; Weaver et al., 2022). The relevance of sustainability has gained importance in pharmaceutical industries (Schneider et al., 2010). This involves how the pharmaceutical industries operate, environmental aspects they follow, and their sustainable approach (Jimenez-Gonzalez et al., 2012; Shaw and Whitney, 2016). The important issues in the pharma sector are represented in Figure 1. The sustainable approach is at micro and macro levels and it is necessary to have it at both these levels. The World Health Organization (WHO) through sustainable approach ensures important health benefits and services for all humans. For this, the management studies on sustainability are important in all pharmaceutical industries (Aquino et al., 2018). Green pharmacy includes the manufacturing of pharmaceutical products in an eco-friendly and economical manner (Clark, 2006). Due to this, there will be reduction of hazardous effects on the human health. "Green" means without disturbing the environment which is very essential. There are additional considerations. Extensive research on the occurrence of pharmaceutical products in environment and its eco-toxicological consequences, European Commission and HELCOM like organizations labeled pharma micro pollutants as developing issue for the world (Caban and Stepnowski, 2021; Deloitte Sustainability 2018; International Initiative on Water Quality-IIWQ 2017).The research process based on the monitoring the pharmaceuticals in environment is often influenced by the Matthew Effect (Iceberg or Bandwagon effect) by limiting the surveys due to the prior studies or the detectable concentration of residues (Daughton, 2014). For the comprehensive management of the pharmaceutical associated eco problems, the initiative must be taken from manufacturing to disposal step. During all this process, every stakeholder is responsible and contributes to have the social management of pharma practices.

PROBLEMS IN PHARMACEUTICAL INDUSTRIES AND NEED FOR SUSTAINABLE APPROACH

India has a population of about 1.2 billion people. The pharmaceutical industries play a very important role to find new drugs, medicines, etc. in order to treat, cure various disorders of the humans. In the year 2017, the Indian pharmaceutical industries had a value of US $ 33 billion (Gujar and Attarwala, 2020). These pharmaceutical industries therefore contribute for the healthy and better health of the humans and hence are important. Both the social health and the economic development depend on the pharmaceutical industry. The pharmaceutical companies or the industries have to adopt sustainable approach to operate. There is a report which shows that pharmaceutical industries produce 52 million metric tons of CO_2 annually (Belkhir and Elmeligi, 2019). There is maximum use of various solvents in pharmaceutical industries and this has to be reduced (Yaseen et al., 2021). For the sustainability approach during manufacturing processes, it is necessary to know which are the factors in the supply chain and manufacturing process that can be replaced or changed to be eco-friendly. The large consumption of energy is also one of the factors which need to be tackled in pharmaceutical industries. The 'reduce, re-use, recycle' term is necessary for this in the pharmaceutical industries, which can be further integrated as part of a circular economy (Alshemari et al., 2021). Reducing or replacing toxic chemical, or solvents can help to achieve eco-friendly and sustainable approach in the pharmaceutical industries. The term sustainability is concerned with social, legal and economic aspects. Addressing the massive

Figure 1. Important Issues in the pharma sector

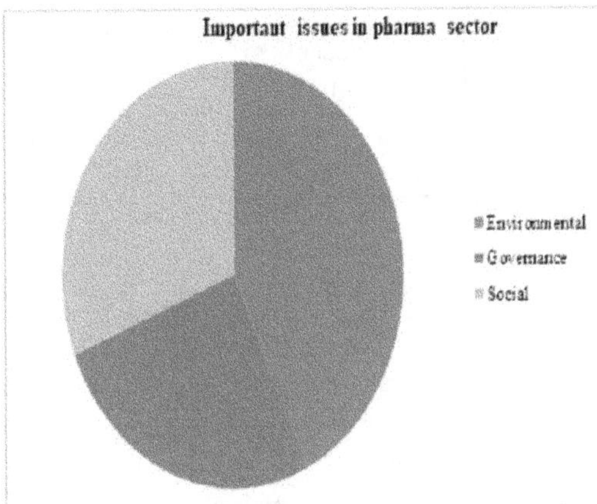

consumption of energy or materials and their consequent emissions is now becoming a factor that is being considered by industries and it is important that the emerging technologies (ET) that will become the gold standard of manufacturing will adhere to sufficient green standards for the future. During the bio fermentation process of antibiotics, production and disposal of antibiotics mycelial dreg (AMD) i.e., residual fermentation substrates, products, mycelia, metal ions etc. also adds the problem of pollution and the selection of proper disposal system (Chen et al., 2021; Li et al., 2016; Ma et al., 2016). In China, AMD has been enlisted as National Catalogue of Hazardous Wastes (under code HW02-276-001-02) (Jiang et al., 2012). The sustainable approach for the pharmaceutical products is represented in Figure 2.

MEASURES TO CONTROL USAGE OF PHARMACEUTICALS

Drugs causing pollution, needs to be properly disposed of by classifying or labeling them as expired, unused, and unwanted medicines (de Campos et al., 2021). Overuse or improper usage of the antibiotics is the main problem which is causing environmentally acquired antibiotic resistance, high health care cost, and eco-toxic effects of drug. Surveillance systems has to be employed for the monitoring of antibiotics management viz., community survey, safety network, health plans and insurance companies, government hospitals, data from private vendors (Demirjian et al., 2015; Shapiro et al., 2014,). Concept to utilize antibiotics in systematic manner is termed as "antibiotic stewardship" for Environmental Fate (Emma et al., 2015). Studies on effect of reduction in restricted use of carbapenem in some institutes, resulted in control of *Pseudomonas aeruginosa* resistance to carbapenems and effective in prevention of *Clostridium difficile* infection (CDI) (Wong and Brad, 2017). Hence in 2017, the 'National Health Policy' suggested antimicrobial resistance as one of the key issues in India and suggested pharmacovigilance through the implementation of Antimicrobial Stewardship Program (AMSP) (Walia et al., 2015) (Figure 3).

Health service sector is one of the important sector for every country. Health sector is responsible for the global warming problem due to release of green house gases. As per the report in United Kingdom (UK), healthcare sector is responsible for 4% of the carbon footprint which suggests implementation of Eco-pharmaco-stewardship program for the sustainable management of pharma products in clinical

Figure 2. Sustainable Approach for the pharmaceutical products

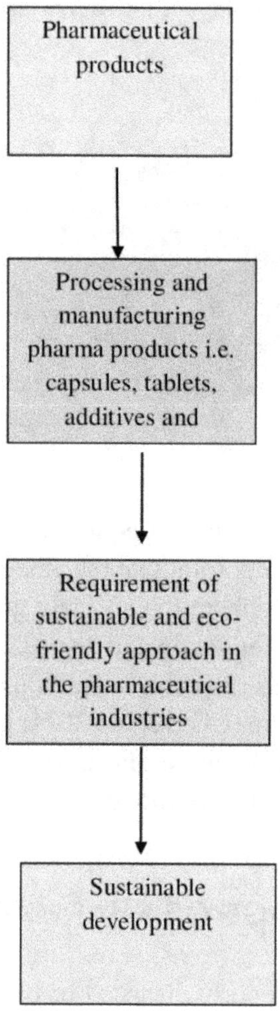

practice (Adeyeye et al., 2022). In Japan, healthcare sector contributed for 72 $MtCO_2e$ (metric tons of CO_2 equivalent) in 2015 suggesting growing and considerable impact of healthcare services on the carbon footprint (Nansai et al., 2020). Karliner and Guenther suggested ten goals for adding green effect to healthcare systems. These goals include sustainable usage of drugs, water, food and adopting the life style by giving priortization to the environmental issues (Karliner and Guenther, 2011).

MODERN METHODS FOR SUSTAINABLE APPROACH IN THE PHARMACEUTICAL INDUSTRIES

The modern methods for sustainable approach in the pharmaceutical industries are represented in Figure 4. The sustainability standards adopted by the pharma sector depends on methods used in manufactur-

Figure 3. Antimicrobial Stewardship Program

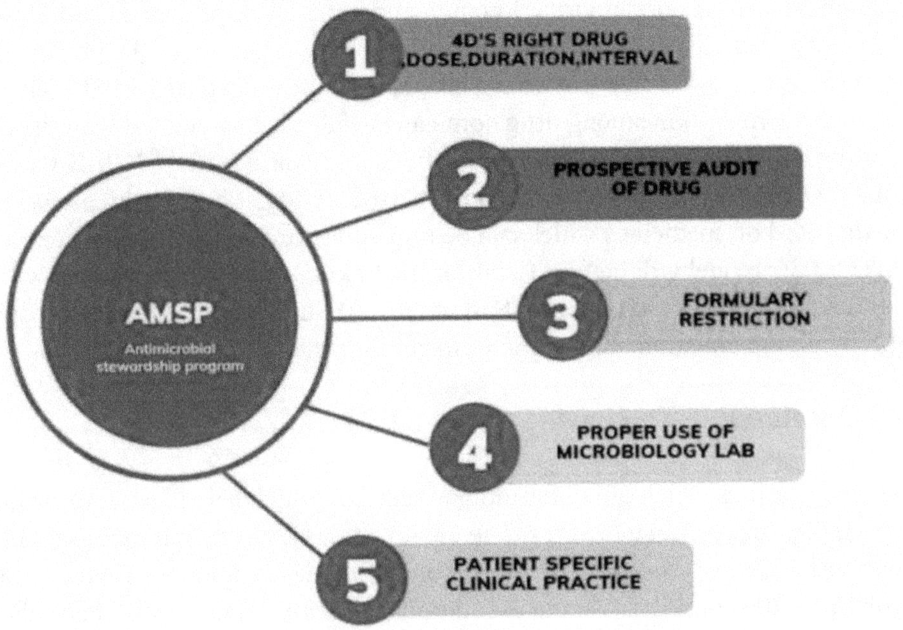

ing pharma products, frameworks created, initiatives for new developments considering environmental aspects, creating baselines and reviews, etc. (Leonard and Schneider, 2004).

Closed-Loop Pharmaceutical Supply Chain (Clpsc)

For every nation it's important to monitor the economy associated with logistic based production, supply, and disposal of pharma products in industries or herbal crops by farmers. Supply chain is of two types open -loop where primary focus is given on the benefit to the producers and closed -loop where circular economy is important. For any type of supply chain, on-time delivery is important criteria (Ishizaka et al., 2022). CLPSC has eco-friendly transportation system as well as industrial waste management

Figure 4. Inter linkage of sustainability with social, economic and environmental

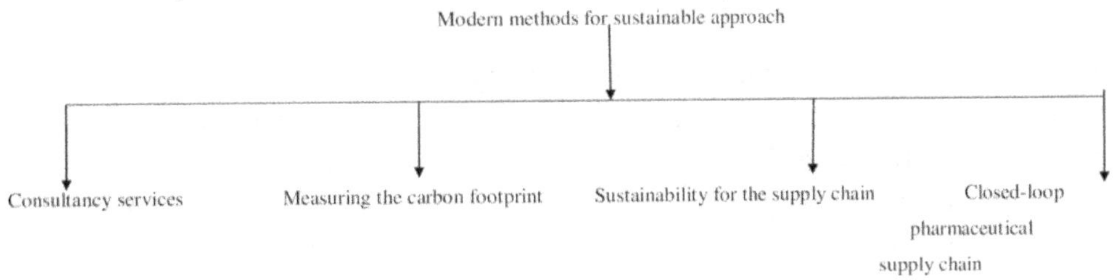

system which assist in controlled forward and reverse flow of the medicines (Amin and Zhang, 2013). During pandemic situation of Covid-19, the role of pharmaceutical supply chain was significant for every nation to combat against corona virus. Recommendations were provided on the use of antiviral and anti-inflammatory medicines as well as vaccines. Major obstacle was of the proper distribution of them to the target location; it was made possible by the cumulative efforts of CLPSC. This chain hardly gives emphasis on the competition among drug companies and price associated with the drugs (Sazvar et al., 2021). For the sustainable operation of this CLPSC, a scenario-based MOMILP model has been suggested for the reverse flows of perished medicines (reverse logistic) into three classes (medicines which has to be disposed of, medicines which can be remanufactured or can be recycled) (Sazvar et al., 2021). Even this CLPSC model will be beneficial for the linkage of herbal medicines with biofuel and having customer centric approach (Garai and Sarkar, 2022). Supply of the proper medicines in right dosage and form by giving attention on the environmental impact is the corporate social responsibility.

Consultancy Services

There are many organizations which offer consultancy services which help to achieve sustainable development goals in the pharmaceutical industries. The organizations assist the pharmaceutical industries to plan and manage sustainability approach. Intertek is one of the United States of America (USA) based organization which provides consultancy services to the pharmaceutical industries. This includes preparing proper regulatory compliances, manage the supply chain, training for proper disposal of pharma products, provide knowledge to the manufacturers regarding to use resources properly, etc. (Cui et al., 2006).

Measuring the Carbon Footprint

The sustainability approach in the pharmaceutical industries can also be achieved by measuring carbon footprint, analytical methods approved by organizations, global reporting initiative (GRI) (Berner and Shike, 1988), and the greenhouse gas method which can determine greenhouse gas emissions.

Sustainability for the Supply Chain

There has to be global green regulatory measures for the management of pharma products. Many organizations help the pharmaceutical industries to check protocols or methods, testing, validation and certification of products to bring in the market. The consulting services and other organizations help the pharma industries to achieve green supply chain management (Jogling et al., 2002).

MODELS FOR SUSTAINABILITY (ROSEN AND KISHAWY, 2012)

There are three various phases of models for sustainability which are -

Research - The first phase for sustainability in the pharmaceutical industries is research which is at pre-competitive level. In this phase, the requirements which are not regulated are checked. The examples include availability and use of energy; resources; impact on the environment, etc. This research phase can be useful to solve manufacturing environmental impacts at immediate stage.

Figure 5.Interlinkage of Sustainability With Social, Economic and Environmental

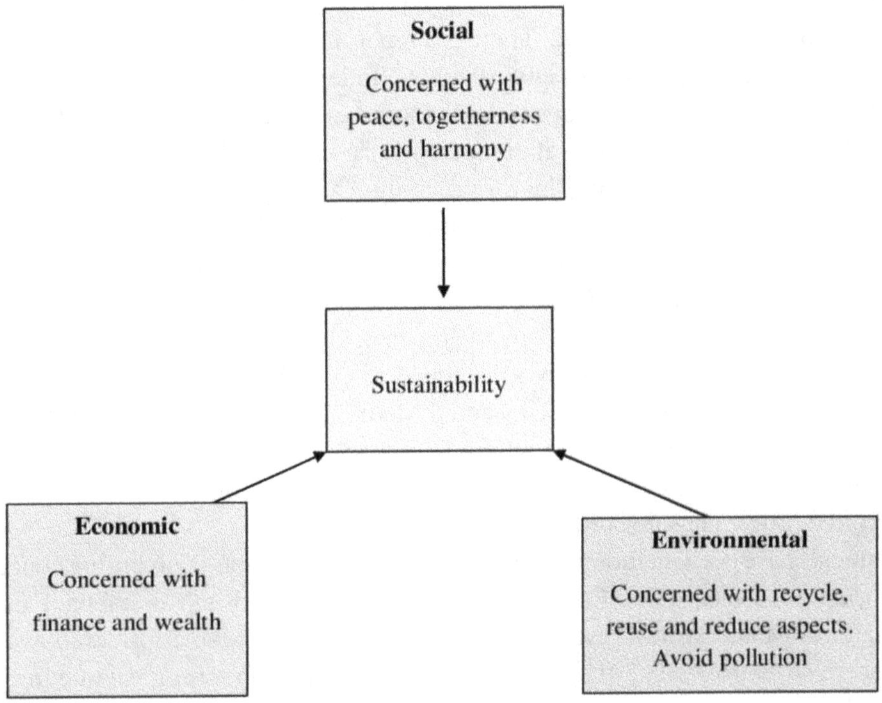

Development - In the development phase, the environmental performance is improved by selecting proper equipment's, methods or protocols for analysis, environmental footprint analysis, etc. The modification in the development phase is high to have sustainability approach.

Commercialization - The modifications and improvements done in development phase are further enlarged in the commercialization phase which includes cooperation with suppliers, vendors and customers.

The inter linkage of sustainability with social, economic and environmental is represented in Figure 5.

DESIGN FOR SUSTAINABILITY

Design for sustainability is the inclusion of sustainability goals in the process and manufacturing sections. The different approaches aimed at design for sustainability are triple bottom-line approach (McDonough and Braungart, 2002) and eco-design approach (Karlsson and Luttropp, 2006). The eco-efficient methods are necessary which takes into consideration balancing the value of economic output and reducing the hazardous impacts on the environment (Braungart et al., 2007). A product development approach which uses eco-design principles without considering economic trade-offs (Grote et al., 2007). The importance of linkage of quality function deployment, life cycle analysis, and TRIZ in the protocols for environment safety is reported by Sakao (2007) and Borea and Wang (2007).

DISPOSAL OF THE PHARMACEUTICAL DRUGS

The method for disposal of the pharmaceutical products needs to be improved. Some of them are disposed to the wastewater, or to the sinks or toilets. There is a report in UK where the disposal of pharmaceuticals through a sink without any impact on the environment (Bound and Voulvoulis, 2005). The same protocol also follows for the disposal of antibiotics (Al-Maadheed et al., 2019). A survey done in 1996 in USA showed that 68% people followed disposal of medicines down the toilets (Kuspis and Krenzelok, 1996). The method for disposal of expired medicines was only 3%. The guidelines to dispose pharmaceutical products in bins at home in 2007 (Glassmeyer et al., 2009). Different countries follow different practices for disposal of pharmaceutical products (Tong et al., 2011b). Some of the medicines or drugs are disposed by burning (Kadam et al., 2016). In 2016, the method for disposal of drugs to home bins and down the toilets were 25 and 1% respectively (Vatovec et al., 2017). In Ghana 1% of the expired drugs or medicines is returned to the pharmacy (Abruquah et al., 2014). There are also national programs such as National Return and Disposal of Unwanted Medicines (NatRUM) Project Audit (Bergen et al., 2013) in Australia and Voluntary Pharmaceutical Take-Back Programs in the Great Lake States (Product Stewardship Institute, 2011). There is need to create awareness among the people for proper disposal of medicines, expired drugs, capsules or tablets.

Pharmaceuticals have been included in the watch list as contaminants of emerging concern by European Union monitoring of surface water. Four pharmaceuticals NSAID drug (diclofenac) and the macrolide antibiotics (azithromycin, clarithromycin and erythromycin) have been considered as contaminants of emerging concern (Ribeiro *et al.*, 2015). Criteria of global usage, poor removal rate in wastewater treatment plants and persistence in the aquatic ecosystem, were considered for the incorporation of six pharmaceuticals (clarithromycin, ciprofloxacin, sulfamethoxazole, venlafaxine, gemfibrozil and diclofenac) as candidates of the watch list (O'Flynn et al., 2021). Potential environmental risk of drugs are given as Risk Quotient (RQ), the data on some drugs is given in Table 1. Non-steroidal anti-inflammatory drugs (diclofenac, ibuprofen, naproxen, and acetylsalicylic acid (ASA)) have been reported to cause mixture toxicity in the environment leading to difficulty in determination of specific drugs environmental risk assessment (Cleuvers, 2004).

For the rejection of pharma micro pollutants in water, researchers are suggesting the techniques like nanofiltration and reverse osmosis processes (Radjenovic et al., 2008). Old methods for the destruction of pharma products are by sewer, combustion, or land disposal (Ivshina et al., 2006). Implementation of physico-chemical methods for the removal of cytostatic compounds (eco-toxic) at the site of origin and utilization is difficult as compared to biological method (Bhattacharyya et al., 2022).

Disposal of Pharma Wastes at Industrial WWTP

Most of the industries associated with the biologically derived antibiotics have adopted the incineration or pyrolysis method for the disposal of AMD (Jiang et al., 2012). During previous years, AMD was recycled as feedstuff and fertilizer due to its contents (Chen et al., 2021). Pharma wastes contain residual concentration of heavy metals which has to be immobilized to avoid leaching effect in the ecosystem. Solar pyrolysis method has been reported for the efficient and economical for the fixation of heavy metals present in Chinese medicine residues (Hou et al., 2022).

Table 1. List of drugs with risk quotient

Drug	Risk Quotient (RQ) (Predicted environmental concentration / predicted no effect concentration)	References
Fluoxetine (Antidepressant drug)	0.03 to 1.55	Yan et al., 2018
Chloroquine, Hydroxychloroquine, Remdesivir, And Ribavirin (Antiviral drug)	>0.1	Kuroda et al., 2021
Favipiravir, Lopinavir, Umifenovir and Ritonavir (Antiviral drug)	>1	Kuroda et al., 2021
Dexamethasone and Oseltamivir (Antiviral drug)	<0.1	Kuroda et al., 2021
Metformin (Anti diabetic drug)	0.01	Jones et al., 2002
Piperacillin, Tazobactam, Flucloxacillin and Ciprofloxacin (Antifungal)	>1	Huschek et al., 2004
Ciprofloxacin, Clarithromycin, Ethinyl estradiol, Acetylsalicylic Acid (Aspirin), Paracetamol and Povidone-Iodine (Pain killer)	>1	Huschek et al., 2004

Disposal of Medical Wastes at Health Care Units

In healthcare units' medical facilities like burial, entombing, removal by municipal containers, burning and dumping etc., are available to dispose medical wastes (Akter, 2000).

Healthcare units must first disinfect the materials to remove the nosocomial infectious agents. Integrated pyrolysis-incineration system is one of the methods widely used for the green removal of hospital medical wastes by heating it to high temperature to carbon black, hydrocarbons, scrap metal like value added products (Khani et al., 2020). Medical waste incinerators are responsible for the release for secondary pollutants like heavy metals (Zn, Cu, As, Pb, Cd), toxic pollutants dibenzofurans and polychlorinated dibenzo-p-dioxins in fly ash (Wang et al., 2012; Xie and Zhu 2013). Considering the cost associated with the disposal of medical waste, some healthcare units prefer steam autoclaves for the safe sterilization of wastes before its landfilling at common places (Tiller and Linscott, 2004). In healthcare units, wastewater treatment facilities should be made available to remove the residual concentration of pharmaceuticals originating from the fecal or urinary excretion system of patients. For the implementation of such facilities cost is the primary factor which limits small units to treat wastewater before its discharge into municipal sewer system. Economical treatment facilities could solve the problem, but most of the efficient methods for the removal of pharmaceutical residues, are costly and must be used in combination. But such facilities must be made compulsory for the healthcare units treating cancer patients and patients with depression.

Disposal of Drugs from Wastewater Treatment Plants

Occurrence of pharmaceuticals in water bodies suggests adoption of method to limit the concentration of the drugs and to avoid the eco-toxicity imposed by drugs or their degradative products. Patients suffering from chemotherapy are administered with cytostatic drugs which excreted as transformed metabolite or untransformed parent compound. Environmental consequences due to such drug residues can be avoided by separating the urine stream and employing the physical methods like advanced oxidation, membrane filtration like techniques (Zhang et al., 2013). Available methods for the removal of drugs in WWTP (waste water treatment plants) are given in Table 2.

ALTERNATE METHODS FOR DISPOSAL OF THE PHARMA PRODUCTS

The toxic wastes and sharps must be burnt. The wastes such as paper, plastics and cardboard can be treated by anaerobic digestion or burning at a very high temperature (Ahmed et al., 2019). The needles and syringes can be sterilized by autoclaving (Zafar, 2019). The expired pharma products can be periodically drained and discarded items can be recycled (Ali et al., 2017). Radioactive wastes can be carefully collected by following proper government rules (Sancho et al., 2013). These policies set by United Nations Sustainable Development Goals must be followed.

SOCIAL LICENSE INITIATIVES IN PHARMA SECTOR

The social issues in pharmaceutical industries require balance between medicines or drugs for the treatment of humans and profit. The social sustainability in the pharma sectors can be achieved by marketing, R & D, supply chains, proper operating methods in the manufacturing process, etc. The Johnson and Johnson pharmaceutical company uses sustainable approach. The pharmaceutical industries must also have profit while achieving sustainability. Many of the pharma companies have prepared their own guidelines related to sustainability. The European Federation of Pharmaceutical Industries and Associations (EFPIA) and Biopharma Investor ESG Communications Guidance 2.0 have mentioned that the pharma sectors should give attention to Environmental, Social and Corporate Governance (ESG).

DIGITAL APPROACH TO MANUFACTURING SUSTAINABILITY

Digital manufacturing is necessary in pharmaceutical processes, products, plants, etc. from end-to-end. The digital tools take into consideration biology, chemistry, physics and engineering to achieve manufacturing sustainability. The platform unites stakeholders, designers, engineers, supply chain vendors, scientists, etc. to make protocols, designs and analysis. The combination of the virtual twin and the power of the 3DEXPERIENCE® platform has been followed since long. The pharma sectors should now have new innovative technologies, methods or protocols to achieve sustainability in aspects of environment, social and economic. The sustainable approach can be achieved by the pharma sectors globally by recycling the medical wastes, etc. There should not be harmful emissions if the pharma products are burnt. There have to policies and legislation to segregate and then treat the pharma products. The materials which can be recycled such as glass vials, plastics, etc. must be properly separated. The methods for segregation and treatment have be eco-friendly and economical (Chisholm et al., 2021).

Table 2. Methods for the removal of drugs in waste water treatment plants

Method		Name of the drug	Efficiency	Reference
Adsorption	Adsorbent: Char from Hair Waste from the Tannery Process	Amoxicillin (AMOX) and Diclofenac (DFC)	80-90%	Rodríguez et al., 2020
Advanced oxidation	AO method: $UV/Fe^{2+} / H_2O_2$	Anticancer drug: Methotrexate	-	Lutterbeck et al., 2015
UV Based advanced oxidation	UV-A homogeneous photo-Fenton process	Antituberculosis drug: isoniazid (INH) and rifampicin (RIF)	70-80%	Stets et al., 2018
Ozonation	-	Anticancer drug: Capecitabine	98.4%	Tang et al., 2021
Electrochemical treatment	Electric energy: 0.87 to 2.29 Wh L^{-1}; Reactive electrochemical membrane (REM) with Ti/SnO_2-Sb anode	Antiretroviral drug: Stavudine	90%	Zhou et al., 2019
Photo catalysis	Photo Fenton process	Anti-inflammatory drug: Ibuprofen	96%	Loaiza-Ambuludi et al., 2014
Biological method	-	Antidepressant sertraline	94%	Gornik et al., 2020
Ozone/H_2O_2 process	-	Antidepressant drug Fluoxetine	86.14%	Aghaeinejad-Meybodi et al., 2015
Membrane bioreactor plus adsorption techniques	Adsorbent: activated carbon	Cytostatic drugs: cancer static platinum compounds (CPC) cisplatin, carboplatin, oxaliplatin, 5-fluorouracil (5-FU) and the anthracyclines doxorubicin, daunorubicin and epirubicin	60%	Lenz et al., 2007
Nano filtration membrane		Non-steroidal anti-inflammatory drugs (NSAIDs): Diclofenac (DIC), Ibuprofen (IBU) and Paracetamol (PARA)	DIC (99.7%) > IBU (81.2%) > PARA (49%)	Maryam et al., 2020

SOLUTIONS AND RECOMMENDATIONS

The pharma sectors can achieve sustainable approach by proper action, monitoring and design in the processes and manufacturing sections. The eco-friendly protocols are the solutions to achieve this to be followed globally.

FUTURE RESEARCH DIRECTIONS

The new methods for recycle and reuse of the pharma products need to be studied in detail. New drugs, medicines for the treatment of human disorders or diseases having safe use must be studied along with their proper method of disposal.

CONCLUSION

The pharmaceutical must adopt sustainable strategies which is very important. The eco-friendly and sustainable approaches in the pharmaceutical industries will be useful to be humans. The environment will also not have hazardous impacts if the sustainable approaches and proper disposal methods of the pharma products is followed. The new methods or protocols should be followed more related to protocols for disposal of syringes, needles, etc. and other pharma products and research needs to be carried out in these areas of aspects.

REFERENCES

Abruquah, A. A., Drewry, J. A., & Taylor, F. (2014). What happens to unused, expired and unwanted medications? A survey of a community-based medication disposal practices. *Int J Dev Sustain*, *3*, 2175–2185.

Adeyeye, E., New, B. J. M., Chen, F., Kulkarni, S., Fisk, M., & Coleman, J. J. (2022). Sustainable medicines use in clinical practice: A clinical pharmacological view on eco-pharmaco stewardship. *British Journal of Clinical Pharmacology*, *88*(7), 3023–3029. doi:10.1111/bcp.15140 PMID:34779524

Aghaeinejad-Meybodi, A., Ebadi, A., Shafiei, S., Khataee, A. R., & Rostampour, M. (2015). Modeling and optimization of antidepressant drug fluoxetine removal in aqueous media by ozone/H_2O_2 process: Comparison of central composite design and artificial neural network approaches. *Journal of the Taiwan Institute of Chemical Engineers*, *48*, 40–48. doi:10.1016/j.jtice.2014.10.022

Ahmed, D., Wagdy, R., & Said, N. (2019). Evaluation of biogas production from anaerobic co-digestion of sewage sludge with microalgae and agriculture wastes. *BioResources*, *14*, 8405–8412.

Akter, N. (2000, January). Medical waste management: A review. Research Reports (1999). *Health Studies, Vol, XXVIII*, 370–394.

Al-Maadheed, S., Goktepe, I., Latiff, A. B. A., & Shomar, B. (2019). Antibiotics in hospital effluent and domestic wastewater treatment plants in Doha, Qatar. *Journal of Water Process Engineering*, *28*, 60–68. doi:10.1016/j.jwpe.2019.01.005

Ali, M., Wang, W., Chaudhry, N., & Geng, Y. (2017). Hospital waste management in developing countries: A mini review. *Waste Management & Research*, *35*(6), 581–592. doi:10.1177/0734242X17691344 PMID:28566033

Alshemari, A., Breen, L., Quinn, G., & Sivarajah, U. (2020). Can we create a circular pharmaceutical supply chain (CPSC) to reduce medicines waste? *Pharmacy (Basel, Switzerland)*, *8*(4), 221. doi:10.3390/pharmacy8040221 PMID:33218038

Aquino, R., Barile, S., Grasso, A., & Saviano, M. (2018). *Envisioning smart and sustainable healthcare: 3D Printing technologies for personalized medication, futures*. Academic Press.

Belkhir, L., & Elmeligi, A. (2019). Carbon footprint of the global pharmaceutical industry and relative impact of its major players. *Journal of Cleaner Production*, *214*, 185–194. doi:10.1016/j.jclepro.2018.11.204

Bergen, P., Kong, D., & George, J. (2013). *The National Return and Disposal of Unwanted Medicines (NatRUM) project audit: Final report*. Academic Press.

Berner, Y. N., & Shike, M. (1988). Consequences of phosphate imbalance. *Annual Review of Nutrition*, *8*(1), 121–148. doi:10.1146/annurev.nu.08.070188.001005 PMID:3060161

Bhattacharyya, P. N., Sonowal, S., Bhattacharyya, L. H., Prasad, R., & Sarma, H. (2022). Bioremediation of cytostatic pharmaceutical and personal care products and emerging technologies. In *Emerging Contaminants in the Environment* (pp. 579-601). Elsevier.

Bom, S., Jorge, J., Ribeiro, H., & Marto, J. (2019). A step forward on sustainability in the cosmetics industry: A review. *Journal of Cleaner Production*, *225*, 270–290. doi:10.1016/j.jclepro.2019.03.255

Borea, M. D., & Wang, B. (2007). Redesign methodology for developing environmentally conscious products. *International Journal of Production Research*, *45*(18-19), 4057–4072. doi:10.1080/00207540701472678

Bound, J. P., & Voulvoulis, N. (2005). Household disposal of pharmaceuticals as a pathway for aquatic contamination in the United Kingdom. *Environmental Health Perspectives*, *113*(12), 1705–1711. doi:10.1289/ehp.8315 PMID:16330351

Braungart, M., McDonough, W., & Bollinger, A. (2007). Cradle-to-cradle design: Creating healthy emissions - A strategy for eco-effective product and system design. *Journal of Cleaner Production*, *5*(13-14), 1337–1348. doi:10.1016/j.jclepro.2006.08.003

Caban, M., & Stepnowski, P. (2021). How to decrease pharmaceuticals in the environment? A review. *Environmental Chemistry Letters*, *19*(4), 3115–3138. doi:10.100710311-021-01194-y

Chen, Y., Du, L., Li, S., Song, W., Jensen, P. A., & Lin, W. (2021). Pyrolysis of antibiotic mycelial dreg and characterization of obtained gas, liquid and biochar. *Journal of Hazardous Materials*, *402*, 123826. doi:10.1016/j.jhazmat.2020.123826 PMID:33254808

Chisholm, J., Zamani, R., Negm, A., Said, N., Abdel daiem, M. M., Dibaj, M., & Akrami, M. (2021). Sustainable waste management of medical waste in African developing countries: A narrative review. *Waste Management & Research*, *39*(9), 1149–1163. doi:10.1177/0734242X211029175 PMID:34218734

Clark, J. H. (2006). Green chemistry: Today and tomorrow. *Green Chemistry*, *8*(1), 17–21. doi:10.1039/B516637N

Cleuvers, M. (2004). Mixture toxicity of the anti-inflammatory drugs diclofenac, ibuprofen, naproxen, and acetylsalicylic acid. *Ecotoxicology and Environmental Safety, 59*(3), 309–315. doi:10.1016/S0147-6513(03)00141-6 PMID:15388270

Cui, C. W., Ji, S. L., & Ren, H. Y. (2006). Determination of steroid estrogens in waste water treatment plant of a contraceptives producing factory. *Environmental Monitoring and Assessment, 121*(1-3), 409–419. doi:10.100710661-005-9139-8 PMID:16758282

Daughton, C. G. (2014). The Matthew Effect and widely prescribed pharmaceuticals lacking environmental monitoring: Case study of an exposure-assessment vulnerability. *The Science of the Total Environment, 466*, 315–325. doi:10.1016/j.scitotenv.2013.06.111 PMID:23911922

de Campos, E. A. R., Ten Caten, C. S., & de Paula, I. C. (2021). End-of-use and end-of-life medicines-Insights from pharmaceutical care process into waste medicines management. *Environmental Science and Pollution Research International, 28*(41), 58170–58188. doi:10.100711356-021-14661-4 PMID:34105077

Deloitte. (2019). *Options for a strategic approach to pharmaceuticals in the environment - Final Report*. Author.

Demirjian, A., Sanchez, G. V., Finkelstein, J. A., Ling, S. M., Srinivasan, A., Pollack, L. A., Hicks, L. A., & Iskander, J. K. (2015). CDC Grand Rounds: Getting smart about antibiotics. *MMWR. Morbidity and Mortality Weekly Report, 64*(32), 871–873. doi:10.15585/mmwr.mm6432a3 PMID:26292205

Garai, A., & Sarkar, B. (2022). Economically independent reverse logistics of customer-centric closed-loop supply chain for herbal medicines and biofuel. *Journal of Cleaner Production, 334*, 129977. doi:10.1016/j.jclepro.2021.129977

Garnier, J. P. (2008). Rebuilding the R&D engine in big pharma. *Harvard Business Review, 86*, 68–70, 72–76, 128. PMID:18543809

Glassmeyer, S. T., Hinchey, E. K., Boehme, S. E., Daughton, C. G., Ruhoy, I. S., Conerly, O., Daniels, R. L., Lauer, L., McCarthy, M., Nettesheim, T. G., Sykes, K., & Thompson, V. G. (2009). Disposal practices for unwanted residential medications in the United States. *Environment International, 35*(3), 566–572. doi:10.1016/j.envint.2008.10.007 PMID:19081631

Gornik, T., Kovacic, A., Heath, E., Hollender, J., & Kosjek, T. (2020). Biotransformation study of antidepressant sertraline and its removal during biological waste water treatment. *Water Research, 181*, 115864. doi:10.1016/j.watres.2020.115864 PMID:32480056

Grote, C. A., Jones, J. M., Blount, G. N., Goodyer, J., & Shayler, M. (2007). An approach to the EUP directive and the application of the economic eco-design for complex products. *International Journal of Production Research, 45*(18-19), 4099–4117. doi:10.1080/00207540701450088

Gujar, G., & Attarwala, A. (2020). Benefits of implementing sustainable business practices for the Indian pharmaceutical industry. *Asian Journal of Management, 11*(1), 26–28. doi:10.5958/2321-5763.2020.00005.0

Hou, X., Deng, Y., Dai, M., Jiang, X., Li, S., Fu, H., & Peng, C. (2022). Migration and transformation of heavy metals in Chinese medicine residues during the process of traditional pyrolysis and solar pyrolysis. *Chemosphere*, *293*, 133658. doi:10.1016/j.chemosphere.2022.133658 PMID:35051513

Huschek, G., Hansen, P. D., Maurer, H. H., Krengel, D., & Kayser, A. (2004). Environmental risk assessment of medicinal products for human use according to European Commission Recommendations. *Environmental Toxicology*, *19*(3), 226–240. doi:10.1002/tox.20015 PMID:15101038

International Initiative on Water Quality-IIWQ. (2017). *Pharmaceuticals in the aquatic environment of the Baltic sea region - A status report. The United Nations Educational, Scientific and Cultural Organization 7*. France and HELCOM.

Ishizaka, A., Khan, S. A., Kheybari, S., & Zaman, S. I. (2022). Supplier selection in closed-loop pharma supply chain: A novel BWM-GAIA framework. *Annals of Operations Research*, 1–24. doi:10.100710479-022-04710-7

Ivshina, I. B., Rychkova, M. I., Vikhareva, E. V., Chekryshkina, L. A., & Mishenina, I. I. (2006). Catalysis of the biodegradation of unusable medicines by alkanotrophic *Rhodococci. Applied Biochemistry and Microbiology*, *42*(4), 392–395. doi:10.1134/S0003683806040090 PMID:17022454

Jiang, X., Feng, Y., Lv, G., Du, Y., Qin, D., Li, X., & Liu, X. (2012). Bioferment residue: TG-FTIR study and co-combustion in a MSW incineration plant. *Environmental Science & Technology*, *46*(24), 13539–13544. doi:10.1021/es3032133 PMID:23163404

Jimenez-Gonzalez, C., Constable, D. J. C., & Ponder, C. S. (2012). Evaluating the "greenness" of chemical processes and products in the pharmaceutical industry-a green metrics primer. *Chemical Society Reviews*, *41*(4), 1485–1498. doi:10.1039/C1CS15215G PMID:22076593

Jobling, S., Coey, S., Whitmore, J. G., Kime, D. E., Van Look, K. J., McAllister, B. G., Beresford, N., Henshaw, A. C., Brighty, G., Tyler, C. R., & Sumpter, J. P. (2002). Wild intersex roach (*Rutilus rutilus*) have reduced fertility. *Biology of Reproduction*, *67*(2), 515–524. doi:10.1095/biolreprod67.2.515 PMID:12135890

Jones, O. A. H., Voulvoulis, N., & Lester, J. N. (2002). Aquatic environmental assessment of the top 25 English prescription pharmaceuticals. *Water Research*, *36*(20), 5013–5022. doi:10.1016/S0043-1354(02)00227-0 PMID:12448549

Kadam, A., Patil, S., Patil, S., & Tumkur, A. (2016). Pharmaceutical waste management an overview. *Indian J Pharm Pract*, *9*(1), 2–8. doi:10.5530/ijopp.9.1.2

Karliner, J., & Guenther, R. (2011). *Global green and healthy hospitals: A comprehensive environmental health agenda for hospitals and health systems around the world*. Health Care without Harm diakses pada laman: http://www. greenhospitals. net/tanggal

Karlsson, R., & Luttropp, C. (2006). Eco-design: What's happening - An overview of the subject area of eco-design and the papers in this special issue. *Journal of Cleaner Production*, *14*(15-16), 1291–1298. doi:10.1016/j.jclepro.2005.11.010

Khani, A., Rasulzade, H., & Aqapur, N. (2020). Green removal of hospital-medical wastes by designed integrated pyrolysis-incineration system. *Journal of Chemistry Letters, 1*, 89–92.

Kuroda, K., Li, C., Dhangar, K., & Kumar, M. (2021). Predicted occurrence, eco-toxicological risk and environmentally acquired resistance of antiviral drugs associated with Covid-19 in environmental waters. *The Science of the Total Environment, 776*, 145740. doi:10.1016/j.scitotenv.2021.145740 PMID:33647647

Kuspis, D. A., & Krenzelok, E. (1996). What happens to expired medications? A survey of community medication disposal. *Veterinary and Human Toxicology, 38*, 48–48. PMID:8825752

Lenz, K., Mahnik, S. N., Weissenbacher, N., Mader, R. M., Krenn, P., Hann, S., & Fuerhacker, M. (2007). Monitoring, removal and risk assessment of cytostatic drugs in hospital waste water. *Water Science and Technology, 56*, 141-149.

Leonard, T., & Schneider, J. (2004, May). Integrated sustainability in the pharmaceutical industry. *Corporate Environmental Strategy: International Journal for Sustainable Business, 11*, 119-128.

Li, C., Zhang, G., Zhang, Z., Ma, D., & Xu, G. (2016). Alkaline thermal pre-treatment at mild temperatures for biogas production from anaerobic digestion of antibiotic mycelial residue. *Bioresource Technology, 208*, 49–57. doi:10.1016/j.biortech.2016.02.064 PMID:26921869

Loaiza-Ambuludi, S., Panizza, M., Oturan, N., & Oturan, M. A. (2014). Removal of the anti-inflammatory drug ibuprofen from water using homogeneous photocatalysis. *Catalysis Today, 224*, 29–33. doi:10.1016/j.cattod.2013.12.018

Lutterbeck, C. A., Baginska, E., Machado, Ê. L., & Kümmerer, K. (2015). Removal of the anti-cancer drug methotrexate from water by advanced oxidation processes: Aerobic biodegradation and toxicity studies after treatment. *Chemosphere, 141*, 290–296. doi:10.1016/j.chemosphere.2015.07.069 PMID:26298026

Ma, D., Zhang, G., Areeprasert, C., Li, C., Shen, Y., Yoshikawa, K., & Xu, G. (2016). Characterization of NO emission in combustion of hydrothermally treated antibiotic mycelial residue. *Chemical Engineering Journal, 284*, 708–715. doi:10.1016/j.cej.2015.08.149

Maryam, B., Buscio, V., Odabasi, S. U., & Buyukgungor, H. (2020). A study on behavior, interaction and rejection of paracetamol, diclofenac and ibuprofen (PhACs) from waste water by nano filtration membranes. *Environmental Technology & Innovation, 18*, 100641. doi:10.1016/j.eti.2020.100641

McDonough, W., & Braungart, W. (2002). Design for the triple top line: New tools for sustainable commerce. *Corporate Environmental Strategy, 9*(3), 1711–1716. doi:10.1016/S1066-7938(02)00069-6

Moldan, B., Janoudkova, S., & Tomas Hak, T. (2012). How to understand and measure environmental sustainability: Indicators and targets. *Ecological Indicators, 17*, 4–13. doi:10.1016/j.ecolind.2011.04.033

Nansai, K., Fry, J., Malik, A., Takayanagi, W., & Kondo, N. (2020). Carbon footprint of Japanese health care services from 2011 to 2015. *Resources, Conservation and Recycling, 152*, 104525. doi:10.1016/j.resconrec.2019.104525

O'Flynn, D., Lawler, J., Yusuf, A., Parle-McDermott, A., Harold, D., Mc Cloughlin, T., & White, B. (2021). A review of pharmaceutical occurrence and pathways in the aquatic environment in the context of a changing climate and the Covid-19 pandemic. *Analytical Methods*, *13*(5), 575–594. doi:10.1039/D0AY02098B PMID:33507166

Product Stewardship Institute. (2011). Report: Lessons learned: Voluntary pharmaceutical take-back programs in the Great Lakes States. Author.

Radjenovic, J., Petrovic, M., Ventura, F., & Barcelo, D. (2008). Rejection of pharmaceuticals in nanofiltration and reverse osmosis membrane drinking water treatment. *Water Research*, *42*(14), 3601–3610. doi:10.1016/j.watres.2008.05.020 PMID:18656225

Ribeiro, A. R., Nunes, O. C., Pereira, M. F., & Silva, A. M. (2015). An overview on the advanced oxidation processes applied for the treatment of water pollutants defined in the recently launched Directive 2013/39/EU. *Environment International*, *75*, 33–51. doi:10.1016/j.envint.2014.10.027 PMID:25461413

Rodriguez, F., Montoya-Ruiz, C., Estiati, I., & Saldarriaga, J. F. (2020). Removal of drugs in polluted waters with char obtained by pyrolysis of hair waste from the tannery process. *ACS Omega*, *5*(38), 24389–24402. doi:10.1021/acsomega.0c02768 PMID:33015455

Rosen, M. A., & Kishawy, H. A. (2012). Sustainable manufacturing and design: Concepts, practices and needs. *Sustainability*, *4*(2), 154–174. doi:10.3390u4020154

Rosi-Marshall, E. J., & Kelly, J. J. (2015). Antibiotic Stewardship should consider environmental fate of antibiotics. *Environmental Science & Technology*, *49*(9), 5257–5258. doi:10.1021/acs.est.5b01519 PMID:25905451

Sakao, T. (2007). AQED-centered design methodology for environmentally conscious product design. *International Journal of Production Research*, *45*(18-19), 4143–4162. doi:10.1080/00207540701450179

Sancho, M., Arnal, J. M., & García-Fayos, B. (2013). Treatment of hospital radio-active liquid wastes from RIA (radioimmunoassay) by membrane technology. *Desalination*, *321*, 110–118. doi:10.1016/j.desal.2013.03.032

Sazvar, Z., Zokaee, M., Tavakkoli-Moghaddam, R., Salari, S. A. S., & Nayeri, S. (2021). Designing a sustainable closed-loop pharmaceutical supply chain in a competitive market Considering demand uncertainty, manufacturer's brand and waste management. *Annals of Operations Research*, *315*(2), 2057–2088. doi:10.100710479-021-03961-0 PMID:33583989

Schneider, J., Wilson, A., & Rosenbeck, J. (2010). Pharmaceutical companies and sustainability: An analysis of corporate reporting. *Benchmarking*, *17*(3), 421–434. doi:10.1108/14635771011049371

Shapiro, D. J., Hicks, L. A., Pavia, A. T., & Hersh, A. L. (2014). Antibiotic prescribing for adults in ambulatory care in the USA, 2007-09. *The Journal of Antimicrobial Chemotherapy*, *69*(1), 234–240. doi:10.1093/jac/dkt301 PMID:23887867

Shaw, B., & Whitney, P. (2016). Ethics and compliance in global pharmaceutical industry marketing and promotion: The role of the IFPMA and self-regulation. *Pharmaceuticals Policy and Law*, *18*(1-4), 199–206. doi:10.3233/PPL-160443

Stets, S., do Amaral, B., Schneider, J. T., de Barros, I. R., de Liz, M. V., Ribeiro, R. R., Nagata, N., & Peralta-Zamora, P. (2018). Antituberculosis drugs degradation by UV-based advanced oxidation processes. *Journal of Photochemistry and Photobiology A Chemistry*, *353*, 26–33. doi:10.1016/j.jphotochem.2017.11.006

Tang, S., Xu, L., Yu, X., Chen, S., Li, H., Huang, Y., & Niu, J. (2021). Degradation of anticancer drug capecitabine in aquatic media by three advanced oxidation processes: Mechanisms, toxicity changes and energy cost evaluation. *Chemical Engineering Journal*, *413*, 127489. doi:10.1016/j.cej.2020.127489

Tiller, T., & Linscott, A. (2004). Evaluation of a steam autoclave for sterilizing medical waste at a university health center. *American Journal of Infection Control*, *32*(3), E9. doi:10.1016/j.ajic.2004.04.013

Tong, A. Y. C., Peake, B. M., & Braund, R. (2011b). Disposal practices for unused medications in New Zealand community pharmacies. *Journal of Primary Health Care*, *3*(3), 197–203. doi:10.1071/HC11197 PMID:21892421

Vatovec, C., Van Wagoner, E., & Evans, C. (2017). Investigating sources of pharmaceutical pollution: Survey of over-the-counter and prescription medication purchasing, use, and disposal practices among university students. *Journal of Environmental Management*, *198*, 348–352. doi:10.1016/j.jenvman.2017.04.101 PMID:28494423

Walia, K., Ohri, V. C., & Mathai, D. (2015). Antimicrobial stewardship program (AMSP) practices in India. *The Indian Journal of Medical Research*, *142*(2), 130. doi:10.4103/0971-5916.164228 PMID:26354210

Wang, Y. F., Wang, L. C., Hsieh, L. T., Li, H. W., Jiang, H. C., Lin, Y. S., & Tsai, C. H. (2012). Effect of temperature and CaO addition on the removal of polychlorinated dibenzo-p-dioxins and dibenzofurans in fly ash from a medical waste incinerator. *Aerosol and Air Quality Research*, *12*(2), 191–199. doi:10.4209/aaqr.2011.06.0079

Weaver, E., O'Hagan, C., & Lamprou, D. (2022). The sustainability of emerging technologies for use in pharmaceutical manufacturing. *Expert Opinion on Drug Delivery*, *19*(7), 861–872. doi:10.1080/17425247.2022.2093857 PMID:35732275

Wong, D., & Brad, S. (2017). Leveraging antimicrobial stewardship into improving rates of carbapenem-resistant Enterobacteriaceae. *Virulence*, *8*(4), 383–390. doi:10.1080/21505594.2016.1188234 PMID:27187821

Xie, Y., & Zhu, J. (2013). Leaching toxicity and heavy metal bioavailability of medical waste incineration fly ash. *Journal of Material Cycles and Waste Management*, *15*(4), 440–448. doi:10.100710163-013-0133-x

Yaseen, G., Ahmad, M., & Zafar, M. (2021). Green sustainable process for chemical and environmental engineering and science. In Current status of solvents used in the pharmaceutical industry. Elsevier.

Zafar, S. (2019). *Medical waste management in developing countries*. Thomé-Kozmiensky Verlag GmbH-Neuruppin. Available at: https://www.vivis. de/wp-content/uploads/WM9/2019_WM_351-358_Zafar.pdf

Zhang, J., Chang, V. W., Giannis, A., & Wang, J. Y. (2013). Removal of cytostatic drugs from aquatic environment: A review. *The Science of the Total Environment*, *445*, 281–298. doi:10.1016/j.scitotenv.2012.12.061 PMID:23337605

Zhou, C., Wang, Y., Chen, J., & Niu, J. (2019). Porous Ti/SnO2-Sb anode as reactive electrochemical membrane for removing trace antiretroviral drug stavudine from wastewater. *Environment International*, *133*, 105157. doi:10.1016/j.envint.2019.105157 PMID:31520959

KEY TERMS AND DEFINITIONS

Carbon Footprint: The carbon footprint denotes the quantity of greenhouse gases generated in the environment due to human activities and industrialization.

Eco-Friendly: The term eco-friendly denotes which is safe to the environment and humans.

Economical: Economical meaning is very cheap.

Supply Chain: A supply chain is the final product which goes to the consumer.

Chapter 12
A Philosophical Reflection of SDG 4 and Our Education Policy: Justified Self-Interest vs. Common Interest

Jahid Siraz Chowdhury
https://orcid.org/0000-0002-1016-0441
Universiti Malaya, Malaysia

Parimal Roy
https://orcid.org/0000-0002-0461-2587
Universiti Malaya, Malaysia

ABSTRACT

No creed has called for education for peace. Instead of revealing the world of injustices, such an assertion emerged since the 1970s by Paulo Freire, Frantz Fanon from French, Syed Hussein Alatas from Malaysia, Vine Deloria from the American Indians. Later, Gayatri Spivak, Walter Mignolo, Eve Tuck, and Yung have pointed out the system's problem. This chapter demonstrates an unorthodox, non-linear discussion with UNESCO's (in effect, the SDG 4) educational program references. The inspiration came from different masterpieces—Spivak's Righting Wrong, Vine Deloria's Indigenous Metaphysics, Frantz Fanon's Black Skin White Mask, Darryl Macer's Bioethics for Love. In terms of gnoseology, the authors followed Sadia Gaon's phrase—a polymath said in 872 AD: 'observe the unobserved' in the new normalcy—a part of practical philosophy—and the analytical or conceptual domain. This chapter contains three parts: first the motivation, then the analytical framework, and finally, established argument. The authors conclude that the education system shapes mental faults that shape our activation.

THE DISCUSSION'S MOTIVATION

What is the Creed of Education when Human Lives are at Stake?

As we are engaged in Education, we try to find the answer—what the creed of Education is! Not that of

DOI: 10.4018/978-1-6684-7499-0.ch012

enlightened philosopher Immanuel Kant's moral Education (Moran, 2009; Dennis, 2020; Webb, 2020) or John Stuart Mill or Rene Descartes' morality (Dale, 2006) all have been 'reasoned' by bloodshed, slavery, and looting (Tricoire, 2017; Heller &McElhinny, 2017). After a few centuries, we cannot avoid Kant (Dennis, 2020). Nor do we see as appropriate the Pragmatist philosopher John Dewey (2010) and John Rawls (Rawls, 2009) utilitarian philosophy or Al Farabi's Oneness as the definitive source (Mahdi, 2020; Imdad, Hafidhuddin & Arif, 2019). Instead, these three names are our ground to deploy this discussion. As 'disciples of social sciences, we are 'conceptually' involved in building and promoting peace, human rights, and justice.

We fully agreed— "Education transforms lives"—however, we ask a few asking. We are a little careful instead of blind participation. Thirty-five years ago, Gustavo Esteva cautioned: *'be aware of participation'—a caution of supranational 'abstract' policies and states' involvement* (Esteva, 1985). Hitherto, Gustavo is essential as a reneged lighthouse to those who think of and act for the marginals. We are here to argue that three schools are not only dominating the education system of modern times. Our asking domain aligned with Vine Deloria Indigenous metaphysics. Deloria was an American Indian activist and philosopher who injected that western Education and epistemology is not providing us a justified common interest.

Hence, the Western notion does not fit in Indigenous (marginal people). Our second motivation came from Frantz Fanon. Fanon has many differences with Paolo Freire (Tuck & Yang, 2012), though both focused on Education. We need an education that does not contribute only to knowledge but a transformation of UNESCO's global aim. Education that enables action, the development of critical thinking, the acquisition of intellectual reflection methods and collective work, which collaborates in the search for a social and political transformation through non-violent methods and the construction of a reality adapted to it region of the world we inhabit. Darryl Macer, a prominent bioethicist (1994, 1998), who also worked for UNESCO, has been grappling that educating human rights and peace is an experience that generates learning and transformation processes in action. In this chapter (read, discussion), the principles that emerge from the UNESCO and global education system's experience for Peace and Education transform lives are elaborated critically. A good number of academic research has appeared with a 'critical' stand on how this global plan will be grounded when the world is already infraction. The voice is not only from one regional country but globally, as seen in table 1.

Table 1 is a part of our ground as it gives us the foundation to raise our voices. Meanwhile, we see scholars are raising voices from a critical stand (Brissett &Mitter, 2017; Ashukem, 2020— along with pointing out particular human indicators that are equally important.

Tables 1 and 2 show the announcement of SDGs that came to the fore in 2015 by former Secretary-General reverend Pope Francis, Malala Yousafzai, and Ugandan President Museveni. With a robust, ambitious, and gigantic set of 17 goals and 169 'targets' to eliminate extreme poverty, about discrimination and throw them out of the globe. In this chapter, it is difficult to point out all these targets that cover almost all spheres of human life; however, our "way of speaking seems both natural and close to the bone (Hacking, 2002, p.2)". However, we will point to Education—even though our discussion may lack sufficient empirical data or debates within, this will provoke some knowledge pool thoughts. These 'Goals' never asked for a radical transformation or covering social, economic, and ecological issues the world faces today caused by colonialism and neoliberalism.

Education—since the human civilization—is playing a significant role in human life (Imdad et al., 2019)—and here are vital means to materialize these grand promises (Dyer &Rajan, 2020).

Table 1. Arguing voices on SDGs. Source: Authors' compilation

Region	Country	Major Works
Africa	Kenya	Cheserek, G. J., & Mugalavai, V. K. (2012). Challenges and reforms facing the Kenyan education system in the 21st century: Integrating the principles of vision 2030 and constitution 2010
	Sub-Sahara	Ilie, S., & Rose, P. (2018). Who benefits from public spending on higher Education in South Asia and sub-Saharan Africa? Ilie, S., & Rose, P. (2016). Is equal access to higher Education in South Asia and sub-Saharan Africa achievable by 2030?
	Africa	Adenle, A. A. (2020). Assessment of solar energy technologies in Africa-opportunities and challenges in meeting the 2030 agenda and sustainable development goals
	Ghana	Osei Kwadwo, V., & Konadu, O. A. (2020). Can Ghana Afford the Sustainable Development Goal on Education?
Europe	Spain	Filippo, D. D., Benayas, J., Peña, K., & Sánchez, F. (2020). Communication on Sustainability in Spanish Universities: Analysis of Websites, Scientific Papers, and Impact in Social Media. Boto-Álvarez, A., & García-Fernández, R. (2020). Implementation of the 2030 Agenda Sustainable Development Goals in Spain
	Romania	Firoiu, D., Ionescu, G. H., Băndoi, A., Florea, N. M., & Jianu, E. (2019). Achieving sustainable development goals (SDGs): Implementation of the 2030 Agenda in Romania
Asia-Pacific	Asia-Pacific	Forlin, C. (2019). Teacher Education and Inclusion in the Asia-Pacific Region
	South Asia	Dyer, C., & Rajan, V. (2020). Educating South Asia's internally migrating children.

SDGs 4 aims "to ensure inclusive and quality education for all and promote lifelong learning" (The United Nations, 2015) and contains ten 'targets' to be achieved by 2030. We echo with many authors (Brissett &Mitter, 2017; Firoiu et al., 2019), "what are the prospects of fulfilling these promises?". Why do we need to see inspite of 'the critical argument (table1 and 2) again? Our question, as stated, is

Table 2. The critical stand pointing to particular human indicators. Source: Authors' compilation

Indicators	Majors works
Human rights	Beiter, K. D. (2017). Is the Age of Human Rights Really over-The Right to Education in Africa-Domestication, Human Rights-Based Development, and Extraterritorial State Obligations
CSR*	Abad-Segura, E., Cortés-García, F. J., & Belmonte-Ureña, L. J. (2019). The sustainable approach to corporate social responsibility: A global analysis and future trends
Education quality	González García, E., Colomo Magaña, E., & Cívico Ariza, A. (2020). Quality education as a sustainable development goal in the context of 2030 agenda: Bibliometric approach
Inclusive Education	Schwab, S. (2020). Inclusive and Special Education in Europe.
Management of University	Paletta, A., &Bonoli, A. (2019). Governing the university from the perspective of the United Nations 2030 Agenda.
Sustainability	Higgins-Desbiolles, F., & Wijesinghe, G. (2018). The critical capacities of restaurants as facilitators for transformations to sustainability.
Finance	Archer, D., &Muntasim, T. (2020). Financing SDG 4: context, challenges, and solutions
Lack of Holism	del Río Castro, G., Fernández, M. C. G., &Colsa, Á. U. (2020). Unleashing the convergence amid digitalization and sustainability towards pursuing the Sustainable Development Goals (SDGs): A holistic review
Gender	Pappu, R. (2020). Gender equity in Education: Changes and challenges in South Asia

ontological—specifically, "[t]he ontological is appealing because it offers a unifying principle for the analytics and poetics of anthropology beyond the human. From this perspective, the whole cosmos is in urgent need of rethinking. Anthropolo[ical discussion here], then, has just begun (Bessire& Bond, 2014, p.341)." Certainly, Ian Hacking's Historical ontology and Michel Foucault's original thought on Ontology are instructive here. Noticeably, in the famous work, what is Enlightenment, Michel Foucault only mentioned the term twice when Ian Hacking has a full-length book, *Historical Ontology. Our second issue is as Alharbi's inference, that is more than critical or speculation, and the stand of "[p]* hilosophical problems are conceptual (Hacking, 2002, p, 36). The reason behind that is, a narration of reverend Pope was instructive and vital for our argument—'development is another name of peace(see Paul II, 1987), for willing readers, see Saint Augustine (1998). A known fact, Saint Augustine is the first man who asserted that society develops on a linear stage. In part three, we will deploy the discussion; meanwhile, we should indicate our analytical guidelines.

ANALYTICAL FRAMEWORK

This segment is our faith, our methodology—we conclude that science is only as good as its adopted worldview or lifeworld, much like a religion. To evaluate our point of view, we used four main streams. Although they appear to be independent, they are all interconnected. We describe the four conceptual streams that will direct the rest of the chapter and, in turn, our thought, becoming, and acting as social scientists. This section also discusses the study's meaning and a reflection on methodological limitations. Our first stream is for our use. As a researcher, we have been rebuilding the 'self.' Then, we went back to Al-Farabi (872-950), Saadia Gaon, and the Critical stance of understanding (882-942). The poststructuralist movement presented us with our third source of information. Our final justification is based on social science's Decolonial Awareness. The order of intellectual trends is based on their sources rather than their influence, but they have all enriched our "being"—methodological acumen.

In 1643's Religio Medici, Zoroastrianism was identified as one of the world's oldest and most commonly practiced religions (Browne, 1852; Hickey, 2019). Contemplative studies as a sub-field of social science have arisen since then, largely due to research into Buddhist and Vedic meditation practices. To discuss some of the most critical current approaches to consciousness research, Presti says that first-person, subjective experience is required to be a full self to achieve the entire—by essence, we are whole. As we previously stated, following Saadia Gaon's stream, Al-Farabi, then in the modern age, Vine Deloria, Frantz Fanon, rather than Immanuel Kant, appears to be important to our project. The Poststructuralist turn is the third stream. Michel Foucault suggested the power-information-commerce nexus (see Foucault, 1980), but the deconstruction thesis (Caputo, 1997), the subaltern movement (Chakrabarty, 2008), and historiography supplemented our intuitions as sources of knowledge. The Decolonial turn is our final stream. This concept was not coined at the seminar in 2015; however, the west's critique and ambiguity of being is a philosophical theme identified by Carlos Maritegui in 1927 and Syed HusseinAlattas in 2010. Edward Said in the 1970s, and Vine Deloria in 1969. Mahatma Gandhi, Frantz Fanon, and Syed Hussein Alattas were anti-colonial pioneers. The second-generation movement, which includes Farid Alatas, Ngugi, Gayatri Spivak, and Walter Mignolo, concludes that imperialism kills socio-culture, academic practice, society as a whole, and even the colony's physical absence.

In the Indigenous setting, Indigenous scholars followed the Critical movement (see Linda Smith, Shawn Wilson, Martin Nakata, Karen Martin) and exercised in various fields. However, universities are crucial in decolonizing a society's many woven colonial fabrics (Walter Mignolo's 'disobeying west in academia,' Gayatri Spivak's 'epistemic terror,' Hussein Alatas's'captive mind').

Then we looked at the study's meaning, which ostensibly involves science and philosophy history. This section delves into the western 'history of science,' or, to put it another way, the history of philosophy, in which the history of science is combined with the history of philosophy, all of which are fraught with bloodshed, looting, ethnic cleansing, and the appropriation of eastern wealth. Since roughly 1492, the genteel and lament construction of the western history of science, philosophy, and/or scientism has dominated the knowledge field (Vandana Shiva, Alfred Crosby). The third segment depicts the methods we used to perform our study. We have weaknesses, such as a lack of empirical evidence, which we address in the last section. On the other hand, a small table could help us understand the chapter's theme.

Our total disparity, and argument, are based on one of the older heated debates, including Foucault's stance, which heavily concerns nominalism: conscious and unconscious. This is an issue in modern science, or as you might call it, western ontology. Ian Hacking defines the fundamental question as making up the definitions that we use "to describe the world (p.39-40)," to which we add the global South. Fanon is unique in that, like Vine Deloria, he takes a stance against scientism. "The issue is that we don't understand why the universe is so comprehensible to our naming schemes." For us, this is a fundamental stance. In her book "Indigenous Research Methodologies," Linda Smith chastised them for coming and naming our universe. When choosing our methodological framework, will we stand for latching on to these doctrines? Is it possible that a stance may be taken to refute strict nominalism? As a result, we used Critical Discourse Analysis (CDA), which is a form of discourse analytical research that focuses on how text and talk in the social and political context enact, perpetuate, and resist social power violence, domination, and inequality (Van Dijk, 2006, 2008). Language is a type of social activity that creates and strengthens societal power relations, according to CDA's underlying philosophy. CDA rejects the idea of a neutral and rationalist view of the world based on this premise, instead considering language usage as highly political. The concept of 'critical' in CDA is derived from the Frankfurt School and Jürgen Habermas; we adopted Al-farabai and Saadia Gaon as our departure points (see table 3). The Frankfurt School, or critical theory, is ontologically western, especially regarding axiology and self-determinism. Let us go about it a little bit more.

The critical framework, for example, naturally explores a broader nature of societies (Rowe, Baldry, &Earles, 2015) and is overtly political (Henry & Foley, 2018). Regarding ontology, Critical theories focus on anthropocentric analogies, which are predominantly western individualistic (Rowe et al., 2015). While IRP, on the other hand, focuses on connectedness, living and non-living worlds (Martin &Mirraboopa, 2003), kin groups (Moreton-Robinson, 2000, 2015), the universe, and land-based relationships (Andrews, 2020; Moreton-Robinson, eds, 2020, also see Wilson, Breen, A, &DuPré, (Eds.). (2019)-and this is against solipsism.

Regarding epistemology, the former informs subjectivists like IRP (Rowe et al., 2015). Still, the subjectivist measurement is well known and focused on the western worldview, rooted in western philosophy, that has misrepresented Indigenous peoples, their understanding, and community sentiment for centuries by western researchers, and even in the presentation, creating, and locating the Other (Indigenous and all colonized people). Put, can any western theory or methodological say or take a position similar to Lynn Lavallee (2009)?" If consulted by the group, even several years after the conclusion of a research project, the research team must be prepared to assist the community with their requests (p.24)," Lavallee explained our view on axiology, which is standing out from the crowd, and reciprocal connection. It is one side of our analysis. However, we seek assistance from Saadia Gaon's (882-942) theory of knowledge (see Efros, 1942; Malek, 2018). Saadia and Alfarabi (Mahdi, 2020) have an immense impact on developing our understanding.

Table 3. Analytical Standpoint. Source: Authors' compilation

THE TOOLS OF METHODOLOGY	
Stream One	**Stream Two**
Presence: Interiority-Self Presence: Praxis-Activity with localized participation Research: Research Engagement with Data: Discernment -Evaluation-choice in relation to data Emerging: Genisis-Brighting an articulated insight: Enactment-Renewed participation in a public forum	Sources of Knowledge Sensation Nous Interference Tradition
Stream Three	**Stream Four**
Textual Presentation of Covid-19 Seeking the relationship of knowledge and power within the Capitalist and Socialist opinion for Combating the New Normal.	Here we follow Walter Mignolo. Naquib Al-Attas' assertion of western 'uncertainty.' Linda Smith's 'Decolonial Tools like Reconciliation and Healing of the community, Development of the people, Recovery the lost history

SOME THESIS ANALYSIS

We segregated this part into a few sub-topics—which may help readers to follow the analysis.

Thesis One: Development and Development IGO'a is the Creation of Globalization when Globalization is a New Form of Colonialism

From where we start this premises, Emma Crewe and Elizabeth Harrison (Crewe & Harrison, 1998) have a magnificent discussion of the present-day activities—nothing but the systematic, sophisticated west heritage. Emma Crewe, and Harrison's second chapter, An Intellectual Heritage of Development, has been considered as "[s]ilent traditions(p.25).".This is such a trend that many critical (Banerjee, 2003), post-colonial thinkers (see Escobar, 2011; Esteva, 2014; Esteva, 2019; Esteva, 2020; Esteva& Escobar, 2017), and Decolonial scholars (such, Sultana, 2019; Massarella, Sallu & Ensor, 2020; Klein, 2017) have pointed this since long to recent time. The problem— some are replacing the Critical stand as decolonizing, which is creating another problem, such Sultana (2019) started with Paolo Freire: "We need critical hope the way a fish needs unpolluted water (Sultana, 2019, p. 32). In doing a Decolonizing Farhana Sultana (of course, Sultana is not alone, Soynni Madison, Linda Smith also) have fallen into the trap. The reason is that authors like Sultana are from Bangladesh, the global South, yet, captive, it would be clearer if we read from Gaytri Spivak: "I have been suggesting, then, that "human rights culture" runs on unremitting Northern-ideological pressure, even when it is from the South; that there is a real epistemic discontinuity between the Southern human rights advocates and those whom they protect (Spivak, 2004, p.36). We will discuss in thesis three

Due to the inherent frustration towards neoliberal capitalism, the prevalent socio-political ideology which consistently portrays (see Hacking, 2002), and the debate on growth, we ask: how much would the SDGs-4 work toward the predominant globalist agenda? Inevitably, we are questioning the degree

Table 4. Philosophical base and practical construction of 'development. Source: Authors' compilations

Philosophical Stand	Dividing concepts	
Descartes:	I think	They do not think
Locke	Enlightened and Developed	Underdeveloped
Ethnography	We	They
Westermarck	Reciprocity in kind	The receiver of reciprocity-in- kind is Christian Commonwealth
CBD	Knowledge Documentation	Benefit sharing
Pope ii	Peace and Development	Agitation
NGOs and IGOs, and SDGs	My, our	Their
CBD: Convention of Biological Diversity, IGOs: Intra Governmental Organizations		

that the SDGs will entirely change educational opportunities for sustainable growth. In this excerpt, we are attempting to make a disclaimer for the jubilation around these aims by pointing out how conflicting the rhetoric of transformational Education, in relation to the SDGs-4, is with social and economic systems characterize the ubiquitous culture purposefully (Hacking, 2002). The whole claim is made by putting SDGs-4 within the framework of two traditionally prevailing narratives:

Education and research and its shifts in curriculum and The Utilitarian moral philosophy.

We find that both narratives integrate and incorporate—inherited, of course—in the SDGs' particular lens. A contribution to environmental progress triggers the presentation of the transition of Education. Concurrently, its discussion of utilitarian theory reflects the all-pervading new responsibility (Education for 2030) to the neoliberal capitalist development paradigm. Ipso facto, our critical objective is to explore the dominance of the SDG-4 and how we—the global South, agree to accept this under the Development Discourse. Development was often named a depoliticization device (read Majid Rahmenma in Ziai, 2017; James Ferguson).

The myths, language, political systems, and creation discourses are frequently imperialist in their overarching philosophies and behaviors. The imperial power structure (Mignolo, 2011) of the past continues as modernity/coloniality today (Mignolo, 2011; Mignolo& Walsh, 2018, pp. 120-123), regenerating colonial relationships of dominance, inequality, and repression, while formally settled. The framings that guide policy and project creation will influence whole individuals and locations' consequences and pathways (as if the west is locating us). Hegemonic proclamations should not often confront the effect of structure and interpretation on other individuals' and subordinates' living conditions. This breakdown contributed to multiple implementation delays, diverse opposition conflicts from academia and communities, and innovative products or services of the global South in the strongest terms. For instance, in the 1960s green revolution ruined the agro-based economy of Bangladesh, Tanzania, and other Latin and Asian countries (see James Scott for agriculture, 1985, 2010, 2020; Vandana Shiva for the ecology and gender, 2014; James Ferguson for oil mining 2005 are few names avid the vast literature). All these happened because of community development, national revenue, and progress.

Our experimentation believed that every educational reform proposal is difficult to serve such contradictory value-added speeches. Therefore, sustainability education and capitalist growth creation education within the SDGs is an incredibly troublesome topic. In its very nature, SDGs express prevailing philosophies (see table 4) and perhaps facets to model and describe development strategies and thereby presumably neglect oppressed ideologies, which may be a problem if you determine who gains from this vision 2030. By defining a particular direction towards "sustainable development," the SDGs are likely to support specific desires over others and may favour certain development philosophies over others. The framework—where the SDGs came from—is in the interests of the SDGs owners, and how the SDGs can affect sustainable development efforts in the world is imperative. We look into how SDGs-4 perpetuates utilitarianism in schooling, that we must be vigilant to engage in these latest projects and the degree to which we commit to social justice. Via CDA, we seek to unveil principles that ultimately form educational results and provide room for promoted but subordinated speeches. In the sense of neoliberalism and globalization, we see the future consequences of predominant rhetoric and its ideals in pursuing "sustainable growth" or sustainability within the system.

Whatever policy ideology accompanies evolutionism has, since its colonization (and, of course, other manifestations historically or simultaneously of imperialism), rhetorically explained interventions in the "backward" nations on the premise that the influence of more sophisticated foreign parties allows them to catch up with traditional cultures. Anti-colonialists like Edward Said, Talal Asad, and Arthuro Escobar remind us that since 'they' were powerless to rule themselves, the compassionate Christian response was to assume care of governing duties in their stead.

Thesis Two: IGOs are Copies of Capitalist Cosmopolitanism

Therefore, *we have to be aware of participation* in caution from Esteva for a long time, and from the capitalist cosmopolitanism is 'centrifugally' made by and for Europe (Mignolo, 2011, p. 23)[1] And a weapon of capitalist and colonial cultural control. States used these foreign policies with other institutions (see Harvey, 2014, pp. 161-64) to control her citizen (Dreyfus &Rabinow, 2014; Agamben, 2005) and prevent communism, too (Rahnema cited in Ziai, 2017, p.10)." We know it needs a long discussion to justify the thesis. Let us give an example.

Regarding the Convention of Biological Diversity (CBD), scholars often admire global leaders and that Indigenous people can save their knowledge and culture. However, are we not repeating Kathleen McAfee in Selling nature to save it? Biodiversity and green developmentalism (1999) showed the historical formation of CBD and its brutality.

Scholars (Shizha, 2017; Banerjee, 2003) see that SDGs are nothing but the implementing guidelines of CBD, and this is such a trap that we are unaware of this. As mentioned before, Sultana, citing Frantz Fanon and Linda Smith, states that "[u]ltimately, decolonizing is about liberation and new ways of valuing, not privileging Eurocentric values as universal or superior (2019, p.34)" -we argue, by trying to establish the decolonial stand, whether Dr. Sultana is reproducing another colonial legacy or not!

The impact is unseen—in the present world—the most repeated word in the academic and political discourse is—the development of the people, specifically of the global South. Indeed, there is always something not visible in the intellectual world. The urgency to make human life 'sustainable' or to 'mobilize' or modern all available interdisciplinarity to learn or act better does not end when these words cease to be in the foreground. Similarly, the need to determine the impact or to assess more than superficially the immediate results of an intervention is still urgent. This is especially so in the context of scarce resources such as the current one, where the word "crisis" justifies cuts in financing essential issues, and the selection of so-called "social investments" is strengthened. The making, development, distribution, and "construction of SDGs -4 is not neutral; it reflects a particular global social and political context and motivations in which different social forces seek to make and remake the world (Sayed & Moriarty,2020)."

What do we need to do? Gayatri Spivak answered:

In order to shift this layered discontinuity, however slightly, we must focus on the quality and end of Education; at both ends, the Southern elite is often educated in Western or Western-style institutions. We must work at both ends—both in Said/ Rorty's utopia and in the schools of the rural poor in the global South (Spivak, p. 380)

As stated, (see Sayed & Moriarty, 2020) contend that the construction of SDGs- 4 is not neutral; we addon, instead, it represents a specific global social and political sense and motivations under which various social movements aim to make and remake the world. As can be observed, the MDGs do not discuss Education for All. Why? Is this not listed in the SDGs? We discovered the response to Mark Fisher's (2009) and Gayatri Spivak's (2004) masterpiece, *Writing Wrongs*. This Neoliberalism, or the global North, has no hegemonic impact on the socio-economic organization; instead, it is the only truth we can foresee (Fisher, 2009; Sayed, & Moriarty,2020) Methodology part, (Spivak, 2004). Spivak or Fisher's thought drives us, but we feel *'unhappy consciousness'* because they neglected to discuss local society's holism. Spivak believed in a move close to Derrida or Foucault but dared to suggest and we need as 'weing.' However, their lens is helpful for us because it is the lens by which everything, including education policy, is now presented, named, made, organized, and marketed to the global South. As if this is the only normal situation, our emotional state, as Syed Hussein Alatas put it, is still a prisoner, as Sultana was (2019).

Aligned to other sustainability goals, the SDGs aim to change, develop, modern, and all human virtues. We have had the same logic since *the Columbian Exchange* (read Hegel, Locke, JS Mill, and Alfred Crosby). This classification pattern is not new (Edward Said), but it was generated by the notion of Saint Augustine, the first society classifier, later advocated by several, including René Descartes, Immanuel Kant, and David Hume. Their promotion was imperial, and the commonwealth was Christian. The historical context, the human influence (read Tribal), social categorization production, promotion of the degree and quality of habitability, and those policies of regulation and preservation under globalization through IGOs are thus required to be evaluated. They are to identify the new sense of place (Homo Bhabha) where Education (SDG -4) takes on greater significance. Human habitability is not just superficially 'holistic' but not radically changed. If so, writers like Edward Said, Hussein Alatas, and Frantz Fanon do not complement it. This study aims to refocus on schooling, national policy, and the identification of a new unification path between 'adult' and natural habitats via empirical methodologies on public education and development strategies. Our epistemic foundation is associated with human existence and not forcing. The basics to estimate the degree of unification between natural, relational, and mutual planning metrics soon. Therefore, integrated schooling is recommended, but we believe it is necessary for human health and preservation. This study concludes that the epistemic re-structure of Education will affect education and future policies to create a harmonized right-based society.

Thesis Three: Social Justice is a Sophisticated Trapping

Conversation with the Rakhain and others leads to asking, is the social justice metonym to 'neo-liberal, 'global political platform'?

[d]ecolonization, which we assert is a distinct project from other civil and human rights-based social justice projects, is far too often subsumed into the directives of these projects, with no regard for how decolonization wants something different than those forms of justice. (Tuck et al., 2014, p.3).

Understandably, it is much easier to defend a notion than rejecting. To start introducing Ihsan and rejecting social justice, we surfed multiple aspects/dimensions such as feminist, libertarian, and Marxist. For conceptual comprehension, we refer (Barry, 2005, pp.3-26; Smith, 2000; Sandel, 2010) for the theoretical understanding (Barry 2005:45-66; Smith, 1997; Sen, 1992; Arrow, 1973). Some texts (Barry, 2005, pp. 47-55; Lee & Smith, 2004, pp. 1-12; Sen, 2009) underpin Social Justice in the world system and/or the neoliberal ideology. Soyini Madison's *Critical Ethnography*, well referred to in IRP, adopted Rawl (2009 [1971]) to justify social justice and distributive 'reciprocity' in ethnography. The grounded logic, following Rawl, Madison says that wealthy people can distribute their wealth towards the poor since they are in a social contract of the society (Can we recall Thomas Hobbes' Reciprocity?). Rawl is an ideological follower of John Dewey, vocal of pragmatism, a dogmatic notion of sustainability of a system instead of changing or transforming. Besides, Dewey and Rawl are both inspired by Mill's utilitarianism (Mill, 2016[1863], pp. 337-383, 1990), a life-long officer of the colonial East India Company. Reciprocity, to Mill, entails precisely such moral action and thus remains beyond the *ken of barbarous* Indian people (Klausen 2016:99 Emphasis ours). Moreover, this kind of reciprocity influenced the liberal neo-liberalism to adjust and maximize personal gain under the capitalist system, and abide by the rules instead of rebelling or revolution or transforming this besmirching system. Therefore, Rawl was criticized by many Marxist philosophers, like Paul Wolf (1977), and even by Amartya Sen (Sen,1992, pp. 81-87, 2009, pp. 52-74), another Noble winner, Kenneth Arrow (1973) for the naked advocacy for capitalism. Moreover, Madison advocated like,

Rawls' social contract is a radical departure from Hobbes and Rousseau, particularly with its emphasis on reciprocity. To begin, Rawls wants us to imagine a group of hypothetical individuals.[2] They come together in a kind of constitutional convention to create a just and fair community in which they and their children will live (Madison 2011:113-114, emphasis and footnote ours).

Let us take a definition of social justice given by critical scholars,

"The ability of social science to be put to policy objectives with the purpose of redressing a variety of historically reified oppressions in modern life: racism, economic injustice, the 'hidden injuries of class,'discrimination in the legal system, gender inequities, and the new oppressions resulting from the restructuring of the social welfare system" (Denzin and Lincoln 2011: 715, also cited in Johnson and Parry 2016, p. 10)

H. L. Goodall, Jr. says, "I have never seen [Denzin] write with such raw, energizing power-- his is the voice of a fine angry angel leading us into the political battle of narratives currently defining, and contesting, qualitative research (Denzin 2010: Back cover)". Given the ground, we excoriate social justice. This is our position. It deploys the message that the Indigenous paradigm is far different from the Critical school; philosophically and practically, this demarcation is marked by a few scholars (Rowe et al., 2015; Henry & Foley, 2018). The critical subjective position of scholars like Madison, Denzin, or Lincoln's epistemology is deeply rooted in the western notion of 'reason' that reason was 'reasoned' by Locke, Mill, and Hobbes.

Thesis Four: SDGs are Becoming and Becoming and Helping to Sustain the System

The Declaration explicitly recognizes "inclusion and equity in and through education as the cornerstone of a transformative education agenda" (UNESCO, 2015, p. 2)

By emphasizing the importance of utilizing technology to develop knowledge societies, the SDGs do, to some extent, promote a utilitarian approach to Education, which is closely linked to a 'pro-growth model of development 'of the 1960s (Rostow, 1959) and in the knowledge economy of neoliberal globalization (Gupta, 2018). Further, the SDGs seemingly endorse a particular form of Western development model, excluding other interpretations of progress.

SDGs-4, in particular, is more utilitarian. For example, Target 4.4 – "By 2030, significantly increase the amount of youth and adults with appropriate skills, like technical and vocational skills, for employment, better jobs, and entrepreneurship" – strongly stresses the employment-oriented emphasis on utilitarian Education, orienting youth and adults to function inside the existing socio-economic framework (Slocum, Dimitrov & Webb, 2019). Three of the ten targets, including this one, emphasized technological knowledge and preparation; this is particularly noticeable in target 9, which calls for an expansion in the number of scholarships accessible to adolescents and adults in developed countries "for enrolment in higher education, including vocational training and information and communications technology, educational, engineering, and science programmes." This goal explicitly emphasizes STEM sectors, emphasizing the role of technology in optimizing output quality. Just one goal, though, specifically proposes a revolutionary solution to schooling, one that is explicitly concerned with problems of social justice – which is target 7:

Target 7 is also the only SDGs-4 target that specifically addresses 'sustainable growth.' Nevertheless, there is little evidence for this aim that this package of goals is much more likely to result in long-term growth than prior educational programs such as the EFA or the MDGs.

The goal's narrow focus on sustainable development represents a departure from various stages

- During the 1992 Earth Summit. For example, the vocabulary used in Chapter 36 of Agenda 21 is much more specific in emphasizing a transformative approach to Education. The platform calls for "integrating climate and sustainability as a cross-cutting topic into curriculum at all levels," as well as "a comprehensive analysis of curricula to ensure a multidisciplinary approach to education" and "respect for complex and conventional information systems" (United Nations, 1992, p. 321).

- Education for Sustainable Development rhetoric prevalent in previous efforts such as the Decade of Education for Sustainable Development (2005-2014) or (Agenda 21). Goal 7 is the nearest SDGs -4 to deal with sustainable growth directly; however, it declines to mention transforming curricula, implementing and validating alternate curriculum frameworks and forms of expertise, or incorporating environmental and/or development problems into education programs' significant limitations.

Point 1: A utilitarian viewpoint depicts schooling as a collective investment intended to ensure that succeeding generations will take their position as responsible people within an existing societal order. This method suggests that social structures can be embraced as they are without prolonged analytical reflection on their inherent prejudices. Such a strategy is not new; in reality, in the 1950s and 1960s, especially through the work of Theodore Schultz, growth and Education efforts occurred within the context of 'human resource theory,' which "rested on the premise that structured education is highly instrumental and even essential to increase a population's output capacity" (Fägerlind and Saha, p. 47). According to Rizvi and Lingard (2009), those assumptions incorporated into human capital theories betray the basic economic rationality that underpins the definition.

Human capital theory, in addition to being focused on the principle of human economic self-interest, "assumes that people are similarly able to choose" and that economic prosperity and comparative advantage are a direct product of levels of expenditure in human capital. Human resources and utilitarian approaches to Education have widespread roots in Christian commonwealth, colonialism, and neo-liberalism. All believe that progress in a certain form of Education leads to economic growth (from St Augustine to Descartes to Morgan to Marx to Rostow); advancement is synonymous with colonization. In this respect, we contend that the utilitarian approach to schooling is mainly pursued to satisfy the needs of workers and the economy (Kopnina, 2020).

SDGs and social justice (thesis 3) are the productions of western notions, SDGs-4 is here as a reference, and power, of course, is an undeniable factor (Shiva, 2014). The rhetorical tone and process of sustainable development priorities have evolved significantly before CBD, Access to Benefit Sharing, and MDGs were formed by a select community of experts (McAfee, 1999).

The implementation of SDGs-4 is another aspect; when 'inclusion' is rhetoric, the 'participatory' approach enhances the beauty of academic discussion, and policy formulation is authoritarian.

Finally, while the SDGs included a diverse variety of stakeholders in the planning phase, the power relations within such parties and the amount of authority they might genuinely wield are unequal. When undertaking a strategic debate study, it is critical to understand that the mechanism of developing the SDGs was heavily intertwined with uneven power relations. Aside from who was in charge of writing the SDGs, it can be claimed that the vocabulary used to compose the SDG System is exclusionary in its western scientific orientation.

Thesis Five: The Altering Ontology of Education

To help comprehend these processes, this research looks at the effect of COVID-19 on the neo-liberal paradigm that has dominated international Education since the early 1900s. This examines the reason for financial neo-growth capitalism in Ecuador, as well as the concept of education as a cross-border service, the state-supervising model, market-oriented mechanisms and profiting ideology, and the consumer mentality. And this whole system encourages, develops, and fosters justified self-interest (Spivak), which serves neither the common good nor the community. Our final thesis is that the looming problems confronting Northern and Southern institutions are not just economic; they expose the flaws inherent in the neo-liberal paradigm of Education but exacerbated by the coronavirus epidemic. While the epidemic should be contained, its residual consequences may change the overall panorama of international educational relations, as the Cold War between the West and China resurrected.

The neoliberal framework of Education is defined by its commodity model of prospective international students. This method is the consequence of the social capital structure and commodification of Education, as well as subnational (e.g., European Union, Middle East) responses to globalization and banking system unification.

The market system for university management is inefficient in dealing with public health crises and their spillover consequences. The coronavirus pandemic exposed two deficiencies in university administration that must be addressed. The first is a dearth of institutional support for international students who need financial assistance and mental health treatment. Managing emotional stress (we avoided discussing here and financial difficulties are two significant difficulties for international students who are staying abroad). It has been observed that some international students had more significant stress when most of their peers returned home and found themselves alone in a foreign setting, which is a result of the Neoliberal educational system. Recognized that in countries such as the United States, the United Kingdom, Canada, and Australia, most international students are permitted to work up to 20 hours per week, and many perform part-time jobs to support themselves. However, due to the lockdowns and social-distancing (stay-at-home) policies, many international students lost their part-time employment or put their plans to find part-time work on hiatus. This is another effect of Education's profiteering strategy.

The second remark highlights the discrepancy in communication between the school admin, the surrounding community, and international students. From our observations, we discovered that students in Malaysia were hungry and lacked nourishment. Students who reported us for receiving food, despite seeing Universiti Malaya arranging food for the first outbreak in March 2020. However, the Universiti Malaya's administration supplied food within a 5-kilometer radius, but what assessment was made of those who lived further? Thus, Universiti Malaya is an example of a well-managed institution, but what about the world's other thousands of universities? Thus, in addition to making quick choices in response to emergencies, host institutions may enhance decision-making consistency and use more effective communication methods to keep students and staff informed about the rapidly changing circumstances. As an immediate response, we propose that academicians' volunteerism can be a spot-solution (Chowdhury et al., 2021a) under the paradigm of Reciprocity (Chowdhury et al., 2021b).

Third, it is fundamentally erroneous to describe international Higher Education, as a subset of the broader Education paradigm, as a market-driven "transnational service" and cross-border tradeable commodity undermining state authority. The globalization of Education has claimed that delivering HE is not international, nor does it wield power that transcends time, place, and authorities. The efficacy of educational delivery may be harmed by geographical border travel bans, authoritarian control of the Internet for regime security, time zone restrictions, and the operational suspension of transnational agents. Geopolitical tensions between China and the West, in particular, may suffocate the recovery of student flows in the long term after the COVID-19 controversy.

Fourth, the state's regulating strategy should be re-examined in light of the revitalized connection between the state and universities in the new global pandemic environment. It is more hazardous than ever for institutions to become specific to a particular source of revenue, namely tuition fees from overseas students, particularly mainly from China. Marginson stated that international Education would become a "buyer's market" in the following years, with institutions competing for limited foreign students.

The state needs to be accountable for alleviating financial pressures on universities caused by declining enrolment and revenue loss by providing additional expenditure on retaining current students, additional funding for teaching and learning facilities, and an all-inclusive configuration tool for public health care for national and international citizens.

CONCLUSION

We are the Lakota's Crazy Horse

We are not negating the message of SDGs-4; we want inclusion but a holistic, material, and spiritual engagement of people's cosmos. Therefore, we are against the white presence in academia, which teaches us justified self-interest, self-development, and self-cantering, either through SDGs or donations or aid. We do not want an alibi that we are unconscious, uncivilized, and tribal to know anything; our land, history, is our learning source. We want *righting* the rights as righting as culture (Wronka, 2020) with the spirit of Lakota's Crazy Horse (Matthiessen, 2012) to center the people, land, living, and non-living things. In effect, we observed the unobserved history and intention in SDGs-4 at the SDGs, CBD, and the whole white prescriptions. We are Crazy Horse, and our pen is our weapon; our paper is the field. We do not want to reproduce or legalize what many of our colleagues have been doing.

As seen in previous development plans, priorities, objectives, and figures are profoundly Western methods of achieving development and reproducing their ideologies.

What our Education is teaching us, let us cite a painful experience with some Bangladesh migrant workers in Malaysia.

Furthermore, this is the utter expression of Education. This pandemic, however, teaches us that all our education lessons have wrongly guided us.

REFERENCES

Abad-Segura, E., Cortés-García, F. J., & Belmonte-Ureña, L. J. (2019). The sustainable approach to corporate social responsibility: A global analysis and future trends. *Sustainability*, *11*(19), 5382. doi:10.3390u11195382

Adenle, A. A. (2020). Assessment of solar energy technologies in Africa-opportunities and challenges in meeting the 2030 agenda and sustainable development goals. *Energy Policy*, *137*, 111180. doi:10.1016/j.enpol.2019.111180

Andrews, S. (2020). Qualitative analysis at the interface of Indigenous and Western knowledge systems: The Herringbone stitch model. *Qualitative Research*.

Archer, D., & Muntasim, T. (2020). Financing SDG 4: Context, challenges, and solutions. In Grading goal four (pp. 170-193). Brill Sense.

Ashukem, J. C. N. (2020). The SDGs and the bio-economy: Fostering land-grabbing in Africa. *Review of African Political Economy, 47*(164), 275–290. doi:10.1080/03056244.2019.1687086

Augustine, S. (1998). *The City of God Against the Pagans*. Cambridge University Press. doi:10.1017/CBO9780511802300.005

Banerjee, S. B. (2003). Who sustains whose development? Sustainable development and the reinvention of nature. *Organization Studies, 24*(1), 143–180. doi:10.1177/0170840603024001341

Beiter, K. D. (2017). Is the Age of Human Rights Really over-The Right to Education in Africa-Domestication, Human Rights-Based Development, and Extraterritorial State Obligations. *Geo. J. Int'l L., 49*, 9.

Bessire, L., & Bond, D. (2014). Ontological anthropology and the deferral of critique. *American Ethnologist, 41*(3), 440–456. doi:10.1111/amet.12083

Boto-Álvarez, A., & García-Fernández, R. (2020). Implementation of the 2030 Agenda Sustainable Development Goals in Spain. *Sustainability, 12*(6), 2546. doi:10.3390u12062546

Brissett, N., & Mitter, R. (2017). For function or transformation? A critical discourse analysis of Education under the Sustainable Development Goals. *The Journal for Critical Education Policy Studies, 15*(1).

Cheserek, G. J., & Mugalavai, V. K. (2012). Challenges and reforms facing Kenyan education system in the 21st century: Integrating the principles of vision 2030 and constitution 2010. *Journal of Emerging Trends in Educational Research and Policy Studies, 3*(4), 471.

Chowdhury, J. S., Abd Wahab, H., Saad, M. R. M., Reza, H., & Ahmad, M. M. (2021b). *Reciprocity and Its Practice in Social Research*. IGI Global.

Chowdhury, J. S., Abd Wahab, H., Saad, M. R. M., Roy, P. K., Hamidi, M., & Ahmad, M. M. (2021a). Ubuntu Philosophy: 'I Am Because We Are'–A Road to 'Individualism' to Global Solidarity. In Handbook of Research on the Impact of COVID-19 on Marginalized Populations and Support for the Future (pp. 361-381). IGI Global.

Crewe, E., & Harrison, E. (1998). *Whose development. An ethnography of aid*. Zed Books.

del Río Castro, G., Fernández, M. C. G., & Colsa, Á. U. (2020). Unleashing the convergence amid digitalization and sustainability towards pursuing the Sustainable Development Goals (SDGs): A holistic review. *Journal of Cleaner Production*.

Dennis, J. K. (2020). The Kantian Effect: Reconceiving the Integration of Knowledge in Interdisciplinary Theory. *Online Submission, 4*(2), 1–14.

Dewey, J. (2010). The need for a philosophy of Education (1934). *Schools, 7*(2), 244–245. doi:10.1086/656072

Dyer, C., & Rajan, V. (2020). Educating South Asia's internally migrating children. Handbook of education systems in South Asia, 1-28.

Escobar, A. (2011). *Encountering development: The making and unmaking of the Third World*. Princeton University Press.

Esteva, G. (1985). Beware of participation. *Development: Seeds of change, 3*, 77.

Esteva, G. (2014). Commoning in the new society. *Community Development Journal: An International Forum, 49*(suppl_1), i144–i159. doi:10.1093/cdj/bsu016

Esteva, G. (2019). Constructing knowledge in the Latin American University. *Compare-a journal of comparative and* Esteva, G. (2020). Alternative paths of transformation. *Globalizations, 17*(2), 225–231. doi:10.1080/14747731.2019.1670959

Esteva, G., & Escobar, A. (2017). Post-Development@ 25: On 'being stuck'and moving forward, sideways, backward and otherwise. *Third World Quarterly, 38*(12), 2559–2572. doi:10.1080/01436597.2017.1334545

Ferguson, J. (1990). *The anti-politics machine: 'Development', depoliticization and bureaucratic power in Lesotho*. CUP Archive.

Ferguson, J. (2005). Seeing like an oil company: Space, security, and global capital in neoliberal Africa. *American Anthropologist, 107*(3), 377–382. doi:10.1525/aa.2005.107.3.377

Filippo, D. D., Benayas, J., Peña, K., & Sánchez, F. (2020). Communication on Sustainability in Spanish Universities: Analysis of Websites, Scientific Papers and Impact in Social Media. *Sustainability, 12*(19), 8278. doi:10.3390u12198278

Firoiu, D., Ionescu, G. H., Băndoi, A., Florea, N. M., & Jianu, E. (2019). Achieving sustainable development goals (SDG): Implementation of the 2030 Agenda in Romania. *Sustainability, 11*(7), 2156. doi:10.3390u11072156

Fisher, M. (2009). *Capitalist realism: Is there no alternative?* John Hunt Publishing.

Forlin, C. (2019). Teacher Education and Inclusion in the Asia-Pacific Region. Oxford Research Encyclopedia of Education. doi:10.1093/acrefore/9780190264093.013.570

González García, E., Colomo Magaña, E., & Cívico Ariza, A. (2020). Quality education as a sustainable development goal in the context of 2030 agenda: Bibliometric approach. *Sustainability, 12*(15), 5884. doi:10.3390u12155884

Gupta, A. (2018). How neoliberal globalization is shaping early childhood education policies in India, China, Singapore, Sri Lanka and the Maldives. *Policy Futures in Education, 16*(1), 11–28. doi:10.1177/1478210317715796

Hacking, I. (2002). Historical ontology. In *In the Scope of Logic, Methodology and Philosophy of Science* (pp. 583–600). Springer. doi:10.1007/978-94-017-0475-5_13

Heller, M., & McElhinny, B. (2017). *Language, capitalism, colonialism: Toward a critical history*. University of Toronto Press.

Henry, E., & Foley, D. (2018). Indigenous research: ontologies, axiologies, epistemologiesand methodologies. In *Handbook of research methods in diversity management, equality and inclusion at work*. Edward Elgar Publishing. doi:10.4337/9781783476084.00019

Higgins-Desbiolles, F., & Wijesinghe, G. (2018). The critical capacities of restaurants as facilitators for transformations to sustainability. *Journal of Sustainable Tourism.*

Ilie, S., & Rose, P. (2016). Is equal access to higher Education in South Asia and sub-Saharan Africa achievable by 2030? *Higher Education, 72*(4), 435–455. doi:10.100710734-016-0039-3

Ilie, S., & Rose, P. (2018). Who benefits from public spending on higher Education in South Asia and sub-Saharan Africa? *Compare: A Journal of Comparative Education, 48*(4), 630–647. doi:10.1080/03057925.2017.1347870

Imdad, M., Hafidhuddin, D., & Arif, S. (2019). Defining Education: al-Farabi and Ibn Sina terminologies. *Ibn Khaldun Journal of Social Science, 1*(1), 1–10.

Klein, E. (2017). The World Bank on mind, behaviour and society. *Development and Change, 48*(3), 481–501. doi:10.1111/dech.12308

Kopnina, H. (2020). Education for the future? Critical evaluation of Education for sustainable development goals. *The Journal of Environmental Education, 51*(4), 280–291. doi:10.1080/00958964.2019.1710444

Lavallée, L. F. (2009). Practical application of an Indigenous research framework and two qualitative Indigenous research methods: Sharing circles and Anishnaabe symbol-based reflection. *International Journal of Qualitative Methods, 8*(1), 21–40. doi:10.1177/160940690900800103

Mahdi, M. S. (2020). *Alfarabi and the foundation of Islamic political philosophy.* University of Chicago Press.

Martin, K., & Mirraboopa, B. (2003). Ways of knowing, being and doing: A theoretical framework and methods for indigenous and indigenist re-search. *Journal of Australian Studies, 27*(76), 203–214. doi:10.1080/14443050309387838

Massarella, K., Sallu, S. M., & Ensor, J. E. (2020). Reproducing injustice: Why recognition matters in conservation project evaluation. *Global Environmental Change, 65*, 102181. doi:10.1016/j.gloenvcha.2020.102181

Matthiessen, P. (2012). *In the spirit of Crazy Horse.* Random House.

McAfee, K. (1999). Selling nature to save it? Biodiversity and green developmentalism. *Environment and Planning. D, Society & Space, 17*(2), 133–154. doi:10.1068/d170133

Mignolo, W. (2011). *The darker side of western modernity: Global futures, decolonial options.* Duke University Press.

Mignolo, W. D., & Walsh, C. E. (2018). *On decoloniality: Concepts, analytics, praxis.* Duke University Press.

Moran, K. A. (2009). Can Kant have an account of moral Education? *Journal of Philosophy of Education, 43*(4), 471–484. doi:10.1111/j.1467-9752.2009.00721.x

Moreton-Robinson, A. (Ed.). (2020). *Sovereign subjects: Indigenous sovereignty matters.* Routledge. doi:10.4324/9781003117353

Osei Kwadwo, V., & Konadu, O. A. (2020). Can Ghana Afford the Sustainable Development Goal on Education? *Africa Education Review*, *17*(2), 177–197. doi:10.1080/18146627.2018.1557532

Paletta, A., &Bonoli, A. (2019). Governing the university in the perspective of the United Nations 2030 Agenda. *International Journal of Sustainability in Higher Education.*

Pappu, R. (2020). Gender equity in Education: Changes and challenges in South Asia. Handbook of education systems in South Asia, 1-27.

Paul, P. J. II. (1987). Development and solidarity: Two keys to peace. *Tablet*, 22.

Rawls, J. (2009). *A theory of justice*. Harvard University Press.

Rostow, W. W. (1959). The stages of economic growth. *The Economic History Review*, *12*(1), 1–16. doi:10.1111/j.1468-0289.1959.tb01829.x

Rowe, S., Baldry, E., & Earles, W. (2015). Decolonising social work research: Learning from critical Indigenous approaches. *Australian Social Work*, *68*(3), 296–308. doi:10.1080/0312407X.2015.1024264

Sayed, Y., & Moriarty, K. (2020). SDG 4 and the 'education quality turn': Prospects, possibilities, and problems. In *Grading Goal Four* (pp. 194-213). Brill Sense. https://brill.com/view/book/edcoll/9789004430365/BP000017.xml

Schwab, S. (2020). Inclusive and special Education in Europe. Oxford Research Encyclopedia of Education. doi:10.1093/acrefore/9780190264093.013.1230

Scott, J. C. (1985). *Weapons of the weak: Everyday forms of peasant resistance*. Yale University Press.

Scott, J. C. (2010). *The art of not being governed: An anarchist history of upland Southeast Asia*. Nus Press.

Scott, J. C. (2020). *Seeing like a state: How certain schemes to improve the human condition have failed*. Yale University Press.

Shiva, V. (2014). *The Vandana Shiva Reader*. University Press of Kentucky.

Shizha, E. (2017). Neoliberal Managerialism of Higher Education and Human Capital Development in Sub-Saharan Africa in the 21st Century. In Re-thinking Postcolonial Education in Sub-Saharan Africa in the 21st Century (pp. 241-260). Brill Sense.

Siraz, J. (2020). *Songs of Corona, songs of Crying. In Legacies of Love, Peace and Hope: How Education can overcome Hatred and Divide*. Eubios Ethics Institute.

Slocum, S. L., Dimitrov, D. Y., & Webb, K. (2019). The impact of neoliberalism on higher education tourism programs: Meeting the 2030 sustainable development goals with the next generation. *Tourism Management Perspectives*, *30*, 33–42. doi:10.1016/j.tmp.2019.01.004

Spivak, G. C. (2004). Righting wrongs. *The South Atlantic Quarterly*, *103*(2), 523–581. doi:10.1215/00382876-103-2-3-523

Sultana, F. (2019). Decolonizing development education and the pursuit of social justice. *Human Geographies*, *12*(3), 31–46. doi:10.1177/194277861901200305

The United Nations. (2015). *4: Ensure inclusive and quality Education for all and promote lifelong learning*. https://www. un. org/sustainabledevelopment/education/

Tricoire, D. (Ed.). (2017). *Enlightened Colonialism: Civilization Narratives and Imperial Politics in the Age of Reason*. Springer. doi:10.1007/978-3-319-54280-5

Tuck, E., & Yang, K. W. (2012). Decolonization is not a metaphor. *Decolonization, 1*(1).

Turner, D. A. (2006). *This is not a peace pipe: Towards a critical indigenous philosophy*. University of Toronto Press.

Van Dijk, T. A. (2006). Ideology and discourse analysis. *Journal of Political Ideologies, 11*(2), 115–140. doi:10.1080/13569310600687908

Van Dijk, T. A. (2008). Critical discourse analysis and nominalization: Problem or pseudo-problem? *Discourse & Society, 19*(6), 821–828. doi:10.1177/0957926508095897

Webb, S. (2020). Interpreting Kant in Education: Dissolving Dualisms and Embodying Mind–Introduction. *Journal of Philosophy of Education, 54*(6), 1494–1509. doi:10.1111/1467-9752.12529

Wilson, S., Breen, A. V., & DuPré, L. (Eds.). (2019). *Research and reconciliation: Unsettling ways of knowing through Indigenous relationships*. Canadian Scholars.

Wronka, J. (2020). Whistleblowing, Human Rights, and Mental Health/Well-being: Implications for Advanced Generalist Practice. *Journal of Human Rights and Social Work, 5*(1), 1–6. doi:10.100741134-019-00112-1

Ziai Aram. (2017). *Post-development 25 years after The Development Dictionary*. Academic Press.

ADDITIONAL READING

Roy, P., Chowdhury, J. S., Abd Wahab, H., Saad, M. R. B., & Parahakaran, S. (2021). Christianity, COVID-19, and marginal people of Bangladesh: An experience from the Santal Community. In Handbook of Research on the Impact of COVID-19 on Marginalized Populations and Support for the Future (pp. 65-82). IGI Global.

Roy, P., Chowdhury, J. S., Abd Wahab, H., & Saad, R. (2022). Social Justice Through BPATC in Bangladesh Under the Shadow of Colonialism: Prospects and Challenges. *Social Justice Research Methods for Doctoral Research*, 303-319.

Roy, P., Chowdhury, J. S., Abd Wahab, H., & Saad, R. B. M. (2022). Ethnic Tension of the Bangladeshi Santal: A CDA of the Constitutional Provision. In Handbook of Research on Ethnic, Racial, and Religious Conflicts and Their Impact on State and Social Security (pp. 208-226). IGI Global. doi:10.4018/978-1-7998-8911-3.ch013

Roy, P. K., & Hamidi, M. (2022). Digital Ethnography: What We Have Done and What We Need to Do in the New Normal. In Practices, Challenges, and Prospects of Digital Ethnography as a Multidisciplinary Method (pp. 278-287). IGI Global.

ENDNOTES

1 A narration of the reverend Pope is important for our argument, 'development is, as Pope says, another name of peace(see Paul II, 1987) for the eager reader, see Augustine (1998).

2 We may recall imagined communities, an inclusionary term for forming a nation-state, and this imagined community has merged Indigenous identity under the majority Benedict Anderson theorized this.

Chapter 13
Community-Based Rehabilitation Programs for the Acid Victims' Community in Bangladesh:
A Conceptual Analysis Aiming to Including the Excluded Into the SDGs Regime

Tahmina Islam
University of Malaya, Malaysia

Siti Hajar Abu Bakar Ah
Universiti of Malaya, Malaysia

Noralina Omar
Universiti of Malaya, Malaysia

ABSTRACT

Acid violence is not only a violation of human rights, women's rights, and humanity, but also a terrible crime regardless of location. The chapter seeks to concentrate the overall picture with a historical description of acid crime across the world with a succinct and critical review of acid violence from an activist's perspective, including its background history, contributing factors, consequences on victims' lives, and national and international perspectives on acid burn rehabilitation and treatment from Bangladesh context. A proposal is given for future study, which, understandably, will be under the SDGs regime and local legal provision in achieve social justice and human rights.

MOTIVATION OF THE STUDY

I (first Author) attended ASF in 2013 to see one of my former students who had been hired by that firm.

DOI: 10.4018/978-1-6684-7499-0.ch013

I visited the organization, met the executive director and other personnel, and saw their acid burn center, where I met acid burn victims. After witnessing their scarred face and hearing their terrible story, I decided to continue my research on the subject. The information was subsequently given with my student, who was the office's programmer. He assured me he will aid me in the future. I was astounded when I met a victim from my area in ASF and learned that her spouse had burnt her with acid and disfigured her beautiful face. In fact, the visit aroused my curiosity in learning more about this topic. In fact, it was this history that motivated me to seek further research on the topic. And this is the idea.

The researcher became interested to work on that issue after an unscheduled visiting to Acid Survivor Foundation (ASF) Dhaka Bangladesh and seeing the cruel reality, decided to devote the academic effort on this issue, this conceptual analysis is the bay-step towards the inhuman activities if the research itself is a form resistance. The study adopts thematic analysis in order to make a systematic presentation of existing literature from the global to the local context. Sources include recent academic articles, journals, books, newspaper, websites, news clipping, photos, even social media coverage etc. These ranges cover the local Acts and legal provisions to show the gaping hole. The primary objective of this chapter is to give an overview of the notion on acid violence and its treatment and rehabilitation procedures throughout the glove and in Bangladesh. The chapter has explored community-based rehabilitation programs in region and globally. Taken a brief historical background of acid crime and then explores different types of rehabilitation and treatment of acid patients in other countries and the world. On significance, this conceptual study may open an arena to work further by social scientists, perhaps, some empirical study is pertinent so that the government of Bangladesh may take some solid and meaningful all-inclusive programs and policies. specially it may have significant influence on SDG goals 1, 5 and 16.

Considering human rights, Women's rights, and humanity, acid violence is not only a type of violence, but also a blatant and brutal violation of the citizen charter, independent of the geographical location. The purpose of this chapter is to contextualize the whole situation by providing a historical description of the nature of acid crime in the area and worldwide. This chapter provides a concise and critical overview, from the perspective of an activist, of the issue of acid violence, its background history, contributing factors, the effects of acid violence on victims' lives, and the national and international perspective on the rehabilitation and treatment of acid burn patients. After an unplanned visit to the Acid Survivor Foundation (ASF) in Dhaka, Bangladesh and witnessing the cruel reality, the researcher became interested in working on this issue and decided to devote academic effort to it. This conceptual analysis is the first step towards the inhumane activities, if research is a form of resistance. The research use theme analysis to portray current literature from a global to a local context in a systematic manner. Sources include contemporary scholarly publications, journals, books, newspapers, websites, news clippings, photographs, and even social media coverage. This scope encompasses the local Acts and legislative provisions that illustrate the gaping void. This chapter's primary purpose is to provide an overview of the concept of acid violence and its treatment and rehabilitation processes worldwide and in Bangladesh. The chapter examined community-based rehabilitation initiatives regionally and internationally. After providing a short historical context for acid crimes, the author examines several kinds of rehabilitation and therapy for acid victims in various nations and regions.

In terms of its importance, this conceptual study may pave the way for additional research by social scientists, and it may be necessary to do some empirical research so that the government of Bangladesh may enact effective and inclusive policies and programs. notably, it may considerably impact SDG targets 1, 5, and 16.

RATIONALE OF THIS STUDY

Concomitantly, violence against women is a widespread disgraceful phenomenon, a severe human rights violation. It has a significant public health concern with substantial consequences on physical, mental, sexual, and reproductive health (Yountet et al., 2014; Hasam & Islam, 2016; Khatun & Rahman, 2012). Noticeable that, one in three women around the globe experience physical, mental, or sexual abuse in her lifetime (Chakraborty & Kumar, 2017). Because of its nature and arrangement, scholars, Das et al. (2014), termed violence against women as gender-based violence. In further to Hasam and Islam (2016), any activity committed by someone to (or 'intending to) hurt or harm anybody physically is violence, and gender violence is a daily and deadly matter of life for millions of women and girls around the world. These violent actions kill, torture, and hurt girls and women in many ways, physically, mentally, sexually, and economically.

HISTORICAL BACKGROUND OF ACID VIOLENCE AGAINST WOMEN

This section addressed worldwide and Bangladeshi acid violence. Women's acid abuse is horrible. The problem is old despite recent crimes—ancient crime. Few books addressed acid attacks. Unknown worldwide acid strikes. Acid attacks against women are on the rise in Bangladesh, but they were prevalent in Europe and the US until police and legal intervention (Halim, 2007). England industrialized sulphuric acid in the 1940s. Western Europe and the US then used it for violence (www.slate.com). Europe's 16th-century vitriol (Harris, 1989). Americans used sodium hydroxide (Harris, 1989). The UK enacted the Person Act-1861 to combat acid violence (Shukhveer, 2015). In 16th-century France, acid violence was first documented. In France, this was a vitriolage wave. Most acid assaults on women were motivated by jealousy or retribution. Acid assaults were nicknamed "La Vitrioleuse" or "crimes of passion" (Tan et al., 2015).

Acid Throwing is a worldwide concern, claims ASTI. South Asia, Sub-Saharan Africa, West Indies, Middle East. Westerners say acid assaults are common in Bangladesh and India. Uganda, Afghanistan, India, Pakistan, Bangladesh, Nepal, China, Ethiopia, and soon have the most acid attacks, according to Ismail, Guriro, and Lakho (2020). Bangladesh, Cambodia, China, Germany, India, Pakistan, Iran, Jamaica, Martinique, Nigeria, Saudi Arabia, South Africa, Taiwan, Uganda, Vietnam, Laos, Hong Kong, Kenya, Afghanistan, South Africa, Ethiopia, and Nepal have acid violence (Khosnami et al., 2017). Acid attacks aren't confined to impoverished nations. Worldwide. John Morrison, chairman and creator of The Acid Survivors Trust International, told The Lancet that incidence rates are high in Southeast Asia, South Asia, sub-Saharan Africa, Turkey, and other places. Malaysia's corrosive assaults have skyrocketed. In 2009, Asia Star/ANN reported 3 acid attacks. 2011 numbers were 11 and 45. 33 people were robbed or jealous. The victim often couldn't identify the culprits.

Acid violence is a dreadful kind of violence common in industrialized and developing countries, but especially in Southeast Asia, Pakistan, India, Cambodia, and Bangladesh (Sharmin et al., 2019). Acid crimes are widespread in Nepal, India, Pakistan, and Bangladesh, according to Jayarantne (2021). Most acid attacks occur in Bangladesh (Rahman et al., 2014). The researcher now evaluates the local circumstances. Acid violence is horrific in most industrialized and developing nations but concentrated in Southeast Asia, notably Pakistan, India, Cambodia, and Bangladesh (Sharmin et al., 2019). Jayarantne

(2021) said acid crimes are most common in Nepal, India, Pakistan, and Bangladesh. Bangladesh has the most acid attacks (Rahman et al., 2014). As part of the review, the researcher examines the local situation.

BANGLADESH CONTEXT

Acid violence is a common societal issue in South and Southeast Asia. Still, a survey of scientific literature and other relevant texts over the last two decades reveals the problem is the most serious in Bangladesh, which has the highest recorded incidence globally. Ismail, Guriro, & Lakho (2020). From 1999 to 2015, the Acid Survivors Foundation (ASF) identified 3,303 incidences of acid assault in Bangladesh. Three thousand six hundred sixty-two people survived throughout this period.

A survey of scientific literature over the last 20 years claims the issue is serious in Bangladesh, which has the highest recorded incidence (Rahman et al., 2014; Tasnim et al., 2020; Sharmin et al., 2019). Bangladesh has the most acid attacks (Rahman, Bhuiya, & Lovely, 2014). Most victims and abusers are girls and women. Acid casualties might be deliberate or unintended, according to Avon Global Centre (2011). Acid victims may sleep with the intended victims.

Acid violence is a recent concern in Bangladesh. No Bangladeshi source reports when acid attacks began. It's controversial. According to Khan et al. (2019), the first acid attack in Bangladesh was observed in 1961 and publicized in 1967. In 1967, a young girl's family refused a marriage proposal, according to UNICEF (2000). Akhter and Islam (2013) said the first acid assault happened in 1983 in Bangladesh. It shows that acid attacks increased in 2002 and the following year, when Bangladesh passed two acid laws. The two acid Acts reduced acid throwing. Two acid laws prevented acid crime.

This research will identify several explanations for such terrible behaviours, which vary by country and civilization. In Taiwan, Colombia, Sri Lanka, and Cambodia, domestic disagreements, family-related concerns, money disputes, marital incompatibility, and extramarital affairs are typical causes for throwing acid (Guerrero, 2013). India, Pakistan, and Bangladesh have proximate causes of acid violence. Bangladesh, Pakistan, and India. Worldwide acid attacks the UK, USA, Germany, and France are affected. Acid violence varies by country, nation, and race. Previous literature couldn't explain US, French, and German assaults. The lack of acid violence in these nations led to little actions. UK's issue is new. 1500 acid assaults happen yearly globally. UK acid violence was triggered by racism, robbery, and assault (Lewis, 2017). Lewis (2017) concluded that UK gangs crave power and criminality. Teen gangs threw acid at male opponents to show off. Acid availability and disfiguring victims to display authority led to gang culture, according to Lewis (2017).

Acid violence was reported online. 2014 had 16, 2015 25, and 2016 32 acid attacks. UK's NHS struggles with acid throwing. NHS England hired BAPRAS (BAPRAS). NHS and BAPRAS advised acid victims. Some London and SE London burn facilities provide eye/plastic reconstructive surgery. Report, Remove, and Rinse are NHS guidelines (with water). The advice helps acid-burn families manage stress. Multiple NHS organizations supported acid-affected people. EMS, RCS, police. ASTI impacts legislation, attitudes, and campaigns. Medical, mental, and financial help globally (ASTI, 2021). Burn sufferers in the UK now get psychological therapy.

Cambodia's acid assaults are escalating, yet relief is inadequate. Phnom Penh has most burn centers. Victims usually pay. Rural victims can't receive city care readily. Patients must sell property for therapy. The study's findings on acid throwing in Cambodia prompted authorities to investigate (Waldron et al, 2014). CASC combats acid attacks. Aiding victims. Uganda, like Cambodia, lacks acid-affected medical care in 2011, according to ASFU. Mulago Hospital built an acid burn unit in 2003. Traditional healers are consulted. ASFU helps Ugandan hospitals treat acid burns. They provide aid, drugs, and acid-resistant clothing. Acid survivors benefit from pressure garments. Hospitalized and homebound ASF volunteers visit. ASF supports acid victims. ASFU social professionals treat and reintegrate survivors. From 2008-2009, researchers studied acid victims in Sri Lanka. Care for acid victims was studied. Sri Lanka's sole acid-burn clinic. Some NGOs assist liberate acid victims (Karunadasa et al., 2010). Pokhara, Kathmandu, Kaski, Tansen, and Palpa have burn units. Acid-burn centers are few outside cities. Nepal's Bir hospital established a burn unit. AusAID funds the hospital. Bir hospital fees. AusAID offers to burn centers physiotherapy, OT, nutrition, and social workers (Massage, Rana, Basnet, 2011). South Asia is acid-hit. The three countries employ acid identically. Hundreds of Pakistani women are burned yearly with acid and kerosene. The government failed acid victims. NGOs help acid victims. Since 2006, Pakistan's ASF. NGO helps acid victims legally, medically, and emotionally. Aurat Foundation, Ansar Burney Trust, HRCP, and DSF help acid victims (Zia, 2013). Pakistan has six government-run burn units, three in civilian hospitals and three in a military hospital. Untreated rural acid victims may die.

Yousaf and Purkayestha (2015) described Pakistani acid burn treatment. Depilex Smile Again Foundation (DSF). DSF helps acid victims in Pakistan. Acid burn holistic treatment. Acid victims are helped. Beauty salon and sewing workshops are free. They help job-seekers. Client Depilex DSF helps a survivor start a beauty business so she may make a livelihood. Any impacted girl who wants to continue learning gets free education, and volunteers teach her neighbourhood. Volunteers visit schools, contact media, and organize survivor groups. DSF president: a victim needs 35 to 40 cosmetic operations. Free DSF surgery. DSF plans a victim sanctuary.

India's acid victim care is seldom studied. India gives less free healthcare than other Asian countries. No nearby hospitals treat burns. Cities lack hospitals. Costly private hospital care (Patel, 2016; ASFI website). Government services help acid victims and their families. Housing, treatment, medical care, education, and jobs are offered. ASFI, ASTI, PCVC, HRLN, Atijeevan Foundation, and MLNS Foundation are essential.

ASFI was created to prevent acid attacks on women. ASFI's Trauma-Informed Care was developed by Acid Survivors Trust India. ASFI recruits online. PCVC provides crisis therapy and legal assistance. HRLN gets victims compensation. Atijeevan teaches acid victims crafts. ASTI developed the TICK. Local acid suffering will benefit (Acid Survivors Trust India). Private burn center MLNS. Safeguards victims of Acid seek legal, psychological, economical, and recreational help. Locals sponsor the group. Dance therapy, yoga, and poetry relieve stress. ASF treats acid victims. After an incident, survivors go through stages. She requires grafts, trauma care, rehabilitation, and reconstructive surgery. ASF helps acid-burn patients. ASFI offers therapy, social and vocational rehabilitation, and legal help. Table 1 lists the name of organizations and their roles in providing some forms of treatments and rehabilitation programs for acid victims in various countries.

This part is divided into some sub-parts. First, it discussed the institutional-based treatment and rehabilitation facilities for acid burn, and the latter part described community-based rehabilitation (CBR) related approaches that are usually performed by different actors like NGOs and the media in Bangladesh. The only specific organisation for the acid victims in Bangladesh is the Acid Survivors Foundation (ASF). The ASF was established in 1999 by UNICEF. The organization provides medical, legal, and rehabilitative services to acid-violence survivors in Bangladesh. In addition, the ASF has worked in collaboration with local NGOs to develop a nationwide notification system to promptly identify acid victims within 24 hours of the occurrence (Haque & Ahsan, 2014). The ASF provides victims with

Table 1. List of Some Organizations Working for Acid Violence. Source: Bharj et al., (2015, p. 7)

Organizations	Role
Cambodian League for the Promotion and Defence of Human Rights (LICADHO)	PAT programme provides financial, counselling, medical, and legal and advocacy assistance - Reporting of incidences
Children's Surgical Centre (CSC); USA-based NGO27	Burn treatment assistance and rehabilitation
Campaign and Struggle Against Acid Attacks on Women (CSAAAW); India29	- Assists survivors with access to legal, medical and social services - Works to prevent further attacks
Acid Survivors Foundation; Bangladesh	- Assistance with treatment, rehabilitation, legal and advocacy for legal reform, increase awareness through research advocacy and prevention measures
Naripokkho, Bangladesh	-Works to advance the situation of women, to struggle against violence and inequity, lobby for women's rights - Brought media attention and initiated a campaign against acid violence in mid 1990s
Acid Survivors Foundation Pakistan ASFP Pakistan	-Stop acid and burn violence and prevent the proliferation of attacks - Ensure survivors receive the best available medical treatment in the long run - Ensure survivors get justice, and exercise their fundamental rights following the Pakistani constitution and international conventions - Enable survivors to end up as proactive, democratic, empowered and autonomous citizens
Human Rights Commission of Pakistan (HRCP) Pakistan	-Collects statistics from newspaper reports pertaining to acid attacks
Human Rights Watch (HRW); International 33	-Investigate and report on human rights violations on global scale
Ansar Burney Trust; Pakistan	-Medical treatment aid and legal support
Acid Survivors Foundation; Uganda	-Funds medical care -Trains and educates the community - Police and other agencies - Provides counselling and advocacy
Cambodian Acid Survivors Charity (CSAC), Cambodia	Surgical, medical and psychological treatment -Vocational training and social reintegration - Legal assistance and advocacy for legal reform - Awareness through research, education, and advocacy

medical care, surgery, psychotherapy, counselling, and physiotherapy to assist them in recovering from physical and psychological trauma. ASF also offers rehabilitation and reintegration services to victims upon their return to the community following treatment.

Sometimes the survivors are sent abroad for better treatment at the organization's cost. ASF has a hospital named Thikana. ASF operates a 24-hour hotline to trace the acid victim from any place inside the country. The organization established a centre for producing pressure garments for acid survivors in 2001. It has gathered both local and international plastic surgeons together for the treatment of the victims of acid. ASF offers the survivors all the support they need for their rehabilitation after the treatment. ASF has some projects for the victims, such as catering, tailoring, and "pressure garments creation." In addition, with the help of the British high commission, the ASF established a 20-bed nursing unit named "Thikana" for the care of the acid burn victims.

Some other organizations also help the acid victims. For example, BRAC (Building Resources Across Communities), Bangladesh's largest NGO, provides health support, Ain O Salish Kendro (ASK), and

Bangladesh National Women Lawyers Association (BNWLA) provide legal aid to the victims. The Prothom Alo Bangladesh a renowned daily newspaper, raises funds for rehabilitating acid victims. Another organization called the Centre for Rehabilitation of Paralyzed (CRP) established a 15-bed operation facility hospital in Mirpur, Dhaka. Dhaka Medical College Hospital (DMCH), one of the largest government hospitals in Bangladesh, established the National Institute of Burn and Plastic Surgery in 2011. It has a 100-bed hospital for burn and plastic surgery patients supervised by the renowned plastic surgeon Dr. Samonta Lal Sen. The Institute is also working to support the acid victims in collaboration with ASF (Solutions, 2022). After receiving treatment from Dhaka medical college, a survivor returns to the Acid survivor foundation for proper nursing. The name of the hospital is "Thikana."

The Government of Bangladesh approved a unique project in 2015 named *"Sheikh Hasina National Burn and Plastic Surgery Institute."* Prime Minister Sheikh Hasina founded the stone for the Institute in 2015. She also laid the foundation stone of a 500-bed hospital in 2019. There is a plan to set up a 500-bed hospital for burn patients in five medical college hospitals in Bangladesh. Those five medical college hospitals are Rajshahi, Faridpur, Rangpur, Sylhet M A G Medical college, and Shere Bangla medical college hospital Barisal. Each hospital unit will be equipped with a 100-bed hospital and 10 Intensive care units and cabins, and 36 beds with two operation theatres (TBS News website, 2022).

Another organisation named Centre for the Rehabilitation of the Paralyzed (CRP) is very close to ASF Bangladesh. CRP established a 15-bed hospital named Jibontara Hospital in 2001 with the help of the Kadri Charity Foundation. The hospital provides 24 hours' treatment, ambulance service, first aid for acid burn, counselling and psychotherapy, physiotherapy, legal aid, and other forms of social support.

There is another government emergency intervention for rescuing women in a violent attack. It is a one-stop crisis centre (OCC) located in a major medical college hospital. OCC operates at the regional level, which provides emergency medical treatment, police assistance, legal support, and referral services for the victims in crisis. OCC provides the first emergency treatment when an acid survivor comes to OCC (Hossen, 2015). OCC is a multisector project under the Ministry of Women and Children affairs.

The other essential programmes run by the government are preventing and protecting women from all forms of violence against them. The other relevant programs are the National Trauma Counselling Centre, One-stop crises cell, National Violence against women database, violence against women helpline, awareness program, and soon. This project of the Ministry of Women and Children Affairs started in 2008. It has been jointly implemented by the government of Bangladesh and the Government of Denmark in collaboration with the Ministry of Law& Justice, Ministry of Home affairs, Ministry of Health and Family Welfare, Ministry of Education, Ministry of Religious Affairs, Ministry of Youth and Sports, Ministry of Local government, and Rural Developments and Co-operatives. However, the project covers all forms of violence against women, not only acid violence.

The Social welfare ministry's Department of social services (DSS) provides special provisions, loans, grants and disability cards to survivors of acid and other burns. DSS implements social services under the subtitles such as social safety net, programs for the disabled and burnt, poverty alleviation, hospital social services, and so on. The Department has been implementing the programs for the burnt and disabled under the name, 'Rehabilitation program for burnt and disabled Person' since 2016. Earlier, the programme's name was 'Rehabilitation program for acid burned women and the physically disabled. The name was changed in 2016. The program plays a significant role in rehabilitating acid-burn women and disabled people. According to the Department of Social Services (DSS), the programme provides microcredit ranging from BDT 5000 to 30,000 taka (62 $ to 375$) to an acid survivor in 20 installments with a 5% service charge. The program also has a provision to provide BDT 20,000 (250$) to a poor acid survivor for her medical treatment. Upazila social service offices transfer the microcredit and the medical fund (DSS, 2022).

Community-Based Rehabilitation and Reintegration Programs

There are no government or community-based acid victim rehabilitation programs in Bangladesh. ASF and other acid crime NGOs develop most community-based rehabilitation projects. In Bangladesh, various NGOs are the major CBR actors for acid violence.

ASF helps survivors with medical care and rehabilitation. ASF strives to rehabilitate survivors so they may live with dignity. ASF is the only national organization that helps acid-attack victims. ASF plans a victim's rehabilitation following treatment. ASF determines a victim's requirements and plans appropriately. ASF defines essential requirements as health care, justice, living standard, family integration, safety, and social support. ASF stresses medical (physical and psychological), legal (legal assistance shelter), rehabilitation, and reintegration (support for economic independence, access to education, family, and community acceptance) to protect a victim's rights.

ASF uses social and economic reintegration to make victims self-sufficient. ASF maintains a national network of partner NGOs for integration. ASF helps victims and their families with short-term, need-based financial assistance. ASF helps victims in many ways. It helps people find employment and offers cooking, tailoring, pressure clothing, government subsidies, emergency family aid, education support, life skill training, leadership training, vocational training, and networking with local partners and other survivors. ASF also organizes school college campaigns, Bazar campaigns, door-to-door visits, workshops, seminars, meetings with acid sellers and users, and International Women's Day festivities to raise awareness. Action Aid, Naripokkho, BRAC, Ain o Salish Kendra, and Bangladesh National Women Lawyer Association (BNWLA) offer programs to reintegrate acid attack victims.

Bangladesh passed two regulations involving violent assault and acid throwing on women to encourage rehabilitation for survivors. The 2002 Acid Control Act and Acid Offense Control Act prohibit acid violence. National Acid Control Council (NACC) and District Acid Control Committee (DACC) help acid sufferers. The committee approves the survivor's treatment funding after considering their application. The group also offers victims financial aid. A victim or family member may apply for a 5000-15,000-taka loan (ASF Website, 2017). The Department of Social Services of the Ministry of Social Welfare Bangladesh provides treatment grants and microloans for acid victims (MSW website, 2021). If the victim's yearly income is less than BDT 60000, she may apply for a 5000-10,000 award (MSW, 2021).

ASF, major NGOs, and Prothom Alo, a reputable newspaper, also helped curb acid crime. Prothom Alo was founded in 2000 to aid individuals and those who desire to help. Prothom Alo fund for Acid Victim Women began in 2000 when acid attacks were at their height. All Prothom Alo employees contributed one day's pay to the charity. The fund was formed with an endowment from people and organizations in Bangladesh (Prothom Alo, 2022). The charity supports acid victims with education, healthcare, and legal aid. The trust helps victims pursue revenue-generating activities. The charity also fights acid violence. This charity has helped 456 acid survivors (Alo, 2022).

GAPING HOLE

After reviewing the literature above analysis, this study argues that previous studies on the topic of acid violence have mainly concentrated on the causes and repercussions of violent crime on the lives of acid victims. Most writers from many regions of the globe have attempted to understand the reasons for this terrible kind of violence from their respective cultural and geographical vantage points. The literature analysis also reveals that many medical professionals have studied acid throwing. They have tried to evaluate the situation from a medical perspective. So, most of the literature so far has concentrated on the medico-legal components of acid violence in the socio-demographic context: health care management, psychological rehabilitation, and coping mechanisms for acid attack victims. The topic of acid victims' recovery is explored in published works. Mittal et al. (2020) said that nothing was known about the needs and problems of victims of acid violence for a long time.

As an added note, the available research mainly focused on the circumstances surrounding acid attacks and their root causes rather than the needs of those who they had victimized. Few studies have examined victims' experiences in trying to recover from their injuries. The present study has tried to close this knowledge gap by cataloging the issues victims confront throughout the recovery process. The project is meant to bridge a knowledge vacuum to create effective community-based rehabilitation programs for victims of acid attacks.

In addition to the above, South Asia's situation is more vulnerable. Violence against women begins immediately after birth and continues throughout their lives. It is viewed as a 'normal' phenomenon. Ismail et al. (2020) claimed that South Asian women suffer from different types of violence in their lives, including domestic violence, rape, dowry tortures, sexual harassment, suicide, forced marriage, trafficking, and other psychological and economic factors of oppression. Violence against women, therefore, has become one of the most prominent social issues in this region. The highest rate of such violence is recorded in Afghanistan, India, Pakistan, Bangladesh, and Nepal (Ismail et al., 2020).

Naoorwing down the context, Bangladesh is no different from its neighbors being a part of the South Asian region (Rahman et al., 2014). To some extent, violence against women in Bangladesh is more severe than in many other countries. Parvin and Naved's study (2016) mentioned that violence against women in Bangladesh occurs in almost every aspect of their lives. It is a grave threat to women's overall development and progress in Bangladesh. Hossen (2014) stated that women in Bangladesh face different forms of violence like physical abuse (i.e., hitting with fists, punching, pushing, kicking, beating/stabbing), psychological abuse, sexual abuse, acid throwing, murder, rape, sexual harassment of multiple types, eve-teasing, abduction, trafficking, and oppression by a fatwa (religious verdict), which sometimes ended in committing suicide.

Acid violence, acid throwing, or acid attack is one of the most brutal types of violence against women in modern history, especially prevalent in South Asia, Africa, and in certain instances, European nations. Dubey (2015) called it a brutal act. Though acid violence is a global problem, this frequency attracts serious, particularly in Bangladesh, India, Pakistan, Nepal, Cambodia, Vietnam, Laos, China, Iran, Hong Kong, Kenya, Uganda, and Ethiopia (Jabeen et al., 2020). In addition, developing countries like Malaysia and China have also experienced such cases in the recent past (Ahmad, 2012).

Acid violence, as seen from the studies mentioned above, is not limited to a specific race, region, or geographical location. It also happens in many countries of South Asia, Sub-Saharan Africa, the West Indies, and the Middle East. In the 18th century, sulphuric acid, in scholarship widely known as vitriolage, was first manufactured for industrial purposes in England in the

1940s. Vitriolage (acid attack) involves an intentional act of violence in which any corrosive is thrown onto the face and body of a person to disfigure them. The most a common type of corrosive used in these attacks is sulfuric acid (oil of vitriol) hence the name "vitriolage" (Kaur & Kumar, 2020, p. 481). However, people later began using it for violent actions in Western Europe and the United States. The Person Act 1861 was formulated to combat crimes like corrosive substance violence, such as acid, in the UK over a century ago. Dubey (2015) added that some other countries like Vietnam, Laos, Hong Kong, Kenya, South Africa, Uganda, and Ethiopia were on the list where the occurrence of acid assault took place several times. While acid violence is most prevalent in Bangladesh, Cambodia, India, and Pakistan, they have also been reported in Afghanistan and parts of Europe. Nevertheless, a high rate of acid throwing is found in countries like Bangladesh, India, and Pakistan (Jabeen et al., 2020).

A PROPOSED RESEARCH FRAMEWORK

This research proposal also shows that a qualified academic can complete the research, significantly impacting how Acid Burning is addressed in policy and beyond. My research proposal will need to discuss relevant toolkits and credentials and prove that the ideas it proposes have academic merit, useful contributions, and real-world implications to be accepted. The validity of the research and my ability to carry it out aren't enough to get the proposal green-lit, though. Therefore, the following components will be addressed in this research proposal: i. The methodology that will be used to conduct the research. Methods of data collection, analysis, and interpretation; ii. Include a description of the local context and any other limitations of conducting the research that arise from working within an institution, department, or academic program.

The suggested study at hand is qualitative. Qualitative research focuses on understanding phenomena and human experiences as they occur in the wild (Yin, 2011, p 8). Researchers using the qualitative approach try to draw on various sources to better understand the social, institutional, and environmental settings in which people operate. According to Creswell (1994), qualitative research "...is a research that assumes, takes a global perspective, potentially employs a theoretical lens, and studies research issues inquiring into the meaning people or groups attach to a social or human situation" (p. 37). Key features of qualitative research are also discussed by Creswell (1994). According to him, qualitative investigations are done in unstructured settings where the researcher plays a crucial role in data analysis. This is inductive research that draws on several different data sets.

According to Merriam (2005), a qualitative researcher is interested in participants' interpretations of events. How do they create this other reality? Moreover, their apply of their knowledge to the actual world (p. 5). Denzin and Lincoln (1994) define this method as one that "seeks to understand phenomena as they occur in their natural contexts by interviewing participants and eliciting narratives about their experiences and perspectives through the use of in-depth personal narratives, archival research, participant observation, and the analysis of archival materials such as photographs, diaries, and oral histories" (p.9).

The participants in this study are acid attack survivors who are helping researchers better understand the problems associated with this kind of violence. Understanding acid violence and acid victims calls for a qualitative method. Qualitative methods were shown to be a good fit for studying complex topics like acid violence. Because of the delicate nature of the topic at hand, researchers needed to conduct their studies in natural environments to gather sufficient data to draw any firm conclusions on the relationship between acid violence and other factors. The present research intended to examine the victim's private life by looking at her pain, and difficulties, and advised community-based rehabilitation. Because of this, a qualitative method was the only option for meeting the criteria.

Proposed Theoretical Outline

Research theories function like glasses, allowing the researcher to perceive everything within a narrower framework. Many different theoretical frameworks might be discussed in evaluating the suggested study. However, the present investigation has considered some ideas, from which the thesis has gotten adequate guidelines and has linked these theories to the study's aims. The researcher uses Urie Bronfenbrenner's Social-Ecological Model as a theoretical framework throughout this investigation. The social determinants of health may be understood, explored, and addressed on several levels with the help of the Social-Ecological Model. In order to better comprehend the myriad of elements that contribute to health or lack thereof, the Social-Ecological Model directs our attention to the individual's actions and actions in the context of the larger community (Healthy Teen Network, 2014).

The Ecological System Theory, often called the Human Ecological Theory, was conceived and popularized by Urie Bronfenbrenner (1917-2005), a Russian-born American psychologist. He originally presented the hypothesis in his book The Ecology of Human Development: Experiment by Nature and Design (1981). Microsystem, Mesosystem, Exosystem, Macrosystem, and Chronosystem are the five components that comprise the overall theory. A proposal would be, as done to investigate the following hypotheses in light of the statement mentioned above:

Proposed domain question,

i. What are the demands and concerns of the victim of an acid attack throughout the recovery process?
ii. Using the roles of the social system, what is the present rehabilitation procedure for acid victims?
iii. Why do victims of acid in Bangladesh have difficulties throughout the rehabilitation process inside their community?
iv. How might a suitable strategy to CBR (Community-based rehabilitation) programs be suggested so that victims of acid attacks can deal with their deficiencies and difficulties?

Significance of the Study

The study's community-based rehabilitation strategies for acid victims in Bangladesh are of enormous value in terms of social well-being, human rights, and social justice. This result is crucial for the main clients of acid-throwing attacks, the victims. Through these programs, acid-abuse sufferers may find relief from their pain. They may be able to reintegrate into society easily. They would profit physically, intellectually, socially, economically, and legally. The study conclusions would assist acid victims in becoming self-reliant and dealing with life's challenges with greater dignity.

Various parties engaged in the prevention and treatment of acid violence might also benefit from the study results. For instance, the Burn Unit of the government-run medical college hospital may adopt a new method of treating patients. The Ministry of Social Welfare has set aside funding for the victims' rehabilitation and may begin life-improving initiatives.

Scope of the Study

The initiative aims to analyze acid victims in Bangladesh and enhance their community-based rehabilitation program to improve their well-being and reintegrate them into society. The study investigates acid victims' barriers and official and informal recovery. Human rights inform current research. Bangladeshis researched acid-affected ladies. The analysis includes acid victims treated by the Acid Survivors Foundation (ASF) of Bangladesh, the only organization collecting data from acid-affected women. Participants were Dhaka and Sylhet people. It heals acid victims. It examines their current rehabilitation system and the problems victims experience during reintegration and recovery. No legal system or victim empowerment. It doesn't include acid-related criminal laws. Urban and rural acid-affected women are studied. It doesn't study criminals' minds. Research employs case studies.

The study employs Bronfenbrenner's Social-Ecological Model. The model includes micro, meso, exo, macro, and Chrono. Systematization helps conceive acid violence. Psychological, social, economic, political, and physical aspects are used to study human issues. Multidimensional examination of acid victims is possible. Microsystems involve people. It integrates two microsystems. Microsystems affect formal and informal exosystems. Macrosystem values and beliefs. The social-ecological approach helps comprehend acid victim healing. The social-ecological model guides data collection.

Dowry, rejected suitors, and property disputes sparked acid assaults. After an acid attack, a victim's family, in-laws, neighbors, students, and colleagues form their microsystem. Unemployment, patriarchy, women's status, and inadequate education are exosystemic variables in acid throwing. Macrosystems help develop cultural and social variables for such terrible deeds. Acid throwing and its causes were studied holistically. The model helps the researcher understand how acid victims became survivors via extensive treatment. The approach helps researchers evaluate victims' physiological, social, psychological, and other requirements. Acid victims' physical, social, economic, and psychological difficulties are identified. Community-based rehabilitation is recommended. The study presents victim-focused ideas using a social-ecological perspective. This study doesn't address victims' macrosystem. More research is needed. The picture shows acid sufferers' requirements, difficulties, and healing recommendations.

REFERENCES

Acid Survivors Foundation. (2013). *Annual Report 2013*. Retrieved from Dhaka: www.acidsurvivors.org

Ahmad, N. (2012). Weak laws against acid attacks on women: An Indian perspective. *The Medico-Legal Journal, 80*(Pt 3), 110–120. doi:10.1258/mlj.2012.012020

Akhter, G. A., & Islam, F. (2013). Acid violence: A burning issue in Bangladesh. *Ibrahim Medical College Journal, 7*(1), 12–15.

ASTI. (2021). *Acid Survivors Trust International*. Retrieved from https://www.asti.org.uk/

Chakraborty, S., Kumar, S., & Subramaniam, M. (2017). Safe city: Analysis of services for gender-based violence in Bengaluru, India. *International Sociology, 32*(3), 299–322. doi:10.1177/0268580917696386

Creswell, J. W., & Poth, C. N. (2018). *Qualitative Inquiry and Research Design Choosing Among Five Approaches by John W. Creswell Cheryl N. Poth* (H. Salmon, Ed.). Sage.

DSS. (2022). *Department of Social Services*. Retrieved from http://www.dss.gov.bd/site/page/06173ded-0bc3-40b0-8166-46f30a3cd690/-

Dubey, D. N. P. (2015). Acid Violence Cases and Its Forensic Aspect *the Indian Police Journal. LXII, l*(3), 82–96.

Guerrero, L. (2013). Burns due to acid assaults in Bogota, Colombia. *Burns*, *39*(5), 1018–1023. doi:10.1016/j.burns.2012.10.022

Halim Chowdhury, E. (2007). Negotiating state and NGO politics in Bangladesh: Women mobilize against acid violence. *Violence Against Women*, *13*(8), 857–873. doi:10.1177/1077801207302046 PMID:17699115

Haque, S. E., & Ahsan, H. (2014). Human rights violations against women: Acid violence in Bangladesh. *American Journal of Preventive Medicine*, *46*(2), 216–217. doi:10.1016/j.amepre.2013.10.013

Islam, M. S., & Hasam, M. A. (2016). Domestic Violence against Women in Bangladesh: A comparative Study on the perception of Educated and Non-Educated Class. *Review of Social Sciences, 1*(6). doi:. v1i6.43 doi:10.18533/rss

Jabeen, S., Riaz, M., & Omer, S. (2021). Applying Socioecological Framework to Acid Attack Violence: An Exploration of Inhabitant Factors. *Journal of Interpersonal Violence*, *36*(23-24), NP12481–NP12503. doi:10.1177/0886260519898442

Jabeen, S., Riaz, M., & Omer, S. (2021). Applying Socioecological Framework to Acid Attack Violence: An Exploration of Inhabitant Factors. *Journal of Interpersonal Violence*, *36*(23-24), NP12481–NP12503. doi:10.1177/0886260519898442

Kaur, N., & Kumar, A. (2020). Vitriolage (vitriolism)-a medico-socio-legal review. *Forensic Science, Medicine, and Pathology*, *16*(3), 481–488.

Lewis, M. (2017). *Acid attacks: A forensic psychiatry perspective*. Retrieved from https://bit.ly/2LrGOuk

Merriam, S. B., & Grenier, R. S. (2019). Qualitative Research in Practice Examples for Discussion and Analysis USA. *Sage (Atlanta, Ga.)*.

MSW. (2021). *Ministry of Social Welfare*. Retrieved from www.msw.gov.bd

Newsletter, A. S. F. (2016). Voice 40-41. Academic Press.

Parvin, K., Sultana, N., & Naved, R. T. (2016). Disclosure and help-seeking behavior of women exposed to physical spousal violence in Dhaka slums. *BMC Public Health*, *16*(1), 1–8.

Rahman, M., Bhuiyan, F. A., & Lovely, F. H. (2014). Acid violence: A burning impact on women of Bangladesh-case study. *International Journal of Advanced Research in Engineering and Applied Sciences*, *3*(3), 40–57.

Rahman, M., Bhuiyan, F. A., & Lovely, F. H. (2014). Acid violence: A burning impact on women of Bangladesh-case study. *International Journal of Advanced Research in Engineering and Applied Sciences*, *3*(3), 40–57.

Sharmin, A., Humayra, Z. U., & Khan, M. A. (2019). Causes and Consequences of Acid Violence among the Victims Attended in Specialized Acid Survivor center in Dhaka City. *Journal of Surgery and Science*, *23*(1), 29–32.

SolutionsF. I. (2022). *Plastic Surgery BD*. Retrieved from http://plasticsurgerybd.com/

Tan, A., Bharj, A. K., Nizamoglu, M., Barnes, D., & Dziewulski, P. (2015). Assaults from corrosive substances and medico legal considerations in a large regional burn centre in the United Kingdom: Calls for increased vigilance and enforced legislation. *Scars Burn Heal*, *1*. doi:10.1177/2059513115612945

Tan, A., Bharj, A. K., Nizamoglu, M., Barnes, D., & Dziewulski, P. (2015). Assaults from corrosive substances and medico legal considerations in a large regional burn centre in the United Kingdom: Calls for increased vigilance and enforced legislation. *Scars Burn Heal*, *1*. doi:10.1177/2059513115612945

Tbs news on Rehabilitaion. (n.d.). Retrieved from www.tbsnews.net/bangladesh/health/5-hospitals-outside-Dhaka-get-500-bed-unit-beds-338413

Yin, R., K. (2018). *Case Study Research and Applications Design and Methods*. Sage.

Yousaf, F. N., & Purkayastha, B. (2016). Beyond saving faces: Survivors of acid attacks in Pakistan. *Women's Studies International Forum, 54*. doi: .2015.10.003 doi:10.1016/j.wsif

Zia, T. (2013). *Acid violence in Pakistan*. UCLA: Centre for the Study of Women. Retrieved from https://escholarship.org/uc/item/65v958z1 www.worldblindunion.org

KEY TERMS AND DEFINITIONS

Acid Violence.: The term "acid violence"—in academia—has been synonymous with different concepts, such as acid assault, acid burns, acid attack, acid throwing, vitriolism or 'vitriolage' (Byard, 2020). The concept is also used to refer to acid survivors in various organisations that help the victims. The terms "acid violence" and "acid attacks" are synonymous and used interchangeably. Violence against women violates human rights and is a worldwide public health issue impacting women in both industrialized and developing civilizations. According to the United Nations Declaration on the Elimination of Violence against Women, the term "violence against women" includes and means any act of gender-based violence that results in, or is likely to result in, physical, sexual, or psychological harm or suffering to women, including threats of such acts, coercion or arbitrary deprivation of liberty, whether occurring in public or private life (United Nations 1993 General Assembly, New York).

Community-Based Rehabilitation: The World Health Organisation (WHO) promoted the concept of community-based rehabilitation (CBR) in the mid-70. However, CBR is a term that has been used in different literature with different names. As Momm and Konig (1998) used 'community integration,' Miles (1998) introduced "information-based rehabilitation". Miles and Medi (1994) used 'community-based support' as CBR in another paper. Frye (1992) applied the term 'community-based integration of rehabilitation instead of CBR in his writings. Samuel (2015) mentioned CBR as a philosophy.

Rehabilitation: The term rehabilitation is synonymous with coming back, healing, mending, recovery, rehab, snapback, recuperation, or restoration. The word is used in various fields to reduce the disability of a person. Any person may need rehabilitation at any time of his life. Different organizations have defined the concept of rehabilitation from their perspective. In the present study, the term rehabilitation has been applied in case of the acid burn victims, and how they are rehabilitated in society after their treatment. Rehabilitation is also associated with the severity of the disease and injury and support from their families. Though the term mainly focuses on the health and mental issues of a person in the present study, it has covered formal and informal support systems from different systems of an acid survivor and how those systems impacted her life after the vicious accident.

Compilation of References

Abad-Segura, E., Cortés-García, F. J., & Belmonte-Ureña, L. J. (2019). The sustainable approach to corporate social responsibility: A global analysis and future trends. *Sustainability*, *11*(19), 5382. doi:10.3390u11195382

Abruquah, A. A., Drewry, J. A., & Taylor, F. (2014). What happens to unused, expired and unwanted medications? A survey of a community-based medication disposal practices. *Int J Dev Sustain*, *3*, 2175–2185.

Accenture. (2022). *Technology. Digital transformation. Understand digital transformation and how our insights can help drive business value.* Retrieved September 27, 2022, from https://www.accenture.com/us-en/insights/digital-transformation-index

Achor, S. (2010). *The happiness advantage: How a positive brain fuels success in work and life.* Currency. Crown Business/Random House.

Acid Survivors Foundation. (2013). *Annual Report 2013.* Retrieved from Dhaka: www.acidsurvivors.org

Adenle, A. A. (2020). Assessment of solar energy technologies in Africa-opportunities and challenges in meeting the 2030 agenda and sustainable development goals. *Energy Policy*, *137*, 111180. doi:10.1016/j.enpol.2019.111180

Adeyeye, E., New, B. J. M., Chen, F., Kulkarni, S., Fisk, M., & Coleman, J. J. (2022). Sustainable medicines use in clinical practice: A clinical pharmacological view on eco-pharmaco stewardship. *British Journal of Clinical Pharmacology*, *88*(7), 3023–3029. doi:10.1111/bcp.15140 PMID:34779524

Aghaeinejad-Meybodi, A., Ebadi, A., Shafiei, S., Khataee, A. R., & Rostampour, M. (2015). Modeling and optimization of antidepressant drug fluoxetine removal in aqueous media by ozone/H_2O_2 process: Comparison of central composite design and artificial neural network approaches. *Journal of the Taiwan Institute of Chemical Engineers*, *48*, 40–48. doi:10.1016/j.jtice.2014.10.022

Agrawal, G., & Jain, M. (2013). Investor's Preference towards Mutual Fund in comparison to other Investment Avenues. *Journal of Indian Research*, *1*(4), 115–131.

Agudelo, M., Jóhannsdóttir, L., & Davídsdóttir, B. (2019). A literature review of the history and evolution of corporate social responsibility. *International Journal of Corporate Social Responsibility*, *4*(1), 1–23. doi:10.118640991-018-0039-y

Aguinis, H., & Glavas, A. (2012). What we know and don't know about corporate social responsibility: A review and research agenda. *Journal of Management*, *38*(4), 932–968. doi:10.1177/0149206311436079

Ahmad, N. (2012). Weak laws against acid attacks on women: An Indian perspective. *The Medico-Legal Journal*, *80*(Pt 3), 110–120. doi:10.1258/mlj.2012.012020

Ahmed, D., Wagdy, R., & Said, N. (2019). Evaluation of biogas production from anaerobic co-digestion of sewage sludge with microalgae and agriculture wastes. *BioResources*, *14*, 8405–8412.

Akhter, G. A., & Islam, F. (2013). Acid violence: A burning issue in Bangladesh. *Ibrahim Medical College Journal, 7*(1), 12–15.

Akter, N. (2000, January). Medical waste management: A review. Research Reports (1999). *Health Studies, Vol, XXVIII,* 370–394.

Ali, M., Wang, W., Chaudhry, N., & Geng, Y. (2017). Hospital waste management in developing countries: A mini review. *Waste Management & Research, 35*(6), 581–592. doi:10.1177/0734242X17691344 PMID:28566033

Al-Maadheed, S., Goktepe, I., Latiff, A. B. A., & Shomar, B. (2019). Antibiotics in hospital effluent and domestic wastewater treatment plants in Doha, Qatar. *Journal of Water Process Engineering, 28*, 60–68. doi:10.1016/j.jwpe.2019.01.005

Alshemari, A., Breen, L., Quinn, G., & Sivarajah, U. (2020). Can we create a circular pharmaceutical supply chain (CPSC) to reduce medicines waste? *Pharmacy (Basel, Switzerland), 8*(4), 221. doi:10.3390/pharmacy8040221 PMID:33218038

Amihud, Y., & Lev, B. (1981). Risk reduction as a managerial motive for conglomerate mergers. *The Bell Journal of Economics, 12*(2), 605–616. doi:10.2307/3003575

Amran, A., & Siti-Nabiha, A. (2009). Corporate social reporting in Malaysia: A case of mimicking the West or succumbing to local pressure. *Social Responsibility Journal, 5*(3), 358–375. doi:10.1108/17471110910977285

Andrews, S. (2020). Qualitative analysis at the interface of Indigenous and Western knowledge systems: The Herringbone stitch model. *Qualitative Research.*

ANGEM. (2019). *Informe de Sostenibilidad* [Sustainability Report]. https://www.anged.es/wp-content/uploads/2021/01/Informe-sostenibilidad-anged-web.pdfv

Aquino, R., Barile, S., Grasso, A., & Saviano, M. (2018). *Envisioning smart and sustainable healthcare: 3D Printing technologies for personalized medication, futures*. Academic Press.

Archer, D., & Muntasim, T. (2020). Financing SDG 4: Context, challenges, and solutions. In Grading goal four (pp. 170-193). Brill Sense.

Ashford, B., & Gibbs, B. (1990). The double-edge of organizational legitimation. *Organization Science, 1*(2), 177–194. doi:10.1287/orsc.1.2.177

Ashukem, J. C. N. (2020). The SDGs and the bio-economy: Fostering land-grabbing in Africa. *Review of African Political Economy, 47*(164), 275–290. doi:10.1080/03056244.2019.1687086

ASTI. (2021). *Acid Survivors Trust International.* Retrieved from https://www.asti.org.uk/

Atan, A., Ozgit, H., & Silman, F. (2021). Happiness at work and motivation for a sustainable workforce: Evidence from female hotel employees. *Sustainability, 13*(14), 1–17.

Atkinson, L., & Galaskiewicz, J. (1988). Stock ownership and company contributions to charity. *Administrative Science Quarterly, 33*(1), 82–100. doi:10.2307/2392856

Augustine, S. (1998). *The City of God Against the Pagans.* Cambridge University Press. doi:10.1017/CBO9780511802300.005

Avetisyan, E., & Ferrary, M. (2013). 'Dynamics of stakeholders' implications in the institutionalization of the CSR field in France and in the United States. *Journal of Business Ethics, 115*(1), 115–133. doi:10.100710551-012-1386-3

Ayala del Pino, C. (2021). La responsabilidad social corporativa: Concepto, ámbito de aplicación, grupos de interés y objetivos [Corporate social responsibility: concept, scope of application, stakeholders and objectives]. *Anuario Jurídico y Económico Escurialense, 54*(54), 173–198. doi:10.54571/ajee.462

Ban, K. (2015). *Launch of new sustainable development agenda to guide development actions for the next 15 years.* Disponible en: https://sustainabledevelopment. un.org/?page=view&nr=1021&type=230&menu=2059

Bandura, A. (1977). Self-efficacy: Toward a unifying theory of behavioral change. *Psychological Review*, *84*(2), 191–215.

Banerjee, S. B. (2003). Who sustains whose development? Sustainable development and the reinvention of nature. *Organization Studies*, *24*(1), 143–180. doi:10.1177/0170840603024001341

Barber, B., & Odean, T. (2008). All that glitters: The effect of attention and news on the buying behavior of individual and institutional investors. *Review of Financial Studies*, *21*(2), 785–818. doi:10.1093/rfs/hhm079

Bardoel, E. A., Pettit, T. M., De Cieri, H., & McMillan, L. (2014). Employee resilience: An emerging challenge for HRM. *Asia Pacific Journal of Human Resources*, *52*(3), 279–297.

Barkat, A. (2016). *Political economy of unpeopling of indigenous peoples: The case of Bangladesh.* Mukto Buddhi Prokasana.

Barnett, M. (2007). Stakeholder influence capacity and the variability of financial returns to corporate social responsibility. *Academy of Management Review*, *32*(3), 794–816. doi:10.5465/amr.2007.25275520

Barnett, M. (2014). Why stakeholders ignore firm misconduct: A cognitive view. *Journal of Management*, *40*(3), 676–702. doi:10.1177/0149206311433854

Barney, J. (1991). Firm resources and sustained competitive advantage. *Journal of Management*, *17*(1), 99–120. doi:10.1177/014920639101700108

Barney, J. (1997). *Gaining and Sustaining a Competitive Advantage*. Addison Wesley.

Baxi, C. V., & Ray, R. S. (2012). *Corporate social responsibility*. Vikas Publishing House.

Bear, S., Rahman, N., & Post, C. (2010). The impact of board diversity and gender composition on corporate social responsibility and firm reputation. *Journal of Business Ethics*, *97*(2), 207–221. doi:10.100710551-010-0505-2

Beiter, K. D. (2017). Is the Age of Human Rights Really over-The Right to Education in Africa-Domestication, Human Rights-Based Development, and Extraterritorial State Obligations. *Geo. J. Int'l L.*, *49*, 9.

Belkhir, L., & Elmeligi, A. (2019). Carbon footprint of the global pharmaceutical industry and relative impact of its major players. *Journal of Cleaner Production*, *214*, 185–194. doi:10.1016/j.jclepro.2018.11.204

BelletC.De NeveJ. E.WardG. (2022). Does employee happiness have an impact on productivity? *Saïd Business School WP*, 1-38. Available at: https://ssrn.com/abstract=3470734

Ben Brik, A., Rettab, B., & Mellahi, K. (2011). Market orientation, corporate social responsibility, and business performance. *Journal of Business Ethics*, *99*(3), 307–324. doi:10.100710551-010-0658-z

Benites-Lazaro, L., & Mello-Théry, N. (2017). CSR as a legitimatizing tool in carbon market: Evidence from Latin America's clean development mechanism. *Journal of Cleaner Production*, *149*, 218–226. doi:10.1016/j.jclepro.2017.02.095

Benjaminsen, T. A., & Svarstad, H. (2021). *Political ecology: A critical engagement with global environmental issues.* Springer Nature. doi:10.1007/978-3-030-56036-2

Bergen, P., Kong, D., & George, J. (2013). *The National Return and Disposal of Unwanted Medicines (NatRUM) project audit: Final report.* Academic Press.

Berle, A., & Means, G. (1932). *The Modern Corporation and Private Property*. Macmillan.

Berman, E. M., West, J. P., & Richter, M. N. Jr. (2002). Workplace relations: Friendship patterns and consequences (according to managers). *Public Administration Review, 62*(2), 217–230.

Berner, Y. N., & Shike, M. (1988). Consequences of phosphate imbalance. *Annual Review of Nutrition, 8*(1), 121–148. doi:10.1146/annurev.nu.08.070188.001005 PMID:3060161

Berrone, P., & Gomez-Mejia, L. (2009). Environmental performance and executive compensation: An integrated agency-institutional perspective. *Academy of Management Journal, 52*(1), 103–126. doi:10.5465/amj.2009.36461950

Besra, L. (2014). *A Critical Review of Democracy and Governance Challenges in Bangladesh with special refences to a human rights-based approach for the Development of marginalized indigenous people* [PhD thesis]. Flinders of Institute of Public Policy Management.

Bessire, L., & Bond, D. (2014). Ontological anthropology and the deferral of critique. *American Ethnologist, 41*(3), 440–456. doi:10.1111/amet.12083

BetterUp. (2021). *Five strategies to build workforce resilience.* https://grow.betterup.com/resources/five-strategies-to-build-workforce-resilience/?hsCtaTracking=aff5cfcb-e1b0-4062-a096-0910197538c0%7C26da8608-a596-4482-9062-7c6bb88d811b

Bhattacharyya, P. N., Sonowal, S., Bhattacharyya, L. H., Prasad, R., & Sarma, H. (2022). Bioremediation of cytostatic pharmaceutical and personal care products and emerging technologies. In *Emerging Contaminants in the Environment* (pp. 579-601). Elsevier.

Black, F. (1986). Noise. *The Journal of Finance, 41*(3), 529–543. doi:10.1111/j.1540-6261.1986.tb04513.x

Boardman, J. D., Blalock, C. L., & Button, T. M. (2008). Sex differences in the heritability of resilience. *Twin Research and Human Genetics, 11*(1), 12–27.

Boddewyn, J., & Brewer, T. (1994). International business political behavior: New theoretical directions. *Academy of Management Review, 19*(1), 119–143. doi:10.5465/amr.1994.9410122010

Bom, S., Jorge, J., Ribeiro, H., & Marto, J. (2019). A step forward on sustainability in the cosmetics industry: A review. *Journal of Cleaner Production, 225*, 270–290. doi:10.1016/j.jclepro.2019.03.255

Bonomi, S., & Ricciardi, F. (2017). Trasformare lo spreco alimentare in risorsa sociale: Una soluzione organizzativa [Transforming food waste in a social resource.An organizational solution]. *Impresa Progetto, 2*, 1–20.

Borea, M. D., & Wang, B. (2007). Redesign methodology for developing environmentally conscious products. *International Journal of Production Research, 45*(18-19), 4057–4072. doi:10.1080/00207540701472678

Boto-Álvarez, A., & García-Fernández, R. (2020). Implementation of the 2030 Agenda Sustainable Development Goals in Spain. *Sustainability, 12*(6), 2546. doi:10.3390u12062546

Bound, J. P., & Voulvoulis, N. (2005). Household disposal of pharmaceuticals as a pathway for aquatic contamination in the United Kingdom. *Environmental Health Perspectives, 113*(12), 1705–1711. doi:10.1289/ehp.8315 PMID:16330351

Bowen, H. (1953). *Social responsibilities of the businessman.* University of Iowa Press.

Brammer, S., & Millington, A. (2003). The effect of stakeholder preferences, organizational structure and industry type on corporate community involvement. *Journal of Business Ethics, 45*(3), 213–226. doi:10.1023/A:1024151528646

Brammer, S., & Millington, A. (2004). The development of corporate charitable contributions in the UK: A stakeholder analysis. *Journal of Management Studies, 41*(8), 1411–1434. doi:10.1111/j.1467-6486.2004.00480.x

Braungart, M., McDonough, W., & Bollinger, A. (2007). Cradle-to-cradle design: Creating healthy emissions - A strategy for eco-effective product and system design. *Journal of Cleaner Production*, *5*(13-14), 1337–1348. doi:10.1016/j.jclepro.2006.08.003

Brissett, N., & Mitter, R. (2017). For function or transformation? A critical discourse analysis of Education under the Sustainable Development Goals. *The Journal for Critical Education Policy Studies*, *15*(1).

Brown, N., & Deegan, C. (1998). The public disclosure of environmental performance information—A dual test of media agenda setting theory and legitimacy theory. *Accounting and Business Research*, *29*(1), 21–41. doi:10.1080/00014788.1998.9729564

Business for Social Responsibility. (2000). *Introduction to Corporate Social Responsibility*. Disponible en: http://www.khbo.be/~lodew/Cursussen/4eingenieurCL/The%20Global%20Business%20Responsibility%20Resource%20Center.doc

Caban, M., & Stepnowski, P. (2021). How to decrease pharmaceuticals in the environment? A review. *Environmental Chemistry Letters*, *19*(4), 3115–3138. doi:10.100710311-021-01194-y

Cámara de Valencia. (2020). *Cuaderno de Comercio y Sostenibilidad: Comercio y la RSE* [Trade and Sustainability Notebook: Tafe and CSR]. https://www.camaravalencia.com/es-ES/informacion/publicaciones-de-interes/publicaciones-y-documentos/comercio-distribucion/Documents/CUADERNOS%20COMERCIO%202011/cuaderno_Comercio_y_Sostenibilidad.pdf

Cameron, K. (2012). *Positive leadership: Strategies for extraordinary performance*. Berrett-Koehler Publishers.

Campbell, D. (2000). Legitimacy theory or managerial reality construction? Corporate social disclosure in Marks and Spencer Plc corporate reports, 1969-1997. *Accounting Forum*, *24*(1), 80–100. doi:10.1111/1467-6303.00030

Campbell, J. (2007). Why would corporations behave in socially responsible ways? An institutional theory of corporate social responsibility. *Academy of Management Review*, *32*(3), 946–967. doi:10.5465/amr.2007.25275684

Carhart, M. (1997). On persistence in mutual fund performance. *The Journal of Finance*, *52*(1), 57–82. doi:10.1111/j.1540-6261.1997.tb03808.x

Carrefour [@Carrefoures]. (2022). *Publicaciones* [Perfil en Instagram]. Recuperado el 15 de marzo de 2022, de https://www.instagram.com/carrefoures/

Carrefour. (2022). *Página web oficial sobre Responsabilidad Social Corporativa para Biodiversidad* [Officla Website on Corporate Social Responsibility for Biodiversity]. https://www.carrefour.es/responsabilidad-social-corporativa

Carroll, A. (1991). The Pyramid of CSR: Toward the Moral Management of Organizational Stakeholders. *Business Horizons*, *34*(4), 39–48. doi:10.1016/0007-6813(91)90005-G

Carroll, A. (1998). The four faces of corporate citizenship. *Business and Society Review*, *100*(1), 1–7. doi:10.1111/0045-3609.00008

Carroll, A. (1999). Corporate social responsibility. *Business & Society*, *38*(3), 268–295. doi:10.1177/000765039903800303

Carroll, A. (2008). A history of corporate social responsibility: concepts and practices. In A. M. Andrew Crane, D. Matten, J. Moon, & D. Siegel (Eds.), *The Oxford handbook of corporate social responsibility* (pp. 19–46). Oxford University Press. doi:10.1093/oxfordhb/9780199211593.003.0002

Carroll, A. (2015). Corporate social responsibility: The centerpiece of competing and complementary frameworks. *Organizational Dynamics*, *44*(2), 87–96. doi:10.1016/j.orgdyn.2015.02.002

Carroll, A. B. (1979). A three-dimensional conceptual model of corporate performance. *Academy of Management Review*, *4*(4), 497–505. doi:10.2307/257850

Carroll, A., & Shabana, K. (2010). The business case for corporate social responsibility: A review of concepts, research and practice. *International Journal of Management Reviews*, *12*(1), 85–105. doi:10.1111/j.1468-2370.2009.00275.x

Castillo, A. (2009). *Relaciones Públicas. Teoría e historia*. Editorial UOC.

Chakma & Maitrot. (2016). *Working paper on how Ethnic Minorities became poor and stay poor in Bangladesh: A Qualitative enquiry*. EEP/Shiree.

Chakraborty, S., Kumar, S., & Subramaniam, M. (2017). Safe city: Analysis of services for gender-based violence in Bengaluru, India. *International Sociology*, *32*(3), 299–322. doi:10.1177/0268580917696386

Chan, L., Chen, H., & Lakonishok, J. (2002). On mutual fund investment styles. *Review of Financial Studies*, *15*(5), 1407–1437. doi:10.1093/rfs/15.5.1407

Chen, Y., Du, L., Li, S., Song, W., Jensen, P. A., & Lin, W. (2021). Pyrolysis of antibiotic mycelial dreg and characterization of obtained gas, liquid and biochar. *Journal of Hazardous Materials*, *402*, 123826. doi:10.1016/j.jhazmat.2020.123826 PMID:33254808

Chen, Y., Lai, S., & Wen, C. (2006). The influence of green innovation performance on corporate advantage in Taiwan. *Journal of Business Ethics*, *67*(4), 331–339. doi:10.100710551-006-9025-5

Cheserek, G. J., & Mugalavai, V. K. (2012). Challenges and reforms facing Kenyan education system in the 21st century: Integrating the principles of vision 2030 and constitution 2010. *Journal of Emerging Trends in Educational Research and Policy Studies*, *3*(4), 471.

Chisholm, J., Zamani, R., Negm, A., Said, N., Abdel daiem, M. M., Dibaj, M., & Akrami, M. (2021). Sustainable waste management of medical waste in African developing countries: A narrative review. *Waste Management & Research*, *39*(9), 1149–1163. doi:10.1177/0734242X211029175 PMID:34218734

Chowdhury, J. S., Abd Wahab, H., Saad, M. R. M., Roy, P. K., Hamidi, M., & Ahmad, M. M. (2021a). Ubuntu Philosophy: 'I Am Because We Are'–A Road to 'Individualism' to Global Solidarity. In Handbook of Research on the Impact of COVID-19 on Marginalized Populations and Support for the Future (pp. 361-381). IGI Global.

Chowdhury, J. S., Abd Wahab, H., Saad, M. R. M., Reza, H., & Ahmad, M. M. (2021b). *Reciprocity and Its Practice in Social Research*. IGI Global.

Christmann, P. (2004). Multinational companies and the natural environment: Determinants of global environmental policy standardization. *Academy of Management Journal*, *47*(5), 747–760. doi:10.2307/20159616

Chuang, S., & Huang, S. (2016). The effect of environmental corporate social responsibility on environmental performance and business competitiveness: The mediation of green information technology capital. *Journal of Business Ethics*, *150*(4), 991–1009. doi:10.100710551-016-3167-x

Chua, S. E., Cheung, V., McAlonan, G. M., Cheung, C., Wong, J. W., Cheung, E. P., Chan, M. T., Wong, T. K., Choy, K. M., Chu, C. M., Lee, P. W., & Tsang, K. W. (2004). Stress and psychological impact on SARS patients during the outbreak. *Canadian Journal of Psychiatry*, *49*(6), 385–390.

Clark, J. H. (2006). Green chemistry: Today and tomorrow. *Green Chemistry*, *8*(1), 17–21. doi:10.1039/B516637N

Clarkson, M. (1995). A stakeholder framework for analyzing and evaluating corporate social performance. *Academy of Management Review*, *20*(1), 92–117. doi:10.2307/258888

Cleuvers, M. (2004). Mixture toxicity of the anti-inflammatory drugs diclofenac, ibuprofen, naproxen, and acetylsalicylic acid. *Ecotoxicology and Environmental Safety*, *59*(3), 309–315. doi:10.1016/S0147-6513(03)00141-6 PMID:15388270

Clifton, J., & Harter, J. (2021). *Wellbeing at work*. Simon and Schuster.

Colbert, B., Wheeler, D., & Freeman, R. (2003). Focusing on value: Reconciling corporate social responsibility, stakeholder theory and sustainability in a network world. *Journal of General Management*, *28*(3), 1–28. doi:10.1177/030630700302800301

Comisión Europea. (2001). *Libro Verde de la Comisión Europea para Fomentar un Marco Europeo para la Responsabilidad Social de las Empresas* [European Commission Green Paper on Promoting a European Framework for Corporate Social Responsibility]. Author.

Comisión Europea. (2011). Estrategia renovada de la UE para 2011-2014 sobre la responsabilidad social de las empresas [Renewed EU Corporate Social Responsibility Strategy 2011-2014]. Author.

Cook, I. (2021, September 15). Who is driving the great resignation? *Harvard Business Review*. https://hbr.org/2021/09/who-is-driving-the-great-resignation

Creswell, J. W., & Poth, C. N. (2018). *Qualitative Inquiry and Research Design Choosing Among Five Approaches by John W. Creswell Cheryl N. Poth* (H. Salmon, Ed.). Sage.

Crewe, E., & Harrison, E. (1998). *Whose development. An ethnography of aid*. Zed Books.

Cuervo, A. (2009). Corporate social responsibility, corporate governance and stakeholders (Corporate social responsibility, corporate governance and stakeholders.). In *Responsabilidad social: una reflexión global sobre la RSE* (pp. 51–61). Pretince Hall.

Cuesta, M., & Valor, C. (2003). Responsabilidad social de la empresa: concepto, medición y desarrollo en España [Corporate social responsibility: concept, measurement and development in Spain]. *Boletín Económico De ICE. Información Comercial Española*, *2755*, 7–20.

Cui, C. W., Ji, S. L., & Ren, H. Y. (2006). Determination of steroid estrogens in waste water treatment plant of a contraceptives producing factory. *Environmental Monitoring and Assessment*, *121*(1-3), 409–419. doi:10.100710661-005-9139-8 PMID:16758282

Darnall, N., Henriques, I., & Sadorsky, P. (2010). Adopting proactive environmental strategy: The influence of stakeholders and firm size. *Journal of Management Studies*, *47*(6), 1072–1094. doi:10.1111/j.1467-6486.2009.00873.x

Daughton, C. G. (2014). The Matthew Effect and widely prescribed pharmaceuticals lacking environmental monitoring: Case study of an exposure-assessment vulnerability. *The Science of the Total Environment*, *466*, 315–325. doi:10.1016/j.scitotenv.2013.06.111 PMID:23911922

Davis, K. (1960). Can business afford to ignore social responsibilities? *California Management Review*, *2*(3), 70–76. doi:10.2307/41166246

Davis, K. (1973). The case for and against business assumption of social responsibilities. *Academy of Management Journal*, *16*(2), 312–322.

Davis, K., & Blomstrom, R. (1966). *Business and its environment*. McGraw-Hill.

Davis, L., & North, D. (1971). *Institutional Change and American Economic Growth*. Cambridge University Press. doi:10.1017/CBO9780511561078

Dawson, J. (2013). Retailer activity in shaping food choice. *Food Quality and Preference*, *28*(1), 339–347. doi:10.1016/j.foodqual.2012.09.012

de Campos, E. A. R., Ten Caten, C. S., & de Paula, I. C. (2021). End-of-use and end-of-life medicines-Insights from pharmaceutical care process into waste medicines management. *Environmental Science and Pollution Research International*, *28*(41), 58170–58188. doi:10.100711356-021-14661-4 PMID:34105077

De Smet, A., Dowling, B., Mugayar-Baldocchi, M., & Schaninger, B. (2021, September 8). *How companies can turn the Great Resignation into the Great Attraction.* McKinsey & Company. https://www.mckinsey.com/businessfunctions/people-and-organizational-performance/our-insights/great-attrition-orgreat-attraction-the-choice-is-yours

Debats, D. L. (1999). Sources of meaning: An investigation of significant commitments in life. *Journal of Humanistic Psychology*, *39*(4), 30–57.

Debnath, M. K. (2010). *Living on the Edge: The predicament of a rural indigenous Santal community in Bangladesh* [Doctoral dissertation].

Debnath. (2020). A community under siege: exclusionary education policies and indigenous Santals in the Bangladeshi context. *Third World Quarterly, 41*(3), 453-469.

Debnath, M. K. (2012). The invisible agenda: Civilising mission or missionizing civilization. *International Journal of Human Rights*, *16*(3), 461–473. doi:10.1080/13642987.2011.572550

Deegan, C. (2002). Introduction - The legitimising effect of social and environmental disclosures - a theoretical foundation. *Accounting, Auditing & Accountability Journal*, *15*(3), 282–311. doi:10.1108/09513570210435852

Deegan, C., Rankin, M., & Tobin, J. (2002). An examination of the corporate social and environmental disclosures of BHP from 1983-1997: A test of legitimacy theory. *Accounting, Auditing & Accountability Journal*, *15*(3), 312–343. doi:10.1108/09513570210435861

Deegan, C., & Unerman, J. (2011). *Financial accounting theory* (2nd ed.). McGraw-Hill.

del Río Castro, G., Fernández, M. C. G., & Colsa, Á. U. (2020). Unleashing the convergence amid digitalization and sustainability towards pursuing the Sustainable Development Goals (SDGs): A holistic review. *Journal of Cleaner Production*.

Deloitte. (2018). *Managing Risk in Digital Transformation.* Retrieved September 27, 2022, from https://www2.deloitte.com/content/dam/Deloitte/za/Documents/risk/za_managing_risk_in_digital_transformation_112018.pdf

Deloitte. (2019). *Options for a strategic approach to pharmaceuticals in the environment - Final Report.* Author.

Deloitte. (2020, January). *Mental health and employers: Refreshing the case for investment.* Deloitte. https:// www2.deloitte.com/content/dam/Deloitte/uk/Documents/consultancy/deloitte-uk-mental-health-and-employers.pdf

Deloitte. (2022). *Future of Digital Transformation in the European Union 2035.* Retrieved August 20, 2022, from https://www2.deloitte.com/de/de/pages/strategy/articles/future-of-digital-transformation-eu-2035.html

Demirjian, A., Sanchez, G. V., Finkelstein, J. A., Ling, S. M., Srinivasan, A., Pollack, L. A., Hicks, L. A., & Iskander, J. K. (2015). CDC Grand Rounds: Getting smart about antibiotics. *MMWR. Morbidity and Mortality Weekly Report*, *64*(32), 871–873. doi:10.15585/mmwr.mm6432a3 PMID:26292205

Dennis, J. K. (2020). The Kantian Effect: Reconceiving the Integration of Knowledge in Interdisciplinary Theory. *Online Submission*, *4*(2), 1–14.

Dentchev, N. (2009). To what extent is business and society literature idealistic? *Business & Society*, *48*(1), 10–38. doi:10.1177/0007650307299222

Dewangga, A., Goldsmith, S., & Pegram, N. (2008). *Social responsibility guidelines & sustainable development: Integrating a common goal of a sustainable society* [Unpublished Masters dissertation]. Blekinge Institute of Technology, Karlaskrona, Sweden.

Dewey, J. (2010). The need for a philosophy of Education (1934). *Schools, 7*(2), 244–245. doi:10.1086/656072

Diana, T. (2006). Doing Business the Socially Responsible Way. *Business Credit, 108*(6), 45–48.

Diener, E., & Biswas-Diener, R. (2011). *Happiness: Unlocking the mysteries of psychological wealth.* John Wiley & Sons.

Diener, E., Sandvik, E., & Pavot, W. (1991). Happiness is the frequency, not the intensity, of positive versus negative affect. In F. Strack, M. Argyle, & N. Schwarz (Eds.), *Subjective well-being: An interdisciplinary perspective.* Pergamon.

Digital Europe. (2022). *A stronger digital industrial Europe - Digital Transformation as its Focus.* Retrieved August 20, 2022, from https://www.digitaleurope.org/policies/a-stronger-digital-industrial-europe-digital-transformation-as-its-focus/

DiMaggio, P., & Powell, W. (1983). The iron cage revisited: Institutional isomorphism and collective rationality in organizational fields. *American Sociological Review, 48*(2), 147–160. doi:10.2307/2095101

Directorate General for Administration and Public Employment and Department for International Relations and Communication. (2021). *Public Employee Motivation in EU Central and Federal Public Administrations. An Exploratory Approach.* Retrieved August 20, 2022, from https://www.eupan.eu/wp-content/uploads/2021/10/Motivation_study_2021.pdf

Doh, J., & Guay, T. (2006). Corporate social responsibility, public policy, and NGO activism in Europe and the United States: An institutional stakeholder perspective. *Journal of Management Studies, 43*(1), 47–73. doi:10.1111/j.1467-6486.2006.00582.x

Dowling, J., & Pfeffer, J. (1975). Organizational legitimacy: Social values and organizational behavior. *Pacific Sociological Review, 18*(1), 122–136. doi:10.2307/1388226

DSS. (2022). *Department of Social Services.* Retrieved from http://www.dss.gov.bd/site/page/06173ded-0bc3-40b0-8166-46f30a3cd690/-

Du Pisani, J. A. (2006). Sustainable Development–historical roots of the concept. *Environmental Sciences, 3*(2), 83–96. doi:10.1080/15693430600688831

Dubey, D. N. P. (2015). Acid Violence Cases and Its Forensic Aspect *the Indian Police Journal. LXII, l*(3), 82–96.

Duncan, D. L. (2020). What the COVID-19 pandemic tells us about the need to develop resilience in the nursing workforce. *Nursing Management, 27*(3), 22–27.

Dyer, C., & Rajan, V. (2020). Educating South Asia's internally migrating children. Handbook of education systems in South Asia, 1-28.

Ebner, D., & Baumgartner, R. (2006). The relationship between sustainable development and corporate social responsibility. In Corporate responsibility research conference (Vol. 4, No. 5.9, p. 2006). Queens University.

Edmunds, L. D., & Pryce-Jones, J. (2008). Relationships between happiness, overtime, sick leave and intention to stay or leave. *Selection and Development Review, 24*(1), 812.

Eells, R., & Walton, C. (1974). Conceptual Foundations of Business. Richard D. Irwin.

Eells, R. (1956). *Corporation giving in a free society.* Harper.

Eilbert, H., & Parket, I. R. (1973). The current status of corporate social responsibility. *Business Horizons, 16*, 5–14.

Eisenhardt, K. (1985). Control: Organizational and economic approaches. *Management Science, 31*(2), 134–149. doi:10.1287/mnsc.31.2.134

Eisenhardt, K. (1989). Agency theory: An assessment and review. *Academy of Management Review, 14*(1), 57–74. doi:10.2307/258191

Ekholm, A., & Pasternack, D. (2008). Overconfidence and investor size. *European Financial Management, 14*(1), 82–98.

ElAlfy, A., Darwish, K. M., & Weber, O. (2020). Corporations and sustainable development goals communication on social media: Corporate social responsibility or just another buzzword? *Sustainable Development, 28*(5), 1418–1430. doi:10.1002d.2095

Elijido-Ten, E., Kloot, L., & Clarkson, P. (2010). Extending the application of stakeholder influence strategies to environmental disclosures. *Accounting, Auditing & Accountability Journal, 23*(8), 1032–1059. doi:10.1108/09513571011092547

Elkington, J. (1998). Partnerships from cannibals with forks: The triple bottom line of 21st-century business. *Environmental Quality Management, 8*(1), 37–51. doi:10.1002/tqem.3310080106

Elton, E., Gruber, M., & Blake, C. (1996). Survivorship bias and mutual fund performance. *Review of Financial Studies, 9*(4), 1097–1120. doi:10.1093/rfs/9.4.1097

Escobar, A. (2011). *Encountering development: The making and unmaking of the Third World*. Princeton University Press.

España, D. [@día_esp]. (2022). *Publicaciones* [Perfil en Instagram]. Recuperado el 25 de marzo de 2022, de https://www.instagram.com/dia_esp

Estanyol, E. (2020). Comunicación de la responsabilidad social corporativa (RSC): Análisis de las campañas más premiadas en 2018 [Communication of Corporate Social Responsibility (CSR): Analysis of the most Awarded Campaigns in 2018]. *El Profesional de la Información, 29*(3), e290334. Advance online publication. doi:10.3145/epi.2020.may.34

Esteva, G. (1985). Beware of participation. *Development: Seeds of change, 3*, 77.

Esteva, G. (2014). Commoning in the new society. *Community Development Journal: An International Forum, 49*(suppl_1), i144–i159. doi:10.1093/cdj/bsu016

Esteva, G. (2019). Constructing knowledge in the Latin American University. *Compare-a journal of comparative and*
Esteva, G. (2020). Alternative paths of transformation. *Globalizations, 17*(2), 225–231. doi:10.1080/14747731.2019.1670959

Esteva, G., & Escobar, A. (2017). Post-Development@ 25: On 'being stuck'and moving forward, sideways, backward and otherwise. *Third World Quarterly, 38*(12), 2559–2572. doi:10.1080/01436597.2017.1334545

Eurofound. (2021). *The digital age: Implications of automation, digitisation and platforms for work and employment, Challenges and prospects in the EU series*. Publications Office of the European Union, Luxembourg. Retrieved August 20, 2022, from https://euagenda.eu/upload/publications/ef21007en.pdf

European Commission (EC). (2020). *White Paper On Artificial Intelligence - A European approach to excellence and trust.* COM(2020) 65 final. https://ec.europa.eu/info/sites/default/files/commission-white-paper-artificial-intelligence-feb2020_en.pdf

European Commission (EC). (2022). *Proposal for a Regulation of the European Parliament and of the Council on the European Health Data Space (Text with EEA relevance)* {SEC(2022) 196 final} - {SWD(2022) 130 final} - {SWD(2022) 131 final} - {SWD(2022) 132 final}. COM(2022). 197 final 2022/0140 (COD). https://health.ec.europa.eu/system/files/2022-05/com_2022-197_en.pdf

European Commission. (2022). *Digital Transformation of European Industry and Enterprises: Report and Recommendations of the Strategic Policy Forum on Digital Entrepreneurship*. Retrieved August 20, 2022, from http://www.eurasiancommission.org/ru/act/dmi/workgroup/materials/Pages/%D0%9F%D1%80%D0%BE%D0%BC%D1%8B%D1%88%D0%BB%D0%B5%D0%BD%D0%BD%D0%BE%D1%81%D1%82%D1%8C/%D0%95%D0%A1_%D0%A6%D0%B8%D1%84%D1%80%D0%BE%D0%B2%D0%B0%D1%8F%20%D1%82%D1%80%D0%B0%D0%BD%D1%81%D1%84%D0%BE%D1%80%D0%BC%D0%B0%D1%86%D0%B8%D1%8F%20%D0%BF%D1%80%D0%BE%D0%BC%D1%8B%D1%88%D0%BB%D0%B5%D0%BD%D0%BD%D0%BE%D1%81%D1%82%D0%B8_2016.pdf

European Investment Bank (EIB). (2022). *Digitalisation in Europe 2021-2022: Evidence from the EIB Investment Survey*. Retrieved August 20, 2022, from https://www.eib.org/attachments/publications/digitalisation_in_europe_2021_2022_en.pdf doi:10.2867/091152

European Parliament (EP). (2021). *EU health data center and a common data strategy for public health. Study Panel for the Future of Science and Technology EPRS*. European Parliamentary Research Service. Scientific Foresight Unit (STOA). PE 690.009 – September 2021. https://www.europarl.europa.eu/RegData/etudes/STUD/2021/690009/EPRS_STU(2021)690009_EN.pdf

European Parliament (EP). (2022a). *Artificial intelligence: MEPs want the EU to be a global standard-setter*. https://www.europarl.europa.eu/news/en/press-room/20220429IPR28228/artificial-intelligence-meps-want-the-eu-to-be-a-global-standard-setter

European Parliament (EP). (2022b). *Special Committee on Artificial Intelligence in a Digital Age*. https://www.europarl.europa.eu/committees/en/aida/home/highlights

European Parliament (EP). (2022c). *Special Committee on Artificial Intelligence in a Digital Age*. Committees. Activity Report. following AIDA Mandate 2020-2022. September 2020 - March 2022. European Union (EU). https://www.europarl.europa.eu/committees/en/aida/home/highlights. https://www.europarl.europa.eu/cmsdata/248838/AIDA_Committee_Activity_Report.pdf

European Social Survey European Research Infrastructure (ESS ERIC). (2022a). ESS20 - integrated file, edition 1.2 [Data set]. Sikt - Norwegian Agency for Shared Services in Education and Research. doi:10.21338/ESS10E01

European Social Survey European Research Infrastructure (ESS ERIC). (2022b). *ESS10 Data Documentation*. Sikt - Norwegian Agency for Shared Services in Education and Research. doi:10.21338/NSD-ESS10-2020

European Social Survey European Research Infrastructure (ESS ERIC). (2022c). *About the European Social Survey European Research Infrastructure (ESS ERIC)*. Retrieved August 15, 2022, from https://www.europeansocialsurvey.org/about/

Eurostat. (2021). *Sustainable development in the European Union: Monitoring report on progress towards the SDGs in an EU context*. European Union. Retrieved August 20, 2022, from https://ec.europa.eu/eurostat/documents/3217494/12878705/KS-03-21-096-EN-N.pdf doi:10.2785/636600

Fama, E. (1970). Efficient capital markets: A review of theory and empirical work. *The Journal of Finance*, *25*(2), 383–417. doi:10.2307/2325486

Fama, E., & French, K. (1992). The cross-section of expected stock returns. *The Journal of Finance*, *47*(2), 427–465. doi:10.1111/j.1540-6261.1992.tb04398.x

Feldstein, M. (2013). *The Reagan-Thatcher revolution*. Disponible en: https://www.dw.com/en/the-reagan-thatcher-revolution/a-16732731

Ferguson, J. (1990). *The anti-politics machine: 'Development', depoliticization and bureaucratic power in Lesotho*. CUP Archive.

Ferguson, J. (2005). Seeing like an oil company: Space, security, and global capital in neoliberal Africa. *American Anthropologist*, *107*(3), 377–382. doi:10.1525/aa.2005.107.3.377

Ferns, B., Emelianova, O., & Sethi, S. (2008). In his own words: The effectiveness of CEO as spokesperson on CSR-sustainability issues. *Corporate Reputation Review*, *11*(2), 116–129. doi:10.1057/crr.2008.11

Ferrari, R. (2015). Writing narrative style literature reviews. *Medical Writing*, *24*(4), 230–235. doi:10.1179/2047480615Z.000000000329

Filippo, D. D., Benayas, J., Peña, K., & Sánchez, F. (2020). Communication on Sustainability in Spanish Universities: Analysis of Websites, Scientific Papers and Impact in Social Media. *Sustainability*, *12*(19), 8278. doi:10.3390u12198278

Firoiu, D., Ionescu, G. H., Băndoi, A., Florea, N. M., & Jianu, E. (2019). Achieving sustainable development goals (SDG): Implementation of the 2030 Agenda in Romania. *Sustainability*, *11*(7), 2156. doi:10.3390u11072156

Fisher, C. D. (2010). Happiness at work. *International Journal of Management Reviews*, *12*(4), 384–412.

Fisher, M. (2009). *Capitalist realism: Is there no alternative?* John Hunt Publishing.

Fitch, H. (1976). Achieving corporate social responsibility. *Academy of Management Review*, *1*(1), 38–46. doi:10.5465/amr.1976.4408754

Fletcher, D., & Sarkar, M. (2013). Psychological resilience: A review and critique of definitions, concepts, and theory. *European Psychologist*, *18*(1), 1–33.

Folkman, S., Lazarus, R. S., Dunkel-Schetter, C., DeLongis, A., & Gruen, R. J. (1986). Dynamics of a stressful encounter: Cognitive appraisal, coping, and encounter outcomes. *Journal of Personality and Social Psychology*, *50*, 992–1003.

Fontaine, M. (2013). Corporate social responsibility and sustainability: The new bottom line? *International Journal of Business and Social Science*, *4*(4), 1–10.

Forlin, C. (2019). Teacher Education and Inclusion in the Asia-Pacific Region. Oxford Research Encyclopedia of Education. doi:10.1093/acrefore/9780190264093.013.570

Foro de Expertos en Responsabilidad Social de las Empresas. (2007). *Informe del foro de expertos en responsabilidad social de las empresas* [Report of the forum of experts in corporate social responsibility]. Established on March 17, 2005 at the initiative of the Ministry of Labor and Social Affairs. Concluded on July 12, 2007.

Foster, K., Roche, M., Giandinoto, J., & Furness, T. (2020). Workplace stressors, psychological well-being, resilience, and caring behaviours of mental health nurses: A descriptive correlational study. *International Journal of Mental Health Nursing*, *29*(1), 56–68.

Fransen, L. (2013). The embeddedness of responsible business practice: Exploring the interaction between national-institutional environments and corporate social responsibility. *Journal of Business Ethics*, *115*(2), 213–227. doi:10.100710551-012-1395-2

Frederick, W. (1960). The growing concern over business responsibility. *California Management Review*, *2*(4), 54–61. doi:10.2307/41165405

Freeman, R. (1984). *Strategic Management - A Stakeholder Approach*. Pitman.

Freeman, R. (2001). A stakeholder theory of the modern corporation. *Perspectives in Business Ethics*, *3*, 144.

Freeman, R., & Reed, D. (1983). Stockholders and stakeholders: A new perspective on corporate governance. *California Management Review*, *25*(3), 88–106. doi:10.2307/41165018

Friedman, M. (1970). The social responsibility of business is to increase its profits. *The New York Times Magazine.*

Friedman, A., & Miles, S. (2002). Developing stakeholder theory. *Journal of Management Studies, 39*(1), 1–21. doi:10.1111/1467-6486.00280

Friedman, M. (1962). *Capitalism and freedom.* University of Chicago Press.

Friedman, M. (2007). The social responsibility of business is to increase its profits. In *Corporate ethics and corporate governance* (pp. 173–178). Springer. doi:10.1007/978-3-540-70818-6_14

Frynas, J. (2015). Strategic CSR, value creation and competitive advantage. In T. C. Lawton & T. S. Rajwani (Eds.), *The Routledge Companion to Non- Market Strategy.* Routledge.

Frynas, J. (2015). Strategic CSR, value creation and competitive advantage. In T. C. Lawton & T. S. Rajwani (Eds.), *The Routledge Companion to Non- Market Strategy: 245-262.* Routledge.

Funk, K. (2003). Sustainability and performance. *MIT Sloan Management Review, 44*(2), 65–70.

Future Workplace. (2021). *2021 HR sentiment survey: Five strategic priorities for the hybrid workplace.* https://futureworkplace.com/ebooks/2021-hr-sentiment-survey/

Galaskiewicz, J. (1985). *Social Organization of an Urban Grants Economy: A Study of Business Philanthropy and Nonprofit Organizations.* Academic Press.

Gallego, I. (2006). The use of economic, social and environmental indicators as a measure of sustainable development in Spain. *Corporate Social Responsibility and Environmental Management, 13*(2), 78–97. doi:10.1002/csr.94

Gallup. (2022). *State of the global workplace: 2022 Report, The voice of the World's employees.* Gallup. https://www.gallup.com/workplace/349484/state-of-the-global-workplace-2022-report.aspx#ite-393218

Garai, A., & Sarkar, B. (2022). Economically independent reverse logistics of customer-centric closed-loop supply chain for herbal medicines and biofuel. *Journal of Cleaner Production, 334*, 129977. doi:10.1016/j.jclepro.2021.129977

García-Marzá, D. (2004). *Ética empresarial. Del diálogo a la confianza (Business ethics. From dialogue to trust).* Trotta.

Garnier, J. P. (2008). Rebuilding the R&D engine in big pharma. *Harvard Business Review, 86*, 68–70, 72–76, 128. PMID:18543809

Gilbert, D., Mckee, A., Spreitzer, G., & Amabile, T. (2017). *Happiness (HBR emotional intelligence series).* Harvard Business Review Press.

Glassmeyer, S. T., Hinchey, E. K., Boehme, S. E., Daughton, C. G., Ruhoy, I. S., Conerly, O., Daniels, R. L., Lauer, L., McCarthy, M., Nettesheim, T. G., Sykes, K., & Thompson, V. G. (2009). Disposal practices for unwanted residential medications in the United States. *Environment International, 35*(3), 566–572. doi:10.1016/j.envint.2008.10.007 PMID:19081631

González García, E., Colomo Magaña, E., & Cívico Ariza, A. (2020). Quality education as a sustainable development goal in the context of 2030 agenda: Bibliometric approach. *Sustainability, 12*(15), 5884. doi:10.3390u12155884

González, A. L., Alkorta, A. B., & Salcedo, J. L. (2022). The Social and Solidarity Economics, Public Policies, and Non-Monetary Economic Practices: The Case of Associative Firms in Loja, Ecuador. In J. Saiz-Alvarez (Ed.), *Handbook of Research on Emerging Business Models and the New World Economic Order* (pp. 242–266). IGI Global. doi:10.4018/978-1-7998-7689-2.ch012

Gornik, T., Kovacic, A., Heath, E., Hollender, J., & Kosjek, T. (2020). Biotransformation study of antidepressant sertraline and its removal during biological waste water treatment. *Water Research, 181*, 115864. doi:10.1016/j.watres.2020.115864 PMID:32480056

Grober, U. (2007). *Deep roots-a conceptual history of 'sustainable development'*. Academic Press.

Grote, C. A., Jones, J. M., Blount, G. N., Goodyer, J., & Shayler, M. (2007). An approach to the EUP directive and the application of the economic eco-design for complex products. *International Journal of Production Research, 45*(18-19), 4099–4117. doi:10.1080/00207540701450088

Grote, G., & Guest, D. (2017). The case for reinvigorating quality of working life research. *Human Relations, 70*(2), 149–167.

Grupo Día. (2022). *Página web oficial sobre Sostenibilidad.* https://diacorporate.com/vision-sostenible/

Guerrero, L. (2013). Burns due to acid assaults in Bogota, Colombia. *Burns, 39*(5), 1018–1023. doi:10.1016/j.burns.2012.10.022

Guest, D. E. (2017). Human resource management and employee well-being: Towards a new analytic framework. *Human Resource Management Journal, 27*(1), 22–38.

Gujar, G., & Attarwala, A. (2020). Benefits of implementing sustainable business practices for the Indian pharmaceutical industry. *Asian Journal of Management, 11*(1), 26–28. doi:10.5958/2321-5763.2020.00005.0

Guler, A., & Crowther, D. (2008). Towards equitable sustainability. *Ivey Business Journal, 72*(1), 1–7.

Gupta, A. (2018). How neoliberal globalization is shaping early childhood education policies in India, China, Singapore, Sri Lanka and the Maldives. *Policy Futures in Education, 16*(1), 11–28. doi:10.1177/1478210317715796

Hacking, I. (2002). Historical ontology. In *In the Scope of Logic, Methodology and Philosophy of Science* (pp. 583–600). Springer. doi:10.1007/978-94-017-0475-5_13

Halim Chowdhury, E. (2007). Negotiating state and NGO politics in Bangladesh: Women mobilize against acid violence. *Violence Against Women, 13*(8), 857–873. doi:10.1177/1077801207302046 PMID:17699115

Hall, P., & Soskice, D. (2001). *Varieties of Capitalism: The Institutional Basis of Competitive Advantage*. Oxford University Press. doi:10.1093/0199247757.001.0001

Hametner, M. (2022). Economics without ecology: How the SDGs fail to align socioeconomic development with environmental sustainability. *Ecological Economics, 199*, 107490. doi:10.1016/j.ecolecon.2022.107490

Hansen, M. T., Amabile, T. M., Snook, S. A., & Craig, N. (2018). *Purpose, Meaning, and Passion (HBR emotional intelligence series)*. Harvard Business Review Press.

Haque, S. E., & Ahsan, H. (2014). Human rights violations against women: Acid violence in Bangladesh. *American Journal of Preventive Medicine, 46*(2), 216–217. doi:10.1016/j.amepre.2013.10.013

Hart, S. (1995). A natural resource-based view of the firm. *Academy of Management Review, 20*(4), 986–1014. doi:10.5465/amr.1995.9512280033

Hasan, M. M. (2020). *Mining Conflict, Indigenous Peoples and Environmental Justice: The Case of Phulbari Coal Project in Bangladesh* [PhD Thesis]. https://www.ilo.org/wcmsp5/groups/public/---ed_norm/ normes/documents/publication/wcms_205225.pdf

Hediger, W. (2010). Welfare and capital-theoretic foundations of corporate social responsibility and corporate sustainability. *Journal of Socio-Economics*, *39*(4), 518–526. doi:10.1016/j.socec.2010.02.001

Heller, M., & McElhinny, B. (2017). *Language, capitalism, colonialism: Toward a critical history*. University of Toronto Press.

Henry, P. (2021, November 19). *Explainer: What's driving 'the Great Resignation'?* World Economic Forum. https://www.weforum.org/agenda/2021/11/greatresignation-career-change-mental-health-covid/

Henry, E., & Foley, D. (2018). Indigenous research: ontologies, axiologies, epistemologiesand methodologies. In *Handbook of research methods in diversity management, equality and inclusion at work*. Edward Elgar Publishing. doi:10.4337/9781783476084.00019

Higgins-Desbiolles, F., & Wijesinghe, G. (2018). The critical capacities of restaurants as facilitators for transformations to sustainability. *Journal of Sustainable Tourism*.

Hill, C., & Jones, T. (1992). Stakeholder agency theory. *Journal of Management Studies*, *29*(2), 131–154. doi:10.1111/j.1467-6486.1992.tb00657.x

Hoepner, A., Aguiar, T., & Majithia, R. (2014). The level of compliance with the international code of marketing of breast-milk substitutes: Does it matter to stock markets? *Journal of Business Ethics*, *119*(3), 329–348. doi:10.100710551-013-1625-2

Holder-Webb, L., & Cohen, J. (2012). The cut and paste society: Isomorphism in codes of ethics. *Journal of Business Ethics*, *107*(4), 485–509. doi:10.100710551-011-1060-1

Hopkins, M. (1998). *The Planetary Bargain: Corporate Social Responsibility Comes of Age*. Macmillan.

Hopkins, M. (2004). *The Planetary Bargain. Corporate Social Responsibility Matters*. Routledge.

Hotho, J., & Pedersen, T. (2012). Beyond the rules of the game: three institutional approaches and how they matter for international business. In M. Demirbag & G. Wood (Eds.), *Handbook of Institutional Approaches to International Business*. Edward Elgar. doi:10.4337/9781849807692.00016

Hou, X., Deng, Y., Dai, M., Jiang, X., Li, S., Fu, H., & Peng, C. (2022). Migration and transformation of heavy metals in Chinese medicine residues during the process of traditional pyrolysis and solar pyrolysis. *Chemosphere*, *293*, 133658. doi:10.1016/j.chemosphere.2022.133658 PMID:35051513

Huang, K., Dyerson, R., Wu, L., & Harindranath, G. (2015). From temporary competitive advantage to sustainable competitive advantage. *British Journal of Management*, *26*(4), 617–636. doi:10.1111/1467-8551.12104

Hui, L. (2008). Combining faith and CSR: A paradigm of corporate sustainability. *International Journal of Social Economics*, *35*(6), 449–465. doi:10.1108/03068290810873429

Huschek, G., Hansen, P. D., Maurer, H. H., Krengel, D., & Kayser, A. (2004). Environmental risk assessment of medicinal products for human use according to European Commission Recommendations. *Environmental Toxicology*, *19*(3), 226–240. doi:10.1002/tox.20015 PMID:15101038

IESE. (2017). *Empresa y objetivos de desarrollo sostenible* [Company and Sustainable Development Goals]. Cuadernos de la Cátedra "la Caixa" de Responsabilidad Social de la Empresa. Nº34. https://media.iese.edu/upload/ST0438.pdf

Ilie, S., & Rose, P. (2016). Is equal access to higher Education in South Asia and sub-Saharan Africa achievable by 2030? *Higher Education*, *72*(4), 435–455. doi:10.100710734-016-0039-3

Ilie, S., & Rose, P. (2018). Who benefits from public spending on higher Education in South Asia and sub-Saharan Africa? *Compare: A Journal of Comparative Education*, *48*(4), 630–647. doi:10.1080/03057925.2017.1347870

Illia, L., Rodríguez, B., González, A., & Romenti, S. (2010). La comunicación de la RSC entre las 250 principales empresas europeas [The CSR Communication Between the Top 250 Euopean Companies]. *Cuadernos de Información*, *27*(27), 85–96. doi:10.7764/cdi.27.25

Imdad, M., Hafidhuddin, D., & Arif, S. (2019). Defining Education: al-Farabi and Ibn Sina terminologies. *Ibn Khaldun Journal of Social Science*, *1*(1), 1–10.

Instituto Nacional de Estadística (INE). (n.d.). https://www.ine.es/

International Business Machines Corporation (IBM). (2022). *What is digital transformation?* Retrieved September 27, 2022, from https://www.ibm.com/topics/digital-transformation

International Initiative on Water Quality-IIWQ. (2017). *Pharmaceuticals in the aquatic environment of the Baltic sea region - A status report. The United Nations Educational, Scientific and Cultural Organization 7.* France and HELCOM.

Ishizaka, A., Khan, S. A., Kheybari, S., & Zaman, S. I. (2022). Supplier selection in closed-loop pharma supply chain: A novel BWM-GAIA framework. *Annals of Operations Research*, 1–24. doi:10.100710479-022-04710-7

Islam, M. S., & Hasam, M. A. (2016). Domestic Violence against Women in Bangladesh: A comparative Study on the perception of Educated and Non-Educated Class. *Review of Social Sciences, 1*(6). doi:.v1i6.43 doi:10.18533/rss

Ismail, M. (2009). Corporate social responsibility and its role in community development: An international perspective. *Journal of International Social Research*, *2*(9), 1–12.

ISO 26000. (2010). *Guidance on social responsibility. Committee Draft ISO/CD26000.* International Standards Organization. https://iso26000.info/wp-content/uploads/2017/06/ISO-26000_2010_E_OBPpages.pdf

Issa, H., & Jaleel, E. (2021). Social isolation and psychological wellbeing: Lessons from Covid-19. *Management Science Letters*, *11*(2), 609–618.

Ivshina, I. B., Rychkova, M. I., Vikhareva, E. V., Chekryshkina, L. A., & Mishenina, I. I. (2006). Catalysis of the biodegradation of unusable medicines by alkanotrophic *Rhodococci. Applied Biochemistry and Microbiology*, *42*(4), 392–395. doi:10.1134/S0003683806040090 PMID:17022454

Jabeen, S., Riaz, M., & Omer, S. (2021). Applying Socioecological Framework to Acid Attack Violence: An Exploration of Inhabitant Factors. *Journal of Interpersonal Violence*, *36*(23-24), NP12481–NP12503. doi:10.1177/0886260519898442

Jahan, F. (2020). *The issue of identity: state denial, local controversies and everyday resistance among the Santal in Bangladesh* [PhD Thesis]. Hale University.

Jamali, D., & Neville, B. (2011). Convergence versus divergence of CSR in developing countries: An embedded multi-layered institutional lens. *Journal of Business Ethics*, *102*(4), 599–621. doi:10.100710551-011-0830-0

Jami Pour, M., & Lotfiyan, Z. (2020). A new framework of electronic word-of-mouth in social networking sites: The system-based approach. *International Journal of Internet Marketing and Advertising*, *14*(1), 48–70. doi:10.1504/IJIMA.2020.106044

Jawahar, I., & McLaughlin, G. (2001). Toward a descriptive stakeholder theory: An organizational life cycle approach. *Academy of Management Review*, *26*(3), 397–414. doi:10.2307/259184

Jeje, Y. (2006). *Southern Alberta Landscapes: Meeting the Challenges Ahead: Export Coefficients for Total Phosphorus, Total Nitrogen and Total Suspended Solids in the Southern Alberta Region: A Review of Literature.* Alberta Environment.

Jennings, P., & Zandbergen, P. (1995). Ecologically sustainable organizations: An institutional approach. *Academy of Management Review*, *20*(4), 1015–1052. doi:10.5465/amr.1995.9512280034

Jensen, M., & Meckling, W. (1976). Theory of the firm: Managerial behavior, agency costs, and ownership structure. *Journal of Financial Economics*, *3*(4), 305–360. doi:10.1016/0304-405X(76)90026-X

Jia, M., & Zhang, Z. (2014). How does the stock market value corporate social performance? When behavioral theories interact with stakeholder theory. *Journal of Management Studies*, *51*(7), 1118–1152. doi:10.1111/joms.12090

Jiang, X., Feng, Y., Lv, G., Du, Y., Qin, D., Li, X., & Liu, X. (2012). Bioferment residue: TG-FTIR study and co-combustion in a MSW incineration plant. *Environmental Science & Technology*, *46*(24), 13539–13544. doi:10.1021/es3032133 PMID:23163404

Jimenez-Gonzalez, C., Constable, D. J. C., & Ponder, C. S. (2012). Evaluating the "greenness" of chemical processes and products in the pharmaceutical industry-a green metrics primer. *Chemical Society Reviews*, *41*(4), 1485–1498. doi:10.1039/C1CS15215G PMID:22076593

Jobling, S., Coey, S., Whitmore, J. G., Kime, D. E., Van Look, K. J., McAllister, B. G., Beresford, N., Henshaw, A. C., Brighty, G., Tyler, C. R., & Sumpter, J. P. (2002). Wild intersex roach (*Rutilus rutilus*) have reduced fertility. *Biology of Reproduction*, *67*(2), 515–524. doi:10.1095/biolreprod67.2.515 PMID:12135890

Jones, O. A. H., Voulvoulis, N., & Lester, J. N. (2002). Aquatic environmental assessment of the top 25 English prescription pharmaceuticals. *Water Research*, *36*(20), 5013–5022. doi:10.1016/S0043-1354(02)00227-0 PMID:12448549

Jones, T. (1980). Corporate social responsibility revisited, redefined. *California Management Review*, *22*(3), 59–67. doi:10.2307/41164877

Kadam, A., Patil, S., Patil, S., & Tumkur, A. (2016). Pharmaceutical waste management an overview. *Indian J Pharm Pract*, *9*(1), 2–8. doi:10.5530/ijopp.9.1.2

Kahneman, D., & Krueger, A. B. (2006). Developments in the measurement of subjective well-being. *The Journal of Economic Perspectives*, *20*, 3–24.

Kang, N., & Moon, J. (2012). Institutional complementarity between corporate governance and corporate social responsibility: A comparative institutional analysis of three capitalisms. *Socio-economic Review*, *10*(1), 85–108. doi:10.1093er/mwr025

Kao, E., Yeh, C., Wang, L., & Fung, H. (2018). The relationship between CSR and performance: Evidence in China. *Pacific-Basin Finance Journal*, *51*, 155–170. doi:10.1016/j.pacfin.2018.04.006

Karliner, J., & Guenther, R. (2011). *Global green and healthy hospitals: A comprehensive environmental health agenda for hospitals and health systems around the world.* Health Care without Harm diakses pada laman: http://www. green-hospitals. net/tanggal

Karlsson, R., & Luttropp, C. (2006). Eco-design: What's happening - An overview of the subject area of eco-design and the papers in this special issue. *Journal of Cleaner Production*, *14*(15-16), 1291–1298. doi:10.1016/j.jclepro.2005.11.010

Kaur, N., & Kumar, A. (2020). Vitriolage (vitriolism)-a medico-socio-legal review. *Forensic Science, Medicine, and Pathology*, *16*(3), 481–488.

Khan, A., Chen, C. C., Suanpong, K., Ruangkanjanases, A., Kittikowit, S., & Chen, S. C. (2021). The Impact of CSR on Sustainable Innovation Ambidexterity: The Mediating Role of Sustainable Supply Chain Management and Second-Order Social Capital. *Sustainability*, *13*(21), 12160. doi:10.3390u132112160

Khani, A., Rasulzade, H., & Aqapur, N. (2020). Green removal of hospital-medical wastes by designed integrated pyrolysis-incineration system. *Journal of Chemistry Letters*, *1*, 89–92.

Khatri, P., & Gupta, P. (2019). Development and validation of employee wellbeing scale–a formative measurement model. *International Journal of Workplace Health Management*, *12*(5), 352–368.

Khoury, G., Rostami, J., & Turnbull, J. (1999). *Corporate Social Responsibility: Turning Words into Action*. Conference Board of Canada.

Klein, E. (2017). The World Bank on mind, behaviour and society. *Development and Change*, *48*(3), 481–501. doi:10.1111/dech.12308

Kleine, A., & Hauff, M. (2009). Sustainability-driven implementation of corporate social responsibility. *Journal of Business Ethics*, *85*(3), 517–533. doi:10.100710551-009-0212-z

Kopnina, H. (2020). Education for the future? Critical evaluation of Education for sustainable development goals. *The Journal of Environmental Education*, *51*(4), 280–291. doi:10.1080/00958964.2019.1710444

Kotler, P., & Lee, N. (2007). *Corporate Social Responsibility: doing the most good for your company and your case*. John Wiley & Sons.

Kraaijenbrink, J., Spender, J., & Groen, A. (2010). The resource-based view: A review and assessment of its critiques. *Journal of Management*, *36*(1), 349–372. doi:10.1177/0149206309350775

Kumar, S., Murphy, M., Talwar, S., Kaur, P., & Dhir, A. (2021). What drives brand love and purchase intentions toward the local food distribution system? A study of social media-based REKO (fair consumption) groups. *Journal of Retailing and Consumer Services*, *60*, 102444. doi:10.1016/j.jretconser.2021.102444

Kuntz, J. R., Näswall, K., & Malinen, S. (2016). Resilient employees in resilient organizations: Flourishing beyond adversity. *Industrial and Organizational Psychology: Perspectives on Science and Practice*, *9*(2), 456–462.

Kuroda, K., Li, C., Dhangar, K., & Kumar, M. (2021). Predicted occurrence, eco-toxicological risk and environmentally acquired resistance of antiviral drugs associated with Covid-19 in environmental waters. *The Science of the Total Environment*, *776*, 145740. doi:10.1016/j.scitotenv.2021.145740 PMID:33647647

Kuspis, D. A., & Krenzelok, E. (1996). What happens to expired medications? A survey of community medication disposal. *Veterinary and Human Toxicology*, *38*, 48–48. PMID:8825752

Lama, D., & Cutler, H. C. (2008). *İş hayatında mutluluk sanatı* (M. Tayga, Trans.). Klan Yayınları.

Lamberti, L., & Lettieri, E. (2009). CSR practices and corporate strategy: Evidence from a longitudinal case study. *Journal of Business Ethics*, *87*(2), 153–168. doi:10.100710551-008-9876-z

Langtry, B. (1994). Stakeholders and the moral responsibilities of business. *Business Ethics Quarterly*, *4*(4), 431–443. doi:10.2307/3857342

Lantos, G. (2001). The boundaries of strategic corporate social responsibility. *Journal of Consumer Marketing*, *18*(7), 595–632. doi:10.1108/07363760110410281

Lavallée, L. F. (2009). Practical application of an Indigenous research framework and two qualitative Indigenous research methods: Sharing circles and Anishnaabe symbol-based reflection. *International Journal of Qualitative Methods*, *8*(1), 21–40. doi:10.1177/160940690900800103

Le Blanc, P. M., & Oerlemans, W. G. (2016). Amplition in the workplace: Building a sustainable workforce through individual positive psychological interventions. *Psychologist Papers*, *37*(3), 185–191.

Lee, M. (2008). A review of the theories of corporate social responsibility: Its evolutionary path and the road ahead. *International Journal of Management Reviews*, *10*(1), 53–73. doi:10.1111/j.1468-2370.2007.00226.x

Lenz, K., Mahnik, S. N., Weissenbacher, N., Mader, R. M., Krenn, P., Hann, S., & Fuerhacker, M. (2007). Monitoring, removal and risk assessment of cytostatic drugs in hospital waste water. *Water Science and Technology, 56*, 141-149.

Leonard, T., & Schneider, J. (2004, May). Integrated sustainability in the pharmaceutical industry. *Corporate Environmental Strategy: International Journal for Sustainable Business, 11*, 119-128.

Lewis, M. (2017). *Acid attacks: A forensic psychiatry perspective*. Retrieved from https://bit.ly/2LrGOuk

Liao, S., Hu, D., & Chung, Y.-C. (2017). LMX and Employee satisfaction: Mediating effect of psychological capital. *Leadership and Organization Development Journal*, *38*(3), 433–449.

Li, C., Zhang, G., Zhang, Z., Ma, D., & Xu, G. (2016). Alkaline thermal pre-treatment at mild temperatures for biogas production from anaerobic digestion of antibiotic mycelial residue. *Bioresource Technology*, *208*, 49–57. doi:10.1016/j.biortech.2016.02.064 PMID:26921869

Lidl [@lidlespana]. (2022). *Publicaciones* [Perfil en Instagram]. Recuperado el 25 de marzo de 2022, de https://www.instagram.com/lidlespana/

Lidl. (2022). *Página web oficial sobre Sostenibilidad* [Offical Website on Sustainability]. https://empresa.lidl.es/sostenibilidad

Lindblom, C. (1983). *The concept of organizational legitimacy and its implications for corporate social responsibility disclosure*. Working Paper. American Accounting Association Public Interest Section.

Lindgreen, A., & Swaen, V. (2010). Corporate social responsibility. *International Journal of Management Reviews*, *12*(1), 1–7. doi:10.1111/j.1468-2370.2009.00277.x

Lips-Wiersma, M., & Wright, S. (2012). Measuring the meaning of meaningful work: Development and validation of the Comprehensive Meaningful Work Scale (CMWS). *Group & Organization Management*, *37*(5), 655–685.

Loaiza-Ambuludi, S., Panizza, M., Oturan, N., & Oturan, M. A. (2014). Removal of the anti-inflammatory drug ibuprofen from water using homogeneous photocatalysis. *Catalysis Today*, *224*, 29–33. doi:10.1016/j.cattod.2013.12.018

Lockett, A., & Thompson, S. (2004). Edith Penrose's contributions to the resource-based view: An alternative perspective. *Journal of Management Studies*, *41*(1), 193–203. doi:10.1111/j.1467-6486.2004.00428.x

Long, J. (2008). From Cocoa to CSR: Finding sustainability in a cup of hot chocolate. *Thunderbird International Business Review*, *50*(5), 315–320. doi:10.1002/tie.20215

Lo, S. F., & Sheu, H. J. (2007). Is corporate sustainability a value-increasing strategy for business? *Corporate Governance*, *15*(2), 345–358. doi:10.1111/j.1467-8683.2007.00565.x

Lourenço, I., Callen, J., Branco, M., & Curto, J. (2014). The value relevance of reputation for sustainability leadership. *Journal of Business Ethics*, *119*(1), 17–28. doi:10.100710551-012-1617-7

Lund, S., Madgavkar, A., Manyika, J., Smit, S., Ellingrud, K., Meaney, M., & Robinson, O. (2021). *The future of work after COVID-19*. McKinsey Global Institute. https://www.mckinsey.com/featured-insights/future-of-work/the-future-of-workafter-covid-19

Luque, A. (2021). Practicality, support or premeditated calculation in the digital age: The case of Ecuador. *Revista Venezolana De Gerencia, 26*(6), 29-46. https://www.produccioncientificaluz.org/index.php/rvg/article/view/37135 doi:10.52080/rvgluz.26.e6.3

Luque, A., & Herrero-García, N. (2019). How corporate social (ir)responsibility in the textile sector is defined, and its impact on ethical sustainability: An analysis of 133 concepts. *Corporate Social Responsibility and Environmental Management*, *26*(6), 1–22. doi:10.1002/csr.1747

Lutterbeck, C. A., Baginska, E., Machado, Ê. L., & Kümmerer, K. (2015). Removal of the anti-cancer drug methotrexate from water by advanced oxidation processes: Aerobic biodegradation and toxicity studies after treatment. *Chemosphere*, *141*, 290–296. doi:10.1016/j.chemosphere.2015.07.069 PMID:26298026

Ma, D., Zhang, G., Areeprasert, C., Li, C., Shen, Y., Yoshikawa, K., & Xu, G. (2016). Characterization of NO emission in combustion of hydrothermally treated antibiotic mycelial residue. *Chemical Engineering Journal*, *284*, 708–715. doi:10.1016/j.cej.2015.08.149

Mahdi, M. S. (2020). *Alfarabi and the foundation of Islamic political philosophy*. University of Chicago Press.

Maignan, I., & Ferrell, O. (2004). Corporate social responsibility and marketing: An integrative framework. *Journal of the Academy of Marketing Science*, *32*(1), 3–19. doi:10.1177/0092070303258971

Málovics, G., Csigéné, N. N., & Kraus, S. (2008). The role of corporate social responsibility in strong sustainability. *Journal of Socio-Economics*, *37*(3), 907–918. doi:10.1016/j.socec.2006.12.061

Mandaric, D., Anica, H., & Goran, K. (2021). Perception of Consumers' Awareness about Sustainability of Fashion Brands. *Journal of Risk and Financial Management*, *14*(12), 594. doi:10.3390/jrfm14120594

Manne, H., & Wallich, H. (1972). *The Modern Corporation and Social Responsibility*. American Enterprise Institute for Public Policy Research.

Marco-Lajara, B., Seva-Larrosa, P., Martínez-Falcó, J., & Sánchez-García, E. (2021j). El clúster vitivinícola de Jumilla: Entre la tradición y la modernidad [The Jumilla wine cluster: Between tradition and modernity]. In XLIII jornadas de viticultura y enología de la Tierra de Barros: III Congreso agroalimentario de Extremadura [XLIII Tierra de Barros Viticulture and Oenology Conference: III Agri-food Congress of Extremadura] (pp. 56-70). Centro Universitario Santa Ana.

Marco-Lajara, B., Zaragoza-Sáez, P. C., Martínez-Falcó, J., & Sánchez-García, E. (2022h). Does green intellectual capital affect green innovation performance? Evidence from the Spanish wine industry. *British Food Journal*, ahead-of-print.

Marco-Lajara, B., Zaragoza-Saez, P., & Martínez-Falcó, J. (2022e). Green Innovation: Balancing Economic Efficiency With Environmental Protection. In Frameworks for Sustainable Development Goals to Manage Economic, Social, and Environmental Shocks and Disasters (pp. 239-254). IGI Global.

Marco-Lajara, B., Zaragoza-Sáez, P., Falcó, J. M., & Millan-Tudela, L. A. (2022f). Corporate Social Responsibility: A Narrative Literature Review. *Frameworks for Sustainable Development Goals to Manage Economic, Social, and Environmental Shocks and Disasters*, 16-34.

Marco-Lajara, B., Zaragoza-Saez, P., Falcó, J. M., & Sánchez-García, E. (2022b). COVID-19 and Wine Tourism: A Story of Heartbreak. In Handbook of Research on SDGs for Economic Development, Social Development, and Environmental Protection (pp. 90-112). IGI Global.

Marco-Lajara, B., Zaragoza-Sáez, P., Martínez-Falcó, J., & Sánchez-García, E. (2022a). Green Intellectual Capital in the Spanish Wine Industry. In Innovative Economic, Social, and Environmental Practices for Progressing Future Sustainability (pp. 102-120). IGI Global. doi:10.4018/978-1-7998-9590-9.ch006

Marco-Lajara, B., Zaragoza-Saez, P., Martínez-Falcó, J., & Sánchez-García, E. (2022c). COVID-19 and Wine Tourism: A Story of Heartbreak. In Handbook of Research on SDGs for Economic Development, Social Development, and Environmental Protection (pp. 90-112). IGI Global.

Marco-Lajara, B., Martínez-Falcó, J., Ruiz-Fernández, L., & Seva-Larrosa, P. (2022k). Evolución del pensamiento en la disciplina de dirección estratégica: la visión de la empresa basada en las capacidades dinámicas y en el conocimiento. [Evolution of thinking in the discipline of strategic management: the vision of the company based on dynamic capabilities and knowledge] In *Investigación y transferencia de las ciencias sociales frente a un mundo en crisis* [Social science research and transfer in the face of a world in crisis]. (pp. 1801–1826). Dykinson.

Marco-Lajara, B., Sánchez-García, E., Martínez-Falcó, J., & Poveda-Pareja, E. (2022l). Regional Specialization, Competitive Pressure, and Cooperation: The Cocktail for Innovation. *Energies*, *15*(15), 5346.

Marco-Lajara, B., Sánchez-García, E., Seva-Larrosa, P., & Martínez-Falcó, J. (2022m). Knowledge creation and diffusion inspecialized environments: What are the factors involved? In *Empresa, economía y derecho. Oportunidades ante un entorno global y disruptivo* [Business, economy and law. Opportunities in a global and disruptive environment]. (pp. 432–459). Dykinson.

Marco-Lajara, B., Seva-Larrosa, P., Martínez-Falcó, J., & García-Lillo, F. (2022i). Wine clusters and Protected Designations of Origin (PDOs) in Spain: An exploratory analysis. *Journal of Wine Research*, *33*(3), 1–22. doi:10.1080/09571264.2022.2110051

Marco-Lajara, B., Seva-Larrosa, P., Martinez-Falco, J., & Sanchez-Garcia, E. (2021a). How Has COVID- 19 Affected The Spanish Wine Industry? An Exploratory Analysis. *Natural Volatiles & Essential Oils Journal*, *8*(6), 2722–2731.

Marco-Lajara, B., Seva-Larrosa, P., Ruiz-Fernandez, L., & Martinez-Falco, J. (2021b). The Effect of COVID- 19 on the Spanish Wine Industry. In *Impact of Global Issues on International Trade* (pp. 211–232). IGI Global., doi:10.4018/978-1-7998-8314-2.ch012

Marco-Lajara, B., Zaragoza Sáez, P., & Martínez-Falcó, J. (2022n). Does Green Intellectual Capital Affect Green Performance? The Mediation of Green Innovation. *Telematique*, *21*(1), 4594–4602.

Marco-Lajara, B., Zaragoza-Saez, P., Martínez-Falcó, J., & Millan-Tudela, L. A. (2022b). Analysing the Relationship Between Green Intellectual Capital and the Achievement of the Sustainable Development Goals. In *Handbook of Research on Building Inclusive Global Knowledge Societies for Sustainable Development* (pp. 111–129). IGI Global. doi:10.4018/978-1-6684-5109-0.ch005

Marco-Lajara, B., Zaragoza-Sáez, P., Martínez-Falcó, J., & Ruiz-Fernández, L. (2022g). The Effect of Green Intellectual Capital on Green Performance in the Spanish Wine Industry: A Structural Equation Modeling Approach. *Complexity*, *2022*, 2022. doi:10.1155/2022/6024077

Marco-Lajara, B., Zaragoza-Sáez, P., Martínez-Falcó, J., & Sánchez-García, E. (2022d). El capital intelectual verde como hoja de ruta para la sostenibilidad: El caso de bodegas Luzón [Green Intellectual Capital as a Roadmap for Sustainability:The case of Luzon Wineries]. *GeoGraphos: Revista Digital para Estudiantes de Geografía y Ciencias Sociales*, *13*(147), 137–146.

Marco-Lajara, B., Zaragoza-Sáez, P., Martínez-Falcó, J., & Sánchez-García, E. (2022d). El capital intelectual verde como hoja de ruta para la sostenibilidad: El caso de bodegas Luzón. *GeoGraphos: Revista Digital para Estudiantes de Geografía y Ciencias Sociales*, *13*(147), 137–146.

Marco-Lajara, B., Zaragoza-Sáez, P., Martínez-Falcó, J., & Sánchez-García, E. (2022o). Las rutas del vino de España: el impacto económico derivado de las visitas a bodegas y museos. [Spain's wine routes: the economic impact of visits to wineries and museums] In *Investigación y transferencia de las ciencias sociales frente a un mundo en crisis* [Social science research and transfer in the face of a world in crisis]. (pp. 1774–1800). Dykinson.

Marquis, C., Glynn, M., & Davis, G. (2007). Community isomorphism and corporate social action. *Academy of Management Review, 32*(3), 925–945. doi:10.5465/amr.2007.25275683

Marsden, C. (2001). *The Role of Public Authorities in Corporate Social Responsibility.* http://www.alter.be/socialresponsibility/ people/marchri/en/displayPerson

Marsiglia, E., & Falautano, I. (2005). Corporate social responsibility and sustainability challenges for a Bancassurance Company. *The Geneva Papers on Risk and Insurance. Issues and Practice, 30*(3), 485–497. doi:10.1057/palgrave.gpp.2510040

Martin, K., & Mirraboopa, B. (2003). Ways of knowing, being and doing: A theoretical framework and methods for indigenous and indigenist re-search. *Journal of Australian Studies, 27*(76), 203–214. doi:10.1080/14443050309387838

Maryam, B., Buscio, V., Odabasi, S. U., & Buyukgungor, H. (2020). A study on behavior, interaction and rejection of paracetamol, diclofenac and ibuprofen (PhACs) from waste water by nano filtration membranes. *Environmental Technology & Innovation, 18*, 100641. doi:10.1016/j.eti.2020.100641

Massarella, K., Sallu, S. M., & Ensor, J. E. (2020). Reproducing injustice: Why recognition matters in conservation project evaluation. *Global Environmental Change, 65*, 102181. doi:10.1016/j.gloenvcha.2020.102181

Matten, D., & Moon, J. (2008). "Implicit" and "explicit" CSR: A conceptual framework for a comparative understanding of corporate social responsibility. *Academy of Management Review, 330*(2), 404–424. doi:10.5465/amr.2008.31193458

Matthiessen, P. (2012). *In the spirit of Crazy Horse.* Random House.

McAfee, K. (1999). Selling nature to save it? Biodiversity and green developmentalism. *Environment and Planning. D, Society & Space, 17*(2), 133–154. doi:10.1068/d170133

McDonough, W., & Braungart, W. (2002). Design for the triple top line: New tools for sustainable commerce. *Corporate Environmental Strategy, 9*(3), 1711–1716. doi:10.1016/S1066-7938(02)00069-6

McGuire, J. (1963). *Business and society.* McGraw-hill.

McKee, A. (2017). *How to Be happy at work: The power of purpose, hope, and friendship.* Harvard Business Press.

McWilliams, A., & Siegel, D. (2011). Creating and capturing value: Strategic corporate social responsibility, resource-based theory, and sustainable competitive advantage. *Journal of Management, 37*(5), 1480–1495. doi:10.1177/0149206310385696

McWilliams, A., Siegel, D., & Wright, P. (2006). Corporate social responsibility: Strategic implications. *Journal of Management Studies, 43*(1), 1–18. doi:10.1111/j.1467-6486.2006.00580.x

Meadows, D. H., Meadows, D. L., Randers, J., & Behrens, W. W. (2018). The limits to growth. In *Green planet blues* (pp. 25–29). Routledge. doi:10.4324/9780429493744-3

Meisinger, S. (2007). HR's role in social responsibility and sustainability. *HRMagazine, 52*(12), 8.

Mellahi, K., Frynas, J., Sun, P., & Siegel, D. (2016). A review of the nonmarket strategy literature: Towards a multi-theoretical integration. *Journal of Management, 42*(1), 143–173. doi:10.1177/0149206315617241

Menguc, B., Auh, S., & Ozanne, L. (2010). The interactive effect of internal and external factors on a proactive environmental strategy and its influence on a firm's performance. *Journal of Business Ethics, 94*(2), 279–298. doi:10.100710551-009-0264-0

Mercadona [@mercadona]. (2022). *Publicaciones* [Perfil en Instagram]. Recuperado el 25 de marzo de 2022, de https://www.instagram.com/mercadona/

Mercadona. (2022b). *Página web oficial sobre Responsabilidad Social Corporativa* [Offical Website on Corporate Social Responsibility]. https://info.mercadona.es/es/cuidemos-el-planeta

Merriam, S. B., & Grenier, R. S. (2019). Qualitative Research in Practice Examples for Discussion and Analysis USA. *Sage (Atlanta, Ga.)*.

Meyer, J., & Rowan, B. (1977). Institutionalized organizations: Formal structure as myth and ceremony. *American Journal of Sociology*, *83*(2), 340–363. doi:10.1086/226550

Microsoft. (2022). *Focus on four areas to unlock value*. Retrieved September 20, 2022, from https://www.microsoft.com/en-us/industry/digital-transformation

Mignolo, W. (2011). *The darker side of western modernity: Global futures, decolonial options*. Duke University Press.

Mignolo, W. D., & Walsh, C. E. (2018). *On decoloniality: Concepts, analytics, praxis*. Duke University Press.

Miles, M., & Covin, J. (2000). Environmental marketing: A source of reputational, competitive, and financial advantage. *Journal of Business Ethics*, *23*(3), 299–311. doi:10.1023/A:1006214509281

Mitchell, R., Agle, B., & Wood, D. (1997). Toward a theory of stakeholder identification and salience. *Academy of Management Review*, *22*(4), 853–886. doi:10.2307/259247

Mobus, J. (2005). Mandatory environmental disclosures in a legitimacy theory context. *Accounting, Auditing & Accountability Journal*, *18*(4), 492–517. doi:10.1108/09513570510609333

Moggi, S., Bonomi, S., & Ricciardi, F. (2018). Against Food Waste: CSR for the Social and Environmental Impact through a Network-Based Organizational Model. *Sustainability*, *10*(10), 3515. doi:10.3390u10103515

Mohr, L., Webb, D., & Harris, K. (2001). Do consumers expect companies to be socially responsible? The impact of corporate social responsibility on buying behavior. *The Journal of Consumer Affairs*, *35*(1), 45–72. doi:10.1111/j.1745-6606.2001.tb00102.x

Mohsin, A. (2001). *The state of "minority" rights in Bangladesh*. International Centre for Ethnic Studies.

Mohsin, A. (2002). *The Politics of Nationalism: The Case of the Chittagong Hill Tracts Bangladesh* (2nd ed.). The University Press Limited.

Moir, L., & Taffler, R. (2004). Does corporate philanthropy exist? Business giving to the arts in the U.K. *Journal of Business Ethics*, *54*(2), 149–161. doi:10.100710551-004-1777-1

Moldan, B., Janoudkova, S., & Tomas Hak, T. (2012). How to understand and measure environmental sustainability: Indicators and targets. *Ecological Indicators*, *17*, 4–13. doi:10.1016/j.ecolind.2011.04.033

Monfort, A., & Villagra, N. (2016). Corporate Social Responsibility and Corporate Foundations in Building Responsible Brands. *El Profesional de la Información*, *25*(5), 767–777. doi:10.3145/epi.2016.sep.07

Monitor Deloitte. (2019). *Digital Transformation in the EU 2035. A Glimpse into the Future*. Center for the Long View. Retrieved August 20, 2022, from https://www2.deloitte.com/content/dam/Deloitte/de/Documents/strategy/deloitte-future-of-digital-transformation-eu-2035.pdf

Monnot, M. J., & Beehr, T. A. (2014). Subjective well-being at work: Disentangling source effects of stress and support on enthusiasm, contentment, and meaningfulness. *Journal of Vocational Behavior*, *85*(2), 204–218.

Montiel, I. (2008). Corporate social responsibility and corporate sustainability: Separate pasts, common futures. *Organization & Environment*, *21*(3), 245–269. doi:10.1177/1086026608321329

Moon, J. (2007). The contribution of corporate social responsibility to sustainable development. *Sustainable Development, 15*(5), 296–306. doi:10.1002d.346

Moore, G. (2001). Corporate social and financial performance: An investigation in the U.K. supermarket industry. *Journal of Business Ethics, 34*(4), 299–315. doi:10.1023/A:1012537016969

Moran, K. A. (2009). Can Kant have an account of moral Education? *Journal of Philosophy of Education, 43*(4), 471–484. doi:10.1111/j.1467-9752.2009.00721.x

Moreton-Robinson, A. (Ed.). (2020). *Sovereign subjects: Indigenous sovereignty matters*. Routledge. doi:10.4324/9781003117353

MSW. (2021). *Ministry of Social Welfare*. Retrieved from www.msw.gov.bd

Myerson, J., & Tidd, P. (2017). *Developing a practical framework for workplace design to affect employee wellbeing: A research study*. Gensler and the Helen Hamlyn Centre for Design at the Royal College of Art.

Nansai, K., Fry, J., Malik, A., Takayanagi, W., & Kondo, N. (2020). Carbon footprint of Japanese health care services from 2011 to 2015. *Resources, Conservation and Recycling, 152*, 104525. doi:10.1016/j.resconrec.2019.104525

Nassif, A. G., Hackett, R. D., & Wang, G. (2021). Ethical, virtuous, and charismatic leadership: An examination of differential relationships with follower and leader outcomes. *Journal of Business Ethics, 172*(3), 581–603.

Nassir, I. (2017). Happiness in the workplace underpins a sustainable business environment. *InBusiness*. https://www.thenationalnews.com/business/comment/happiness-in-the-workplace-underpins-a-sustainable-business-environment-1.683369

Navarro-Espigares, J. L., & González-López, J. M. (2006). Corporate social responsibility and economic growth. *Estudios de Economía Aplicada, 24*, 637–665.

Neu, D., Warsame, H., & Pedwell, K. (1998). Managing public impressions: Environmental disclosures in annual reports. *Accounting, Organizations and Society, 23*(3), 265–282. doi:10.1016/S0361-3682(97)00008-1

Newsletter, A. S. F. (2016). Voice 40-41. Academic Press.

North, D. (1990). *Institutions, Institutional Change and Economic Performance*. Cambridge University Press. doi:10.1017/CBO9780511808678

Novak, J. J. (1993). Bangladesh: Reflections on the water. Indiana University Press.

O'Flynn, D., Lawler, J., Yusuf, A., Parle-McDermott, A., Harold, D., Mc Cloughlin, T., & White, B. (2021). A review of pharmaceutical occurrence and pathways in the aquatic environment in the context of a changing climate and the Covid-19 pandemic. *Analytical Methods, 13*(5), 575–594. doi:10.1039/D0AY02098B PMID:33507166

Observatorio de RSC. (2014). *Introducción a la Responsabilidad Social Corporativa* [Introduction to Corporate Social Responsibility]. Observatorio de RSC.

Oh, W., Chang, Y., & Martynov, A. (2011). The effect of ownership structure on corporate social responsibility: Empirical evidence from Korea. *Journal of Business Ethics, 104*(2), 283–297. doi:10.100710551-011-0912-z

Oikonomou, I., Brooks, C., & Pavelin, S. (2014). The financial effects of uniform and mixed corporate social performance. *Journal of Management Studies, 51*(6), 898–925. doi:10.1111/joms.12064

Ojo, A., Fawehinmi, O., & Yusliza, M. (2021). Examining the predictors of resilience and work engagement during COVID-19 pandemic. *Sustainability, 13*(5), 2902–2923.

Okafor, A., Adeleye, B. N., & Adusei, M. (2021). Corporate social responsibility and financial performance: Evidence from US tech firms. *Journal of Cleaner Production, 292*, 126078. doi:10.1016/j.jclepro.2021.126078

Oliver, P. (2012). *Succeeding with your literature review. A handbook for students.* McGraw-Hill, Open University Press.

Oracle. (2022). *What is Digital Transformation?* Retrieved September 20, 2022, from https://www.oracle.com/cloud/digital-transformation/

Orebech, P., Bosselman, F., Bjarup, J., Callies, D., Chanock, M., & Petersen, H. (2005). *The role of customary law in sustainable development.* Cambridge University Press.

Organization for Economic Cooperation and Development (OECD). (2019a). *Measuring the Digital Transformation. A Roadmap for the Future.* Retrieved August 20, 2022, from https://www.oecd-ilibrary.org/science-and-technology/measuring-the-digital-transformation_97dc0edb-en

Organization for Economic Cooperation and Development (OECD). (2019b). *Characterising innovation in the digital age.* Retrieved August 20, 2022, from https://www.oecd-ilibrary.org/science-and-technology/digital-innovation_2f5d36df-en

Organization for Economic Cooperation and Development (OECD). (2020a). *Chapter 5: The role of international co-operation in the digital age.* Retrieved August 20, 2022, from https://www.oecd-ilibrary.org/docserver/7d3929e1-en.pdf?expires=1663745432&id=id&accname=guest&checksum=4792067EFB409431E5D8B29BBABACC6B

Organization for Economic Cooperation and Development (OECD). (2020b). *Education in the Digital Age: Healthy and Happy Children.* Retrieved August 20, 2022, from https://www.oecd-ilibrary.org/sites/1209166a-en/index.html?itemId=/content/publication/1209166a-en

Organization for Economic Cooperation and Development (OECD). (2021). *OECD Report on Public Communication. The Global Context and the Way Forward.* Retrieved August 20, 2022, from https://www.oecd-ilibrary.org/governance/oecd-report-on-public-communication_f68023c0-en

Organization for Economic Cooperation and Development (OECD). (2022). *Health Data Governance for the Digital Age. Implementing the OECD Recommendation on Health Data Governance.* Retrieved August 20, 2022, from https://www.oecd-ilibrary.org/social-issues-migration-health/health-data-governance-for-the-digital-age_68b60796-en

Orjuela, S. (2011). La Comunicación en la gestión de la Responsabilidad Social Empresarial [Communication in the Managment of Corporate Societal Responsibility]. *Correspondencias & Análisis, 1.*

Osei Kwadwo, V., & Konadu, O. A. (2020). Can Ghana Afford the Sustainable Development Goal on Education? *Africa Education Review, 17*(2), 177–197. doi:10.1080/18146627.2018.1557532

Pabón, M. V., Jiménez, V., & Sierra, A. (2013). Relación entre la responsabilidad social y la publicidad social en las organizaciones. *Revista Comunicación, 30*, 67–76.

Pagani, G. (2012). ¿Se puede ser una empresa socialmente responsable sin comunicar? In M. Cuervo (Ed.), *Relaciones Públicas al sur de Latinoamérica II. Una mirada regional de los nuevos escenarios y desafíos de la comunicación* (pp. 117-125). Cuaderno 40: Facultad de Diseño y Comunicación. Centro de Estudios en Diseño y Comunicación Univ. de Palermo. http://www.scielo.org.ar/pdf/ccedce/n40/n40a11.pdf

Paletta, A., &Bonoli, A. (2019). Governing the university in the perspective of the United Nations 2030 Agenda. *International Journal of Sustainability in Higher Education.*

Panapanaan, V., Linnanen, L., Karvonen, M., & Phan, V. (2003). Roadmapping corporate social responsibility in Finnish companies. *Journal of Business Ethics, 44*(2), 133–148. doi:10.1023/A:1023391530903

Pappu, R. (2020). Gender equity in Education: Changes and challenges in South Asia. Handbook of education systems in South Asia, 1-27.

Parris, T. M., & Kates, R. W. (2003). Characterizing and measuring sustainable Development. *Annual Review of Environment and Resources*, *28*(1), 559–586. doi:10.1146/annurev.energy.28.050302.105551

Parvin, K., Sultana, N., & Naved, R. T. (2016). Disclosure and help-seeking behavior of women exposed to physical spousal violence in Dhaka slums. *BMC Public Health*, *16*(1), 1–8.

Patten, D. (1992). Intra-industry environmental disclosures in response to the Alaskan oil spill: A note on legitimacy theory. *Accounting, Organizations and Society*, *17*(5), 471–475. doi:10.1016/0361-3682(92)90042-Q

Paul, B. D. (2008). A history of the concept of sustainable Development: Literature review. The Annals of the University of Oradea. *Economic Sciences Series*, *17*(2), 576–580.

Paul, P. J. II. (1987). Development and solidarity: Two keys to peace. *Tablet*, 22.

Peters, M., Siller, L., & Matzler, K. (2011). The resource-based and the market-based approaches to cultural tourism in Alpine destinations. *Journal of Sustainable Tourism*, *19*(7), 877–893. doi:10.1080/09669582.2010.547198

Pilar, L., Kvasnicková Stanislavská, L., & Kvasnicka, R. (2021). Healthy Food on the Twitter Social Network: Vegan, Homemade, and Organic Food. *International Journal of Environmental Research and Public Health*, *18*(7), 3815. doi:10.3390/ijerph18073815 PMID:33917406

Pilar, L., Stanislavská, L. K., Kvasnicka, R., Hartman, R., & Tichá, I. (2021). Healthy Food on Instagram Social Network: Vegan, Homemade and Clean Eating. *Nutrients*, *13*(6), 1991. doi:10.3390/nu13061991 PMID:34207910

Popescu, C. R. G. (2018). "Intellectual Capital" - Role, Importance, Components and Influences on the Performance of Organizations - A Theoretical Approach. *32nd Conference of the International-Business-Information-Management-Association (IBIMA). Vision 2020: Sustainable Economic Development And Application Of Innovation Management.*

Popescu, C. R. G. (2019a). Business Development Opportunities: Demonstrating Present And Future Performance, Auditing Intellectual Capital: A Case Study On Romanian Organizations. *33rd International-Business-Information-Management-Association (IBIMA) Conference. Vision 2025: Education Excellence and Management of Innovations through Sustainable Economic Competitive Advantage.*

Popescu, C. R. G. (2019b). Intellectual Capital, Integrated Strategy and Performance: Focusing on Companies' Unique Value Creation Mechanism and Promoting Better Organizational Reporting In Romania: A Framework Dominated By the Impact of Green Marketing and Green Marketing Strategies. *33rd International-Business-Information-Management-Association (IBIMA) Conference. Vision 2025: Education Excellence and Management of Innovations through Sustainable Economic Competitive Advantage.*

Popescu, C. R. G. (2019c). Demonstrating How Universities Extend Value Creation And Performance: Convergence Between Intellectual Capital Contributions And Research Quality - A Romanian Collective Intelligence Framework. *11th International Conference on Education and New Learning Technologies (EDULEARN). EDULEARN19: 11th International Conference On Education And New Learning Technologies.*

Popescu, C. R. G. (2019d). Using Intellectual Capital Measurements In Universities To Assess Performance - Evidence From The Romanian Education System. *11th International Conference on Education and New Learning Technologies (EDULEARN). EDULEARN19: 11th International Conference On Education And New Learning Technologies.*

Popescu, V. A., Popescu, G. N., & Popescu, C. R. G. (2011). "Liquid Assets" Or Turning Fine Wines In A Very Profitable Investment. *Crises After The Crisis: Inquiries From A National, European And Global Perspective, Vol. IV. 18th International Economic Conference on Crisis After the Crisis - Inquiries from a National European and Global Perspective.*

Popescu, V. A., Popescu, G. N., & Popescu, C. R. G. (2012a). Building a culture for innovation through competitive intelligence and accountability: case of Romania. *Innovation And Sustainable Competitive Advantage: From Regional Development To World Economies,* Vols. 1-5. *18th International-Business-Information-Management-Association Conference (IBIMA).*

Popescu, V. A., Popescu, G. N., & Popescu, C. R. G. (2012b). Knowledge And Knowledge Management - New Challenges And Future Perspectives. *EDULEARN12: 4th International Conference On Education And New Learning Technologies. Book Series: EDULEARN Proceedings. 4th International Conference on Education and New Learning Technologies (EDULEARN),* 1011-1019.

Popescu, V. A., Popescu, G. N., & Popescu, C. R. G. (2013). The Impact Of Higher Education On The Development Of Nowadays Society - A Case Study On Romania's Experience. *7th International Technology, Education And Development Conference (INTED2013). Book Series: INTED Proceedings. 7th International Technology, Education and Development Conference (INTED),* 4988-4996.

Popescu, V. A., Popescu, G. N., & Popescu, C. R. G. (2014). The Economic And Social Dimensions Of Romania's Metallurgical Industry. *Metalurgija. Croatian Metallurgical Socberislaviceva, 53*(1), 113-115.

Popescu, V. A., Popescu, G. N., & Popescu, C. R. G. (2015a). The Relation Productivity - Environment In The Context Of Sustainable Development - Case Study On The Romanian Industry. *Metalurgija. Croatian Metallurgical Socberislaviceva, 54*(1), 286-288.

Popescu, V. A., Popescu, G. N., & Popescu, C. R. G. (2015b). Competitiveness And Sustainability - A Modern Economic Approach To The Industrial Policy. *Metalurgija. Croatian Metallurgical Socberislaviceva, 54*(2), 426-428.

Popescu, V. A., Popescu, G. N., & Popescu, C. R. G. (2015c). The Impact Of Global Crisis On The Dominant Sectors Of The Economy At The Romanian Industry. *Metalurgija. Croatian Metallurgical Socberislaviceva, 54*(2), 289-291.

Popescu, C. R. G. (2020a). Developing a Model for Entrepreneurship Competencies: Innovation, Knowledge Management, and Intellectual Capital – Success Competences for Building Inclusive Entrepreneurship and Organizational Performance. In J. Šebestová (Ed.), *Developing Entrepreneurial Competencies for Start-Ups and Small Business* (pp. 1–22). IGI Global. doi:10.4018/978-1-7998-2714-6.ch001

Popescu, C. R. G. (2020b). Analyzing the Impact of Green Marketing Strategies on the Financial and Non-Financial Performance of Organizations: The Intellectual Capital Factor. In V. Naidoo & R. Verma (Eds.), *Green Marketing as a Positive Driver Toward Business Sustainability* (pp. 186–218). IGI Global. doi:10.4018/978-1-5225-9558-8.ch008

Porcelli, A. (2020). El valor de las redes sociales en el progreso de los objetivos de desarrollo sostenible [The Value of Social Media in Advancing the Sustainable Development Goals]. *Lex Social, 10*(2), 2. doi:10.46661/lexsocial.5078

Porter, M., & Kramer, M. (2006). Strategy & Society. *Harvard Business Review, 84*(12), 1–16. PMID:17183795

Porter, T. (2008). Managerial applications of corporate social responsibility and systems thinking for achieving sustainability outcomes. *Systems Research and Behavioral Science: The Official Journal of the International Federation for Systems Research, 25*(3), 397–411. doi:10.1002res.902

Preston, L., & Post, J. (1975). *Private Management and Public Policy.* Prentice-Hall.

Product Stewardship Institute. (2011). Report: Lessons learned: Voluntary pharmaceutical take-back programs in the Great Lakes States. Author.

Pryce-Jones, J. (2010). *Happiness at work: Maximizing your psychological capital for success*. John Wiley & Sons.

Pryce-Jones, J., & Lindsay, J. (2014). What happiness at work is and how to use it. *Industrial and Commercial Training, 46*(3), 130–134.

PWC-PricewaterhouseCoopers. (2022). *Redefining a post-pandemic world: Challenges in today's employee wellbeing and how to alleviate them.* https://www.pwc.com/mt/en/publications/humanresources/redefining-wellbeing-in-a-post-pandemic-world.html

Radjenovic, J., Petrovic, M., Ventura, F., & Barcelo, D. (2008). Rejection of pharmaceuticals in nanofiltration and reverse osmosis membrane drinking water treatment. *Water Research, 42*(14), 3601–3610. doi:10.1016/j.watres.2008.05.020 PMID:18656225

Rahman, M. M. (2020). *Organizational gap analysis in achieving SDGs in Bangladesh*. Academic Press.

Rahman, M., Bhuiyan, F. A., & Lovely, F. H. (2014). Acid violence: A burning impact on women of Bangladesh-case study. *International Journal of Advanced Research in Engineering and Applied Sciences, 3*(3), 40–57.

Rajarajan, V. (2003). Investors' demographics and risk bearing capacity. *Finance India, 17*(2), 565.

Rawls, J. (2009). *A theory of justice*. Harvard University Press.

REBA. (2020, July). *REBA / AXA PPP healthcare employee wellbeing research report*. https://reba.global/ reports/reba/axa-ppp-healthcare-employee-wellbeing-research-2020

Rego, A., Owens, B., & Leal, S. (2017). How leader humility helps teams to be humbler, psychologically stronger, and more effective: A moderated mediation model. *The Leadership Quarterly, 28*, 639–658.

Ribeiro, A. R., Nunes, O. C., Pereira, M. F., & Silva, A. M. (2015). An overview on the advanced oxidation processes applied for the treatment of water pollutants defined in the recently launched Directive 2013/39/EU. *Environment International, 75*, 33–51. doi:10.1016/j.envint.2014.10.027 PMID:25461413

Rist, G. (2014). *The history of Development: from western origins to global faith*. Bloomsbury Publishing.

Roberts, R. (1992). Determinants of corporate social responsibility disclosure: An application of stakeholder theory. *Accounting, Organizations and Society, 17*(6), 595–612. doi:10.1016/0361-3682(92)90015-K

Rodriguez, F., Montoya-Ruiz, C., Estiati, I., & Saldarriaga, J. F. (2020). Removal of drugs in polluted waters with char obtained by pyrolysis of hair waste from the tannery process. *ACS Omega, 5*(38), 24389–24402. doi:10.1021/acsomega.0c02768 PMID:33015455

Rosen, M. A., & Kishawy, H. A. (2012). Sustainable manufacturing and design: Concepts, practices and needs. *Sustainability, 4*(2), 154–174. doi:10.3390u4020154

Rosi-Marshall, E. J., & Kelly, J. J. (2015). Antibiotic Stewardship should consider environmental fate of antibiotics. *Environmental Science & Technology, 49*(9), 5257–5258. doi:10.1021/acs.est.5b01519 PMID:25905451

Rosso, B. D., Dekas, K. H., & Wrzesniewski, A. (2010). On the meaning of work: A theoretical integration and review. *Research in Organizational Behavior, 30*, 91–127.

Rostow, W. W. (1959). The stages of economic growth. *The Economic History Review, 12*(1), 1–16. doi:10.1111/j.1468-0289.1959.tb01829.x

Rowe, S., Baldry, E., & Earles, W. (2015). Decolonising social work research: Learning from critical Indigenous approaches. *Australian Social Work, 68*(3), 296–308. doi:10.1080/0312407X.2015.1024264

Roy, P., Chowdhury, J. S., Abd Wahab, H., & Saad, R. B. M. (2022). Ethnic Tension of the Bangladeshi Santal: A CDA of the Constitutional Provision. In Handbook of Research on Ethnic, Racial, and Religious Conflicts and Their Impact on State and Social Security (pp. 208-226). IGI Global. doi:10.4018/978-1-7998-8911-3.ch013

Royal Government of Bhutan. (2012). *The report of the high-level meeting on wellbeing and happiness: Defining a new economic paradigm.* The Permanent Mission of the Kingdom of Bhutan to the United Nations.

Roy, P. K., Hamidi, M., & Roy, S. (2022). Internet as a Field: An Analysis of the Santal Online Communities. In *Practices, Challenges, and Prospects of Digital Ethnography as a Multidisciplinary Method* (pp. 124–137). IGI Global. doi:10.4018/978-1-6684-4190-9.ch009

Ruf, B., Muralidhar, K., Brown, R., Janney, J., & Paul, K. (2001). An empirical investigation of the relationship between change in corporate social performance and financial performance: A stakeholder theory perspective. *Journal of Business Ethics, 32*(2), 143–156. doi:10.1023/A:1010786912118

Rugman, A., & Verbeke, A. (2002). Edith Penrose's contribution to the resource-based view of strategic management. *Strategic Management Journal, 23*(8), 769–780. doi:10.1002mj.240

Russo, M., & Fouts, P. (1997). A resource-based perspective on corporate environmental performance and profitability. *Academy of Management Journal, 40*(3), 534–559.

Ryff, C. D., & Keyes, C. L. M. (1995). The structure of psychological well-being revisited. *Journal of Personality and Social Psychology, 69*(4), 719–727.

Ryff, C. D., & Singer, B. H. (2006). Best news yet on the six-factor model of well-being. *Social Science Research, 35*(4), 1103–1119.

Sakao, T. (2007). AQED-centered design methodology for environmentally conscious product design. *International Journal of Production Research, 45*(18-19), 4143–4162. doi:10.1080/00207540701450179

Salas-Vallina, A., & Alegre, J. (2021). Happiness at work: Developing a shorter measure. *Journal of Management & Organization, 27*(3), 460–480.

Salas-Vallina, A., López-Cabrales, Á., Alegre, J., & Fernández, R. (2017). On the Road to Happiness at Work (HAW): Transformational Leadership and Organizational Learning Capability as Drivers of HAW in a Healthcare Context. *Personnel Review, 46*(2), 314–338.

Samoggia, A., Bertazzoli, A., & Ruggeri, A. (2019). Food retailing marketing management: Social media communication for healthy food. *International Journal of Retail & Distribution Management, 47*(9), 928–956. doi:10.1108/IJRDM-08-2018-0178

Sánchez-Torné, I., Morán-Álvarez, J. C., & Pérez-López, J. A. (2020). The importance of corporate social responsibility in achieving high corporate reputation. *Corporate Social Responsibility and Environmental Management, 27*(6), 2692–2700. doi:10.1002/csr.1993

Sancho, M., Arnal, J. M., & García-Fayos, B. (2013). Treatment of hospital radio-active liquid wastes from RIA (radioimmunoassay) by membrane technology. *Desalination, 321*, 110–118. doi:10.1016/j.desal.2013.03.032

Santesmases, M. (2012). *DYANE. Versión 4.* Editorial Pirámide.

Sarkar, S., & Searcy, C. (2016). Zeitgeist or chameleon? A quantitative analysis of CSR definitions. *Journal of Cleaner Production, 135*, 1423–1435. doi:10.1016/j.jclepro.2016.06.157

Sarker, M. A. R., Khan, N. A., & Musarrat, K. M. (2016). Livelihood and vulnerability of the Santals community in Bangladesh. *The Malaysian Journal of Social Administration, 12*(1), 38–55. doi:10.22452/mjsa.vol12no1.2

Sarvaiya, H., & Wu, M. (2014). An integrated approach for corporate social responsibility and corporate sustainability. *Asian Social Science, 10*(17), 57. doi:10.5539/ass.v10n17p57

Sayed, Y., & Moriarty, K. (2020). SDG 4 and the 'education quality turn': Prospects, possibilities, and problems. In *Grading Goal Four* (pp. 194-213). Brill Sense. https://brill.com/view/book/edcoll/9789004430365/BP000017.xml

Sazvar, Z., Zokaee, M., Tavakkoli-Moghaddam, R., Salari, S. A. S., & Nayeri, S. (2021). Designing a sustainable closed-loop pharmaceutical supply chain in a competitive market Considering demand uncertainty, manufacturer's brand and waste management. *Annals of Operations Research, 315*(2), 2057–2088. doi:10.100710479-021-03961-0 PMID:33583989

Schmitt, E., Galli, F., Menozzi, D., Maye, D., Touzard, J. M., Marescotti, A., Six, J., & Brunori, G. (2017). Comparing the sustainability of local and global food products in Europe. *Journal of Cleaner Production, 165*, 346–359. doi:10.1016/j.jclepro.2017.07.039

Schneider, J., Wilson, A., & Rosenbeck, J. (2010). Pharmaceutical companies and sustainability: An analysis of corporate reporting. *Benchmarking, 17*(3), 421–434. doi:10.1108/14635771011049371

Schuler, D., & Cording, M. (2006). A corporate social performance-corporate financial performance behavioral model for consumers. *Academy of Management Review, 31*(3), 540–558. doi:10.5465/amr.2006.21318916

Schwab, S. (2020). Inclusive and special Education in Europe. Oxford Research Encyclopedia of Education. doi:10.1093/acrefore/9780190264093.013.1230

Schwartz, M., & Carroll, A. (2008). Integrating and unifying competing and complementary frameworks: The search for a common core in the business and society field. *Business & Society, 47*(2), 148–186. doi:10.1177/0007650306297942

Schwepker, C. H., Valentine, S. R., Giacalone, R. A., & Promislo, M. (2021). Good barrels yield healthy apples: Organizational ethics as a mechanism for mitigating work-related stress and promoting employee well-being. *Journal of Business Ethics, 174*(1), 143–159.

Scott, J. C. (1985). *Weapons of the weak: Everyday forms of peasant resistance*. Yale University Press.

Scott, J. C. (2010). *The art of not being governed: An anarchist history of upland Southeast Asia*. Nus Press.

Scott, J. C. (2020). *Seeing like a state: How certain schemes to improve the human condition have failed*. Yale University Press.

Scott, R. (2001). *Institutions and Organizations*. Sage Publications.

Selekman, B. (1959). *A moral philosophy for management*. McGraw-Hill.

Sen, A. (2009). *The Idea of Justice*. Allan Lane Penguin Books.

Seres-Deloitte. (2022). *VIII Informe del impacto social de las empresas* [VIII Report on the Social Impact of Companies]. https://www2.deloitte.com/es/es/pages/about-deloitte/articles/informe-impacto-social-empresas.html

Sethi, S. (1975). Dimensions of corporate social performance: An analytical framework. *California Management Review, 17*(3), 58–64. doi:10.2307/41162149

Seva-Larrosa, P., Martínez-Falcó, J., & Ruiz-Fernández, L. (2022). Analizando las principales variables empresariales en los clusters vinícolas españoles teniendo en cuenta la localización de las empresas y su pertenencia a una marca colectiva. [Analyzing the main business variables in Spanish wine clusters taking into account the location of the companies and their membership in a collective brand] In *Miradas sobre el emprendimiento ante la crisis del coronavirus* [Perspectives on entrepreneurship in the face of the coronavirus crisis]. (pp. 629–634). Dykinson.

Shafie, H., & Kilby, P. (2003). *Including the excluded: ethnic inequality and Development in Northwest Bangladesh.* Academic Press.

Shanmugham, R. (2000). Factors influencing investment decisions. In Indian Capital Markets–Trends and Dimensions. Tata McGraw-Hill Publishing Company Limited.

Shapiro, D. J., Hicks, L. A., Pavia, A. T., & Hersh, A. L. (2014). Antibiotic prescribing for adults in ambulatory care in the USA, 2007-09. *The Journal of Antimicrobial Chemotherapy*, *69*(1), 234–240. doi:10.1093/jac/dkt301 PMID:23887867

Sharma, S., & Rudd, A. (2003). On the path to sustainability: Integrating social dimensions into the research and practice of environmental management. *Business Strategy and the Environment*, *12*(4), 205–214. doi:10.1002/bse.366

Sharmin, A., Humayra, Z. U., & Khan, M. A. (2019). Causes and Consequences of Acid Violence among the Victims Attended in Specialized Acid Survivor center in Dhaka City. *Journal of Surgery and Science*, *23*(1), 29–32.

Shaw, B., & Whitney, P. (2016). Ethics and compliance in global pharmaceutical industry marketing and promotion: The role of the IFPMA and self-regulation. *Pharmaceuticals Policy and Law*, *18*(1-4), 199–206. doi:10.3233/PPL-160443

Sheehy, B. (2015). Defining CSR: Problems and solutions. *Journal of Business Ethics*, *131*(3), 625–648. doi:10.100710551-014-2281-x

Shiva, V. (2014). *The Vandana Shiva Reader*. University Press of Kentucky.

Shizha, E. (2017). Neoliberal Managerialism of Higher Education and Human Capital Development in Sub-Saharan Africa in the 21st Century. In Re-thinking Postcolonial Education in Sub-Saharan Africa in the 21st Century (pp. 241-260). Brill Sense.

Shleifer, A. (2000). *Inefficient markets: An introduction to behavioural finance*. OUP. doi:10.1093/0198292279.001.0001

Shu-Chuan, C., & Hsuan-Ting, C. (2019). Impact of consumers' corporate social responsibility-related activities in social media on brand attitude, electronic word-of-mouth intention, and purchase intention: A study of Chinese consumer behavior. *Journal of Consumer Behaviour*, *18*(6), 453–462. doi:10.1002/cb.1784

Shu-Chuan, C., Hsuan-Ting, C., & Gan, C. (2020). Consumers' engagement with corporate social responsibility (CSR) communication in social media: Evidence from China and the United States. *Journal of Business Research*, *110*, 260–271. doi:10.1016/j.jbusres.2020.01.036

Sikidar, S. (1996). Equity and Mutual Funds—A Behavioural Study. *Management of Financial Services*, 136.

Singh, K., & Misra, M. (2021). Linking corporate social responsibility (CSR) and organizational performance: The moderating effect of corporate reputation. *European Research on Management and Business Economics*, *27*(1), 100139. doi:10.1016/j.iedeen.2020.100139

Singh, S., & Aggarwal, Y. (2018). Happiness at work scale: Construction and psychometric validation of a measure using mixed method approach. *Journal of Happiness Studies*, *19*(5), 1439–1463.

Siraz, J. (2020). *Songs of Corona, songs of Crying. In Legacies of Love, Peace and Hope: How Education can overcome Hatred and Divide.* Eubios Ethics Institute.

Sison, A. (2009). From CSR to corporate citizenship: Anglo-American and continental European perspectives. *Journal of Business Ethics, 89*(3), 235–246. doi:10.100710551-010-0395-3

Skare, M., & Golja, T. (2014). The impact of government CSR supporting policies on economic growth. *Journal of Policy Modeling, 36*(3), 562–577. doi:10.1016/j.jpolmod.2014.01.008

Slocum, S. L., Dimitrov, D. Y., & Webb, K. (2019). The impact of neoliberalism on higher education tourism programs: Meeting the 2030 sustainable development goals with the next generation. *Tourism Management Perspectives, 30*, 33–42. doi:10.1016/j.tmp.2019.01.004

Smith, N. (2001). Changes in corporate practices in response to public interest advocacy and actions. In Handbook of Marketing and Society. Sage.

Smith, N. (2003). Corporate social responsibility: Whether or how? *California Management Review, 45*(4), 52–76. doi:10.2307/41166188

Sneddon, C., Howarth, R. B., & Norgaard, R. B. (2006). Sustainable Development in a post-Brundtland world. *Ecological Economics, 57*(2), 253–268. doi:10.1016/j.ecolecon.2005.04.013

Soeftestad, L. T. (1994). *Workshop on participatory development.* Academic Press.

Soeftestad, L. T. (2004). Biodiversity conservation, communication and language–is English a solution, a problem or both? *Policy Matters, 13*, 281–283.

SolutionsF. I. (2022). *Plastic Surgery BD.* Retrieved from http://plasticsurgerybd.com/

Sommovigo, V., Setti, I., & Argentero, P. (2019). The role of service providers' resilience in buffering the negative impact of customer incivility on service recovery performance. *Sustainability, 11*(1), 1–22.

Sotorrío, L. L., & Sánchez, J. L. F. (2008). Corporate social responsibility of the most highly reputed European and North American firms. *Journal of Business Ethics, 82*(2), 379–390. doi:10.100710551-008-9901-2

Spence, A., & Zeckhauser, R. (1971). Insurance, information, and individual action. *The American Economic Review, 61*(2), 380–387.

Spivak, G. C. (2004). Righting wrongs. *The South Atlantic Quarterly, 103*(2), 523–581. doi:10.1215/00382876-103-2-3-523

Stets, S., do Amaral, B., Schneider, J. T., de Barros, I. R., de Liz, M. V., Ribeiro, R. R., Nagata, N., & Peralta-Zamora, P. (2018). Antituberculosis drugs degradation by UV-based advanced oxidation processes. *Journal of Photochemistry and Photobiology A Chemistry, 353*, 26–33. doi:10.1016/j.jphotochem.2017.11.006

Steurer, R., Langer, M., Konrad, A., & Martinuzzi, A. (2005). Corporations, stakeholders and sustainable development I: A theoretical exploration of business-society relations. *Journal of Business Ethics, 61*(3), 263–281. doi:10.100710551-005-7054-0

Suchman, M. (1995). Managing legitimacy: Strategic and institutional approaches. *Academy of Management Review, 20*(3), 571–610. doi:10.2307/258788

Sultana, F. (2019). Decolonizing development education and the pursuit of social justice. *Human Geographies, 12*(3), 31–46. doi:10.1177/194277861901200305

Surroca, J., Tribo, J., & Zahra, S. (2013). Stakeholder pressure on MNEs and the transfer of socially irresponsible practices to subsidiaries. *Academy of Management Journal, 56*(2), 549–572. doi:10.5465/amj.2010.0962

Swanson, D. (1995). Addressing a theoretical problem by reorienting the corporate social performance model. *Academy of Management Review*, *20*(1), 43–64. doi:10.2307/258886

Tan, A., Bharj, A. K., Nizamoglu, M., Barnes, D., & Dziewulski, P. (2015). Assaults from corrosive substances and medico legal considerations in a large regional burn centre in the United Kingdom: Calls for increased vigilance and enforced legislation. *Scars Burn Heal*, *1*. doi:10.1177/2059513115612945

Tang, S., Xu, L., Yu, X., Chen, S., Li, H., Huang, Y., & Niu, J. (2021). Degradation of anticancer drug capecitabine in aquatic media by three advanced oxidation processes: Mechanisms, toxicity changes and energy cost evaluation. *Chemical Engineering Journal*, *413*, 127489. doi:10.1016/j.cej.2020.127489

Tbs news on Rehabilitaion. (n.d.). Retrieved from www.tbsnews.net/bangladesh/health/5-hospitals-outside-Dhaka-get-500-bed-unit-beds-338413

The Global Goals. (2022). *Climate Change: Take Urgent Action to Combat Climate Change and its Impacts*. Retrieved August 20, 2022, from https://www.globalgoals.org/goals/13-climate-action/

The United Nations. (2015). *4: Ensure inclusive and quality Education for all and promote lifelong learning*. https://www. un. org/sustainabledevelopment/education/

Thompson, A., & Bruk-Lee, V. (2021). Employee happiness: Why we should care. *Applied Research in Quality of Life*, *16*(4), 1419–1437.

Tiller, T., & Linscott, A. (2004). Evaluation of a steam autoclave for sterilizing medical waste at a university health center. *American Journal of Infection Control*, *32*(3), E9. doi:10.1016/j.ajic.2004.04.013

Tong, A. Y. C., Peake, B. M., & Braund, R. (2011b). Disposal practices for unused medications in New Zealand community pharmacies. *Journal of Primary Health Care*, *3*(3), 197–203. doi:10.1071/HC11197 PMID:21892421

Torstensson, L., Johansson, R., & Mark-Herbert, C. (2021). Food Dishes for Sustainable Development: A Swedish Food Retail Perspective. *Foods*, *10*(5), 932. doi:10.3390/foods10050932 PMID:33922742

Torugsa, N., O'Donohue, W., & Hecker, R. (2012). Capabilities, proactive CSR and financial performance in SMEs: Empirical evidence from an Australian manufacturing industry sector. *Journal of Business Ethics*, *109*(4), 483–500. doi:10.100710551-011-1141-1

Tranfield, D., Denyer, D., & Smart, P. (2003). Towards a methodology for developing evidence-informed management knowledge by means of systematic review. *British Journal of Management*, *14*(3), 207–222. doi:10.1111/1467-8551.00375

Trapp, N. (2012). Corporation as climate ambassador: Transcending business sector boundaries in a Swedish CSR campaign. *Public Relations Review*, *38*(3), 458–465. doi:10.1016/j.pubrev.2012.03.004

Tricoire, D. (Ed.). (2017). *Enlightened Colonialism: Civilization Narratives and Imperial Politics in the Age of Reason*. Springer. doi:10.1007/978-3-319-54280-5

Tripura, J. (2016). Reflection of the Santal Rebellion and the Situations of the Indigenous Peoples of Bangladesh. *Unread Voice*.

Tripura, P. (2020). *Colonial Shadow in Bangladesh*. Bangla Books. www.mochta.gov.bd

Tripura, P. (2018). *Prantikotar Khaad Theke Mohaakashe*. Samhati Publication.

Tuck, E., & Yang, K. W. (2012). Decolonization is not a metaphor. *Decolonization*, *1*(1).

Turner, D. A. (2006). *This is not a peace pipe: Towards a critical indigenous philosophy*. University of Toronto Press.

United Nations (UN). (2015a). *Sendai Framework for Disaster Risk Reduction 2015–2030.* Retrieved August 20, 2022, from https://sustainabledevelopment.un.org/frameworks/sendaiframework and https://sustainabledevelopment.un.org/content/documents/2157sendaiframeworkfordrren.pdf

United Nations (UN). (2015b). *Addis Ababa Action Agenda of the Third International Conference on Financing for Development (Addis Ababa Action Agenda).* Retrieved August 20, 2022, from https://sustainabledevelopment.un.org/frameworks/addisababaactionagenda and https://sustainabledevelopment.un.org/content/documents/2051AAAA_Outcome.pdf

United Nations (UN). (2015c). *Transforming our world: the 2030 Agenda for Sustainable Development.* Retrieved August 20, 2022, from https://sdgs.un.org/2030agenda

United Nations (UN). (2015d). *Paris Agreement on Climate Change.* Retrieved August 20, 2022, from https://sdgs.un.org/frameworks/parisagreement

United Nations (UN). (2022). *Do you know all 17 SDGs?* Department of Economic and Social Affairs. Sustainable Development. Retrieved August 20, 2022, from https://sdgs.un.org/goals

United Nations (UN). (2022). *Sustainable Development Goals (SDGs). Goal 3: Ensure healthy lives and promote well-being for all at all ages.* https://www.un.org/sustainabledevelopment/health/

United Nations Environment Programme (UNEP). (2021). *For people and planet: the United Nations Environment Programme strategy for 2022–2025 to tackle climate change, loss of nature and pollution.* United Nations Environment Assembly of the United Nations Environment Programme. Retrieved August 20, 2022, from https://wedocs.unep.org/bitstream/handle/20.500.11822/35162/Doc3%20Reve1%20EnglishK2100501.pdf?sequence=1&isAllowed=y

United Nations Environment Programme (UNEP). (2022). *Learn more about SDG 13: Take Urgent Action to Combat Climate Change and its Impacts.* Retrieved August 20, 2022, from https://www.unep.org/explore-topics/sustainable-development-goals/why-do-sustainable-development-goals-matter/goal-13

United Nations Environment Programme (UNEP). (2022a). *Digital Transformation.* Retrieved August 20, 2022, from https://www.unep.org/explore-topics/technology/what-we-do/digital-transformation

United Nations Environment Programme (UNEP). (2022b). *What is UNEP's ambition?* Retrieved August 20, 2022, from https://www.unep.org/explore-topics/technology/what-we-do/digital-transformation/what-uneps-ambition

United Nations Environment Programme (UNEP). (2022c). *Digital Transformation: Becoming an Innovative, Agile and Collaborative Organization, Fit for Purpose in the Digital Age - 2022 Version 1.0.* Retrieved August 20, 2022, from https://www.unep.org/resources/policy-and-strategy/digital-transformation-becoming-innovative-agile-and-collaborative

United Nations Framework Convention on Climate Change (UNFCCC). (2022). *Action on Climate and SDGs.* Retrieved August 20, 2022, https://unfccc.int/topics/action-on-climate-and-sdgs/action-on-climate-and-sdgs

Vadakkepatt, G., Shankar, V., & Varadarajan, R. (2021). Should firms invest more in marketing or R&D to maintain sales leadership? An empirical analysis of sales leader firms. *Journal of the Academy of Marketing Science, 49*(6), 1088–1108. doi:10.100711747-021-00774-2

Van Dijk, T. A. (2006). Ideology and discourse analysis. *Journal of Political Ideologies, 11*(2), 115–140. doi:10.1080/13569310600687908

Van Dijk, T. A. (2008). Critical discourse analysis and nominalization: Problem or pseudo-problem? *Discourse & Society, 19*(6), 821–828. doi:10.1177/0957926508095897

Van Marrewijk, M. (2003). Concepts and definitions of CSR and corporate sustainability: Between agency and communion. *Journal of Business Ethics, 44*(2), 95–105. doi:10.1023/A:1023331212247

Van Marrewijk, M., & Hardjono, T. (2003). European corporate sustainability framework for managing complexity and corporate transformation. *Journal of Business Ethics*, *44*(2), 121–132. doi:10.1023/A:1023335414065

Van Marrewijk, M., & Werre, M. (2003). Multiple levels of corporate sustainability. *Journal of Business Ethics*, *44*(2), 107–119. doi:10.1023/A:1023383229086

Vatovec, C., Van Wagoner, E., & Evans, C. (2017). Investigating sources of pharmaceutical pollution: Survey of over-the-counter and prescription medication purchasing, use, and disposal practices among university students. *Journal of Environmental Management*, *198*, 348–352. doi:10.1016/j.jenvman.2017.04.101 PMID:28494423

Votaw, D. (1973). Genius becomes rare: A comment on the doctrine of social responsibility Pt. II. *California Management Review*, *15*(3), 5–19. doi:10.2307/41164435

Vyas, R. (2012). Mutual fund investor's behaviour and perception in Indore city. *Researchers World*, *3*(3), 67.

Wald, J., Taylor, S., Asmundson, G. J., Jang, K. L., & Stapleton, J. (2006). *Literature review of concepts: Psychological resiliency*. Defence R&D Canada.

Waldman, D., Luque, M., Washburn, N., & House, R. (2006). Cultural and leadership predictors of corporate social responsibility values of top management: A GLOBE study of 15 countries. *Journal of International Business Studies*, *37*(6), 823–837. doi:10.1057/palgrave.jibs.8400230

Walia, K., Ohri, V. C., & Mathai, D. (2015). Antimicrobial stewardship program (AMSP) practices in India. *The Indian Journal of Medical Research*, *142*(2), 130. doi:10.4103/0971-5916.164228 PMID:26354210

Walton, C. (1967). *Corporate social responsibilities*. Wadsworth Publishing Company.

Walton, R. (1974). Improving the quality of working life. *Harvard Business Review*, *54*(3), 12–16.

Wang, H., & Choi, J. (2013). A new look at the corporate social-financial performance relationship: The moderating roles of temporal and interdomain consistency in corporate social performance. *Journal of Management*, *39*(2), 416–441. doi:10.1177/0149206310375850

Wang, R., & Huang, Y. (2018). Communicating corporate social responsibility (CSR) on social media: How do message source and types of CSR messages influence stakeholders' perceptions? *Corporate Communications*, *23*(3), 326–341. doi:10.1108/CCIJ-07-2017-0067

Wang, Y. F., Wang, L. C., Hsieh, L. T., Li, H. W., Jiang, H. C., Lin, Y. S., & Tsai, C. H. (2012). Effect of temperature and CaO addition on the removal of polychlorinated dibenzo-p-dioxins and dibenzofurans in fly ash from a medical waste incinerator. *Aerosol and Air Quality Research*, *12*(2), 191–199. doi:10.4209/aaqr.2011.06.0079

Wankel, C. (2008). *21st century management: a reference handbook*. SAGE Publications. doi:10.4135/9781412954006

Warr, P. (1999). Well-being and the workplace. In D. Kahneman, E. Diener, & N. Schwarz (Eds.), *Well-being: The foundations of hedonic psychology* (pp. 392–412). Russell Sage Foundation.

Warr, P. B. (2013). Jobs and Job-Holders: Two sources of Happiness and Unhappiness. In S. A. David, I. Boniwell, & A. C. Ayers (Eds.), *The Oxford Handbook of happiness* (pp. 733–750). Oxford University Press.

We Are Social. (2022). *Digital Spain 2022*. https://wearesocial.com/es/blog/2022/01/digital-2022/

Weaver, E., O'Hagan, C., & Lamprou, D. (2022). The sustainability of emerging technologies for use in pharmaceutical manufacturing. *Expert Opinion on Drug Delivery*, *19*(7), 861–872. doi:10.1080/17425247.2022.2093857 PMID:35732275

Webb, S. (2020). Interpreting Kant in Education: Dissolving Dualisms and Embodying Mind–Introduction. *Journal of Philosophy of Education*, *54*(6), 1494–1509. doi:10.1111/1467-9752.12529

Wee, B. V., & Banister, D. (2016). How to write a literature review paper? *Transport Reviews*, *36*(2), 278–288. doi:10.1080/01441647.2015.1065456

Wernerfelt, B. (1984). A resource-based view of the firm. *Strategic Management Journal*, *5*(2), 171–180. doi:10.1002mj.4250050207

Werther, W. Jr, & Chandler, D. (2005). Strategic corporate social responsibility as global brand insurance. *Business Horizons*, *48*(4), 317–324. doi:10.1016/j.bushor.2004.11.009

Whitley, R. (1999). *Divergent Capitalisms: The Social Structuring and Change of Business Systems*. Oxford University Press.

Willett, W., Rockström, J., Loken, B., Springmann, M., Lang, T., Vermeulen, S., Garnett, T., Tilman, D., DeClerck, F., Wood, A., Jonell, M., Clark, M., Gordon, L. J., Fanzo, J., Hawkes, C., Zurayk, R., Rivera, J. A., De Vries, W., Majele Sibanda, L., ... Murray, C. J. L. (2019). Food in the Anthropocene: The EAT–Lancet Commission on healthy diets from sustainable food systems. *Lancet*, *393*(10170), 447–492. doi:10.1016/S0140-6736(18)31788-4 PMID:30660336

Wilson, M. (2003). Corporate sustainability: What is it and where does it come from? *Ivey Business Journal*, *67*(6), 1.

Wilson, S., Breen, A. V., & DuPré, L. (Eds.). (2019). *Research and reconciliation: Unsettling ways of knowing through Indigenous relationships*. Canadian Scholars.

Wong, D., & Brad, S. (2017). Leveraging antimicrobial stewardship into improving rates of carbapenem-resistant Enterobacteriaceae. *Virulence*, *8*(4), 383–390. doi:10.1080/21505594.2016.1188234 PMID:27187821

Wood, G., Dibben, P., & Ogden, S. (2014). Comparative capitalism without capitalism, and production without workers: The limits and possibilities of contemporary institutional analysis. *International Journal of Management Reviews*, *16*(4), 384–396. doi:10.1111/ijmr.12025

World Economic Forum (WEC). (2018). *Fourth Industrial Revolution for the Earth Series. Harnessing Artificial Intelligence for the Earth*. PwC and Stanford Woods Institute for the Environment. https://www3.weforum.org/docs/Harnessing_Artificial_Intelligence_for_the_Earth_report_2018.pdf

World Economic Forum (WEC). (2020a). *Responsible Limits on Facial Recognition. Use Case: Flow Management. Part II Pilot phase: Self-assessment, the audit management system and certification*. White Paper. https://www.weforum.org/whitepapers?platform=shaping-the-future-of-technology-governance-artificial-intelligence-and-machine-learning. https://www3.weforum.org/docs/WEF_Responsible_Limits_on_Facial_Recognition_2020.pdf

World Economic Forum (WEC). (2020b). *Ethics by Design: An organizational approach to responsible use of technology*. White Paper. https://www.weforum.org/whitepapers?platform=shaping-the-future-of-technology-governance-artificial-intelligence-and-machine-learning. https://www3.weforum.org/docs/WEF_Responsible_Limits_on_Facial_Recognition_2020.pdf

World Economic Forum (WEC). (2021a). *Responsible Use of Technology: The IBM Case Study*. White Paper. https://www.weforum.org/whitepapers?platform=shaping-the-future-of-technology-governance-artificial-intelligence-and-machine-learning. https://www3.weforum.org/docs/WEF_Responsible_Use_of_Technology_The_IBM_Case_Study_2021.pdf

World Economic Forum (WEC). (2021b). *Harnessing Artificial Intelligence to Accelerate the Energy Transition.* White Paper. https://www.weforum.org/whitepapers?platform=shaping-the-future-of-technology-governance-artificial-intelligence-and-machine-learning. https://www3.weforum.org/docs/WEF_Harnessing_AI_to_accelerate_the_Energy_Transition_2021.pdf

World Economic Forum (WEC). (2021c). *Responsible Use of Technology: The Microsoft Case Study.* White Paper. https://www.weforum.org/whitepapers?platform=shaping-the-future-of-technology-governance-artificial-intelligence-and-machine-learning. https://www3.weforum.org/docs/WEF_Responsible_Use_of_Technology_2021.pdf

World Economic Forum (WEC). (2022a). *A Blueprint for Equity and Inclusion in Artificial Intelligence.* White Paper. https://www.weforum.org/whitepapers?platform=shaping-the-future-of-technology-governance-artificial-intelligence-and-machine-learning. https://www3.weforum.org/docs/WEF_A_Blueprint_for_Equity_and_Inclusion_in_Artificial_Intelligence_2022.pdf

World Economic Forum (WEC). (2022b). *Unpacking AI Procurement in a Box: Insights from Implementation.* White Paper. https://www.weforum.org/whitepapers?platform=shaping-the-future-of-technology-governance-artificial-intelligence-and-machine-learning. https://www3.weforum.org/docs/WEF_Unpacking_AI_Procurement_in_a_Box_2022.pdf

World Economic Forum (WEF). (2022a). *Digital Transformation Initiative (DTI).* Retrieved September 20, 2022, from https://reports.weforum.org/digital-transformation/

World Economic Forum (WEF). (2022b). *Digital Consumption.* Retrieved September 20, 2022, from https://reports.weforum.org/digital-transformation/digital-consumption/

World Economic Forum (WEF). (2022c). *Introducing Digital Value to Society.* Retrieved September 20, 2022, from https://reports.weforum.org/digital-transformation/unlocking-trapped-value/?doing_wp_cron=1664281325.0679690837860107421875

World Economic Forum (WEF). (2022d). *The digital transformation of logistics: Threat and opportunity.* Retrieved September 20, 2022, from https://reports.weforum.org/digital-transformation/the-digital-transformation-of-logistics-threat-and-opportunity/

World Economic Forum (WEF). (2022e). *The Digital Transformation Of Business. Automation can empower workers and enhance productivity. Here's how.* Retrieved September 20, 2022, from https://www.weforum.org/agenda/2022/09/how-to-transform-your-company-with-lean-augmentation-regardless-of-size/

World Economic Forum (WEF). (2022f). *Infrastructure. Digital public infrastructure can help solve global challenges. This is how to implement it.* Retrieved September 20, 2022, from https://www.weforum.org/agenda/2022/09/6-first-principles-for-making-digital-public-infrastructure-impactful/

World Economic Forum (WEF). (2022g). *Cybersecurity. Cybersecurity: 5 ways to make your business more cyber secure.* Retrieved September 20, 2022, from https://www.weforum.org/agenda/2022/09/cybersecurity-business-cyber-secure/

Wright, P., & Ferris, S. (1997). Agency conflict and corporate strategy: The effect of divestment on corporate value. *Strategic Management Journal, 18*(1), 77–83. doi:10.1002/(SICI)1097-0266(199701)18:1<77::AID-SMJ810>3.0.CO;2-R

Wright, T. A., & Doherty, E. M. (1998). Organizational behavior 'rediscovers' the role of emotional well-being. *Journal of Organizational Behavior, 19*, 481–485.

Wronka, J. (2020). Whistleblowing, Human Rights, and Mental Health/Well-being: Implications for Advanced Generalist Practice. *Journal of Human Rights and Social Work, 5*(1), 1–6. doi:10.100741134-019-00112-1

Xie, Y., & Zhu, J. (2013). Leaching toxicity and heavy metal bioavailability of medical waste incineration fly ash. *Journal of Material Cycles and Waste Management*, *15*(4), 440–448. doi:10.100710163-013-0133-x

Xu, S., & Yang, R. (2010). Indigenous characteristics of Chinese corporate social responsibility conceptual paradigm. *Journal of Business Ethics*, *93*(2), 321–333. doi:10.100710551-009-0224-8

Yaseen, G., Ahmad, M., & Zafar, M. (2021). Green sustainable process for chemical and environmental engineering and science. In Current status of solvents used in the pharmaceutical industry. Elsevier.

Ye, N., Kueh, T. B., Hou, L., Liu, Y., & Yu, H. (2020). A bibliometric analysis of corporate social responsibility in sustainable development. *Journal of Cleaner Production*, *272*, 122679. doi:10.1016/j.jclepro.2020.122679

Yin, R., K. (2018). *Case Study Research and Applications Design and Methods.* Sage.

Yousaf, F. N., & Purkayastha, B. (2016). Beyond saving faces: Survivors of acid attacks in Pakistan. *Women's Studies International Forum, 54*. doi: .2015.10.003 doi:10.1016/j.wsif

Zafar, S. (2019). *Medical waste management in developing countries.* Thomé-Kozmiensky Verlag GmbH-Neuruppin. Available at: https://www.vivis. de/wp-content/uploads/WM9/2019_WM_351-358_Zafar.pdf

Zhang, J., Chang, V. W., Giannis, A., & Wang, J. Y. (2013). Removal of cytostatic drugs from aquatic environment: A review. *The Science of the Total Environment*, *445*, 281–298. doi:10.1016/j.scitotenv.2012.12.061 PMID:23337605

Zhou, C., Wang, Y., Chen, J., & Niu, J. (2019). Porous Ti/SnO2-Sb anode as reactive electrochemical membrane for removing trace antiretroviral drug stavudine from wastewater. *Environment International*, *133*, 105157. doi:10.1016/j.envint.2019.105157 PMID:31520959

Zia, T. (2013). *Acid violence in Pakistan.* UCLA: Centre for the Study of Women. Retrieved from https://escholarship.org/uc/item/65v958z1 www.worldblindunion.org

Ziai Aram. (2017). *Post-development 25 years after The Development Dictionary*. Academic Press.

Zink, K. J. (2005). Stakeholder orientation and corporate social responsibility as a precondition for sustainability. *Total Quality Management & Business Excellence*, *16*(8-9), 1041–1052. doi:10.1080/14783360500163243

About the Contributors

Cristina Raluca Gh. Popescu is Full-Professor Habil. at the University of Bucharest, Bucharest, Romania, PhD. Supervisor and Doctoral School Member at The Bucharest University of Economic Studies, Bucharest, Romania, and an award-winning Scientific Researcher. Having more than 21 years of experience, focuses on helping students learn and apply the subjects more effectively, and centers on improving scientific research excellence. Values a special environment where her in-depth knowledge of creative thinking and academic writing can help deliver accurate research results. She is skilled in Business Administration, Economics, Management, Accounting, and Audit. Collaborations: The National Institute for Research and Development in Environmental Protection (I.N.C.D.P.M.), Romania; National Research and Development Institute for Gas Turbines COMOTI, Romania; University of Craiova, Romania; Ministry of Research and Innovation, Romania. She is Member of Chamber of Financial Auditors of Romania (CAFR), Romania as Financial Auditor, and Member of Authority for the Public Oversight of the Statutory Audit Activity (ASPAAS), Ministry of Public Finance, Romania as Financial auditor. Single author and coauthor of more than 300 scientific works, with national and international publishers, having national and international coauthors: books, book chapters, articles, congress and conference papers. She has more than 1200 citations in national and international publications. Member of Scientific Committee (SC), 2022: International Congress of Management, Economy and Policy (ICOMEP), Turkey; Symposium on Migration and Asylum in Turkey, Tekirdağ Namık Kemal Üniversitesi (Tekirdag Namık Kemal University), Turkey; International Congress "Multidimensional Sustainability: Transitions and Convergences", Instituto Superior Politécnico Gaya (ISPGAYA), Portugal; 6th International Academic and Professional Congress on Happiness "Happiness Management. A Social Well-being multiplier. Social Marketing and Organizational Communication", Universidad de Salamanca, Spain. Editor and Editorial Advisory Board (EAB) member: IGI Global – Publishing House (Pennsylvania, USA). Guest Editor for Emerald Publishing Limited (Bingley, Bradford District, United Kingdom): Journal of Management Development (MD). Guest Editor and Academic Editor for Multidisciplinary Digital Publishing Institute (MDPI, Basel, Switzerland): Mathematics, Journal of Risk and Financial Management (JRFM), Businesses, Sustainability. Topic Editor for Multidisciplinary Digital Publishing Institute (MDPI, Basel, Switzerland): Mathematics, Businesses. Associate Editor for The International Academy of Organizational Behavior Management (IAOBM): International Journal of the Academy of Organizational Behavior Management (IJAOBM); The International Journal of Management Science and Information Technology (IJMSIT). Editorial Advisory Board (EAB) Member for North American Institute of Science and Information Technology (NAISIT) (The International Journal of Management Science and Information Technology (IJMSIT)); Journal of Emerging Economies and Policy (JOEEP). Review Board member: IBIMA Conferences and IBIMA Publishing, USA (Journal of E-Government

Studies and Best Practices, The MENA Journal of Business Case Studies); International Conference on Decision Making for Small and Medium-Sized Enterprises (DEMSME 2021); International Congress "Multidimensional Sustainability: Transitions and Convergences", Instituto Superior Politécnico Gaya (ISPGAYA), Portugal (2022); IGI Global – Publishing House (Pennsylvania, USA); University of Bucharest (International Journal of Health Economics (IJHE)); Multidisciplinary Digital Publishing Institute (MDPI, Basel, Switzerland) (Sustainability, Microorganisms, Businesses, Forests, Energies, Computation, Agriculture, Water, International Journal of Environmental Research and Public Health, Urban Science, Mathematics, Journal of Open Innovation: Technology, Market, and Complexity (JOItmC), Journal of Risk and Financial Management (JRFM), Risks, Agronomy, Economies, Symmetry, Administrative Sciences, World, Informatics). Invited reviewer: Management Decision (MD), Sustainable Development (SD), Corporate Social Responsibility & Environmental Management (CSREM), Journal of Business Economics and Management (JBEM), Engineering Economics (Inzinerine Ekonomika), International Journal of Sustainable Development and Planning (IJSDP), Transformations in Business & Economics (TIBE), Open Research Europe (ORE), Coffee Science (CS), Journal of Management and Economics Research (JMER).

* * *

Siti Binti Abu Bakar Ah is a professor in the department of Social Administration & Justice University of Malaya, Malaysia. Her major area of expertise is social policy. Over the last 22 years, she has been involve in developing and promoting the teaching, learning and research opportunity in the field of social policy and Social Work. Her research interest focus on social care program for the at-risk children in Malaysia, children well being and social development for vulnerable social groups.

Jahid Siraz Chowdhury is a PhD Fellow at the Universiti Malaya. Before that, he served as an anthropology faculty at Shahjalal University of Science and Technology, Sylhet, Bangladesh. On COVID-19, jahid contributed a Trilogy, The 2020 Pandemic and Social Science: Some Insights from the South, University Malaya Press, Malaysia (Eds); Handbook of Research on the Impact of COVID-19 on Marginalized Populations and Support for the Future, IGI Global, USA(Eds); UBUNTU Philosophy in the New Normalcy, Palgrave Macmillan, Singapore. He is trying to make space for Reciprocity in Social research, for which jahid is engaged with few book projects, such are 'Reciprocity and Its Practice in Social Science', In progress with IGI Global, USA.2nd Book: 'Philosophy to Practice of Reciprocity' In progress, and 'A Reciprocal Ethnography of the Bangladeshi Rakhain: Seeing with Ubuntu in the New Normal', Under the Australia Pacific Publisher (2021 Upcoming). He is a creative writer, published 13 books in Bengali. One Book is 'Purbo-Prantic' Eastern Corner'¬¬ a historical novel traced back from 600 to 1304 AD in the eastern part of Bangladesh. His ethnographic Book on Abortion, "Stigmatised Girl" (Bengali) will be published in English, Hindi, and Malaya.

Pedro Cuesta-Valino holds a PhD in Economics and Business and is a Professor of Marketing at University of Alcalá (Spain) since 1996. His priority lines of research are the marketing strategies and the consumer and organizational behavior. He is the author of more than 80 research papers that have been published in several academic journals (Technological Forecasting and Social Change, Corporate Social Responsibility and Environmental Management, Journal of Business Research, Journal Retailing and Consumer Services, Economic Research, Journal of Business & Industrial Marketing, International

Journal of Environmental Research and Public Health, British Food Journal, Media and Communication, Corporate Governance, Corporate Communications, etc.). Among others, he is the Executive Editor of the International Journal of Internet Marketing and Advertising, Associate Editor of Humanities & Social Sciences Communication and member of the Editorial Board of International Journal of Consumer Studies, Spanish Journal of Marketing, Revista, Portuguesa de Estudos Regionais, Retos, International Review of Communication And Marketing Mix, ADResearch ESIC International Journal of Communication Research and ESIC Digital Economy & Innovation Journal. Finally, he is founder and promoter of the International University Network of Happiness.

Patricia Durán-Álamo has a double degree in Journalism and Audiovisual Communication from the Rey Juan Carlos University of Madrid and specialized in Communication and Corporate Identity from the International University of La Rioja. As a teacher, since 2019 she has been a professor in the Marketing and Market Research Area of the University of Alcalá. Additionally, she teaches master classes at private universities such as the IE Business School or the European University of Madrid, among other private specialized training centers. As a professional, she manages the communication of companies through offline communication strategies (press releases, PR, among others) and online (Social Networks, chatbots, SEO, SEM, among others) of technology-based companies. Specifically, during her career, she has worked in private sector in different companies of the Spanish entrepreneurial ecosystem such as Wazypark or Coches.com. Currently, she leads the Communication Department of Planeta Chatbot, a communication medium specialized in Artificial Intelligence and conversational technology, from which she collaborates with private companies (Amazon, Google, BBVA, IBM, among others) and different public entities such as SEGITTUR, an organization that potential introduction of new technologies in the tourism sector, or municipalities such as Malaga or Gran Canaria. Additionally, she leads the conversational design department of the technology consultancy Chatbot Chocolate, from which she works on digitization processes and new commercial communication strategies for companies such as Teka, Mahou San Miguel, Pernod Ricard, Metro Bilbao, Metro Sevilla, REALE Seguros, among other.

Tugba Erhan, PhD, is an assistant professor of business at Suleyman Demirel University. Tugba earned her BA in English Language from Uludag University and her PhD in business from Suleyman Demirel University. Her research interests focus on employee behaviors, approaches to work as calling, and decent work. Tugba loves spending time in nature, taking photos of nature and swimming. She lives with her husband Mustafa and their daughter in Isparta, Turkey.

Aparna Gunjal has 132 publications to her credit and 8 years of teaching experience. She is reviewer and editorial board member for many journals. She has received travel grants and national and international awards for paper presentation in the conferences.

Mashita Binti Hamida is Senior lecturer in Department of Social Administration and Justice of Universiti Malaya, Malaysia. She Obtained PhD from the University of La Trobe, Australia. Her areas of research include Development studies, Social Services System, Migration, and stateless group of people (Refugee).

Tahmina Islam is a PhD fellow in the department of Social Administration & Justice in the University of Malaya, Malaysia. She is also a professor in the department of Social Work, Shahjalal University Science & Technology Sylhet, Bangladesh. Besides these she is involve in various social welfare activities in her country. She is also a motivational speaker, trainer, and play role as a psycho social counselor. Her research interests are on violence against women, couple conflict, indigenous people, mental health, counseling.

Arturo Luque is full professor at the Technical University of Manabí, Ecuador, and member of Euro-Mediterranean Observatory on Public Policies and Democratic Quality at the University King Juan Carlos (Spain) and visiting Professor at the University of Rosario, Colombia. He holds a Ph.D. in Social Sciences and Law and a Master of two years about Labor Relations. He supervises several doctoral theses (Ph.D.) in Córdoba (Spain) and in the Basque Country (GEZKI Institute) like a director and co-director. It has 80 indexed articles and his latest publications includes topics about digitalization (Practicality, support or premeditated calculation in the digital age: the case of Ecuador), Globalization (Analysis of the concept of informal economy through 102 definitions: legality or necessity), corporate social (Ir)responsibility (How corporate social (ir)responsibility in the textile sector is defined, and its impact on ethical sustainability: An analysis of 133 concepts), transnational companies (The transnational textile companies relationship with environment: a Delphi analysis approach) and their relations with ethics (Corruption in the transnational textile industry: an exception or the rule?), social economy and cooperative system like economic alternative (Socially responsible public management: case spinning development in Ecuador), media analysis and social conflicts (Analysis of the indigenous uprising of Ecuador, 2019: between a measured legal response and lawfare, 2019) and sustainability (Public Strategy and Eco-Social Engagement in Latin American States: An Analysis of Complex Networks Arising from Their Constitutions).

Bartolomé Marco-Lajara is Professor of Business Organization at the University of Alicante (Spain). He holds a PhD in Economics and his doctoral dissertation focused in strategic alliances management. His research interests are on Strategic Management and Tourism Management. He is author of several books, book chapters and international articles related to teaching methodology and the areas above mentioned. On the other hand, he is member of the Tourism Research Institute at the University of Alicante since its foundation. He has participated in many public- and private-funded projects, being the main researcher in many of them. He was assistant dean of the Economics Faculty at the University of Alicante during eight years, holding now the position of Head of the Department of Business Organization at this University.

Javier Martínez Falcó is Assistant Professor in the Department of Management at the University of Alicante. In the field of research, he focuses his interest on issues related to the Strategic Management of the Company, specifically in the areas of Knowledge Management and Corporate Sustainability of wine companies, on which he has written several publications in the form of articles, book chapters and contributions to conferences. He has also participated in several national research projects and teaches Strategic Management on the ADE, TADE and DADE degree courses.

Noralina Omar is a Senior Lecturer in the department of Social Administration & Justice, in the University of Malaya, Malaysia. Her core area of expertise is Family social Work.Over 10 years she has been involved in research and publications focusing on family and children. Her research interest focus on child well-being, family ecology and parent child relationship.

Neha N. Patil is HOD of the Department of Microbiology at Annasaheb Magar Mahavidyalaya, Hadapsar, Pune, Maharashtra, India. She has 35 years of research experience. She has 35 research publications, 2 books and 9 book chapters to her credit.

Azucena Penelas-Leguía is a Ph. D in Business Administration from the University of Alcalá (Madrid) and a degree in Business Administration from the University of Alcalá (Madrid). Regarding University, she has been working as a Professor of the Marketing area at the University of Alcalá, as well as a Professor of Marketing in several Master degrees. As a professional, she has been a consultant in the marketing department of several public and private organizations. She has been Assistant Dean in the Economic and Business School and Assistant Director of the Economic and Business Administration Department (University of Alcala). Currently, she is the Academic Coordinator of the Marketing area. As a researcher, she has directed several research projects focused on marketing management in companies, public and nonprofit organizations, and the tourist sector. She is member of a scientific committee, author and coordinator of several marketing articles and marketing case studies, in journals in the area of economics and business. In addition, she is a founding member of several international association on Marketing.

Parimal Roy, PhD candidate at Department of Social Administration & Justice, Universiti Malaya, Malaysia. studied in Anthropology. Later he obtained papers on MBA, Project management, and Criminology (paper is better than a certificate) to enhance his knowledge. He is currently working in a state own institution in the field of Training & Development. Decolonizing, Marginal community, subaltern voice, Project management - all are interest arena in academic world. His written book is Extra-marital love in folk songs. Co-author of Captive minded intellectual; Quantitative Ethnography in Indigenous Research Methodology; and so many book chapters and journals.

Hasan Huseyin Uzunbacak, PhD, is an associate professor at Suleyman Demirel University. Hasan Huseyin earned his BA in economics and his PhD in Business from Suleyman Demirel University. His research interests focus on organizational behavior specifically leadership, positive organizational behavior, HRM, employee empowerment, and career planning.

Meghmala Waghmode has 15 years of teaching experience and currently she is pursuing her Ph.D degree. She has 30 research papers, 2 books and 9 book chapters to her credit.

Haris Wahab is a Professor at the Department of Social Administration and Justice, Universiti Malaya, Malaysia. His core area of expertise is Community Development. Over the 19 years, he has been involved in developing and promoting teaching, learning, and research opportunities in community development and social work. He teaches social problems, social work, community development, social marketing, research methodology and social theories. His research interests focus on community well-being, social care programs for the at-risk children in Malaysia, children's well-being and social development for vulnerable social groups.

Seher Yastioglu, PhD, is an assistant professor at the department of Management and Organization, Burdur Mehmet Akif Ersoy University, Turkey. She earned her MA in management and organization and PhD in Business Administration. Her research interests include positive organizational behavior, work, and organizational psychology especially leadership, workplace happiness, meaning of work, life meaning, and culture. Also, she is interested in applied psychometrics and quantitative research methodology. Seher dedicates her spare time to her family and motorcycle touring. She lives with her husband Can in Burdur, Turkey.

Patrocinio Zaragoza-Sáez (PhD, University of Alicante, Spain) is a Professor at the Department of Business Management at the University of Alicante, Spain. She holds the position of Coordinator of the University Master's Degree in Tourism Management and Planning. Her primary research interests are knowledge management and intellectual capital, strategic management and tourism management. She has published research papers in international journals including Journal of Business Research, Regional Studies, Journal of Knowledge Management, Knowledge Management Research and Practice, Journal of Intellectual Capital, International Journal of Knowledge Management Studies, Business Strategy & Environment, Intangible Capital, International Journal of Contemporary Hospitality Management Current Issues in Tourism, Cornell Hospitality Quarterly, Tourism Economics and Tourism Management. She has been involved in several national and international scientific and academic research projects.

Index

A

B

C

D

E

G

H

I

J

K

L

N

O

P

R

S

T

U

W

www.ingramcontent.com/pod-product-compliance
Lightning Source LLC
LaVergne TN
LVHW062146300926
849161LV00010B/2640
9781668474990